WHO'S WHO

A PLAYER BY PLAYER GUIDE TO WEST HAM UNITED F.C.

WEST HAM UNITED

100

1895 - 1995

YEARS

Centenary Edition

THAMES IRONWORKS • WEST HAM UNITED

By Tony Hogg & Tony McDonald

Published by
INDEPENDENT UK SPORTS PUBLICATIONS

First published in Great Britain by
Independent UK Sports Publications
7-9 Rathbone Street, London W1P 1AF
England.

Telephone: 0171 636 5599 Fax: 0171 636 1617

Text Copyright Independent UK Sports Publications

Design Copyright ACL & Polar

ISBN No. 1-899429-01-8

Designed and Printed by
ACL Colourprint & Polar Publishing (UK) Ltd
2, Uxbridge Road, Leicester, LE4 7ST.
Telephone: (0116) 2610800

Photographs courtesy of:
Richard Austin, Steve Bacon, Colorsport, Empics, Albert York, Malcolm Craig, Mick Jones.
Many of the photographs reproduced are from the private collections of the authors or
from albums owned by various Hammers' supporters or players.

Cover Photographs:

FRONT:
(Top): The day West Ham United 'won' the World Cup! Jubilant Hammers trio Bobby Moore, Geoff Hurst (raising the Jules Rimet Trophy) and Martin Peters on a victory lap of honour around Wembley after beating West Germany in the 1966 World Cup Final.
(Bottom left): Frank McAvennie, one of the most popular Hammers, who signed twice for West Ham.
(Bottom centre): Len Goulden, a goal-scoring legend of the 1930's.
(Bottom right): Cult hero Julian Dicks, who rejoined the club during the printing of this book in October 1994.

BACK:
(Top left): Jackie Morton, Hammers' wing-flier of the 1930's.
(Centre): Tony Cottee, a goalscoring sensation at 17 and now back at Upton Park after six years at Everton.
(Right): The legendary Billy Bonds - 27 years a Hammer as player, coach and manager.
(Bottom): Six of the best - our collection of 1982 internationals on parade at the Chadwell Heath training ground (left to right): Paul Goddard, Alan Devonshire, Alvin Martin, Trevor Brooking (all England), Ray Stewart (Scotland), Francois Van Der Elst (Belgium).

INTRODUCTION

THERE are two major ingredients essential in the making of a great football club. A ready supply of quality players and a passionate public willing to support them.

Over the last 100 years, West Ham United and their forebears, Thames Ironworks, have been blessed with an abundance of both.

Not all of the players have possessed the ultimate in skill, but the majority that have not, have been able to commit enough effort and endeavour to compensate for what they might have lacked in the finer points of the game.

While the fans have followed the team and their fluctuating fortunes through thick and thin over 10 decades, remaining constant in their support on but few and exceptional occasions.

Some of the players have been true greats like Dick Walker, 'Big' Jim Barrett, Billy Bonds, Frank Lampard, Alvin Martin, Ray Stewart and Tony Gale.

Some, like Geoff Hurst, had greatness thrust upon them, almost as if destiny decreed it their right.

One, Bobby Moore, aspired to greatness and became almost an icon. So completely did he learn his art.

Others, like Syd Puddefoot, Danny Shea, Jimmy Ruffell, Len Goulden, Johnny Byrne, Martin Peters, Trevor Brooking and Alan Devonshire, were the quintessential exponents of what Pele called 'The beautiful game.'

More recently, players like Frank McAvennie and Julian Dicks have attained cult status, having captured the imagination of an adoring public, ever ready to acclaim a new star.

But this book is not just about those players, important though their contribution to the history of West Ham United undeniably is.

It's also about the unsung heroes, like Andy Malcolm, Ken Brown, Ronnie Boyce, Pat Holland, Geoff Pike and Peter Butler, without whose 100% work-rate, the

glittering prizes could not have been attained and promotion goals realised.

Within these 256 pages lay the career details of over 640 players who pulled on the famous claret and blue shirt.

Some were content to do their bit in Irons' cause without making the headlines. A select few found fame and fortune and all the trappings associated with success. Many flitted briefly across the Memorial Ground and Upton Park stage, hardly to be heard of again.

Some players are remembered more for their off-field antics, than what they achieved on it.

Great characters and practical jokers like Jackie Wood, who always made sure he was last out of the bath so he could give the players who had changed a good soaking as they walked past.

Until, that is, he did it to Dick Walker, who was wearing Jackie's suit!

A talented few, like Alan Dickens, had a glittering future, but inexplicably failed to fulfil their potential.

Most tragic of all, are those like Mark Smith, whose future seemed assured, only to be tragically and prematurely terminated by injury.

This book is also about Paul Marquis, who played for just one minute against Manchester City at Maine Road and in doing so achieved what few men can lay claim to: he played for West Ham United.

While researching the popular 'Where are they now?' and 'Vintage Claret' features for the official club publication, *Hammers News,* the publishers have been constantly amazed at the amount of players interviewed who listed their time at West Ham as the happiest of their careers.

Their testimonies have been reinforced by the number of players who have returned to the club a second time, most recently Tony Cottee and Julian Dicks, who are just part of a list of returnees which almost warrants a Who's Who of their own and includes famous names like Billy Grassam, George Hilsdon, Danny

Shea, Syd Puddefoot, Brian Dear and of course, Frank McAvennie.

All returned like prodigal sons for a second spell at the club they regarded as 'home'.

The club became renowned for its youth policy, although they were glad to take on board some famous faces who had already made their names elsewhere. Jimmy Greaves and Liam Brady are two 'Vintage Clarets' who spent their twilight days with Hammers.

When the original *Who's Who of West Ham United* was written by Tony Hogg and Jack Helliar back in 1986, there were very few books of its type in circulation. The intervening years have witnessed a huge output by club historians and statisticians, however, resulting in a publishing boom which has given football fans a far clearer insight into the history and playing staff of their particular club.

Many gaps still exist, although despite the fact that invaluable records were lost in the blitz of the last war, Hammers have fared better than most in this field - thanks to a small, though very enthusiastic, group of people who have painstakingly 're-researched' the 100-year history of West Ham United Football Club.

Without claiming to have covered every detail, this special centenary edition of the Who's Who includes a biographical account of every player to have pulled on a claret and blue shirt since West Ham United was formed in 1900, in addition to many of the even earlier pioneers of the Thames Ironworks team which began life in 1895. We have also included a number of players who, although they did not make an official first team appearance, went on to establish themselves in the game, either in another capacity at Upton Park or as a player with another club. Tony Carr and Harry Cripps are two typical examples.

Fan-tastic: supporters at Villa Park on the occasion of the ill-fated FA Cup semi-final against Nottingham Forest in 1991.

This edition is not simply an update of the original Who's Who. In the majority of cases, the biographical detail is much more comprehensive and the additional number of pages has created scope for more extensive use of pictures. Obviously, errors that appeared in the original edition have been corrected.

We make no excuse for allocating the legendary Bobby Moore, OBE, six pages for his entry, but consider every player equal in one respect . . . they all had the honour of playing for a club rightly revered throughout the world of football.

To many of us West Ham is not simply our favourite football club, it is a way of life. The influence successes like the Cup Final victories have on people's lives cannot be underestimated. The fans who were at Wembley to see Moore lift the FA Cup in 1964 and then the European Cup Winners' Cup a year later, will cherish the memories forever. When Bonds climbed the same steps to hoist the FA Cup again in 1975 and 1980, the feeling of pride filled the hearts of all Hammers' fans.

Anyone who watched, fingers crossed, as Ray Stewart stepped up to slam home the dramatic late penalty equaliser in the 1981 League Cup Final against Liverpool, will have experienced fewer more magical moments.

Books of this kind evoke a million memories . . . of matches triumphantly won against the odds, and others that somehow got away. In 100 years, the highest West Ham have ever achieved in the top flight is third place, in 1985/86, when only the two mighty Merseyside giants, Liverpool and Everton, proved the barrier to that elusive first championship.

It is a cause of deep disappointment to many supporters that the club has rarely mounted another serious title challenge, before or since. Indeed, to many there could be no more appropriate anthem than 'I'm Forever Blowing Bubbles'. Very few clubs have been able to sustain success over a long period, but the dreams of thousands have 'faded and died' more often than they care to remember. This has particularly applied to more recent seasons: promotion in May 1991 followed

by relegation a year later, then promotion again in May 1993. High and lows . . . supporting the Hammers is like a roller-coaster ride through life itself.

Yet Hammers have been at their most enigmatic in cup competitions. Hopes of adding to four FA Cup successes were cruelly shattered by Keith Hackett's infamous red card and classy Nottingham Forest in 1991. The club must consider itself fortunate to have enjoyed such solid, loyal support over the years, and this was never more evident than on that fateful day at Villa Park, where thousands displayed a remarkable, non-stop show of unity as the chant of 'Billy Bonds' Claret and Blue Army' reverberated around the ground.

That is why this book is dedicated to the lifeblood of any football club - the supporters. We hope you gain as much pleasure from reading it as we did in compiling it.

Tony Hogg & Tony McDonald

CONTENTS

CARRERAS CIGARETTES

J. BARRETT
WEST HAM U. (2ND DIVISION)

PROMINENT FOOTBALLERS.

L. JARVIS.
WEST HAM UNITED.

WILLS'S CIGARETTES

I. GOULDEN (WEST HAM UNITED)

PROMINENT FOOTBALLERS.

G. KITCHEN,
WEST HAM UNITED.

F. BLACKBURN,
WEST HAM UNITED.

YOUNG. LEFT FULL BACK.
WEST HAM UNITED. F.C-13.

W. GRASSAM,
WEST HAM UNITED.

F. PIERCY,
WEST HAM UNITED.

Acknowledgements

A NY work on this scale would be impossible to achieve without the help and encouragement of a number of people. In our case dedicated historians like Roy Shoesmith, whose information on early players was both timely and invaluable; Terry Connelly, for providing photographs (often at short notice) and his unique knowledge on the whereabouts of past players, gleaned while pursuing his hobby of tracking down former favourites; his friend Stephen Marsh for also providing pictures, drawing cartoon caricatures and giving us unlimited access to his incredible collection of memorabilia accumulated in his years as founder of the West Ham United Autograph Society (hence the signed pics in this book!); Brian Taylor, for lending his priceless cigarette card collection for use in the colourful 'Hall of Fame' section; John Helliar and his late father Jack, who helped to lay the foundations for the Who's Who story; Steve Bacon, the official club photographer, and Richard Austin for their superb pictures; the late Albert York for his legendary 'tunnel shots'; Steve Blowers, of *Hammers News Magazine*, for his 'reminders' and encouragement; Ray Hutson, for helping to compile the WW2 guest players' list and player research; Russell Stander, for additional research (even though he supports Spurs!); Danny Francis, for formulating the mountain of statistical information into an accessible system; Tracey Carlton, for typesetting; John Cornell, Fred Loveday, Dennis Lamb, Gary Robson, W.J. Goodall, George Randall, Pat Fitzpatrick, Keith Creamer, Bill and Sue of Ashley Road, Forest Gate, and John Northcutt of the West Ham United Statisticians' Group . . . all for their help on the 1986 edition which is incorporated in this revision. Also, thanks to Martin Penton, who was missed out in 1986! Thanks, for the programmes.

Thanks, too, to Gerald Toon at ACL for his constant (but necessary) 'badgering' to ensure this was published before Christmas, to our patient book-binder, Brian Martin (who is, thankfully, a West Ham fan!), to Trevor Hartley for his creative skills in the design room, and to Alvin Martin for his foreword.

Finally, thanks to Philip Evans, Managing Director of Independent UK Sports Publications, for his unfaltering faith in this project, and to Andrew Farley and Mark O'Connor for their sterling efforts in the marketing and distribution department.

We couldn't have done it without you!

John Lyall, a loyal club servant for 34 years, carries off the FA Cup after his Second Division side toppled Arsenal 1-0 in May 1980 - the last major honour Hammers won.

6

FOREWORD

By Alvin Martin
West Ham United & England

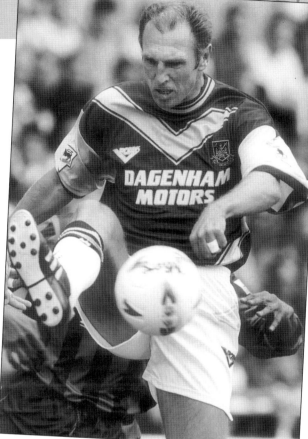

IT'S 20 years ago now that I first walked down the forecourt that leads to the main stand, a skinny 16 year old hoping to be taken on as an apprentice professional, and not knowing what West Ham was really all about.

I think at this moment in time it's fair to say that I understand what makes Upton Park a special place. It's a club with a tremendous history of players and a great reputation in the world of football, so it's a privilege to be asked to write the foreword to this excellent book.

There have been many ups and downs during my time here, but not many regrets. Not being able to watch the 'great man' first hand was perhaps something I lost out on - 'Mooro' left the club a few months before I arrived - but every player, without exception, that I spoke to about Bobby is full of nothing but admiration for him. He has always been held up to every youngster at the club as the perfect example and it would have been something to have been around the place when 'Mooro' was here.

Well, if I didn't get to play with Bobby, I certainly got the chance to run out with some other great players - Trevor, Dev, Parksey, Frank, Van Der Elst, Stewart, McAvennie, Cottee, Dicks, all great players in their own right. But the best for me was Bonzo, an inspirational leader and the one player above all that I would pick first on my team-sheet week in, week out. The John Lyall team of the early 80's, led by Bill, was probably the most enjoyable era of all . . . three Wembley visits in quick succession and a European campaign to boot.

Young Alvin Martin with dad Albert at Upton Park in 1980

Of course there have been times when I'm sure every West Ham supporter has asked themselves the question, why? - relegation, promotion, relegation, promotion in the late 80's and early 90's, this period certainly tested their faith to the full. There can be some explanation when I tell you that over the years, the quote that sums up our supporters is one that they themselves have given me when I've asked them why: "Because Alv, we're West Ham, and that is that."

One thing is for sure, the support we have is unique and without it West Ham would not be the club it is today, and when my playing career is over I expect to be shouting with the rest . . . because I'm West Ham, and that is that.

ALVIN MARTIN
October 27, 1994

THE MASTER SIGNS.
The legendary Bobby Moore obliges a young fan during a break in training at West Ham Stadium, Custom House, prior to the 1964 FA Cup Final.

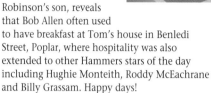

ADAMS, William 1936-37

Born: Tynemouth. 3.11.02
Lge apps: 3 (1 gl)

■ Bill made a sensational start in West Ham's colours when he scored against his old club, Southampton, in Hammers' 2-0 victory at the Dell on 21 November 1936 - quite a feat for a right-half! He had a slow start at the Dell - after making his debut against Stoke City in Aug. 1927, he had to wait over three years until his next first team outing. But once in the Saints side, he went on to make 205 League and Cup outings and was appointed captain. However, he was destined for only a brief stay at Upton Park, transferring to Southend United in Jan. 1937. He began his career with Sunderland Colliery and then Guildford City before transferring to Southampton. Bill returned to Hampshire in 1937 and was mine host of the Half Way Inn at Chandlers Ford for 26 years until his death in Mar. 1963.

ALLAN, Robert 1889-03

Born: Dundee, Scotland
Lge apps (TIW): 21 (1 gl)
SL apps (WHU): 52 (1 gl)
Cup apps: 5

■ In common with his colleague and fellow-countryman Charlie Craig, Bob hailed from Dundee and made his TIW debut in a 3-1 reverse at Southampton in Dec.1889, playing at outside-right. He held that position on all but two occasions during Hammers' last campaign under the Ironworks banner, switching to inside-left against Sheppey United and trying out the right-half berth he was later to fill with such distinction in a victorious Hermit Road encounter with Gravesend. His time on the wing prompted the following testimonial in a 1900-01 club handbook: "Shows excellent judgment in everything he does, and can take hard knocks and play on as game as ever. Centres on the run, and occasionally contributes a long shot with plenty of steam behind it. Doesn't neglect his inside man, and although weighty, can show a rare turn of speed when necessary." A letter sent to the late Jack Helliar from an old supporter (now deceased), who used to play schools football with trainer Tom Robinson's son, reveals that Bob Allen often used to have breakfast at Tom's house in Benledi Street, Poplar, where hospitality was also extended to other Hammers stars of the day including Hughie Monteith, Roddy McEachrane and Billy Grassam. Happy days!

ALLEN, Clive 1992-94

Born: Whitechapel, East London. 20.5.61
Lge apps: 38 (17 gls)
Cup Apps: 6 (1 gl)

■ One of the game's most prolific goalscorers, Clive joined his sixth London club when he was transferred from Chelsea for £250,000 on the eve of the transfer deadline in Mar. 1992 to begin a two-year spell with Hammers. The son of former Tottenham and QPR star Les Allen, and the third member of the famous family to wear claret and blue, Clive first proved his insatiable appetite for goals as a young star with Havering, Essex and London Schools teams. Although West Ham were the nearest club to his Hornchurch home, and he trained with Spurs, Clive signed apprentice for QPR in 1976 and pro two years later. In the summer of 1980, aged only 19 and after one full League season, Clive became the youngest million pound player when he moved from Rangers to Arsenal for £1.25m . . . but moved on to Terry Venables' Crystal Palace before the following season started, having played only three friendlies for the Gunners! He was swapped for Kenny Sansom in another deal valued at £1.25m! Within eight weeks of signing Clive, Venables moved to QPR and after a difficult 10 months at Selhurst Park, the striker was reunited with "Venners" at Loftus Road, in a £700,000 deal. His first season back in West London brought him an appearance in the 1982 FA Cup Final v Spurs, but Clive withdrew through injury after only 10 minutes and was forced to miss the replay, which Spurs won. Tottenham was his next port of call, in 1984, at a cost of £700,000. A spate of injuries hampered his contribution but in the third of his four seasons at White Hart Lane Clive reached his peak. In a glorious 1986/87 campaign he broke Jimmy Greaves' club record by scoring 33 League goals and 49 overall, including the first in the 1987 FA Cup Final v Coventry City after just two minutes. Unfortunately, Clive had to settle for a second loser's medal, but there was an immediate tonic as he collected both the Football Writers' Association and PFA's Player of the Year awards. In addition to youth and under-21 caps, Clive made five full appearances for England. His debut came as substitute against Brazil in the Maracana Stadium in 1984. His turbulent spell at

Clive Allen

White Hart Lane ended in March 1988, when, ironically, that man Venables sold him to French club Bordeaux for £1m - his third million pound transfer - although he remained with the north Londoners until the end of that season. He stayed in France for only a year before yet another £1m deal brought him back to England to play for newly-promoted Manchester City. Despite maintaining an impressive scoring record, it became evident soon after the start of his second season at Maine Road that he did not figure in their future plans, so he returned to London in December 1991 to join another of his father's former clubs, Chelsea, for a modest £250,000. The same fee took him to Upton Park 14 months later when Clive celebrated his debut with a goal . . . at Stamford Bridge! Unfortunately injury restricted Clive to just three more outings that season and his late arrival could not save Hammers from relegation from the old First Division in May 1992. A year later, though, Clive was a hero again, as he netted the crucial second goal, as substitute, in the final home game against Cambridge United. That 2-0 victory ensured Hammers pipped Portsmouth for the runners-up spot behind Newcastle United, and automatic promotion to the newly-named Premier League, by a single goal! Although Clive made only two sub. appearances between January and the promotion party, his 12 goals before Christmas proved crucial. Clive's third season with Hammers was also marred by injury but his ratio of almost a goal every other game made him a successful short-term success. A goal-taker who did all his work in the penalty area, where he found space and had the knack of being in the right place at the right time. Clive's farewell game for Hammers was as sub in the goalless FA Cup quarter-final tie v Luton Town at Upton Park (14.3.94). Millwall - Clive's seventh London club - paid £75,000 for him on transfer deadline day, Mar. 1994.

ALLEN, Martin   1989-

Born: Reading, Berks. 18.8.65.
Lge apps: 158 (23 gls)
Cup apps: 28 (9 gls)

■ The most successful midfield goalscorer since Martin Peters, Martin became the second member of the Allen family (cousins Paul and Clive completed the trio) to play for Hammers when Lou Macari paid £660,000 to make him his first signing after succeeeding John Lyall as manager. The former QPR midfielder capped his debut with a goal in the 3-1 Second Division home win v Plymouth Argyle (26.8.89) and added another 10 in his first season. Although he earned the nickname "Mad Dog" for his tenacious ball-winning efforts, Martin's surging runs from deep, and eye for the long-range strike, have yielded a good ratio of goals and scoring opportunities. In five seasons at Upton Park, Martin has scored 32 goals. He was particularly effective in Hammers' 1992/93 promotion-winning campaign when he forged a fearless new central midfield partnership with Peter Butler and netted 10 times. And an

Martin Allen

impressive spell that produced five goals in six games near the end of the 1993/94 campaign placed him third in the team's goal-scoring chart, behind Morley and Chapman. The return to the top flight also marked a significant improvement to Martin's disciplinary record - just three bookings compared to the previous season's tally of 13 yellow cards, which resulted in an FA fine and five-match suspension. Martin first showed his competitive strength as captain of England Schoolboys in 1980, the year in which he signed apprentice forms for QPR. Terry Venables gave him his first pro contract three years later, although it was Alan Mullery who called up Martin for his first team debut, in a UEFA Cup, first round, tie against KR Reykjavik (Iceland) at Highbury in Sept. 1984 (the game was switched because UEFA banned the use of Rangers' plastic pitch). He made his League debut for R's as sub. at Luton in Mar. 1985. A year later Martin was sub at Wembley when QPR were beaten 3-0 by Oxford United in the Milk (League) Cup Final. An intense, demonstrative character at times, Martin likes to celebrate his goals - especially the spectacular ones - by running towards the corner flag. His father Dennis, who travels all over the country to watch his son, played for Charlton Athletic, Reading and AFC Bournemouth.

ALLEN, Paul   1979-85

Born: Aveley, Essex. 28.8.62
Lge apps: 149 (6 gls)
Cup apps: 43 (5 gls)

■ The subject of a shock transfer to Tottenham Hotspur for a fee set at £425,000 by the Football League Tribunal during the summer of 1985, this little midfield dynamo was already the proud holder of two national football records. In May 1980 he became (at 17 years and 256 days) the youngest player ever to appear in an English FA Cup Final, collecting a winners' medal to boot. He also smashed Bobby Moore's long-standing record of 18 England Youth caps the following year. Before joining his cousin Clive Allen at White Hart Lane, Paul signed apprentice in July 1978 and full professional forms for Hammers in Aug. 1979, after a spell at QPR, where his uncle, Les Allen, - also a former Spurs' star, was once manager. A one-time Essex

Paul Allen

and Thurrock Boys starlet, he returned to West Ham's First Division side in 1984 after a long lay-off through injury and made a major contribution towards the club's successful fight against relegation, displaying the kind of form which saw him blossom into one of the finest midfield players in the country and led to Spurs and Liverpool battling for his signature. The eventual winners from North London paid Hammers 50 per cent of the profit on his £550,000 move to Southampton in September 1993, because of a clause in his contract. Paul appeared in both the 1987 and 1991 FA Cup Finals for Spurs and amassed a total of 376 League and Cup games while at White Hart Lane, scoring 28 goals. Paul was the first of the 'Allen Dynasty' to play for Hammers, being followed by cousins Martin and Clive Allen. England Under-21 international. Paul's original transfer from West Ham was one of several player moves, which were the subject of an FA inquiry in the summer of 1994, and which led to Spurs' severe punishment: They were banned from the 1994/95 FA Cup, deducted six Premiership points and fined £600,000 plus costs.

ALLEN, Percy   1919-23

Born: West Ham, London. 2.7.1895
Lge apps: 80 (5 gls)
Cup apps: 6

Percy Allen

■ Joining Hammers from local amateur soccer for the club's initial League season of 1919/20 (after being commissioned during WW1 army service), Percy made his Second Division debut at outside-right in a 1-2 home defeat to Birmingham on 1 November 1919. Although he was tried in the centre-forward spot, it wasn't until he converted to right-half that he found his true role to become an ever-present in the 1921-22 campaign and prompted the following comment in a club handbook of that period: "A class player who would do admirably in First League Football." Unfortunately he was never put to the test in the higher grade, as he was transferred to Northampton Town before Hammers' promotion to Division One in 1923, later seeing service with Peterborough, Lincoln City, Weymouth and Stamford Town before retiring from the game. He then returned to his roots working for West Ham Corporation, while continuing to support their footballing counterparts at Upton Park. Eventually the owner of a newsagent's in Barking Road, East Ham, Percy passed away at the age of 74 in Oct. 1969; but his son Don continued to keep the family name alive at the Boleyn Ground by his presence in the press box as a sports reporter with the South Essex Recorder Group of Newspapers.

ALLEN, Robert H.   1919-20

Born: Dundee.

■ A mysterious figure from Hammers' first League season who, according to the record books, came from Dundee and made only one Second Division appearance - albeit a scoring one. His moment of glory came on 1 November 1919, when he netted from the centre-forward position in the 1-2 home defeat v Birmingham.

Malcolm Allison

ALLISON, Malcolm   1951-1957

Born: Dartford, Kent. 5.9.27.
Lge apps: 238 (10 gls)
Cup apps: 17

■ Signed from Charlton Athletic (22.2.51) after seven seasons at The Valley. Malcolm's influence on West Ham United cannot be underestimated. During manager Ted Fenton's reign, it was Malcolm who - with Ted's blessing - took charge of the coaching sessions that helped pave the way for aspiring youngsters such as Bobby Moore, who, ironically, went on to take Malcolm's place in the heart of defence. A master tactician and innovator, Malcolm was years ahead of his time in his coaching and fitness routines, some of which were based on continental ideas. Fellow pro and former England youth coach, John Cartwright, once said of Mal: "He should be revered. They should have a statue to him at West Ham . . . he laid the foundation for the success of the club - not by what he did on the field, but the knowledge he gave to other people." Widely recognised as the founder of the so-called West Ham Academy, which met regularly in the afternoons, after training, at Cassetarri's Cafe in the nearby Barking Road and at local dog

Malcolm Allison (centre) enjoys a cuppa with Jimmy Andrews, Dave Sexton, Noel Cantwell, John Bond, Frank O'Farrell and Mal Musgrove at Cassettari's Cafe in the Barking Road

tracks. His successes as a leading coach have tended to eclipse his fine career as a centre-half in the fifties. But Malcolm's cherished ambition to play in the First Division was cruelly shattered when he struck down by tuberculosis eight games into the club's 1957/58 promotion season. Malcolm's last-ever senior appearance for Hammers came at Sheffield United (16.9.57). He was taken ill after the game and had a lung removed in hospital. Although he battled tremendously hard to beat T.B., making a steady comeback in the reserves, Malcolm had to accept the bitter truth that his first team days were over. The night he finally realised this (8.9.58) will forever remain etched on the memories of all those who were present. Fenton had to make a choice for the number six shirt: Allison, having fought his way back to fitness; or Bobby Moore, the young pretender hungry for his first big chance. It was Malcolm's great friend and team mate, Noel Cantwell, who, when asked for his opinion by Fenton, nominated Moore for his debut v Manchester United. Let Moore himself tell the story of that emotional night under the Upoton Park lights. In Jeff Powell's book, Bobby Moore, The Life and Times of a Sporting Legend, Moore says: "I'd been a professional for two and a half months and Malcolm had taught me everything I knew. For all the money in the world I wanted to play. For all the money in the world I wanted Malcolm to play because he'd worked like a bastard for this one game in the First Division. It would have meant the world to him. Just one more game, just one minute in that game. I knew that on the day Malcolm with all his experience would probably do a better job than me. But maybe I'm one for the future. It somehow had to be that when I walked into the dressing room and found out I was playing, Malcolm was the first person I saw. I was embarrassed to look at him. He said "Well done. I hope you do well." I knew he meant it but I knew how he felt. For a moment I wanted to push the shirt at him and say "Go on, Malcolm. It's yours. Have your game. I can't stop you. Go on, Malcolm. My time will come. But he walked out and I thought maybe my time wouldn't come again. Maybe this would be my only chance. I thought: you've got to be lucky to get the chance, and when the chance comes you've got to be good enough to take it. I went out and played the way Malcolm had always told

me to play. Afterwards I looked for him back in the dressing room. Couldn't find him. When Malcolm was coaching schoolboys. He took a liking to me when I don't think anyone else at West Ham saw anything special in me. Just for that, I would have done anything for him. Every house needs a foundation and Malcolm gave me mine. It went beyond that. He was the be-all and end-all for me. I looked up to the man. It's not too strong to say I loved him. Malcolm said one simple thing which was to stay in my life forever. We sometimes used to get the same bus from the ground and we were sitting upstairs one day when Malcolm said very quietly: "Keep forever asking youself: If I get the ball now, who will I give it to?" He told me that was di Stefano's secret at Real Madrid." Malcolm Shunned medical advice to continue his playing career with Romford in the Southern League. Soccer coach at Cambridge University and Toronto (Canada) before taking his first step up the managerial ladder with Bath City. From there he moved further west to Plymouth Argyle, followed by a successful period with Joe Mercer at Manchester City, where the pair won all the game's major honours. After those days "Big Mal's" career took some diverse points of call, numbering among them Crystal Palace (where his flamboyance was characterised by his fedora, kingsize cigars and champagne lifestyle), Man. City again, FC Sporting Lisbon (whom he steered to championship success), Middlesbrough and non-league Durham side Willington. Was in Kuwait coaching the national side until March 1986. He was briefly back in the big-time in 1992/93 as boss of Bristol Rovers who gained a shock FA Cup draw at Aston Villa and a 4-0 victory over deadly rivals Bristol City under his management. But he was later dismissed and his unique talent is once again going to waste. Now based in Cleveland.

Played	League		FAC		LC		Europe		Total	
	App	Gls	App	Gls	App	Gls	App	Gls	App	Gls
1950-51	10	0	0	0	0	0	0	0	10	0
1951-52	38	0	3	0	0	0	0	0	41	0
1952-53	39	2	1	0	0	0	0	0	40	2
1953-54	42	0	3	0	0	0	0	0	45	0
1954-55	25	0	2	0	0	0	0	0	27	0
1955-56	40	3	6	0	0	0	0	0	46	3
1956-57	39	4	2	0	0	0	0	0	41	4
1957-58	5	1	0	0	0	0	0	0	5	1
TOTAL	238	10	17	0	0	0	0	0	255	10

ALLISON, Tommy   1903-09

Born: Edinburgh, Scotland. 1875
SL apps: 156 (7 gls)
Cup apps: 9

■ Tom began his career with New Brighton Tower, who staged Second Division football at the Tower Athletic Grounds between 1888 and 1901. When they folded he transferred to Southern League Reading, but after two successful seasons with the Berkshire club, he led a four-strong delegation of the Biscuitmen's playing staff to join Hammers for the last campaign at the old Memorial Grounds. By far the most successful of the quartet, he became a regular member of the senior side and was appointed vice-captain and awarded the proceeds of a Western League match against Portsmouth in recognition of his services. From a scoring debut against Kettering Town in Sept. 1903, until his last appearance v Watford in April 1909, he never gave less than his best, and could consider himself unfortunate in not adding to the Scottish junior cap he won with Strathclyde, at senior level. Died Mar. 4, 1961.

PROMINENT FOOTBALLERS.

T. ALLISON,
WEST HAM UNITED.

AMBLER, Charles   1901-02

Born: 1868.
SL apps: 1

■ This reserve team goalkeeper won a place in the limelight almost by default when an administrative mistake meant Hammers playing host to Spurs in a Southern League clash at the Memorial Grounds as well as receiving Leyton for an FA Cup third qualifying match. With the prospect of larger gate receipts from the meeting with the more illustrious opponents from Tottenham, Hammers solved the problem by conceding home advantage in the Cup and sending their reserve X1 to Leyton, where Charlie kept a clean sheet in a 1-0 victory. Back at the Memorial Grounds the first team lost by the same margin - a result which prompted the West Ham management to rest the great Hughie Montieth from a post both he and his many admirers regarded as his by right. So Charles duly made his Southern League debut the following week v QPR. There was to be no fairytale ending, however, as West Ham went down 2-1 at Rangers' Latimer Road, North Kensington, home after having to change in the Latimer Arms pub and run down the road to the pitch. So ended Charles Ambler's less-than-glamourous taste of first-class football 1901-

style. There was one further irony the next week (Nov. 16, 1901) when West Ham's full-strength first-team crashed out of the FA Cup on their own ground, beaten by Essex village team Grays. Charlie had begun his career with Bostal Rovers and signed pro for Royal Arsenal in 1891. He moved to Clapton (where he reverted to amateur status) in 1892; Dartford, 1893; Luton Town, Sept. 1894; and after making 133 first team apps for Spurs between 1894/1900, moved again to Gravesend and New Brompton in 1900. After leaving Irons he joined Millwall in the summer of 1902. Charles passed away in 1952.

ANDERSON, Edward   1933-35

Born: Durham
Lge apps: 26
Cup apps: 2

■ A big broad-shouldered right-half signed from Torquay United, Ted made 24 Second Division appearances during the 1933-34 season after making his debut on the opening day of that campaign against Bolton Wanderers at Upton Park. The following season he lost the first team spot to Ted Fenton, and was subsequently transferred to Chester after only two more League outings. Ted played for Jarrow before joining Wolves in Dec.1929 and had two seasons with Tranmere Rovers before WW2.

ANDREW, George   1967

Born: Glasgow, Scotland. 24.11.45
Lge apps: 2

■ Fair-haired young Scot who arrived at Upton Park via Glasgow junior side Possilpark YMCA, in Sept. 1963. One of several players tried in the centre-half position as a replacement for Ken Brown, he made the first of only two League appearances at home to Sunderland in Feb. 1967. After a short spell at Cyrstal Palace, he joined Southern League Romford and found his true niche at Brooklands. Then became a teacher in Cornwall where he played in the county league with St. Blaizey. George died suddenly in July 1994.

ANDREWS, Jimmy   1951-55

Born: Invergordon, Scotland. 1.2.27
Lge apps: 114 (21 gls)
Cup apps: 6

■ Another Scot, this flying left-winger was signed from Dundee FC for £4,750 in Nov. 1951 - quite a substantial fee those days! Jimmy proved to be a worthwhile investment, giving the club great service before leaving for near-neighbours Leyton Orient in 1956. After winding up his player career at QPR, he went on to gain a fine reputation as a coach and later managed Cardiff City after another ex-Hammer - Frank O'Farrell - vacated the post. Now scouting for Southampton.

ARMSTRONG, Eric   1946-53

Born: Hebburn-on-Tyne, Northumberland. 25.5.21
Lge apps: 1

■ Whole-hearted wing-half who rarely played in the first XI, but inspired everyone with his devotion to the game. Signed from Cramlington Welfare FC after service in the Royal Navy in WW2, he had played for East Northumberland Boys before progressing to senior soccer. A member of the Combination championship side of 1947-48, he turned his attention to coaching Hammers' junior sides and became coach of Harwich and Parkeston FC in 1954. Spent over a decade as the Essex club's manager until his untimely death in 1969.

ARNOTT, John H.   1953-55

Born: Sydenham, London. 6.9.32.
Lge apps: 6 (2 gls).

■ Played four League games as an amateur, but made only two further first XI appearances after turning pro for the 1954-55 season. Later had spells with Shrewsbury Town. AFC Bournemouth and Gillingham; finishing his playing career in the Southern League with Dover, where he was still playing until well into his forties.

The £4,750 fee West Ham paid Dundee for winger Jimmy Andrews (below) in 1951 turned out to be money well spent

ASHTON, Herbert   1908-15

Born: Blackburn, Lancashire. 1887.

■ With 226 Southern League outings, "Tiddler" Ashton holds Hammers' all-time appearance record in that competition, totalling nine more than his nearest rival - team-mate and fellow Blackburn lad, the aptly named Fred Blackburn. He joined Hammers from Accrington in 1908, after helping them win the Lancashire Combination in 1905/06. As his nickname would indicate, Herbert was small in stature, but the diminutive winger had plenty of fans ready to help him out when the going got rough, a section of whom took their protective instincts too far when they invaded the pitch to do battle on their hero's behalf in a particularly tough Upton Park encounter with Syd King's old team, New Brompton. Luckily West Ham chairman Bill White was able to placate the fans and order was restored. The incident seemed to underline the fact that Ashton could do little wrong in Hammers' fans' eyes. Herbert joined the Royal Flying Corps during WW1 as a mechanic, but still managed to turn out on 63 occasions in the old London Combination. He was also chosen to represent the Southern League v the Irish League in 1915.

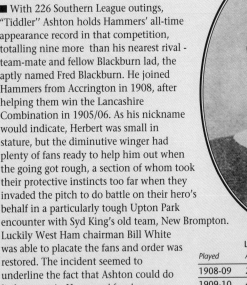

Played	League		FAC		LC		Europe		Total	
	App	Gls	App	Gls	App	Gls	App	Gls	App	Gls
1908-09	27	1	2	0	0	0	0	0	29	1
1909-10	42	4	5	0	0	0	0	0	47	4
1910-11	37	6	4	0	0	0	0	0	41	6
1911-12	33	3	5	0	0	0	0	0	38	3
1912-13	36	6	4	0	0	0	0	0	40	6
1913-14	35	3	4	1	0	0	0	0	39	4
1914-15	14	0	1	0	0	0	0	0	15	0
TOTAL	224	23	25	1	0	0	0	0	249	24

ASKEW, William   1912-15

Born: London
SL apps: 104 (2 gls)
Cup apps: 8

■ Although relatively short (5ft 9ins) for a centre-half, Bill was a steady performer and became something of a fixture in Hammers' defence in the season leading up to the outbreak of WW1. Previously with Aston Villa and Norwich he was an ever-present in the Southern League team in 1913-14 and was absent on only two occasions the following campaign. He continued to help the club in the initial war-time season by turning out 28 times in the London Combination and also underlined the seriousness with which this makeshift tournament was regarded by the players by managing to get himself sent off twice!

William Askew

ATKINS, C.   1908-09

SL apps: 2 (1 gl)

■ This centre-forward's brief flirtation with first X1 football saw him among the scorers in a 4-0 Boleyn Castle romp over Essex rivals Southend United. His appearance in the following week's 3-1 reverse v Coventry City at Highfield Road proved to be his last Southern League outing.

ATTEVELD, Ray   1992

Born: Amsterdam, Holland. 8.9.1966.
Lge apps: 1.
Cup apps: 2.

■ Made a slice of Hammers' history when, in Feb. 1992, he became the first Dutchman to make his League debut (in the last season before the old First Division became the Premier League) for West Ham. But apart from that outing, in a 2-1 defeat at Sheffield Wednesday (22.2.92), the midfielder's only other appearances during his month's loan from Everton were in the two FA Cup fifth round clashes against Sunderland - a 1-1 draw at Roker Park (Feb. 15) and the replay at Upton Park (Feb. 26) which Hammers lost 3-2. Unable to regain favour at Goodison Park, where he played 51 League games, he joined two former Hammers, Nicky Morgan and Leroy Rosenior, at Bristol City.

ATWELL, Reg   1938-46

Born: Oakengates, Wellington, Shrops. 23.3.20
Lge apps: 4.

■ Tough-tackling wing-half. Signed from Denaby United. Served with Essex Regt. and RA through WW2, during which he guested with Burnley. Made a big name for himself when transferred to the Turf Moor club. Son of a former Shrewsbury player, Reg played over 250 games for the Lancastrians (including a 1947 Cup final appearance) before moving to Bradford City in 1954.

Reg Atwell

AYRIS, John   1970-76

Born: Wapping, London. 8.1.53
Lge apps: 57 (gls. 1)
Cup: 8 (gls. 1).

■ Flying young right-wing prospect who didn't quite fulfil early promise after experiencing injury problems. Signed as a full pro in Oct. 1970, and made his League debut the same month v Burnley. He was selected for the England Youth team seven times in 1971. Given a free transfer at the end of the 1976-77 season, he first joined Wimbledon and then went on trial to Brentford.

John Ayris

BAILEY, Dan   1912-21

Born: East Ham, London. 26.6.1893
SL apps: 49 (13 gls)
Cup apps: 4 (3 gls)
Lge apps: 35 (9 gls)
Cup apps: 3 (1 gl)

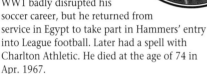
Dan Bailey

■ Signed from Custom House FC, Dan took over Dany Shea's inside-right position when the latter transferred to Blackburn Rovers for a record £2,000 in 1913; he was a member of the side which went from Jan. 1, 1913 to Sept. 16, the same year without defeat in the Southern League. WW1 badly disrupted his soccer career, but he returned from service in Egypt to take part in Hammers' entry into League football. Later had a spell with Charlton Athletic. He died at the age of 74 in Apr. 1967.

BAILLIE, David   1925-29

Born: Ilford, Essex. 1906
Lge apps: 16
Cup apps: 1

■ This locally-born goalkeeper was with Hammers for around six seasons, mostly as understudy to the great Ted Hufton, but enjoyed a fair amount of first team outings. Signed from Coryton FC, he was given the following testimony in a 1920's club handbook: "There are few goalies in the country who can hold and field a wet ball like him." He transferred to Chester in 1929, where he was under the managership of Charlie Hewitt, but returned to the Boleyn when he retired from playing to take up the post of assistant groundsman. Dave passed away in Nov. 1967, aged 61.

BAINBRIDGE, Ken   1946-49

Born: Barking, Essex. 15.1.21
Lge apps: 79 (16 gls)
Cup apps: 4 (1 gl)

■ A prominent member of Hammers' senior side in the immediate post-war period, this speedy winger was a handful for his opponents and not averse to having a crack at goal. His scoring exploits became even more pronounced when transferred to Reading and later Southend United, where he ended his League career. Ken holds the record for scoring the quickest goal at Upton Park - in the Second Division match v Barnsley (29.8.49). It was timed at nine seconds from the kick-off. Hammers won 2-1.

BALL, John   1929-30

Born: Stockport, Cheshire. 29.9.1899
Lge apps: 15 (9 gls)

■ A former miner, who first made his mark with Silverwood Colliery FC in the Sheffield Association League. It was not long before League clubs began to notice his goalscoring prowess and he subsequently joined Sheffield United. Fortune didn't smile on him at Bramall Lane, however, a bad injury forcing him back into non-League soccer for a season with Wath Athletic in the Midland League. His career underwent a remarkable transformation when he signed for First Division Bury and his fairytale comeback was completed in 1927 when he was chosen to play for England v Ireland in Belfast. Also lining-up against the Irish that day were his two team mates-to-be, Stan Earle and Ted Hufton (the latter sustained a broken arm and despite carrying on for far longer than was wise, eventually left the field). There were no substitutes allowed in those days, but Johnny Ball gave a creditable performance as makeshift 'keeper as England's 10 men went down 0-2. Whether this incident played any part in the sharp-eyed inside-left joining Hammers is not known, but his nine goals in 15 First Division appearances certainly paid dividends. John joined Coventry City when he left the Boleyn Ground.

BAMLETT, Tommy   1904-05

SL apps: 18
Cup apps: 1

■ Along with goalkeeper Matt Kingsley and full-back partner Dave Gardner, Tommy made up a trio of former Newcastle United defenders who were on duty for Hammers' inaugural Upton Park match against Millwall on September 1, 1904. A Geordie by birth, he made his Newcastle debut against those other footballing Magpies, Notts County, at Trent Bridge in Oct. 1901, after his signing from local league Kibblesworth. Only one more League outing in the famous black and white stripes followed, however, before his move south. Also known as Herbert, the left-back's 18 Southern League outings for Irons in 1904-05 represented his best spell of first X1 football before his return to non-league soccer with West Stanley in his native North-East.

BANKS, Steven   1992

Born: Hillingdon, Middlesex 9.2.72

■ Young 5ft 11ins goalkeeper who made only one first team appearance for Hammers - in a low-key 2-2 draw with Bristol Rovers in the Anglo-Italian Cup, preliminary round, at Upton Park (2.9.92). Steve represented Berkshire Schools and after progressing through the youth ranks, he made his Reserve team bow for West Ham at Fulham (11.10.89). Spent a while on loan to his home town club, non-league Wokingham, where he came under the watchful eye of former mentor and Hammers' 'keeper Phil Parkes. Steve was given a free transfer in May 1993 and joined Gillingham.

BANNER, Arthur   1938-48

Born: Sheffield, Yorkshire. 28.6.18
Lge apps: 27

■ A strong, sturdy full-back who was one of quite a number of players who managed to play for the club before, during and after the war. Originally signed from Doncaster Rovers before hostilities broke out, he saw army service in the Essex Regt. and R.A., attaining rank of sergeant. He moved to Leyton Orient in 1948. When he left Brisbane Road he became player/manager of Sittingbourne in Kent, and later coached Ilford to the Amateur Cup Final in 1958.

Arthur Banner

BANTON, Dale   1979-80

Born: Kensington, London. 15.5.61
Lge apps: 5
Cup apps: 1

■ Promising midfielder who was reluctantly allowed to leave Upton Park owing to intense competition for places. The former Middlesex Schools star grabbed the headlines when scoring five goals in one match at the end of the 1982-83 season for Aldershot, the club he joined on leaving Hammers. He then joined FA Cup giant-killers York City in 1984-85. He completed 138 League appearances for the Minstermen (49 gls) before transferring to Walsall in Oct. 1988, but made only 10 outings there, moving on to Grimsby Town in Mar. 1989, where he totalled only eight appearances before returning to Aldershot in Aug. 1989.

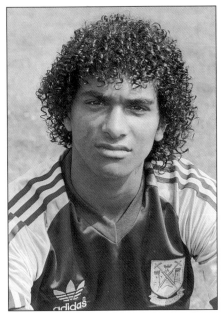

Bobby Barnes

Billy Barnes

BARNES, Bobby   1980-85

Born: Kingston, Surrey. 17.12.62
Lge apps: 22 (3 gls)
Cup apps: 7 (1 gl)

■ Fast, skilful winger with the ability to take on and beat opponents, he scored on his League debut v Watford in Sept. 1980. Won an extended run in the first team during Hammers' injury crisis of 1983-84, and staked a regular claim in 1984-85. A member of the Youth Cup-winning team of 1981, he also had England Youth honours. Had a spell on loan to Scunthorpe United in 1985-86 before being transferred to Aldershot for £15,000 in Mar. 1986. In 1987 Bobby moved to Swindon Town where he scored 13 goals in 45 League games for The Robins, before moving on again to Bournemouth in Mar. 1989. He made only 14 appearances at Dean Court, however, and was on his travels again in October the same year to join Northampton Town where he played 98 times for the League side, scoring 37 goals in the process. In Feb. 1992 he joined Peterborough United but the following season he tried his luck north of the border with Scottish Premier Partick Thistle. Bobby was training with Ipswich Town, under his old Upton Park bosses John Lyall and Mick McGiven on Mondays and Tuesdays, before jetting off from Stansted Airport, flying home after each match on Saturday!

BARNES, William   1902-04

SL apps: 48 (5 gls)
Cup apps: 5

■ A Cup Final hero with Sheffield United, Billy joined Hammers from the Yorkshiremen in the summer of 1902 having previously gained an unexpected place in the Blades' line-up at outside-right for the FA Cup Final replay of 1902 v Southampton at Crystal Palace; he replaced Bennett who was injured in the first drawn game and scored the decisive goal in a 2-1 victory. After two years regular service in West Ham's Southern League X1 Billy moved to Luton and then across London to Queens Park Rangers, who were then playing at Park Royal. He later became something of a pioneer in his role as a trail-blazing coach on the continent with Spanish club Bilbao, thus beginning a trend with which ex-Hammer Malcolm Allison was also familiar with in more recent times. Hammers met Billy's club on their first-ever continental tour in 1921 and set a good example by winning 2-0. While Billy was finding fame in international football circles, his brother Alfred (who lived at Dale Road, Canning Town) was making a name for himself in a different sphere. being Labour M.P. for East Ham South, later attaining Cabinet rank. He began his pro career with Leyton.

BARRETT, Jim, Snr.   1925-38

Born: West Ham, London. 1907

CARRERAS CIGARETTES

J. BARRETT
WEST HAM U. (2ND DIVISION)

■ A name to conjure with, and one inextricably entwined in Hammers' heritage. A "larger than life" character, "Big Jim" - as he was affectionately known - first played at Upton Park as a member of the West Ham Boys team which met Liverpool in the English Shield Final of 1920-21. The then Duke of York (later H.M. King George VI) was among the crowd which broke the existing attendance record at the Boleyn. A team-mate of Jim's that day was Billy "Bubbles" Murray, so-called because of his uncanny resemblance to the boy in the famous painting by Millais entitled "Bubbles" and used to advertise Pears Soap - hence the origin of Hammers' theme song. Although Billy Murray had no connection with West Ham United, he had been a colleague of Jim's in the renowned Park School side, to whom Jim had transferred from Abbey School because the latter had no football team. Also involved with Jim's early development was the Fairbairn House Boys' Club, which also produced other players of Football League standard such as Ted Fenton, Jack Townrow, George Barber (of Chelsea fame) and Alf "Snowball" Barrett of Fulham. Jim's namesake had also played for Park School and was a member of the West Ham Boys team which won the 1916-17 English Shield Final, defeating Grimsby 2-0.

Signing professional forms in Hammers' Cup Final year of 1923 at the age of 16, Jim had to wait two years to make his League debut v Spurs at White Hart Lane on March 28, 1925. It was the first of a total which stand (in 1994) as the seventh highest appearance record in the club's history. Big Jim's solitary international appearance v Ireland in 1928 constituted a record at the other end of the scale. His four minutes on the field, before injury ended his aspirations, remains the shortest recorded international career. He continued to be an invaluable asset to his club, however, not least because of his remarkable versatility which had seen him perform in every position for the first and second XI's. His ability to switch from defence to attack was borne out by his tally of more than 50 League and Cup goals whilst a Hammer. A story worth telling was that during a Hammers' tour of Holland he deliberately aimed at a clock behind the goal and hit the target to put it out of action! In 1945-46 Jim was in charge of the "A" team, and actually played in the same side as his son, Jim Barrett junior. After his retirement he had the satisfaction of seeing "Young Jim" carry on the family tradition in the League side. His later life was beset with ill-health, and following a long stay in hospital he passed away on Nov. 25, 1970 at the age of 63. England cap: 1929 v Northern Ireland, (1).

Played	League App	Gls	FAC App	Gls	LC App	Gls	Europe App	Gls	Total App	Gls
1924-25	5	0	0	0	0	0	0	0	5	0
1925-26	42	6	1	0	0	0	0	0	43	6
1926-27	42	1	3	0	0	0	0	0	45	1
1927-28	34	5	0	0	0	0	0	0	34	5
1928-29	22	1	2	3	0	0	0	0	24	4
1929-30	40	7	4	1	0	0	0	0	44	8
1930-31	40	4	1	0	0	0	0	0	41	4
1931-32	38	3	2	0	0	0	0	0	40	3
1932-33	40	8	6	0	0	0	0	0	46	8
1933-34	38	5	2	0	0	0	0	0	40	5
1934-35	41	5	2	0	0	0	0	0	43	5
1935-36	40	2	2	0	0	0	0	0	42	2
1936-37	11	1	0	0	0	0	0	0	11	1
1937-38	8	1	0	0	0	0	0	0	8	1
1938-39	1	0	0	0	0	0	0	0	1	0
TOTAL	442	49	25	4	0	0	0	0	467	53

Jim Barrett Jnr

BARRETT, Jim, Jnr.   1949-54

Born: West Ham, London. 5.11.30
Lge apps: 85 (24 gls)
Cup apps: 2 (1 gl)

■ From Juniors 2/49. Son of the illustrious "Big" Jim Barrett, Jim junior made a good impression at the Boleyn in the early fifties. Sold for a substantial fee to Nottingham Forest at Christmas 1954, he was their top scorer in 1956-57 and played a big part in their rise to the First Division. After a short spell with Birmingham City, he returned to the fold as a player/manager of Hammers' "A" team until 1968, when he left again to serve under another ex-Hammer, Ben Fenton, at Millwall. Later became a publican at the Napier Arms in Halstead, Essex.

BEAUCHAMP, Joey   1994

Born: Oxford. 13.3.71

■ Exciting youngster who joined West Ham at the second attempt from Oxford United for £1 million in June 1994, pipping Swindon Town for his signature. Billy Bonds had tried to sign Joey three months earlier, on transfer deadline day, but withdrew his interest when it became clear that the player was reluctant to leave the city where he was born and bred. Joey had attracted the attention of a number of top clubs but preferred to stay at the Manor Ground to help Oxford's vain fight to avoid relegation from Division One at the end of 1993/94. His decision even surprised Oxford who, expecting him to move to Upton Park, signed winger Jimmy Carter as his loan replacement! Joey joined the U's straight from school and, apart from a six-match spell on loan to Swansea at the end of 1991, has spent all his early career with his local club. Made 124 League (20 gls) and 15 (1 gl) cup appearances, including a brilliant performance v West Ham at Upton Park (21.11.92) when he got the better of Julian Dicks and was the pick of the visitors. But, amazingly, the bewildering Beauchamp never did make an official appearance for the club. The shy youngster confessed after his first day's training at Chadwell Heath that he had made a mistake in not joining Swindon originally. He simply couldn't cope with travelling to and from his Oxford home each day and new manager Harry Redknapp had no option but to offload the £1 million misfit as quickly as possible. After several friendly outings in claret and blue (he is pictured below in action in his first game at Oxford City), Beauchamp finally got his wish to join Swindon - in exchange for defender Adrian Whitbread plus around £300,000. A most unsatisfactory end to a bizarre sequence of events.

BEALE, R   1913-14

SL apps: 1

■ Geoff Hurst once perceived that one bad game at the beginning of a career can prove fatal for future prospects. For a goalkeeper just making his way in the game, the dangers are heightened and the debut of R. Beale proved to be a perfect example of this pitfall. Spending most of the 1913-14 season as understudy to regular first X1 'keepers Hughes and Lonsdale, the ill-fated custodian was given his Southern League baptism in the very last match of the campaign v Portsmouth at Fratton Park, where a 5-1 scoreline ensured it was the last in every sense for our subject in a West Ham shirt.

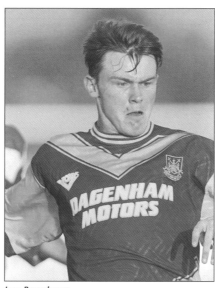

Joey Beauchamp

BEESLEY, Mick   1960-62

Born: High Beech, Essex. 10.6.42.
Lge apps: 2 (1 gl)

■ Despite scoring on his League debut v Everton at Goodison Park in Sept. 1960, and heavily for the reserves, this inside-forward failed to win a regular place in the League side. Transferred to Southend United in July 1962, where he joined up with former Hammers' manager Ted Fenton, he moved on to Peterborough United in 1965; returned to Roots Hall two years later to finish his career with the Essex club. He had received London and FA Youth honours while with Hammers.

Dick Bell

BELL, Dick   1938-39

Born: Aberdeen, Scotland
Lge apps: 1 (1 gl)

■ This Scottish inside-forward scored on his League debut for Hammers v West Bromwich Albion at Upton Park on April 15 1939, in what was to be his first, and last, first team appearance. Signed from Sunderland in 1937, he is one of the few to be able to claim the 100% record: played one, scored one. Joined the Essex Regt. T.A. in April 1939, and saw war service with the R.A. Known to his Army mates as "Brindie."

BELL, George   1911-12

SL apps: 2

■ In an age when centre-forwards were expected to average a goal a game, George Bell was given two opportunities wearing the number nine shirt - against the two Towns, Swindon and Northampton respectively. Both matches ended in defeat for Hammers with George failing to get on the scoresheet. An amateur from the Barking club, he sustained a serious knee injury in an Amateur Cup tie v Ilford that ended his career in 1913.

BENNETT, Les   1954-56

Born: Wood Green, London. 10.1.18
Lge apps: 26 (3 gls)
Cup apps: 2 (1 gl)

■ In spite of his relatively brief period at the club, this popular player made a big impact during his stay at Upton Park. Formerly with Spurs (for whom he signed pro. in May 1939), he was skipper for many of his appearances in the claret and blue, and was a frequent member of the side which narrowly missed promotion in 1954-55. Made his debut for Hammers v Derby County at Upton Park on Christmas Day 1954. Became player/manager of Clacton Town and later joined up briefly with Malcolm Allison at Southern League Romford. Later manager of a caravan site at Point Clear, near Clacton, and afterwards had a business post at the University of Essex, near Colchester. His WW2 service with the Devon Regt. was in India, Egypt and Burma.

BENNETT, Peter   1964-70

Born: Hillingdon, Middlesex. 24.6.46
Lge apps: 42 (3 gls)
Cup apps: 5

■ Adaptable inside-forward who found it difficult to hold a regular place in the senior side. Nevertheless, he managed a fair total of appearances during his six years in contention. Signing pro during the summer of 1963 after two years of apprenticeship, he made his League debut v Bolton Wanderers at Upton Park (4.4.64). A member of the FA Youth Cup-winning team of 1963, he joined Orient in 1970 in the deal that brought Tommy Taylor in the opposite direction.

BEST, Clyde   1969-75

Born: Somerset, Bermunda. 24.2.51.
Lge apps: 186 (47 gls)
Cup apps 32 (11 gls)

■ A powerful striker who didn't quite realise his full potential. Deceptively fast for his size, he possessed a lethal shot and fearsome heading ability. Signed pro. in Apr. 1969 and made his League bow v Arsenal in August the same year. A full Bermudan international, he later played in the North American Soccer League for Tampa Bay Rowdies and Portland Timbers after transferring from Hammers to the Florida-based club in Feb. 1976; also had a spell with Feyenoord in the Dutch First Division during 1977/78 before returning to Portland. Clyde is now a successful businessman in the USA, running his own cleaning company in Florida. Only the second black player to make Hammers' first team after John Charles.

Clyde Best (left) picks up Mick Jones whilst Bobby Moore guards the post... Hammers v Leeds, April 1973. Best had to take over in goal after 'keeper Bobby Ferguson went off injured.

Dave Bickles

BETTS, Eric   1950

Born: Coventry, Warwicks. 27.7.25
Lge apps: 3 (1 gl)

■ Signed from Walsall in Apr. 1950 after service with Mansfield, Coventry and Nuneaton. Eric, an outside-left, made his first appearance in West Ham's colours in a 5-0 win over Watford Reserves at Upton Park (22.4.50). Scoring a goal in that match which also featured Hammers' subsequent chief executive-secretary Eddie Chapman (another scorer), he went on to make a trio of Second Division appearances for the club before continuing his transfer travels with Rochdale, Crewe, Wrexham and Oldham where he ended his League career in 1956.

BICKLES, Dave   1963-67

Born: West Ham, London. 6.4.44
Lge apps: 25

■ Tall, commanding pivot. First blooded in the senior side during the American Soccer League Tournament in 1963, he made his initial League appearance in Sept. of that year v Liverpool at Anfield - the last occasion, incidentally, Hammers managed to win there (as at August

1994). Transferred to Crystal Palace in Oct. 1967, he later had a spell with Colchester United before becoming player/manager of the now defunct Romford FC in the Southern League. He was managing Havering side Collier Row in the Spartan League in the 1982-83 season. For the last two decades Dave's main vocation has been P.E. teacher at Brampton Manor School in East Ham, from where he recommended pupil Lee Hodges, the Essex, London and England schoolboy international midfielder, to Hammers. As well as running Newham District schools team, Dave is now employed on a part-time basis with West Ham United, supervising the under-16's at Chadwell Heath.

BICKNELL, Charles   1936-47

Born: Pye Bridge, Chesterfield. 6.11.05
Lge apps: 137
Cup apps: 12

■ A strong, powerful full-back who had made 244 consecutive appearances for Bradford City when Hammers signed him in Mar. 1936. Continued his ever-present record by playing in every match except one until the outbreak of WW2 - by which time he had been appointed

club captain. Served in the Police Specials during the War, and played many games in regional football. Skippered the Hammers in the 1940 War Cup Final at Wembley, when they beat Blackburn Rovers 1-0. He managed a further 19 Second Division appearances after the resumption of normal League activities in 1946-47. Given a free transfer at the end of that campaign, he then became manager of Southern League Bedford Town.
Died in Cambridgeshire 6.9.94, aged 88.

BIGDEN, James
1901-04

Born: London
SL apps: 91 (3 gls)
Cup apps: 5

■ James made his first appearance in West Ham's colours in the opening game of the 1901/02 season which was won 2-0 v Bristol Rovers at East-ville, thanks to goals from Grassam and Corbett. A product of local football, he made the majority of his near 100 Southern League and FA Cup appearances at wing-half, although he sometimes played at inside-forward. By 1906 Jim had moved across London to serve Woolwich Arsenal, then playing at the Manor Ground, Plumstead, and with the assistance of two other ex-Hammers in MacEachrane and Satterwaite, helped the Gunners to oust his former club from that year's FA Cup in the first round proper.

BIGGAR, William
1902-03

Born: Blayden-on-Tyne, Newcastle. 1877.
SL apps: 8

■ Bill began the 1902/03 season as Hammers' first choice 'keeper following his transfer from Sheffield United, along with winger Billy Barnes. But a 5-1 reverse in his third match at Wellingborough Town saw him lose his place to Welsh international Fred Griffiths, and although he regained it at the tail-end of the season, he was on his way at the end of the campaign. Joined Fulham for 1903-04 and then Watford 1904/05. Moved from Watford to Rochdale in 1910 where he won a Lancashire Combination medal in 1910/11. Stayed with the Lancastrians up to WW1.

BIGGIN, H.
1919

Lge apps: 2

■ Embarked on his League career in an infamous 7-0 defeat at the hands of Barnsley at Oakwell (7.9.19) from the inside-right position; switched to the right-wing for his only other first team appearance in a 1-1 draw with Stoke City at Upton Park on Oct. 4 the same year.

BING, Doug
1951-55

Born: Broadstairs, Kent. 27.10.28
Lge apps: 29 (3 gls)

■ Had National Service in the army. Signed from Margate on New Year's Day 1951 on the recommendation of former Hammer Almer Hall, the Seasiders' manager at that time. Doug was originally an inside or wing-forward, but was successfully converted to half-back at the Boleyn. Although never a first team regular, he was a capable deputy when called upon. Making his League debut v Hull City at Boothferry Park in 1951-52, he enjoyed four happy years as a Hammer until returning to his former club in the summer of 1955 - where he was medically advised to give up the game four years later.

Above: Dougie Bing

Left: Charlie Bicknell

BIRCHENOUGH, W. 1920

Lge. apps: 1

■ A goalkeeper who made a solitary Second Division appearance in a 2-1 defeat v Nottingham Forest at the City Ground (5.4.20).

BIRNIE, Alexander 1903-04

Born: 1884.

■ Very little can be ascertained about the career of Alex other than that he was probably a Scotsman and made his solitary Southern League appearance in the inside-right position in a 1-0 defeat at the hands of Brentford at the Memorial Grounds. His only other senior appearance also came against opponents from West London, Fulham, and ended in another 1-0 reverse in that season's intermediate round of the FA Cup. A reserve team regular, he later played for Norwich City, Maidstone United and Southend United (1908/09).

BISHOP, Ian 1989-

Born: Liverpool. 29.5.65
Lge apps: 156 (9 gls)
Cup apps: 26 (3 gls)

■ Long-haired midfield creator who achieved the notable distinction of playing in all four divisions of the Football League when Manchester City signed him from Harry Redknapp's AFC Bournemouth for £465,000 in the summer of 1989. But by the following Christmas, popular "Bish" was back in Division Two - valued at £650,000 when he arrived at Upton Park with Trevor Morley in the exchange deal that took unsettled Mark Ward to Maine Road. The classy midfielder began his pro career close to home, at Everton, who he joined straight from school. After four league outings on loan to Crewe Alexandra towards the end of 1982/83, Ian made his only first team appearance for the Toffees, as sub v Manchester United at Goodison in May 1983, before resuming his battle to make his mark in the lower divisions. He was sold by Howard Kendall to Carlisle United for £15,000 in Oct. 1984 at the age of 19 and played 132 League games for England's most northerly club, enduring two consecutive relegation campaigns, before moving to the south coast club Bournemouth for £35,000 four years later. He played 44 League games in his one and only season for the Cherries. Although he was at Manchester City for only 19 games in a four-month spell, Bish quickly established himself as a firm favourite with the fans who appreciated his silky skills and ability to spray accurate passes all over the field. He and Morley starred in a memorable 5-0 victory over arch rivals United but when manager Mel Machin was sacked, the arrival of Kendall (who released him at Everton), in December 1989, spelled the end of the City line for this talented youngster with the long, flowing mane. At West Ham, Ian has proved equally popular with the fans,

although he has not always been an automatic choice since Billy Bonds succeeded Lou Macari. He made his debut, along with Morley, at Leicester City (30.12.89) and capped his first full season in claret and blue by captaining Hammers to promotion in May 1991, having taken over the skipper's armband from the injured Julian Dicks.. A few days later, he gained his first - and so far only - England B cap v Switzerland at Walsall. Ian's turbulent career took another twist a year later when he found himself back in Division Two. And his frustration further increased in December 1992 when, along with several other players, he was placed on the transfer list as the club tried to cut its wage bill in the wake of the ill-fated bond scheme. The likeable Scouser maintained that he had no wish to leave and his loyalty was rewarded when he returned to the side and played an influential part in clinching promotion back to the top flight in May 1993. Even so, he remained unsettled during that summer and it was only after Ian had been on the brink of joining Southampton that West Ham reacted by signing him on a new three-year contract in Sept. 1993. With his future

happily settled, Bish celebrated his, and Hammers', first season in the Premiership by claiming an automatic first team place and playing consistently with all the style and grace of so many of his illustrious midfield predecessors.

BISHOP, Sidney 1920-26

Born: Stepney, London. 10.2.1900.
Lge apps: 159 (8 gls)
Cup apps: 14

■ After a humble beginning as a forward with Isthmian League Ilford and a spell with Crystal Palace reserves, Sydney Macdonald Bishop, to give him his full title, rose to the pinnacle of his profession after signing for West Ham United in 1920 and playing for the RAF during WW1. Born at the turn of the century in Stepney, during the very year of the formation of West Ham United, he was affectionately nicknamed "Sticks" by the Boleyn crowd in recognition of his slender frame. A member of the side which gained near immortality by appearing in the

Ian Bishop

first Wembley Cup Final of 1923, Syd was one of the few utility players of his generation; playing in nearly every position for Hammers - including goal when Ted Hufton was injured on one occasion! It has been often said that the best half-backs are those who have had experience in the forward positions, gaining first-hand knowledge of the type of service the men up front need in the process. Syd's career certainly benefited from this drill. Well known as a big occasion player, he was named as reserve for England v Ireland at Liverpool in 1924, but was destined to wait until after he had left Upton Park before gaining full international recognition. His departure from the Boleyn to Leicester City was regretted by his many admirers long after he had left; but there could be no denying that this great player had lost form during his last season with Hammers. He even reverted to his old positions in the forward-line in a desperate effort to regain his lost sparkle. All this changed with his move to Filbert Street, however.

Although he continued to live in London (a decision which must have brought its own difficulties in the days before motorways), his form improved to such an extent that he won four full caps for his country in 1927 - v Scotland, Belgium, Luxembourg and France. This success was followed by disappointment the next year when he had to cry off through illness after being named England's captain v Scotland - yes, the side which was to become famous through-out the world of football as the "Wembley Wizards" with their 5-1 victory in 1928. Whether or not Syd would have been able to stem the Scottish tide, we will never know, but his former Hammers' team mate in goal for England that fateful day - Ted Hufton - would have doubtless been happier with him playing in front of him, and it is doubtful that Alex James & Co. would have had it quite so much their own way had Sticks played. It was a more mature Syd Bishop who returned to his beloved London to sign for Chelsea in 1928 for £4,000, with brain rather than brawn being the hallmark of his play. Some of his thoughts of those days are worth repeating some half-century later: "I think it is a mistake to enter into a game with fixed ideas on tactics. If you are a half-back the first thing you should try to find out is what sort of form each front-line man happens to be in, and see to it that the fellows on top of their game see most of the ball." It would be interesting to hear the comments of some of the coaches of today on such a refreshingly simple approach. Syd Bishop was in the Chelsea team which won promotion to the First Division in 1930, and came back to Upton Park as a member of the Blues' side which knocked Hammers out of the FA Cup in

a fourth round tie in 1933. A subsequent report in a West Ham match programme opined that Syd looked "as good as ever." Injuries forced him to give up the game soon afterwards, and at the sadly premature age of 49 he died at his Chelsea home in 1949.

BLACK, Robert 1937-38

Lge. apps: 2

■ A rugged right-half, Bobby made his Second Division debut for Hammers v Nottingham Forest (2.2.37); he made one more first team appearance the following season before moving on to near-neighbours Clapton Orient.

BLACKBURN, Alan 1954-57

Born: Pleasley, Mansfield, Notts. 4.8.35
Lge. apps: 15 (3 gls)

■ A former Barnardo's Boy, he was discovered playing in Hertfordshire junior soccer. A centre or inside-forward, he caused a sensation by scoring 13 goals for Hammers in the FA Youth Cup during the 1953-54 season. A prolific scorer for the reserves, he was a member of the Combination championship team of 1954 and made his initial first XI appearance v Derby County in December of the same year. Served in the Forces from Mar. 1955 on National Service. Later transferred to Halifax Town, he carried on his goalscoring exploits at The Shay and also later saw service with non-league Margate and Wellington Town.

BLACKBURN, Fred 1905-13

Born: Blackburn, Lancashire. 1879
SL apps: 217 (24 gls)
Cup apps: 20 (4 gls)

■ Fred began his first-class career as an out-side-left with his home-town club, Blackburn Rovers, where he joined from Mellor and was a great favourite with the Ewood Park fans. He won three Lancashire Cup medals while with Rovers and was playing in their First Division team at the age of 17. Represented the English League v Scottish League and also The North v South. First capped for England v Scotland in 1901, he made another appearance versus the "Old Enemy" the following year and also one v Northern Ireland to complete a trio of international outings. He came south to join Hammers in the summer of

F. BLACKBURN, WEST HAM UNITED.

1905 and when he reported for training he scaled 10st 10lb and his height was recorded as 5ft 6ins. A switch to the wing-half positions during the later stages of his time at Upton Park undoubtedly helped him to establish the second highest total of Southern League appearances for Hammers and in doing so gain a well-deserved benefit match v Coventry - along with goalkeeper George Kitchen - in 1911. He had another couple of seasons in the claret and blue after that recognition of his services but did not re-sign for the 1913/14 season. The brother of a former Blackburn and Southampton full-back, Arthur Blackburn, Fred joined the merchant navy when he finished playing, but later returned to the game as coach to Barking in the 1930s - the middle part of which decade saw the Athenian League Championship won by the Vicarage Field club.

Played	League		FAC		LC		Europe		Total	
	App	Gls	App	Gls	App	Gls	App	Gls	App	Gls
1905-06	30	5	2	0	0	0	0	0	32	5
1906-07	29	4	0	0	0	0	0	0	29	4
1907-08	36	4	2	1	0	0	0	0	38	5
1908-09	40	6	6	3	0	0	0	0	46	9
1909-10	42	3	5	0	0	0	0	0	47	3
1910-11	16	2	0	0	0	0	0	0	16	2
1911-12	22	0	5	0	0	0	0	0	27	0
1912-13	2	0	0	0	0	0	0	0	2	0
TOTAL	**217**	**24**	**20**	**4**	**0**	**0**	**0**	**0**	**237**	**28**

BLACKWOOD, John 1904-05

SL apps: 4 (1 gl)

■ John had the unfortunate experience of making his first X1 baptism in the middle of one of Hammers' worst-ever losing runs, in the initial campaign at the Boleyn Ground. He began promisingly enough with his side's only counter in a 4-1 defeat at Portsmouth, after taking over the number nine shirt from Billy Bridgeman, but failed to score in his next three outings (all defeats). His lack of further success led to the recall of Bridgeman and the end of his Southern League opportunities with West Ham. An experienced player, John had seen service with Queens Park Rangers, Partick Thistle, Glasgow Celtic and Reading (1902/03), before joining Irons.

BLOOMFIELD, Jimmy 1965-66

Born: Kensington, London. 15.2.34
Lge. apps: 9
Cup apps: 4 (1 gl)

■ A former Brentford (where he played with Ron Greenwood), Arsenal and Birmingham City inside-forward, he was signed by Hammers in Oct. 1965, after a second spell at Griffin Park. Jimmy left Upton Park to continue his playing career with Plymouth Argyle and became player-manager of Leyton Orient in 1968. Took over from fellow ex-Hammer Frank O'Farrell as boss at Leicester City after guiding O's out of the Third Division. Later returned to Brisbane Road as manager until serious illness

Vincent Blore

forced him to relinquish the post. He was still actively involved in scouting business for Luton Town almost right up to his tragically premature death in Apr. 1983.

BLORE, Vincent   1935-36

Born: Uttoxeter, Staffordshire
Lge. apps: 9

■ Hammers signed this acrobatic goalkeeper from Derby County in the summer of 1935 and he contested the first team spot with Herman Conway the following season. With the arrival of Jack Weare from Wolves effectively relegating Vince to third choice 'keeper, he didn't hesitate when Crystal Palace offered him the opportunity of regular first team football, and he did well with the Glaziers up to the outbreak of WW2. Known as "Vic" Blore by some Hammers' fans.

BLYTHE, Joe   1902-04

Born: Berwick-on-Tweed. 1881.
SL apps: 52
Cup apps: 5

■ A left-half of average height and weight, Joe joined Hammers from Everton during the close season of 1902/03 and made his debut v Reading in the opening fixture of the ensuing campaign at the Memorial Grounds. Strictly a defender, he never managed to get on the score-sheet during the two troubled seasons leading up to the move to the Boleyn Ground, but nevertheless proved to be a stubborn fixture in Irons' often beleaguered defence. Left to join Millwall in Aug. 1904, but is not to be confused with a 'Blythe' already at that club. In a second spell with Hammers, records show that Joe made another three Southern League appearances in 1906/07. In 1911/12 he was playing for Watford.

BOERE, Jeroen   1993-

Born: Arnhem, Holland. 18.11.67
Lge apps: 4
Cup apps: 1 (1gl)

■ Gained immediate notoriety by becoming the first Hammer to be sent off on his first team debut. Jeroen (pronounced Yeron, although the English translation is Jeremy) made his solitary League appearance of the 1993/94 Premiership season at Newcastle United on (25.9.93). A 64th minute sub for Trevor Morley, the powerful Dutch striker lasted just 24 minutes before he was controversially shown the red card by Birmingham referee Mike Reed after clashing with Magpies' defenders Scott and Venison. Jeroen made his mark in the next away game, too, when he scored after coming on in the Coca-Cola League Cup tie at Chesterfield. But Boere, a typical old-fashioned target man, made only two more sub appearances in the season before joining First Division Portsmouth on a month's loan in Feb. 1994. Jeroen, who signed a three-year contract in Sept. 1993, came from Dutch First Division side Go-Ahead Eagles for £165,000 and scored twice for the Reserves in an impressive debut at Arsenal. Kicked off his career with Rotterdam side Excelsior, then had spells with Graafschap, VVV and Roda before joining Go-Ahead in his home town of Deventer. Has also represented Holland at Under-21 and Olympic level. Turned down offers from Scottish Premier

Jeroen Boere

League Dundee United, as well as clubs in France, Germany, Greece and Turkey, to join West Ham. Joined West Bromwich Albion on loan in September 1994.

BOND, John   1951-65

Born: Colchester, Essex
Lge. apps: 381 (33 gls)
Cup apps: 47 (2 gls)

■ A great character and first class full-back. Signed as an amateur from Colchester Casuals in 1950, he made his League debut in the 1951/52 season. Penalty expert and dead-ball kicker, he was in the Second Division championship-winning team of 1957/58 and the FA Cup-winning side of 1964. Transferred to Torquay United from West Ham in 1965, he later managed AFC Bournemouth, Norwich City, Manchester City and Burnley (where one of his first purchases was Hammers' centre-back Joe Gallagher). John afterwards became manager of Swansea City, but following the Swans' domestic problems he took over at St. Andrew's with Birmingham City. He was manager of Shrewsbury Town until the end of the 1992/93 season where his assistant was fellow ex-Hammer Mal Musgrove.

John Bond

Played	League		FAC		LC		Europe		Total	
	App	Gls	App	Gls	App	Gls	App	Gls	App	Gls
1951-52	2	0	0	0	0	0	0	0	2	0
1952-53	14	0	1	0	0	0	0	0	15	0
1953-54	18	0	3	0	0	0	0	0	21	0
1954-55	25	1	1	0	0	0	0	0	26	1
1955-56	34	1	6	0	0	0	0	0	40	1
1956-57	30	1	2	0	0	0	0	0	32	1
1957-58	41	8	3	1	0	0	0	0	44	9
1958-59	42	7	1	0	0	0	0	0	43	7
1959-60	35	7	2	0	0	0	0	0	37	7
1960-61	34	4	1	0	2	0	0	0	37	4
1961-62	37	2	1	0	2	0	0	0	40	2
1962-63	14	0	0	0	2	0	0	0	16	0
1963-64	26	0	7	0	6	1	0	0	39	1
1964-65	29	1	2	0	1	0	4	1	36	2
TOTAL	381	32	30	1	13	1	4	1	428	35

Stanley Bourne

BOURNE, Stanley   1906-12

Born: East Ham, London.
SL apps: 13
Cup apps: 3

■ A distinguished amateur left-back whose commitment to the non-paid ranks resulted in only a somewhat meagre total of appearances for Hammers spread over six seasons. Making his initial appearance for West Ham in a 1-1 draw v Watford at Upton Park in Dec. 1906, he was noted in a 1947 history of the club as: "a notable amateur player, who rejoices in the distinction of having been the only footballer, other than goalkeepers, to wear spectacles in professional football matches." Stan made his final appearance in a West Ham shirt in a 2-2 draw v Norwich at their picturesque ground, The Nest, in Apr. 1912. Played in six London Combination matches in 1915/16 and also turned out occasionally for Arsenal during the conflict.

BOURNE, W   1913-14

Born: Sittingbourne, Kent.

■ This outside-left played only one match in Hammers' Southern League side - a 0-0 draw at Reading's Elm Park (23.3.14). First played for his local club, Sittingbourne, in the Kent League.

BONDS, Billy   1967-88

Born: Woolwich, London.
Lge apps: 663 (48 gls)
Cup apps: 130 (11 gls)

■ A legend of Upton Park, Billy Bonds has spent 27 years with the club as player and manager. In a playing career spanning an incredible 21 seasons, "Bonzo" played a record 793 senior games. Billy's first appearance in claret and blue, following his £49,500 move from Charlton Athletic, was in Ken Brown's testimonial at Upton Park (15.5.67) v Select XI. It was v Sheffield Wednesday (19.8.67) that Billy made his Hammers' League debut. Ron Greenwood's purchase of the swashbuckling right-back proved one of the greatest bargains of all-time. He cost the club the equivalent of around £62.00 a match - a paltry sum when you consider his vast contribution. Billy played for Kent schoolboys before signing for Bob Stokoe at Charlton, making his League debut v Northampton Town (20.2.65). Went on to make 95 League appearances for Charlton before his transfer to Upton Park (13.5.67). A tremendously loyal servant, who never gave less than 100%, Bill always led by example on the field. Courageous in the tackle, he grafted hard for possession and would often defy painful injuries, roll up his sleeves and slog it out in the heart of midfield or, in his latter playing days, the centre of defence. Fearless in the tackle, Bill always let the opposition know they had been in a match - win, lose or draw. Yet he used the ball more intelligently and effectively than perhaps he was sometimes given credit for. He also weighed in with his fair share of goals, including a hat-trick v Chelsea in Mar. 1974, on his way to topping the scorechart with 13 that season. In 1974 he succeeded Bobby Moore as captain and went on to lead the club to FA Cup Final victories in 1975 and 1980, as well as appearances in the finals of the European Cup Winners' Cup (1976) and League Cup (1981). Billy was skipper, too, when West Ham won the Second Division championship (1981). He won two England Under-23 caps and was poised for his full England debut v Brazil at Wembley (12.5.81), when a rib injury, sustained in a collision with 'keeper Phil Parkes in Hammers' last match of the season, cruelly ruled him out. Billy was certain to play in that prestige friendly, having been in two of Ron Greenwood's previous England squads. But the nearest Bonzo got to a full cap was as non-playing sub for a World Cup qualifier against Italy at Wembley (16.11.77). After joining West Ham Billy quickly established himself as a huge crowd favourite with his surging forward runs, which is reflected in the fact that he was voted Hammer of the Year four times - a distinction he shares with Moore. This "Peter Pan" of football was still playing in the First Division at the age of 41 - a remarkable feat recognised by The Queen, who honoured him with the MBE (1.1.88), and his fellow pro's, who presented Billy with the PFA Merit Award in April of the same year. Time and again Billy defied the passing years by returning to play at top level - he officially retired on the same day as Trevor Brooking, in May 1984! But Bill's astonishing playing career had still not run its course. It was not until the summer of 1988 that, nursing a knee injury that forced him to miss the last two games of that season, he finally decided to hang up his boots. His 663rd, and final, League game for the club came in the First Division match at Southampton (30.4.88). If you include European, Charity Shield and Full Members' Cup fixtures, Billy Bonds made 795 official matches for West Ham. John Lyall, eager to make use of Billy's experience and influence, appointed him youth team manager in June 1988. Gillingham offered Bill the position of manager, and he applied (unsuccessfully) for the first team manager's job at Upton Park when Lyall was sacked in July 1989. Instead, the Hammers' board opted for an 'outsider' in Lou Macari but when he resigned just seven months after arriving from Swindon, the ever-popular Bonzo was the People's Choice to take charge of the first team. His appointment (22.2.90) heralded a new wave of optimism and a resurgence of fortunes saw Hammers finish just one place off the play-off zone in Division Two. But Bill marked his first full season in charge by taking Hammers back to the top flight, as runners-up to Oldham Athletic in 1990/91. Billy made history again (12.11.90) when he became the first person to be awarded two Testimonials by the club, Spurs providing the opposition. Already in his brief managerial career, Bonzo has experienced a series of highs and lows. Following the euphoria of his first

Chairman Martin Cearns makes a presentation to commemorate Billy's second testimonial, in 1990

full season, he faced a season-long battle at the foot of the First Division that culminated in relegation at the end of 1991/92. His efforts to produce results on the field were undermined by events off it, where irate fans waged war on the club's ill-conceived bond scheme. Bill's helter-skelter career took another twist a year after the drop, when - having been joined by his old mate Harry Redknapp - Hammers bounced straight back to the senior league, as First Division runners-up to Newcastle United. Despite being the bookies' favourites to go straight back down again in 1993/94, Hammers proved many wrong by attaining a respectable 13th place in their first Premiership campaign. It is impossible to imagine West Ham without Billy Bonds, yet the seemingly impossible happened on Wednesday, August 10, when the legend stunned the fans by announcing his resignation, just 10 days before the start of the new season. Bonds turned down the offer to become a paid director of the club after the Board indicated their preference for Redknapp to take over the top job. Few saw Bonds as manager, long-term, and he himself admitted the demands of modern-day management could never compare with the pleasure he got from playing. So when he sensed that circumstances were changing at Upton Park, it was hardly surprising that he didn't wish to hang around. The club paid up the remaining three years of his contract (said to be worth £500,000) and duly installed Redknapp as the new No.1. As a player Bonds was the rock on which the team was built. A magnificent leader whose wholehearted commitment on the field contrasted with his off-field image as a private man who shys away from the bright lights. At the end of matchday, Bill would not hang about the players' bar for long. Instead he would grab his four-pack of beers and head back through the Blackwall Tunnel to what he has always enjoyed most - time spent at home in Kent with his wife and two daughters.

Played	League		FAC		LC		Europe		Total	
	App	Gls	App	Gls	App	Gls	App	Gls	App	Gls
1967-68	37	1	3	0	2	0	0	0	42	1
1968-69	43	1	3	0	2	0	0	0	47	1
1969-70	42	3	1	0	2	0	0	0	45	3
1970-71	37	0	1	0	2	0	0	0	40	0
1971-72	42	3	4	0	10	2	0	0	56	5
1972-73	39	3	2	0	2	0	0	0	43	3
1973-74	40	13	2	0	1	0	0	0	43	13
1974-75	31	7	8	0	3	2	0	0	42	9
1975-76	18	1	0	0	5	1	9	2	32	4
1976-77	41	3	2	0	3	0	0	0	46	3
1977-78	29	1	3	1	0	0	0	0	32	2
1978-79	39	4	1	0	1	0	0	0	41	4
1979-80	34	1	5	0	9	0	0	0	48	1
1980-81	41	0	3	0	8	1	6	1	58	2
1981-82	29	1	2	1	4	0	0	0	35	2
1982-83	34	3	1	0	4	0	0	0	39	3
1983-84	27	0	1	0	2	0	0	0	30	0
1984-85	22	3	0	0	4	0	0	0	26	3
1985-86	0	0	0	0	0	0	0	0	0	0
1986-87	17	0	4	0	3	0	0	0	24	0
1987-88	22	0	2	0	0	0	0	0	24	0
TOTAL	663	48	48	2	67	6	15	3	793	59

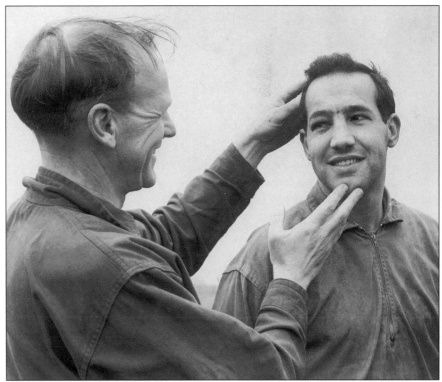

Ron Greenwood inspects Eddie Bovington's bruised eye before an FA Cup replay with Leyton Orient

BOVINGTON, Eddie 1960-67

Born: Edmonton, London. 23.4.41
Lge apps: 138 (1 gl)
Cup apps: 45 (1 gl)

■ From Juniors, signed 5/59. Abrasive, dependable wing-half in the Andy Malcolm mould. His reinstatement to the side after the Boxing Day 1963 debacle against Blackburn Rovers did much to bring about the improved form and stability which led to the team's Cup Final triumph. Made his League debut v Manchester United at Old Trafford in 1960. He now runs a menswear shop at Archway, North London.

Ronnie Boyce

BOYCE, Ronnie 1960-72

Born: East Ham, London. 6.1.43
Lge. apps: 282 (21 gls)
Cup apps: 57 (8 gls)

■ The vital engine room of the successful cup sides of the mid-sixties, Ronnie was known as "Ticker" because he was the heartbeat of the team. He played the game simply, feeding the likes of Hurst, Byrne and Sissons with his accurate passes. Guaranteed himself a permanent place in Upton Park folklore with his two goals v Manchester United in the 1964 FA Cup semi-final at Hillsborough and his Wembley headed winner against Preston North End - the same side he made his League debut against at Upton Park, aged 17 (22.10.60). That was a year after manager Ted Fenton gave the East Ham Grammar School kid his first senior game for the club in a Southern Junior Floodlit Cup tie v Millwall (13.10.59). It was not until 1962/63 season that the unselfish and hard-working Ronnie gained a regular first team place, but from then on he became one of the stalwarts for some eight years (although injury kept him out for a while in 1965/66). A year after experiencing the thrill of scoring his injury-time winner in the FA Cup Final, Ronnie was back at Wembley celebrating Hammers' 1965 European Cup Winners Cup triumph over TSV Munich 1860. Although he was not among the scorers on that classic night, Ron had played a big part in getting the team to Wembley. In what many have described as his best-ever game for the club, Ronnie took over the skipper's role from the injured Bobby Moore, in Czechoslovakia, and steered the side to a brilliant 3-2 aggregate win over Spartak Prague in round one. Team mate Geoff Hurst once said of Boycie: "He is a players' player - a

Ronnie Boyce (centre) heads home Peter Brabrook's cross for the FA Cup winning goal against Preston in 1964

tremendous worker but people do not appreciate his value to the team." Manager Ron Greenwood, who saw Ronnie as the perfect replacement for Phil Woosnam, added: "In other people's eyes he was a most underrated player, but to us he was invaluable. The thing that impressed me most about his play was his ability to do the simple things quickly and efficiently." Ron played schoolboy soccer for East Ham, London, Essex and England, and also won England Youth honours. The closest he came to a full cap was as reserve for an Under-23 fixture. West Ham awarded him a well-earned testimonial in Nov.1972, when George Best's Man. Utd were the opponents. Although not renowned as a goalscorer, Ron scored one of the most bizarre and spectacular goals of all-time at Maine Road in Mar. 1970 (Jimmy Greaves' debut), when he volleyed home from the mud-baked centre circle following 'keeper Joe Corrigan's drop-kick! That was typical Boycie - a quick reader of the game. His last League appearance for Hammers was as sub at Leicester City (30.12.72). After serving John Lyall and Billy Bonds as first team coach, "Boycie" did in fact take charge of one game as caretaker manager in Feb. 1990 - between the resignation of Lou Macari and the appointment of Bonzo. A popular, loyal, one-club man, Ronnie still has his heart and soul in the Hammers, having succeeded Eddie Baily as chief scout in Sept. 1991.

Played	League		FAC		LC		Europe		Total	
	App	Gls	App	Gls	App	Gls	App	Gls	App	Gls
1960-61	3	0	0	0	0	0	0	0	3	0
1961-62	4	1	0	0	0	0	0	0	4	1
1962-63	27	3	5	2	1	0	0	0	33	5
1963-64	41	6	7	3	7	2	0	0	55	11
1964-65	41	4	2	0	1	0	9	1	53	5
1965-66	16	2	1	0	2	0	4	0	23	2
1966-67	37	4	1	0	5	0	0	0	43	4
1967-68	38	0	1	0	3	0	0	0	42	0
1968-69	39	0	3	0	3	0	0	0	45	0
1969-70	20	1	1	0	1	0	0	0	22	1
1970-71	13	0	0	0	0	0	0	0	13	0
1971-72	1	0	0	0	0	0	0	0	1	0
1972-73	2	0	0	0	0	0	0	0	2	0
TOTAL	282	21	21	5	23	2	13	1	339	29

Peter Brabrook

BRABROOK, Peter   1962-68

Born: Greenwich, London. 8.11.37
Lge apps: 167 (33 gls)
Cup apps: 47 (10 gls)

■ This brilliantly talented winger slipped through the club's scouting net after he had played schoolboy soccer for East Ham, Essex and London. Nine years later, it cost £35,000 to sign him from Chelsea, for whom he scored 47 goals in over 250 League games and meanwhile won England Youth and full caps. Even so, it was money well spent. Played in 1964 FA Cup winning team and won a League Cup runners-up medal in 1966. He ended his League career at Orient where he made 72 League appearances and was a vital member of the side which won the Third Division championship in 1970 in company with Hammer-to-be Tommy Taylor under the managership of another ex-Iron, Jimmy Bloomfield, before appearing for Southern League Romford. Relinquished his post as coach to Essex Senior League side Ford United in 1985, but is still involved with local football with Billericay Town from where he recommended striker Steve Jones to West Ham. Peter is also employed as a scout by Hammers. Made a post-soccer career as a butcher in East Ham.

BRADFORD, T.   1911-12

This outside-right made his solitary Hammers' appearance in a Southern League fixture v Stoke City at the Victoria Ground on (20.4.12). The match was drawn 0-0 before an attendance of 8,000.

Below: Liam Brady

BRADSHAW, Harry   1919-21

Born: Lancashire
Lge apps: 14
Cup apps: 1

■ Originally a winger, he converted to wing-half with Irons. Harry won his greatest honour outside football when he was awarded the Military Medal while serving as a brigade runner in France during WW1. Signing pro for the 1919/20 season, he was also a member of the club's relay-team which won the Professional Footballers' 4 x 440 yards at Stamford Bridge, in an era when such races were a popular part of the entertainment at sports meetings. An active member of the Old Players' Association, he was living at Hockley Avenue, East Ham at the time of his death in Oct. 1967, at the age of 71.

BRADSHAW, Tom   1889-1900 TIW

Born: Liverpool. 24.8.1873
SL apps: 5

■ A fast, direct left-winger who began his career with Northwich Victoria and was a regular member of Liverpool's Second Division championship-winning teams of 1894 and 1896 and played on two occasions for the Football League in addition to winning a solitary England cap v Ireland in Feb. 1897. Joining Spurs in May 1898, he actually made his debut and scored against Thames Ironworks in a Thames and Medway League fixture. Virtually an ever-present during that 1888/89 campaign, it proved to be a busy one for him, as he was chosen to represent the United League against the Thames and Medway League, was selected for the South v the North in the annual international trial match and also played for an England X1 v a Scotland X1 in a match to benefit the players' union. After making 69 appearances in all competitions for Spurs that season, he transferred to TIW in the summer of 1899 along with team-mates Kenny McKay and Bill Joyce in a transfer coup masterminded by Irons' secretary George Neil. The highlight of Tom's all too short Irons' career was destined to be his four goals in a 11-1 Thames and Medway Combination thrashing of Grays United, for tragically, both Tom Bradshaw and the man who signed him, George Neill, were dead before they had reached the age of 30. Tom died on Christmas Day 1899 of consumpsion resulting in Spurs and Ironworks meeting (2.4.1900) in a match to raise funds for his dependants.

BRADY, Liam   1987-90

Born: Dublin, Republic of Ireland.
Lge apps: 89 (9 gls)
Cup apps: 26 (1 gl)

■ Regarded world-wide as the Republic of Ireland's greatest-ever player, Brady's record of 72 Irish caps was finally overhauled by Pat Bonner in June 1994. Although Liam was in the twilight of his illustrious career when he ended his seven-year reign in Italy to join Hammers in March 1987, he is still recognised as one of the most accomplished players ever to perform in claret and blue. Yet Liam made his name in Britain with London rivals Arsenal, who he joined as an apprentice in the summer of 1971 after starring in his homeland for St. Kevin's Boys. He made his debut at Highbury as a 17 year-old sub v Birmingham City (6.10.73) and went on to play 235 League games for the Gunners as well as appearing in three consecutive

FA Cup Finals. He was on the losing side v Ipswich Town (1978) and West Ham United (1980), but gained a winner's medal against Manchester United (1979). Also in the Gunners side beaten by Valencia (after penalties - Liam missed the first one!) in the European Cup Winners' Cup Final of May 1980. It was a sad British farewell for the Irish genius but he had so many more big games to look forward to as, aged 24, he broadened his horizons in Italy's tough Serie A. Liam's reputation as a creative midfielder, with an equisite left foot and eye for goal, was enriched by his Italian experience. He ended his first campaign in the famous black and white stripes of Juventus as the team's leading scorer and a championship medal-winner. The Turin club pipped Fiorentina for the title a year later after Brady scored the match-winning penalty in their final game at Catanzaro but, for Liam, the celebrations were muted. Three games prior to that dramatic finale, he had been devastated to learn that he would be replaced as Juve's second foreigner the following season by French superstar Michel Platini. But it was a measure of Liam's character that instead of turning his back on Italy, he stayed and went on to play two seasons for both Sampdoria and Inter Milan, while also spending half a season with his fourth Serie A side, Ascoli. When Liam was ready to return to England, West Ham stole a march on their rivals by snapping him up for £100,000. Liam made his debut at home v Norwich City (14.3.87) and scored the first of his 10 West Ham goals in a 3-1 home win over . . . Arsenal! (8.4.87). But his second season was marred by a knee ligament injury sustained at Derby in Feb. 1988 which forced him to miss the rest of the term and the following summer's European Championship finals. When Liam decided to quit playing at the end of 1989/90 many thought he had retired prematurely. But he went out in a blaze of glory - scoring a spectacular goal in the dying seconds of his farewell game against Wolves at Upton Park (5.5.90). Eleven days later the Football Association of Ireland honoured Liam with a testimonial game v Finland in Dublin. It was the last of his 72 caps - the first was against USSR at Dalymount Park (30.10.74) - and during his stint with Hammers Liam played for his country 11 times. The only sad aspect is that Ireland's leading player was not around when his country enjoyed their greatest moments on the European and World Cup stages.. After a break of a year, Liam returned to football as manager of Glasgow Celtic in July 1991 but boardroom wrangles undermined his efforts and, as the team slipped further into the shadow of great rivals Rangers, he resigned in November 1993. A month later he returned to management, at Brighton, steering the Seagulls clear of the Second Division relegation zone.

☆ *Irish caps*: 1987 v Bulgaria, Belgium, Brazil, Luxembourg, Luxembourg, Bulgaria; 1989 v France, Hungary, Hungary, West Germany; 1990 v Finland.

Tim Breacker

BREACKER, Tim   1990-

Born: Bicester, Oxfordshire. 2.7.65.
Lge apps: 137 (8 gls)
Cup apps: 28

■ Powerful, attacking right-back, Tim became Billy Bonds' first signing, in Oct. 1990, when he joined from Luton Town in a £600,000 deal. Hammers were in Division Two at the time but so confident was Tim that he would soon be returning to the top flight, he had no hesitation leaving the club he joined as a schoolboy and where he made 208 League appearances. The blond full-back made his League debut for Luton at Ipswich Town (31.3.84) and his Hammers' debut as sub at Swindon Town (10.10.90). He took over the right-back role, allowing Steve Potts to switch to central defence. Strong, muscular defender, Tim has also played at centre-back as cover a number of times, but it is as an adventurous, overlapping full-back that he is best known. A placid, unassuming man, Tim is nevertheless a tough, though fair, opponent and was unlucky to be sent off for the first time in his career, after two bookable offences, at Everton in Dec. 1991. Tim has been involved in many vital cup ties in his career. Played for Luton in their 1988 League Cup Final victory over Arsenal, but was on Hatters' losing side when Nottingham Forest snatched the cup a year later. Ironically, Luton returned to Wembley after beating West Ham in the 1989 semi-final. In the FA Cup, he has endured the heartbreak of three semi-final defeats - twice with Luton, v Everton (1985) and Wimbledon (1988), and once with West Ham, v Nottingham Forest (1991). Tim's two England Under-21 caps were both against Italy - at Pisa (9.4.86) and Swindon (23.4.86).

BRANDON, Tommy 1913-20

Born: Blackburn, Lancashire. 1893
SL apps: 34
Cup: 3

■ Essentially a right-back, Tommy began his career with his home-town Blackburn Rovers at the age of 16, in 1909. Represented Lancashire in inter-county matches and stayed loyal to his roots with South Liverpool until joining up with Hammers in the close-season of 1913. Playing his first game for West Ham in a fine 2-1 win over Bristol Rovers at their former Eastville ground (13.9.13), he went on to make 31 Southern League appearances that season, his best by far. With only three outings the following campaign in the uncustomary number two shirt, Tom had to wait until the tail-end of the last war-time season in the old London Combination to make his final appearances in home and away clashes with Fulham. Unable to command a first team place after Hammers' elevation to the Second Division of the Football League, he went back north to serve Hull City in June 1920, and made 56 appearances (some at inside-right) during his stay at Anlaby Road. One of his most outstanding appearances with the Tigers came in 1921 when he was the architect of a sensational 3-0 FA Cup victory over all-conquering Burnley and scorer of one of the goals with a cracking shot from 25 yards. Transferring to Bradford in June 1922, and then on to Wigan Borough in 1925, he was the son of Scottish international, Tom Brandon senior. Died May 1, 1956.

BRETT, Ron 1960-61

Born: Stanford-le-Hope, Essex. 4.9.37
Lge apps: 12 (4 gls)
Cup apps: 1

■ A strong, old-fashioned type of centre-forward who was signed from Crystal Palace in a straight exchange deal which took Malcolm Pyke to Selhurst Park. He rejoined his former club on a similar basis, after nearly three seasons at Upton Park, this time being valued at £7,000 in the record-breaking transaction which made Johnny Byrne a Hammer. Ron died only five months after his transfer when his car collided with a lorry in Clerkenwell. Poignantly, the last match he played in was between Hammers and Palace in a reserve fixture at Upton Park on the Saturday before his tragic death.

BRETT, Frank 1898 TIW

Born: 1877.
SL apps: 1

■ Came from Swanscombe and played in first-ever TIW professional match at inside-right in a 3-0 win at Shepherds Bush (10.9.1898).

BRIDGEMAN, Billy 1903-06

Born: Bromley-by-Bow, London. 1884.
SL apps: 71 (19 gls)
Cup apps: 3 (1 gl)

■ A pupil of Marner Street School where he played in the school XI with another legendary figure, George 'Gatling Gun' Hilsdon, he was chosen to represent Tower Hamlets School League at centre-forward or occasionally inside or outside-right. Joined Irons from the local Adam & Eve FC.

Legend has it that Bill scored all three of West Ham's goals in their emphatic 3-0 victory over deadly local rivals Millwall during the first Southern League fixture to be staged at Upton Park in September, 1904. Although first-class material for folklore and fable, and backed up by no less an authority than Charlie Paynter in later years, the claim is not substantiated by contemporary newspaper reports, which credited Jack Flynn with one of the goals.

Tommy Brandon

He did, however, score a hat-trick in the opening public trial match at Upton Park a few days prior to the meeting with Millwall, a fact which probably helped to blur memories and create confusion over the years. But wherever the truth of the matter lies, one thing can't be denied: He scored West Ham's first-ever goal at Boleyn Castle in that match v Millwall, and served Hammers well as they struggled to establish themselves in Southern League football and deserves his little niche in the club's history. Mostly a centre-forward with Hammers, he had been tried briefly as a rightwinger, a position he was destined to fill with even more distinction on his move to his next club,

Chelsea, most notably in helping the Pensioners to promotion back to the First Division in 1912. After totalling more than 150 senior appearances for the West Londoners, Bill saw out the remainder of his career with Southend United in 1915.

BRIGNULL, Phil 1979

Born: Stratford, London. 2.10.60
Lge apps: 1

■ A useful defender whose first team opportunities were extremely limited. His sole appearance in the senior side was made as sub v Cardiff City at Ninian Park in May 1979. Transferred to AFC Bournemouth in 1981, where his cousin, former Chelsea star David Webb, was then assistant manager. Later moved to Wrexham where he played five times (1 goal), before moving to South Wales via Cardiff City and made a more respectable 49 appearances for the Bluebirds. He then made it a 'hat-trick' of clubs in the Principality by signing for Newport County where he played three times before they left the League.

BRITT, Martin 1963-65

Born: Leigh-on-Sea, Essex. 17.1.46
Lge apps: 20 (6 gls)
Cup apps: 6 (1 gl)

■ A former England Youth international who had been apprenticed in July 1966, this talented centre-forward found competition for a place in the free-scoring West Ham attack of the mid-sixties a stumbling block for his advancement. An indication of his potential can be found in his transfer to Blackburn Rovers, who splashed out £25,000 to take him to Ewood Park. His career was prematurely cut short by injury after only six appearances for Rovers - against whom he had made his Hammers' debut in May 1963.

Phil Brignull

Martin Britt

BROOKING, Trevor   1965-84

Born: Barking, Essex. 2.10.48
Lge apps: 528 (88 gls)
Cup apps: 108 (14 gls)

■ One of the true greats in Hammers' hall of fame. Having signed apprentice after leaving Ilford County High School in July 1965, Trevor turned pro in May 1966 and made his initial League appearance at Burnley (29.8.67). Moore, Hurst and Peters were Hammers' scorers in a 3-3 draw that day and little did the shy, young Brooking realise then that he would go on to join the famous trio among the ranks of West Ham legends. Indeed, Trevor took his time to establish himself in the first team, initially as a centre-forward. He did not start more than 30 League games in a season until after Peters' transfer to Tottenham in March 1970. In fact, he was so disillusioned after being dropped and then left out for a long period by Ron Greenwood, that he went on the transfer list at the end of 1970/71. During the 1972/73 campaign Derby County manager Brian Clough offered £400,000 for Bobby Moore and Trevor, but Greenwood blocked the move. Derby's loss was certainly Hammers' gain, as the tall, elegant Trevor emerged as one of the classiest midfield players in the world. He was regularly outstanding even when the team performance was way below par, as Hammers came to rely so heavily upon the man many doubted would ever make the top grade when he first got his big chance. A marvellous reader of the game, Trevor bemused opponents and enthralled Hammers' fans with his silky skills in the heart of midfield. He passed accurately with both feet, threaded through-balls into gaps that did not appear to exist and also scored his fair share of spectacular goals from distance. Although he was creator much more than ball-winner (Billy Bonds did much to complement him in this respect), Trevor's tall, strong physique still enabled him to hold off his marker - he was expert at shielding the ball and turning his opponents, having already glanced over his shoulder to assess the scene. His speciality 'trick' was letting the ball run on the blind side of his opponent when receiving a throw-in. His control of the ball was incomparable. And he was as immaculate off the pitch as he was on it. A real gentleman of football, Trevor was nicknamed "Hadleigh" by his team mates after a TV character of similar status. First voted Hammer of the Year by the fans in 1971/72, Trevor is the only player to win the award in three consecutive years (1975-78). Had to wait eight years to win a major honour with his club, leading them with his unique midfield skills to victory in the 1975 FA Cup Final v Fulham (3.5.75). Ironically, a major influence on young Trevor had been his schoolboy favourite, the former Fulham great Johnny Haynes. After collecting a runners-up medal in the 4-2 European Cup Winners' Cup Final defeat by Anderlecht (5.5.76) the following year, Trevor was back at Wembley scoring the FA Cup Final winner against Arsenal (10.5.80). Although never renowned as a particularly effective header of the ball, he stooped low to guide Stuart Pearson's shot past Pat Jennings and into the Gunners' net after only 13 minutes. Within a year he was back at Wembley again to face Liverpool in the 1981 League Cup Final, which was drawn 1-1 before the Reds took the replay at Villa Park 2-1. These big occasions, the record-breaking 1980/81 Second Division promotion campaign and his award of the MBE, were appropriate reward for Trevor's admirable loyalty to the club. While many people outside Upton Park expected the England star to move on after Hammers were relegated from Division One in May 1978, he stayed faithful to the club he supported as a kid and went on to enjoy the biggest highlights of his long and illustrious career. England manager Ron Greenwood - who signed Trevor as a schoolboy when he was in charge at Upton Park - reassured the midfield maestro that his international future would not be affected by his club's slide into Division Two. Capped once at Under-23 level, Trevor went on to achieve 47 full England caps. The highspot came during the World Cup qualifying match with Hungary in Budapest in 1981, when his two match-winning goals proved so vital in taking England to Spain for the finals in 1982. By now recognised as a world class performer, Trevor was bitterly disappointed that a long-term groin injury virtually ruled him out of the tournament. He and Kevin Keegan - they had almost a telepathic understanding - were both introduced as subs late in the dramatic match v Spain, but not even these two England greats, still nursing bad injuries, could save Greenwood's side from elimination on a heart-breaking night in Madrid. Trevor missed all but the penultimate match of 1982-83 season due to recurring injury problems, but returned in 1983-84 for 43 League and cup appearances in his final season. Although many believed that he could have continued at the top for at least a couple more seasons, Trevor decided to quit at the top and it was an emotional Upton Park crowd that saluted their hero on his triumphant lap of honour following the game v Everton (14.5.84). That was his 528th League match for Hammers - only Billy Bonds, Frank Lampard and Bobby Moore have played more times for the club. A shrewd and intelligent businessman with a number of directorships, Trevor put his school qualifications to full use. Even while still playing at his peak, he built up business interest outside the game. But he has maintained a strong involvement with football, as a successful radio and television commentator with the BBC and newspaper columnist, often returning to Upton Park in these capacities. And he has not yet finished playing the game. Within months of retiring as a pro at Upton Park, Trevor signed for Havering Nalgo . . . and is now in his tenth season with the Brentwood Sunday League club!

☆ **England caps:** *1974 v Argentina, Portugal (twice), East Germany, Bulgaria, Yugoslavia, Czechoslovakia (sub); 1975 v Portugal: 1976 v Wales, Brazil, Italy (twice), Finland (twice), Republic of Ireland; 1977 v Holland, Northern Ireland, Wales, Italy; 1978 v West Germany, Wales, Scotland (sub), Hungary, Denmark, Republic of Ireland; 1979 v Northern Ireland (twice), Wales (sub), Scotland, Bulgaria, Sweden (sub), Austria, Denmark; 1980 v Argentina (sub), Wales, Northern Ireland, Scotland, Belgium, Spain, Switzerland; 1981 v Spain, Romania, Hungary (twice); 1982 v Scotland, Finland, Spain (sub) (47).*

Played	League		FAC		LC		Europe		Total	
	App	Gls	App	Gls	App	Gls	App	Gls	App	Gls
1967-68	25	9	3	0	0	0	0	0	28	9
1968-69	32	7	2	0	3	1	0	0	37	8
1969-70	21	4	0	0	2	0	0	0	23	4
1970-71	19	2	0	0	1	0	0	0	20	2
1971-72	40	6	4	0	10	1	0	0	54	7
1972-73	40	11	0	0	4	0	0	0	44	11
1973-74	29	6	0	0	2	0	0	0	40	6
1974-75	36	3	8	1	3	1	0	0	47	5
1975-76	34	5	1	0	4	1	7	3	46	9
1976-77	42	4	2	0	2	0	0	0	47	4
1977-78	37	4	2	0	0	0	0	0	39	4
1978-79	21	2	1	0	0	0	0	0	22	2
1979-80	37	3	7	2	8	1	0	0	52	6
1980-81	36	10	3	0	7	0	5	0	51	10
1981-82	34	8	2	0	5	1	0	0	41	9
1982-83	1	0	0	0	0	0	0	0	1	0
1983-84	35	4	3	0	5	2	0	0	43	6
TOTAL	528	88	40	3	55	8	12	3	635	102

Ken Brown and (above) in action against Leeds at Elland Road in April 1964.

BROWN, Ken
1952-67

Born: Forest Gate, London. 16.2.1934
Lge apps: 386 (4 gls)
Cup apps: 69

■ Signed from Dagenham-based Neville United in Oct. 1951 and did army service from 1952-54. Finest of a long tradition of West Ham centre-halves. A stalwart in the promotion year of 1958, he made his first team debut in 1952-53 and played until 1967. The obvious highlights were the winners medals he collected at Wembley for victories in the 1964 FA Cup Final and 1965 European Cup Winners' Cup Final, where he played alongside Bobby Moore in the heart of defence. A crowd of 14,695 turned out at Upton Park (15.5.67) to pay tribute to big Ken on the night of his well-deserved testimonial v Select XI (in which Billy Bonds made his Hammers' debut). Joined fellow exHammer John Bond at Torquay United and gained the unusual distinction of drawing wage packets from two clubs when he continued to manage the pools promotion at Upton Park! Ken won one full cap for England v Northern Ireland at Wembley (18.11.59) and gave a good account of himself in a 2-1 victory. One of nine new caps tried in a three-match spell, Ken was unfortunate to be overlooked in the future as manager Walter Winterbottom continued his search for a successor to Billy Wright. Became manager of Norwich City and led them to victory over Sunderland in the 1985 Milk (League) Cup Final, although that success was dilluted by relegation to Division Two at the end of the same season. But a smile is never missing from Ken's face for long and within a year he led the Canaries back into the top flight, playing the entertaining brand of football he had been involved in at Upton Park for so long. With a decision which shocked the usually tough-skinned football world, Norwich dismissed Ken after a shaky start to the 1987/88 season. But he bounced back as boss of Plymouth Argyle where he had his good friend and former Hammers' winger, Malcolm Musgrove, as assistant. He relinquished the Home Park post in 1991 and is now director of Lakenham Leisure Centre, near Norwich, but he can often be seen at Upton Park watching his son Kenny, continuing the family tradition in claret and blue.
☆ ***England cap:*** *1959 v Northern Ireland (1).*

Played	League		FAC		LC		Europe		Total	
	App	Gls	App	Gls	App	Gls	App	Gls	App	Gls
1952-53	3	0	0	0	0	0	0	0	3	0
1953-54	0	0	0	0	0	0	0	0	0	0
1954-55	23	0	0	0	0	0	0	0	23	0
1955-56	2	0	0	0	0	0	0	0	2	0
1956-57	5	0	0	0	0	0	0	0	5	0
1957-58	41	0	3	0	0	0	0	0	44	0
1958-59	42	0	1	0	0	0	0	0	43	0
1959-60	40	0	2	0	0	0	0	0	42	0
1960-61	42	0	2	0	2	0	0	0	46	0
1961-62	38	0	1	0	2	0	0	0	41	0
1962-63	40	2	5	0	2	0	0	0	47	2
1963-64	36	0	7	0	6	0	0	0	49	0
1964-65	33	1	2	0	1	0	9	0	45	1
1965-66	23	1	3	0	9	0	6	0	41	1
1966-67	18	0	0	0	6	0	0	0	24	0
TOTAL	**386**	**4**	**26**	**0**	**28**	**0**	**15**	**0**	**455**	**4**

BROWN, Kenny J.   1991-

Born: Barking, Essex. 11.7.67.
Lge apps: 51 (5 gls)
Cup apps: 9

■ Followed in the footsteps of his father, Ken senior, and became the third father and son pairing (following the Barretts and Lansdownes) to play for Hammers. Yet Kenny initially joined the club, in Aug. 1991, only as a stop-gap measure following a spate of pre-season injuries to other first team squad members. This tenacious right-back made his debut in the 6-1 drubbing by Italian giants Sampdoria in the Makita Tournament at Highbury and his League bow at home against Luton Town a week later (17.8.91). Versatile Kenny, who also operates effectively in midfield when required, has a fierce shot. Indeed, it was after such a super-strike, v Aston Villa, under the Upton Park lights, that prompted Hammers to make his signing from Plymouth Argyle permanent just a month after his arrival. The West Country club collected a down-payment of £175,000, plus £60,000 after Kenny's 50th appearance. Although not yet establishing himself as a first team regular, Kenny has scored some important goals. It was his winner at Upton Park v Manchester United (22.4.92) that shattered Alex Ferguson's title dream that season, while his goal in a 3-1 win at Swindon (2.5.93) proved vital as Hammers clinched promotion ahead of Portsmouth by one goal's difference! Kenny began his career at Norwich City, who were managed by his Dad at the time, making his debut as sub v Oxford United at Carrow Road (29.11.86). He made 25 League appearances for the Canaries without scoring, then moved on a free to join his father at Plymouth Argyle (Aug. 1988). Kenny played a further 126 League matches for the Pilgrims, scoring four times.

Kenny Brown Jnr

BROWN, William   1907-09

Born: Newmilnes, Ayrshire, Scotland.
SL apps: 19 (4 gls)

■ Although mostly at home in the inside-left position, Billy appeared in all the forward berths for West Ham following his transfer from Vale of Leven, who were founder members of the Scottish League as well as being among the earliest contestants for the Scottish Cup. He made his debut v Swindon Town at the County Ground in the third fixture of the 1907/08 season, but had to wait until the later stages of the campaign before he established himself in the side. His four goals for the claret and blue cause came in seperate bursts of two, his first brace earning a 2-2 draw at the then professional Leyton, and his second helping towards a 4-2 home victory over Southampton. There was little success for him the next season, however; his two Southern League outings reflecting a sad fade-out. Begining his football education with Newmilnes Juniors, he made a big step up with Partick Thistle before transferring to Vale.

BROWN, William   1921-24

Born: Hetton-le-Hole, Co. Durham. 22.8.1900
Lge apps: 60 (15 gls)
Cup apps: 11 (5 gls)

■ A play-anywhere utility man when West Ham plucked him from local football in his native North-East with Hetton, Billy eventually settled down in the inside-right position to partner Dick Richards in the 1923 Cup Final and promotion side. He made his Hammers debut virtually in his own backyard, at South Shields in the final fixture of the 1920/21 season. It wasn't until 1922/23 that he won a regular first team place, and a month after appearing in Hammers' losing Wembley XI gained England honours as reserve against France. A year later he won his solitary full cap v Belgium at the Hawthorns. Transferring to Chelsea shortly afterwards, he later played for Fulham, Stockport and Hartlepool United. Kept in trim in later life as a bath superintendent at Easington Colliery and as a cricket umpire. He died at Easington, Co. Durham aged 85 in Jan. 1985.
☆ *England cap: 1923 v Belgium (1).*

BRUNTON, Fred   1904-05

Lge apps: 1

■ Frederick made only one appearance for Hammers - in the 4-1 Southern League defeat at Portsmouth on Boxing Day 1904. He played at right-half in front of the biggest crowd to watch West Ham that season, 16,000 at Fratton Park.

BRUSH, Paul   1977-85

Born: Plaistow, London. 22.2.58
Lge apps: 151 (1 gl)
Cup apps: 34

■ A fine club-servant and highly-valued member of Hammers' senior squad who proved invaluable during the 1984-85 injury crisis. Coming up for his tenth year with the club before transferring to Crystal Palace, Paul made his League bow v Norwich City (20.8.77) and was the only League ever-present the following season when Hammers began rebuilding the team that would take them back into the top

Paul Brush

BURGESS, Daniel/Dick   1922

Born: Stafford, Staffs
Lge apps: 2

■ After two seasons with Arsenal this inside-right opted to follow his friend and former Gunners' team-mate George Pattison to Upton Park. He was quickly given a chance in the first team, and made two Second Division appearances in rapid succession v Bradford City at Valley Parade (2.9.22) and v Derby County at the Baseball Ground two days later. Dick joined Welsh club Aberdare Athletic in 1922, who staged Football League fare at the Athletic Ground, Ynis between 1921-27, when they were replaced by Torquay United. Later with Queens Park Rangers.

BURKETT, Jack   1962-67

Born: Edmonton, London. 21.8.42
Lge apps: 142 (4 gls)
Cup apps: 39

■ From Juniors 7/58. Quick, tenacious full-back. A product of the successful West Ham youth policy of the late fifties. Liked nothing better than to join in attacks, his speed off the mark enabling him to get back to his defensive duties

Alex Bunbury

flight two years later. By then, Paul had lost his regular full-back spot to Ray Stewart, although he continued to prove excellent cover for both Stewart and Frank Lampard. Paul's solitary League goal came in his last season with the club - v QPR at Upton Park (1.1.85). He was 12th man for the 1980 FA Cup Final. After leaving Palace, Paul played for Enfield in the Diadora Premier League and was still playing in 1993/94 season for Essex Senior League side Heybridge Swifts. His only claim to fame in football management so far is the distinction of being Basil Brush's boss in the BBC TV programme, Fantasy League Football!

Portuguese club Sporting Maritimo for just £50,000 in Nov. 1993. Billy Bonds signed Alex after a trial appearance, although his record for Canada at international level was impressive. He was leading scorer in their qualifying bid for the 1994 World Cup finals that only just failed in a decisive clash with Mexico, but could not reproduce this form for Hammers.
☆ *Canadian caps:* 1993 v Honduras (twice), El Salvador (twice), Mexico (twice). (6)

BUNBURY, Alex   1992-93

Born: British Guyana.18.6.67.
Lge apps: 4
Cup apps: 1

■ A gamble that turned out to be rather expensive, Canadian international Alex cost £200,000 when signed from Montreal Supra in Dec. 1992 after battling to gain a work permit. He made his debut as sub at Brentford (20.12.92) and appeared as sub in two other first team games. But, apart from one Anglo-Italian Cup outing (v Pisa), his only first team starts were v Bristol City (27.1.93) and at Sunderland (27.2.93). He struggled to gain a place in the Reserves before moving on to

Jack Burkett playing for West Ham v Sparta Prague

Dennis Burnett has to step over Jim Standen after the West Ham 'keeper's save from Chelsea's Barry Bridges.

berth when he deputised for the injured Shea. His two appearances the following campaign saw him in the number 10 shirt and open his goalscoring account in a 3-4 reverse at Northampton Town. 1913/14 saw him back at inside-right and scoring his second - and final - goal for the club in a 3-1 win over Gillingham at Upton Park (22.11.13). Mostly a reserve, he played two further matches in the Supplementary Tournament of the London Combination in 1915/16 v Spurs and Millwall. He transferred to Southend United for 1919/20 and became their leading scorer before being signed by Wolves for £800 to form a triumvirate of ex-Southend players at Molineux, with Maurice Woodward and George Marshall, who all played for Wolves in the 1921 FA Cup Final v. Spurs at Stamford Bridge. So he was very much 'one that got away' as far as Hammers were concerned. Frank came back to London in cs 1923 to join Charlton Athletic and scored three goals in 14 games, before moving on to Walsall the following summer, where he became their leading scorer with 14 goals in 38 appearances.

BURROWS, David   1993

Born: Dudley, West Midlands. 25.10.68
Lge apps: 25 (1 gl)
Cup apps: 6 (1 gl)

■ It is a measure of David's qualities as a tough-tackling defender who uses the ball well, that he instantly won the approval of the Upton Park crowd despite replacing their former hero, Julian Dicks. Black Country lad "Bugsy" arrived from Liverpool in Sept. 1993, along with Mike Marsh, in the £2.5 million value swap deal that took Dicks to Anfield. He made his debut in the shock 2-0 win at Blackburn Rovers (18.9.93) and netted his first goal for the club in the live televised match v Manchester City (1.11.93). Although hampered by a knee injury during his first season with Hammers, David settled in very quickly at left-back, and also showed his versatility by covering in the centre of defence when required. A good dead-ball kicker with a ferocious shot - just like the man he replaced. His pro career began at his local club, West Bromwich Albion, in Nov. 1986. He played 46 League games for The Baggies before his big £550,000 move to Liverpool (20.10.88). Capped at Under-21 and B level, and a member of previous full England squads, David enjoyed five successful seasons with the Reds. In 145 League and 47 cup matches for the Merseysiders, he won First Division championship (1990) and FA Cup (1992) winners medals, as well as the Charity Shield (1989 and 1990). But David's stint with Hammers lasted only a year. Harry Redknapp's desperate need to sign a new striker saw 'Bugsy' swapped for Everton's Tony Cotee in September 1994 - a move that also suited the defender, who was keen to return to Merseyside.

See overleaf for David Burrows picture

without being stretched. Collected medals with the Cup-winning sides of 1964-65. Transferred to Charlton Athletic for £10,000 in 1968, and later saw service with Millwall and Southend United before embarking on a spell as a player/manager with St. Patrick's Athletic in the League of Ireland. He returned to the UK in 1976 for a short spell as player/coach back at Southend but got the wander lust again and travelled to the oil-rich Saudi Arabia to manage their Under-18 side. Then he swapped sand for snow when he took up the post of manager of Norwegian Third Division side Orsta in 1980. In 1982 he returned to Southend as youth coach under his old skipper Bobby Moore, and in 1984 took up a similar position at Fulham. He now has a full-time job in charge of the YTS boys in the South of England on behalf of the PFA. Won England Youth honours while with Hammers.

BURNETT, Dennis   1965-67

Born: Bermondsey, London. 27.9.44.
Lge apps: 50
Cup apps: 16 (3 gls)

■ From Juniors 10/62. Constructive defender. Always performed capably when drafted into the side. Enjoyed 24 League outings in 1965/66, the most he managed in any one season. Made his League debut v Fulham at Craven Cottage in Oct. 1965 and won a League Cup runners-up medal the following year. Joined Millwall for £15,000 in 1967 and had a second spell at The Den after two seasons at Hull City, before finishing his League life with Brighton & Hove Albion.

Now running a painting and decorating firm in the south coast town where he lives with his wife and two daughters. Dennis still keeps fit by playing amateur soccer and competing in marathons. Now assistant manager with Sussex side Lancing F.C., Dennis went on as sub in the closing minutes of their 2-1 defeat v. Horsham YMCA in the preliminary round of the F.A. Cup in August 1994 ... a month before his 50th birthday and 28 years after his first appearance in the competition. He was player/manager of Norwegian team Hagur after playing in the States with St. Louis.

BURRILL, Frank   1911-14

Born: Manor Park, London
Lge apps: 17 (2 gls)

■ A pupil of Fourth Avenue School, Manor Park, Frank was signed from local junior football. Frank's 17 appearances for Hammers were spread over three seasons prior to WW1. He made his Southern League debut at centre-forward v Queens Park Rangers (12.3.12), in a 3-0 win at Boleyn Castle, as Hammers' midden was often called then. It was a remarkable match: Irons scoring three times in the last 12 minutes to defeat the visitors after Burrill had swapped positions with the great Danny Shea. His six other outings that season were made from the inside-right

Frank Burrill

35

David Burrows

BURTON, John, H   1908-09

Born: Derby. 1876
Lge apps: 15 (3 gls)
Cup apps: 4

■ Some historians have muddled John's career details up with those of his namesake, and Hammers full-back of a later period, Frank "Broncho" Burton. In some cases the two players' appearance totals have been added together, to give a confusing and wholly inaccurate impression. So let's set the record straight: John H. Burton signed for West Ham United from Blackburn Rovers in the summer of 1908, made his debut against Queens Park Rangers at Upton Park in the season's opening fixture and four days later opened his goalscoring account v Brighton from his favourite inside-left position. He went on to make 15 Southern League appearances that season, his last as a West Ham United player. John had begun his career with his home-town club Derby St. Andrews and stepped up to the town's premier club, Derby County, in Oct. 1896. Unable to win a regular place with The Rams, John moved south to join Chatham in cs 1898 and moved to Spurs in March 1901 after the Kent club had been forced to withdraw from the Southern League. A wing-half at that stage of his career, he made his SL debut for Spurs - although as the North Londoners were preparing for a semi-final match with West Bromwich Albion five days later, it was in all bar name, a reserve line-up. As were all of Burton's senior outings that season as Spurs rested key players for vital cup-ties. A policy vindicated when they became the first (and only) SL club to win the FA Cup in 1901. He managed 72 appearances and five goals in his five years at Northumberland Park but could never command a regular place and in Oct. 1906 moved to Preston North End and later Blackburn. His brother, Oliver, also played for Spurs and survived him in the first team until 1910. Mostly a reserve at Irons, John joined Cardiff City for 1911/12 and was the Bluebirds' captain when they won the SL Second Division Championship in 1912/13. John joined Southend United in cs 1914, the club for whom West Ham waived a £50 transfer fee (for Frank Burrill) to help the Shrimpers gather their playing strength in 1919. He died 14.5.49.

BURTON, Frank   1912-21

Born: Luapanso, Mexico. 1891
Lge apps: 64 (2 gls)
Cup apps: 5

■ Better-known by his nickname "Bronco," Frank was a long-legged full-back whose loping gait and extraordinary on-field contortions apparently likened him to a cowboy's horse. Despite an unorthodox approach he was popular with the fans and formed a fine partnership with Jim Rothwell and later Billy Cope. Served with the Royal Fusiliers in WW1 and was hospitalised at Whitchurch in 1916 suffering from shrapnel wounds, but still managed to turn out in 36 war-time matches for Hammers when he was not fighting the Germans. A regular member of the team in the club's first two League seasons, he was succeeded by Jack Hebden after making the journey across the Thames to join Charlton Athletic, from where he joined Grays in 1925 to become player/coach.

Frank Burton

Stan Burton

BURTON, Stan   1939

Born: Yorkshire. 1912
Lge apps: 1

■ Signed from Wolves five days after playing for them in the 1939 FA Cup Final v Portsmouth at Wembley, he became the first player in history to appear in a Final and play for another club before the end of the season. Making his Hammers' debut along with Cliff Hubbard against Manchester City at Upton Park in the final match of 1938-39, it was destined to be his first - and last - officially recognised League appearance, although he did play a handful of games at the beginning of the following season before League Football was scrapped because of WW2. He began his career with Thurnscoe Victoria, joining Doncaster Rovers in 1932, from where he transferred to Wolves. A dashing winger, he was affectionately nicknamed "Dizzy" by the Wolves crowd. He passed away in Sheffield in 1977.

BUSH, Robert   1902-06

Born: West Ham, London. 1879
SL apps: 20 (1 gl)
Cup apps: 1

■ Discovered literally on the club's doorstep playing Sunday morning football for Brittania FC on the pitch adjoining the Boleyn Ground, Robert scored on his Southern League debut for Hammers in a 1-1 draw at Kettering Town (28.4.03) from the outside-right position. Inexplicably, he didn't play for the first team for the next two seasons, before reappearing on a more permanent basis in the 1905/06 season at left-half. He played 18 times in the SL side that campaign, in addition to an FA Cup tie v Woolwich Arsenal at Plumstead which was drawn 1-1. A pupil of Abbey Road Board School, he played his first football with West Ham Football Club (no connection to W.H.U.F.C) which won the Woodford & District Football League. Transferred to Chelsea, cs 1906.

BUTCHART, J.   1903-04

Born: 1882
SL apps: 3

■ Although listed in the club's 1903/04 handbook as a centre-forward, J. Butchart made his three appearances in Irons' Southern League side in the inside-right position. He figured in two consecutive Memorial Ground victories against Kettering Town (4-1) and Queens Park Rangers (1-0), followed by a 0-2 reverse at Plymouth Argyle. A Scotsman who joined the Hammers from Greenock Morton, he was not called upon after that trip to the West Country.

BUTCHER, George   1910-20

SL apps: 62 (9 gls)
Cup apps: 9 (3 gls)
Lge apps: 34 (8 gls)
Cup apps: 4 (2 gls)

■ A famous name from the old Southern League days, George came from St. Albans City. He scored on his debut at Watford (2.3.10) and went on to make over 70 senior appearances up to the outbreak of WW1. Adding another handful of appearances during the conflict, he notched up 33 Second Division

outings during Hammers' initial Football League season of 1919-20, but played only once in the following campaign. His weight of 11st and height of 5ft 8ins. was just right for a nippy inside-forward, and also stood him in good stead when he became amateur lightweight boxing champion of Hertfordshire. George left the club in Jan. 1921 for Luton Town, and had five years with the Hatters before retiring to carry on the family business of building Artesian Wells. He died (11.1.70) at the age of 80.

George Butcher

BUTLER, Peter   1992-

Born: Halifax, West Yorkshire. 27.8.66
Lge apps: 65 (3 gls)
Cup apps: 7

■ Typically tenacious Yorkhireman who brought steel and grit to Hammers' 1992/93 promotion campaign, Peter completed a long journey through all four divisions when he

Peter Butler

Johnny Byrne playing for West Ham v Sparta Prague ECWC 1964

made his Premiership bow in Aug. 1993. This industrious midfielder proved a bargain £175,000 signing when a League tribunal fixed his fee following his move from Southend United, where "Butts" had established his reputation for honest endeavour and tough tackling. In four seasons at Roots Hall, Peter featured prominently in two consecutive promotion-winning successes, making 142 League appearances. Began his career with local club Huddersfield Town, where he made five sub appearances in two seasons between 1984 and 1986. Had a 14-game loan spell with Cambridge United at the start of 1986, then moved on a free to Bury at the start of 1986/87. But after just 11 League games, the diminutive Butts was on the move again in Dec. 1986, on another free transfer back to Cambridge. He played 55 League matches for them in two years before joining Southend in Feb. 1988. Peter's last season there was hampered by a knee injury and he spent the closing weeks of the 1991/92 term on loan to his first club, Huddersfield. His first game in a claret and blue shirt was in Frank Yallop's Testimonial at Ipswich Town (9.8.92). He made his First Division debut for Hammers the following weekend (16.8.92) at Barnsley - ironically, one of the clubs interested in signing him when his Southend contract expired. Unfortunately, Butts was again plagued by knee problems in his second season with West Ham, an operation causing him to miss the last month of the Premiership term. But not before he'd impressed the legendary Ferenc Puskas in a 'man of the match' display v Coventy City at Upton Park (11.12.93). Moved to Notts County in October 1994 for £350,000.

BYRNE, Johnny 1962-67

Born: West Horsley, Surrey
Lge apps: 156 (79 gls)
Cup apps: 34 (28 gls)

■ One of the most revered of all Hammers' big-money signings. His transfer from Crystal Palace in Mar. 1962 for £58,000 (plus Ron Brett, valued at £7,000) broke the existing record between English clubs. An interesting sidelight to the deal was that the man who first brought John to attention of the then Palace manager (Cyril Spiers) was himself a pre-war player with both clubs -goalkeeper Vincent Blore. Made his debut for Palace against Swindon Town while still on National Service and played in the same army XI as Alan Hodgkinson (Sheffield United), Bill Foulkes (Manchester United) and the great Duncan Edwards. Already a full England international when he arrived at Upton Park as one of the few Third Division players to win a full cap, "Budgie" (nicknamed thus because of his constant chattering on and off the field!) chalked up another 11 appearances for his country while with West Ham. This included a hat-trick v Portugal in 1964, the year in which he collected an FA Cup winners' medal for his starring role as an inside-forward blessed with great skills and a fine shot. Unfortunately, Budgie was forced to miss the 1965 European Cup Winners' Cup Final due to a knee injury sustained while playing for his country v Scotland a few weeks earlier. However, he played in the 1966 League Cup Final defeat by West Bromwich Albion. Johnny's strike ratio was most impressive, particularly in cup ties. His last League appearance in the familiar

number nine shirt for West Ham came v Sunderland at Upton Park (11.2.67), when he netted - along with Geoff Hurst - in a 2-2 draw. This, after Budgie had scored in another 2-2 draw at the Boleyn, v West Bromwich Albion, in the League Cup semi-final (second leg) three days earlier. Talk about going out in style! Tagged the "English Di Stefano" by manager Ron Greenwood, he was sold back to Palace in 1967 for a staggering £45,000, giving Hammers five years distinguished service for a total cash outlay of only £13,000! He left Selhurst Park for Fulham a little over a year later for a vastly deflated fee of £18,000, and spent only a year with the Cottagers before being given a free transfer. He then emigrated to South Africa where he became manager of Durban City whom he led to S.A. Cup and League triumphs in the seventies. Now manager of Greek side Hellenic, Johnny was voted "Coach of the Year" in 1993 and won a free trip back to the UK to see the Arsenal/Sheffield Wednesday FA Cup Final. He was back in the country again in March 1994 to play tribute to his former West Ham and England skipper and great friend Bobby Moore, at the memorial match v FA Premier League in his honour.
☆ *England caps:* 1963 v Switzerland; 1964 v Scotland, Uruguay, Portugal (twice), Republic of Ireland, Brazil, Argentina, Wales, 1965 v Scotland (10).

CADWELL, Albert 1923-33

Born: Edmonton, London. 1.11.1900
Lge apps: 272
Cup apps: 25

■ A real unsung hero who served West Ham United consistently well for 10 seasons. Signed from Nunhead during Hammers' initial season in the First Division, Albert eventually took the place of that other great West Ham left-half, Jack Tresadern. Although small in stature, his superb ball control, allied to his tenacious tackling and work-rate, won him a fine reputation at the highest level. Representative honours, however, were few and far between, although he did play for the Football League v Irish League in 1930 and was honoured by Surrey and London. Quiet and unassuming, Albert was a keen motorist in his off-field moments. He died 13.7.44 aged only 43.

Played	League		FAC		LC		Europe		Total	
	App	Gls	App	Gls	App	Gls	App	Gls	App	Gls
1923-24	29	0	3	0	0	0	0	0	32	0
1924-25	40	0	6	0	0	0	0	0	46	0
1925-26	18	0	0	0	0	0	0	0	13	0
1927-28	27	0	2	0	0	0	0	0	29	0
1928-29	40	0	5	0	0	0	0	0	45	0
1929-30	38	0	4	0	0	0	0	0	42	0
1930-31	31	0	1	0	0	0	0	0	32	0
1931-32	26	1	2	0	0	0	0	0	28	1
1932-33	10	0	2	0	0	0	0	0	12	0
TOTAL	272	1	25	0	0	0	0	0	297	1

CALDWELL, Tommy 1909-12

Born: 1886.
SL apps: 84 (12 gls)
Cup apps: 12 (2 gls)

■ Tom was signed from the infant Southend United, having previously been with Clapton Orient, in time for Hammers' opening fixture of the 1909/10 season v Exeter City at Upton Park. The speedy left-winger then proceeded to make 32 consecutive Southern League appearances before injury hindered his progress. His finest achievement during that run of success was a celebrated hat-trick in a 5-0 win over Bristol Rovers at the Boleyn, for which he was feted by the fans. Although his goalscoring output was cut by half the next season, he was an ever-present throughout the campaign and scored a vital goal in a 2-1 FA Cup third round win over Manchester United in East London. After scoring his last Southern League goal for Hammers v Queens Park Rangers (2.3.12), he made his final appearance in a 5-1 defeat at Millwall for a somewhat inglorious ending to what had been a successful three years in the claret and blue. Later with New Brompton.

CALLADINE, John 1921

Lge apps: 1

■ This right-winger made his solitary League appearance in a 0-0 draw in the last game of the 1920/21 season v South Shields at their Horsley Hill ground.

CAMPBELL, Greg 1984

Born: Portsmouth. 13.7.65
Lge apps: 5

■ AP 7/81 after trials at Manchester United. Son of former Portsmouth and Liverpool star, Bobby Campbell, young Greg's advancement at senior level suffered a big blow when he broke his jaw v Watford in Sept. 1984 and after only two appearances at the sharp end of Hammers' attack, he knew only too well of the physical demands of First Division football. Greg went on loan to Brighton in Feb. 1987 where he made two sub appearances before transferring to Plymouth Argyle in Nov. 1988 and scored six goals in 35 outings for the Pilgrims. The following year he gained experience playing for Sparta Rotterdam in Holland, but returned to the UK for 1990/91 to join Northampton Town. He teamed up with ex-Hammer Bobby Barnes at the County Ground and scored seven times in 45 games for the Cobblers that campaign.

Greg Campbell

CAMPBELL, John 1902-03

Born: 1878
SL apps: 18 (1 gl)

■ A jinking right-winger in the true Scottish tradition, John joined Hammers from that year's Scottish League champions, Glasgow Rangers, and was said to have been part of the Gers' sale of players to raise funds to help pay for damage following the Ibrox Disaster of April 15, 1902. A mere 5ft 5ins in height and tipping the scales at the just 10 stone, he made his debut in the opening game of the 1902-03 season v Reading at the Memorial Grounds and added some much needed guile to an attack which otherwise relied on brawn rather than brain. His single goal while in Hammers' employ came in a 2-1 defeat at Watford (24.1.03), and he was tried in all the forward positions - with the exception of centre-forward - before finding himself on the not retained list at the end of the season.

CAMPBELL, John 1924-29

Born: South Shields, Co. Durham. 12.5.1902
Lge apps: 28 (8 gls)

■ A schoolboy goalkeeper who turned centre-forward with some success for his local works team, before continuing his career north of the border with Berwick Rangers. Jarrow soon stepped in to bring him back "home," after being impressed with his performance in the Scottish Border League. It was from the North-Easterners that he joined Hammers for the 1923/24 season, and although he was never a first team regular, he was nevertheless a valued member of the Upton Park playing staff during the twenties. His finest feat in the claret and blue came in a Reserve fixture, however; Johnny's five goals against Fulham in Dec. 1928 contributing to a 13-2 victory which still stands as a West Ham record in a Football Combination match. John transferred to Clapton Orient in 1929. Passed away in Jan. 1983 at the age of 81.

CANNON, Frank 1909-10

Born: 8.11.1885
SL apps: 3 (1 gl)

■ It would have been nice to be able to say that Frank possessed a cannon-ball shot, but that would be taking journalistic licence too far. What is known for sure is that the former Queens Park Rangers inside-left was not on a losing side during his three-match run in Hammers' Southern League side at centre-forward, and he got on the scoresheet in a 5-0 Upton Park romp over Norwich. Began his career at 15 with Hitchin Town in 1900 and spent seven seasons with the Hertfordshire club before his move to QPR. Worked as a solicitor's clerk in Hitchin and continued in that capacity after turning pro with Rangers in 1907. Represented Herts in numerous county matches between 1902/08 and won several gold medals while with Hitchin. Described as a 'dashing player and good dribbler with a fine shot.' Scored a hat-trick v West Ham for QPR in a 4-0 SL win (20.4.08) at The Park Royal Ground, a performance which obviously prompted Irons to sign him, although he had part of a season with New Brompton before coming to Upton Park in 1909. Assisted Fulham in the early part of 1914/18 war, but was to become yet another player with West Ham connections to perish tragically in that conflict in Feb. 1916.

CANTWELL, Noel   1952-60

Born: Cork, Republic of Ireland. 28.2.32
Lge apps: 248 (11 gls)
Cup apps: 15

■ Swashbuckling, attack-minded full-back whose 17 international appearances for his native Republic of Ireland while with the Hammers bore ample testimony to his skill. Signed from Cork United in 1952, he joined a veritable colony of fellowcountrymen at Upton Park. His classic partnership with John Bond formed one of the best full-back pairings ever seen at the club and was a major factor in the promotion-winning team of 1958. Made his last League appearances for Hammers at Everton (24.9.60) before his transfer to Manchester United for £29,500 (a record at that time for a full-back). Noel, of course, went on to even greater triumphs with United, captaining their 1963 FA Cup-winning side and then in the European Cup Winners Cup against holders Spurs the following season. He also showed his skills were not just confined to the field of play when he took over the chairmanship of the Professional Footballers' Association where he honed the administrative skills later to stand him in good stead with First Division Coventry City and Peterborough United with whom he had two spells as manager and led into Division Three. He later broadened his horizons with the Boston Tea Men in the NASL. Noel made 36 appearances for the Republic of Ireland and captained them on many occasions. He was also player/manager of the Republic towards the end of his international career but had to relinquish the post of manager when the dual responsibilities of the national side and Coventry City proved incompatible. Noel is now mine host at the New Inn public house at Lincoln Road, Peterborough, where he welcomes football fans of all nominations with typical Irish hospitality.
☆ **Republic of Ireland caps:** *1953 v Luxembourg; 1955 v Spain; 1956 v Holland, Denmark, West Germany; 1957 v England (twice), Denmark; 1958 v Austria, Poland (twice); 1959 v Czecholslovakia (twice), Sweden, 1960 v Chile, Sweden, Norway (17).*

Played	League		FAC		LC		Europe		Total	
	App	Gls	App	Gls	App	Gls	App	Gls	App	Gls
1952-53	4	0	0	0	0	0	0	0	4	0
1953-54	23	0	0	0	0	0	0	0	23	0
1954-55	17	0	2	0	0	0	0	0	19	0
1955-56	40	0	6	0	0	0	0	0	46	0
1956-57	39	1	2	0	0	0	0	0	41	1
1957-58	33	4	2	0	0	0	0	0	35	4
1958-59	42	3	1	0	0	0	0	0	43	3
1959-60	40	3	2	0	0	0	0	0	42	3
1960-61	10	0	0	0	0	0	0	0	10	0
TOTAL	248	11	15	0	0	0	0	0	263	11

Noel Cantwell

CARNELLY, Albert   (1899-1900) TIW

SL apps: 27 (8 gls)
Cup apps: 6 (5 gls)

■ A much-travelled inside, cum-centre-forward who joined Irons from Bristol City having previously seen service with Notts County, Loughborough, Nottingham Forest and Leicester Fosse. Albert was a consistent scorer who missed only one SL match and one FA Cup tie in his solitary season with the club. He was an instant hit with the Memorial Ground crowd when he scored twice on his home debut v Chatham who succumbed 4-0. He also scored four goals v Grays United in a Thames and Medway Combination (6.11.1899). Irons got some much needed relief from their season-long fight against relegation with a strong run in the FA Cup, in which, with Carnelly scoring in four of the five rounds played, Hammers reached the fifth qualifying round where they lost 2-1 at home to arch rivals Millwall, the team he joined when he left the Memorial Grounds. Transferred from the Lions to Ilkeston Town in Oct. 1901.

CARR, Franz   1991

Born: Preston, Lancashire. 24.9.66.
Lge apps: 3

■ Speedy right-winger who started just one League game, at Oxford United (13.3.91) and came on as sub in two others during a brief spell on loan from Sheffield Wednesday in Mar. 1991. England Youth and Under-21 international Franz's best days were under Brian Clough at Nottingham Forest, who signed him for £100,000 from Blackburn Rovers and where he won Simod Cup and League Cup medals. After failing to make it in loan stints at West Ham and Sheffield Wednesday, Franz moved to Newcastle United in a £250,000 deal in the summer of 1991. After just 22 League games for Magpies, Carr went on to play for the Sheffield United side that was relegated from the Premiership at the end of 1993/94. Joined promoted Leicester City for 1994/95.

CARR, James   1914-15

Born: Maryhill, Glasgow, Scotland. 19.12.1893
Lge apps: 5 (1 gl)

■ This outside-left made his initial Southern League appearance in a 0-0 draw against his former club Watford at Cassio Road (28.11.14). He scored on his Boleyn baptism the following week in the 2-0 win over Plymouth Argyle. His last appearance in the claret and blue saw him on the opposite flank in the 1-1 draw at Swindon (30.1.15). He is listed in the 1914/15 club handbook as J.E.C. Carr, with no mention of the initial 'I' which has appeared in previous works. He was then 19 years of age, 5ft 7ins and tipped the scales at 10st. Just right for a winger! He began his Football League career at Watford as a 16 year-old and had a spell at Clapton Orient before returning to the Hertfordshire club. During WW1 he guested for Portsmouth and Kilmarnock in between his duties in the army as a private. His career really took off at Reading whom he joined in 1919 to form an exciting partnership with Len Andrews, which was resumed when Jimmy transferred to Southampton in June 1923. He was a valued member of the Saints side which progressed to the FA Cup semi-finals in 1924/25. In May 1926 he joined Swansea Town after scoring 10 times in 96 games for the Saints but with the end of his career approaching he took the unprecedented step of placing an advertisement in the "Athletic News", stating that he would 'assist a club outside the League in exchange for a business.' It worked, because he was soon playing for Southall and running The Red Lion Hotel in the Middlesex town! Jimmy passed away at Harrow, Middlesex 26.6.80.

CARR, Tony

Born: Bow, London. 5.9.1950.

■ Attended St. Paul's Way School and was captain of the East London Boys side which won the English Trophy. Tony was centre-forward and a prolific goalscorer. He had three years as an apprentice with the Hammers and two seasons as a pro., playing in the Reserves. Then moved to Barnet in the Southern League for a season before breaking a leg and being out of the game for 18 months. Meanwhile he qualified as a P.E. instructor and sports master and spent part of his profession at Holloway School and Woodberry Down School in North London. He served as a part-time coach with the youth squad under John Lyall in 1980 and guided the kids to their first-ever South-East Counties League title in 1985. Tony Cottee, Paul Ince and Alan Dickens are among the youngsters who emerged as stars under Tony's management. Appointed manager of the Reserves in 1988, Tony reverted to youth team management duties at the start of 1992/93 and now has considerable responsibilty for youth development, through the school of excellence, at Upton Park.

CARRICK, Christopher   1904-05

Born: Stockton, Teesside. 8.10.1882
SL apps: 18 (6 gls)

■ Christopher's inclusion in the side at outside-left helped to halt a disastrous nine-match losing run which included a home FA Cup defeat by Brighton. It all came right when Chris scored a timely hat-trick in a 6-2 win over Luton to spark off a revival which saw Hammers find the net 30 times in their last 15 matches, as against only 18 in the first 19 games. In Apr. 1905 he transferred to Southern League rivals Spurs, and in a year at White Hart Lane he netted four times in 19 League and Cup matches. Spurs had signed him to replace John Kirwan, who had transferred to Chelsea, but it was only around the middle of the 1905/06 season that he was able to command a regular place. However, in Mar. 1906 Spurs visited the West Country to fulfil two Western League fixtures against Bristol Rovers and Plymouth Argyle and between the two matches Carrick and a team-mate were involved in a mis-demeanour. When they got back to London, the pair were suspended for ignoring training rules. He never played for Spurs again, transfer-ring to fellow Southern League club Reading. He later served Bradford City during the Yorkshire club's geographically confusing dalliance with Southern League football in 1907/08. In Sept. 1908 he crossed the Irish Sea to join Glentoran. Described by a contemporary journalist as being 'a parcel of strength and muscle. Sturdy little winger who is quick off the mark and has the rare gift of taking chances.' Died at Middlesbrough (1927), aged 44.

CARROLL, Johnny   1948-49

Born: Republic of Ireland.
Lge apps: 5

■ One of the lesser-known of the considerable Irish contingent in the immediate post-war period at Upton Park, this centre-forward joined the club at the same time as fellow compatriots Danny McGowan and Fred Kearns. Signed from Limerick, he made only five Second Division appearances in season 1948/49, without getting on the scoresheet.

CARTER, George   1919-27

Born: West Ham, London
Lge apps: 136 (1 gl)
Cup apps: 19

George Carter

■ An East-Ender born and bred, who first came to notice as a member of the West Ham Boys team which contested the Final of the Schools Shield with Sheffield Boys in 1914. He then progressed to his works team, where he combined his duties as an apprentice engineer with playing under the unlikely banner of Green Silley Weir in the London Munitions League. Before the end of WW1 he became one of the early members of the RAF Officer Training Corps, joining Hammers for their intial season of League Football in 1919/20. Equally at home in any of the half-back positions, he often proved to be an invaluable deputy for Syd Bishop, George Kay or Jack Tresadern. A keen tennis player in his off-field moments, George was granted a well deserved benefit by the club in 1925. Just as he seemed set to stake a claim for regular First Team recognition he fell victim to a bad knee injury in a match v Blackburn Rovers at Ewood Park. Despite having a cartilage operation and bravely signing on for the 1927/28 season, the incident effectively ended his first class football career although he did have a brief spell with Fulham in 1928 and then Grays Thurrock. Hiding his disappointment, George found employment with the sugar people. Tate & Lyle, remaining there until he retired to live at Leigh-on-Sea in 1965. A great organiser and soccer ad-ministrator, he kept his interest alive with Lyle Sports FC as honorary secretary and coach, and was also an executive committee member of the London Business Houses League. He later organised the West Ham Six-a-Side Tournament and was Hon. Secretary to the East Ham Memorial Hospital competition. So George Carter put a fair bit back into the game during his time.

CARTER, H   1912-14

Born: Bristol. 1889
SL apps: 10

■ While not being particularly big for a goalkeeper - he tipped the scales at a mere 11st and measured only 5ft 9ins in height when he joined West Ham as a 23 year old from Barrow in 1912 - he was a competent 'keeper nevertheless. Good enough, in fact, not to have been on the losing side in any of his 10 senior appearances while a Hammer - an achievement which might well constitute a club record and one which we felt worthy of setting out, match by match:- Feb 7, 1913 Plymouth (h), W 2-0, Feb 15, Southampton (h) D 1-1; Mar 24, Brighton (a) D 0-0; Mar 29,

Brentford (h) W 2-1; April 5, Millwall (a) W 3-1; April 12, Bristol Rovers (h) W 3-1; April 19, Swindon (a) D 1-1; April 23, Reading (a) D 1-1; April 26, Portsmouth (h) W 2-1; November 22, Gillingham (h) W 3-1. Despite his proud record, Carter was not retained at the end of the 1913-14 season. Team mate of Arhtur Winterhalder and Harold Halse in the Wanstead XI of 1904/05.

CARTWRIGHT, Johnny   1959-61

Born: Northampton. 5.11.40
Lge apps: 4
Cup apps: 1

■ Pro 11/57 after Juniors. Vastly talented insideforward whose first team opportunities were limited by the signing of Welsh inter-national Phil Woosnam and the emergence of Ron Boyce. His subsequent transfer to Crystal Palace bore little success, and he later played for Bath City and Wimbledon in the Southern League. He has since made a name for himself as manager of the England Youth team and a leading coach who, as well as enjoying a good reputation in England, has also gained experience in Kuwait. Became assistant manager of Arsenal in 1985, but resigned - together with Don Howe - in March 1986. Now youth team manager at Charlton Athletic.

CASEY, Jack   1912-15

Born: Liverpool.
SL apps: 74 (12 gls)
Cup apps: 9 (1 gl)

■ Jack was signed from Bromley, where he had played a prominent role in the Kent club's run of success between 1908 and 1911 when they won the Spartan League championship, the Isthmian League (twice) and the FA Amateur Cup. Not one for grabbing the headlines, he nevertheless proved an invaluable asset as the team's regular outside-left up to WW1 and made a further 30 appearances during the conflict, scoring six times. Became a schoolmaster in West Ham and was a fine amateur sprinter with the Polytechnic Harriers in his youth. 'Controls the ball well when at top speed and centres accurately'.

H Carter

CATER, Ron
1946-49

Born: Fulham, London. 2.2.22
Lge apps: 63
Cup apps: 7

■ Joined the ground-staff as a 15-year-old pre WW2, and was in the Essex Regiment and RA from Apr. 1939. A utility defender who played as an amateur for Leytonstone before joining Hammers. Although he was born in West London, Ron turned out for East Ham Boys as well as the London side as a youngster and was also a member of the same army team as 16 other West Ham players. He took the same short journey as so many other former Hammers when he left the club to join Leyton Orient.

CATON, Harold
1912-15

Born: Berkshire
SL apps: 14

■ An amateur with the Barking Curfew club, Harry made his Hammers' debut in an abysmal 6-2 defeat at Merthyr Tydfil in Jan. 1913. But the Berkshire-born right-winger was given another chance to shine in an altogether more fruitful journey west the next month, as a member of the side which brought the points back from Plymouth Argyle. Another call-up for the home encounter with Brentford brought his total of appearances for the season to three; the same figure he reached in 1913/14. A switch to the opposite flank enabled him to more than double his appearance total in the last peace-time season, although he enjoyed his best

campaign, appearance-wise, during the first war-time season, making 18 outings in the London Combination and Supplementary Tournament, in which he also scored his only goal at senior level.

CHALKLEY, George
1908-09

SL apps: 7
Cup apps: 4

■ A centre-half who played the first of a seven match run in the first team in a 1-0 Christmas Day win over Southampton at Upton Park. His final outing was in a 0-1 reverse at Luton (30.1.09). He joined West Ham as an amateur from Custom House FC. Later played for Hastings and Southend United (Oct. 1910). His more famous brother, Alf, played more than 200 games for the club between 1931-37. Not to be confused with F.C. Chalkley who came to TIW in Aug. 1896 from the local Park Grove FC and later played for Clapton Orient (1901-02).

Harry Caton

CHALKLEY, Alfred
1931-37

Born: Plaistow, London
Lge apps: 188 (1 gl)
Cup apps: 14

■ The product of a well-known footballing family - both his brothers played the game; George being an early century Hammers centre-half, while Charlie played left-back for Dartford. A goalscoring outside-left in schools soccer, young Alf was capped for England Boys v Scotland at Liverpool in 1917. There was to be a long gap between that early success and his signing for West Ham United in 1931, with army duty as an Artillery man and his trade as a steel erector taking up much of the intervening years. After impressing in a trial game, Alf played one League match as an amateur before signing pro forms for the 1931/32 season. By now converted to the full-back position, he had to curb his goalscoring bent, although his solitary goal for Hammers was a remarkable one. It came in a re-arranged League match v Manchester City at Upton Park (2.3.32). In a fixture which also marked the reappearance of Syd Puddefoot after a 10-year absence, Alf kicked the ball from near his own penalty area, and his intended clearance sailed over the head of City goalkeeper Langford for the only goal of the game. Although major honours passed him by, Alf did represent the London Combination on three occasions v London Central League and was also honoured by the London FA v Diables Rouges of Belgium.

CHAPMAN, Eddie
1937-56

Born: East Ham, London. 3.8.23
Lge apps: 7 (3 gls)

■ Eddie joined West Ham as an amateur in 1936 before signing on the groundstaff in 1937 and played for Romford until signing pro in 1942, eventually becoming one of the longest-serving members on the club payroll. He took up the position of club secretary when he retired from playing in 1956, and added the title of chief executive in 1979. Blooded in war-time soccer by Charlie Paynter when he was only 16, Eddie had to wait until 1948 before making his League debut in the Second Division after being de-mobbed by the army (where he served in the R.E.). A man with a multitude of memories, he once scored five goals in a 7-0 victory over QPR in a Combination fixture, just after WW2, and was the recipient of the Football League long-service award in 1978. He made one guest appearance for Spurs during the War, against Crystal Palace. Retired from West Ham in June 1986 after an astonishing 49 years service, Eddie was awarded a testimonial by the club and he is still a regular visitor to Upton Park.

CHAPMAN, Lee
1993-

Born: Lincoln, Lincolnshire. 5.2.59.
Lge apps: 30 (7 gls)
Cup apps: 9 (4 gls)

■ Lee Chapman's career as a striker has been full of highs and lows, much like his first season with West Ham

e Chapman

in 1993/94. When Leeds United released 'Chappie' at the end of the previous season, he stepped down a division to join Portsmouth. But Lee soon missed the challenge and atmosphere of the big-time and was relieved to end up at Upton Park - a month into the new campaign and despite originally failing to agree terms with the club in the summer! He enjoyed a fairytale debut, scoring a simple tap-in in a stunning 2-0 victory at Blackburn Rovers (18.9.93), who went on to finish second in the title race. In his next appearance, Lee scored twice on his home debut v Chesterfield in the Coca-Cola (League) Cup but the Upton Park crowd did not always appreciate his qualities as a target man, whose main strength is in the air (lack of wingers did not help his cause). A difficult opponent in the penalty area, Chapman (who was born in Scorer Street!) can find the space to maximise his asset as a tall, lean striker and his headed goals, that carried Hammers through successive FA Cup ties against Notts County and Kidderminster Harriers, to the quarter-final stage, must have been worth, in financial terms, the £250,000 he cost from Pompey. At 35, and with 11 goals to his name, Lee did as well could be expected. Yet he has still to win the fans' approval and, as the season, neared its end, he was relegated to the subs' bench as the management duo experimented with a five-man midfield formation. It is by no means the first challenge 'Chappie' has faced. After an encouraging start at Stoke City (99 League appearances, 34 goals) in 1978, when he also spent a four-match spell on loan to Plymouth Argyle, Lee made - what he described in his own autobiography, More Than A Match - as a 'disastrous' move to Arsenal (23 apps, 4 gls) in 1982 and hardly enjoyed himself any more at Sunderland (15 apps, 3 gls). His career was revitalised under Howard Wilkinson at Sheffield Wednesday (149 apps, 63 gls) in 1984 before it suffered another setback, in 1988, when he endured a bad time with struggling French club Niort. Nottingham Forest (48 apps, 15 gls) rescued Lee from his French ordeal in 1988 and two

years later he began the most successful chapter of his career, with Leeds United (137 apps, 63 gls). Back under Wilkinson's wing at Elland Road, Lee helped Leeds win the Second Division title in his first season. In May 1992, his 16 League goals elevated the Yorkshire club to become the last-ever winners of the old First Division championship. One of football's intellectuals, 'Chappie' complements his playing activities with regular appearances as a soccer TV pundit and quality newspaper columnist. He is also a wine connoisseur and regularly visits the vineyards of Europe. Married to TV actress Lesley Ash.

CHARLES, Clive   1972-73

Born: Bow, London. 3.10.51
Lge apps: 14
Cup apps: 1

■ Younger brother of more famous Hammer John, Charles junior was a useful full-back and a valued member of the Upton Park playing staff in the early 70s, making his debut against

Clive Charles

Coventry City at Highfield Road in Mar. 1972. Clive was never able to call a first team place his own owing to the fine form of Frank Lampard and John McDowell. The signing of Keith Coleman from Sunderland limited his prospects even further and he subsequently transferred to Cardiff City. Now coaching in Oregon, USA.

CHARLES, John   1963-69

Born: Canning Town, London. 20.9.44
Lge apps: 118 (1 gl)
Cup apps: 24 (1 gl)

■ One of the first black players to really break-through in London soccer, "Charlo" was a good full-back and always strove to live up to one of the most famous names in football! He captained West Ham's Youth Cup-winning side, won England Youth honours and made his League bow in a 1-0 home defeat v Blackburn Rovers (4.5.63) - all in 1963. Played all his Hammers' career in the same defence as Bobby Moore. John's final appearance was in a 2-2 draw v the all-conquering Leeds United team at Upton Park (2.4.70). John's solitary League goal came in a memorable match v Manchester United on the day (6.5.67) Best, Charlton, Law and co. clinched the First Division title with a superb 6-1 victory at Upton Park. East Ender John was released by west Ham in the summer of 1971. He was still only 26, but turned down the chance to join Orient to run his own greengrocery market stall.

CHARLTON, William   1922

William Charlton

Born: Sunderland. 10.10.1900
Lge apps: 8.

■ This dashing former England Schoolboy international was signed from South Shields (later Gateshead) on the strength of several impressive displays against Hammers in their formative League seasons. The brother of former Fulham and Carlisle full-back Edward Charlton, Bill made his West Ham debut on the opening day of the 1922/23 season v Bradford City at Upton Park, and played in the first eight matches at outside-right before being superceded by Welsh international Dick Richards. Later played for Newport and Cardiff. Bill died in his hometown in the spring of 1981.

CHISWICK, Peter   1954-56

Born: Dagenham, Essex. 19.9.29
Lge apps: 19

■ This fine goalkeeper signed pro forms during the summer of 1947 after he had appeared as an amateur with Colchester United as well as Hammers. He had to wait until

John Charles

Feb. 1954 before making his League baptism at home to Leeds United. In all he completed 10 years at the Boleyn before moving on to Gillingham in 1956. He later joined the ever-growing colony of ex-Hammers under Almer Hall at Southern League Margate, before being appointed manager/coach to Barking, where his experience as a P.T. teacher (in the RAF) and a fully-qualified FA coach stood him in good stead. Peter died at the tragically early age of 32 in Aug. 1962 after being struck down with a throat infection. It was a loss football could ill-afford.

CHURCH, William   1903-04

SL apps: 2

■ Bill made his Southern League bow in a 0-1 defeat at Swindon Town from the outside-left position (12.3.04). His only appearance in a first team fixture at the Memorial Grounds came the following week (19.3.04), in a 0-2 reverse v London rivals Spurs. A local amateur who played mostly for Leytonstone, but Clapton Orient also made use of his services. Still with the Stones in Apr. 1908.

CLARK, Alexander "Sandy"   1982-83

Born: Airdrie, Scotland. 28.10.56
Lge apps: 26 (7 gls)
Cup apps: 8 (3 gls)

■ Better known as "Sandy" to his colleagues, this Scottish striker cost £200,000 from Airdrie in 1982. A prolific scorer north of the border, he found the transition from part-time football to the much more physically demanding First Division difficult to make and he didn't last a full season at Upton Park. Faced with the daunting prospect of trying to replace popular David Cross in the number nine shirt, Sandy's partnership with Paul Goddard got off to a promising start: He scored five times in a five-match winning spell in Sept./Oct. 1992, but managed to add just two more to that tally before being replaced by Dave Swindlehurst and

the emerging Tony Cottee. His final outing came v Southampton at Upton Park (26.2.83). Former skipper of the Broomfield club and Scottish Footballer of the Year, he returned to his native country with Glasgow Rangers for a hefty fee and was back among the goals after a further move to Hearts. Sandy lost his job as manager at Tynecastle when new chairman Chris Robinson took over in June 1994.

CLARK, David   1906-09

Lge apps: 17

■ Understudy goalkeeper to George Kitchen, David was thrown in at the deep end for the London derby match v Spurs at the Boleyn (29.12.06). Hammers won 4-2 but he was back in the reserves the next week and had to wait until the following season before being given an extended run in the side, after Kitchen was injured at Newcastle. Again taking over from Kitchen, he played in the last 15 games of the 1907/08 season.

Deputising for Kitchen again, Clarke was on the receiving end of a 6-0 drubbing at Northampton (27.2.09) in what proved to be his last first team appearance. He was previously with Bristol Rovers and Glossop. Moved to Bradford Park Avenue with James Dyer for the start of 1909/10. Later with Southend United.

D. CLARK. WEST HAM UNITED.

Simon Clarke in his only first team game at Maine Road

COCKROFT, Joe   1933-39

Born: Barnsley, Yorkshire. 1911
Lge apps: 151 (3 gls)
Cup apps: 12

■ A wonderfully consistent wing-half, Joe was an ever-present in West Ham's Second Division side for four consecutive seasons and probably the finest uncapped player of his generation. Signed at the tail-end of the 1932/33 season on a month's trial from Midland League Gainsborough Trinity, after seeing service with Yorkshire Paper Mills, Barnsley Old Boys, Ardsley Athletic and Wombwell, he was pitched into the first XI after playing just four reserve matches when injuries to Albert Cadwell and Joe Musgrave left Hammers short of a left-half. Although Chesterfield won that Good Friday 1933 clash by the only goal of the game, Joe held his place in a side which managed to win its next four matches and, in doing so, avoided relegation to the Third Division by one point. He missed only three League matches up to the outbreak of WW2, and played in the 1940 League War Cup win over Blackburn Rovers at Wembley. Direction of labour regulation during the early part of hostilities saw him sent back north to do his bit for the war effort at Edgar Allen's Steelworks, Sheffield. While there he guested for Sheffield Wednesday and transferred to the Hillsborough club when the war was over. In 1949 he moved over to rivals Sheffield United, for a fee of £4,000, and played in the First Division for the first time at the age of 37, but only had a year with the Blades before accepting an offer to manage Wisbech Town. He had three years with the Cambridgeshire club after which he retired from the game to go into the Licensed Victualler Trade. He later became a printer. As a boy, Joe played in the same Barnsley school team as the pre-war Spurs' forward George Hunt and Hydes of Leeds United.

Curiously, his first professional club - Rotherham United - let him go. At Upton Park he was often involved in a ploy instigated by that wily old tactician Charlie Paynter, in which he switched roles during a match with Len Goulden to throw the opposition; it worked well by all accounts.

Played	League App	Gls	FAC App	Gls	LC App	Gls	Europe App	Gls	Total App	Gls
1932-33	6	0	0	0	0	0	0	0	6	0
1933-34	42	0	2	0	0	0	0	0	44	0
1934-35	42	0	2	0	0	0	0	0	44	0
1935-36	42	1	2	0	0	0	0	0	44	1
1936-37	42	1	2	0	0	0	0	0	44	1
1937-38	38	0	1	0	0	0	0	0	39	0
1938-39	39	1	3	0	0	0	0	0	42	1
TOTAL	**251**	**3**	**12**	**0**	**0**	**0**	**0**	**0**	**263**	**3**

CLARKE, Simon   1991-93

Born: Chelmsford, Essex. 23.9.71.
Lge apps: 3

■ Represented Chelmsford Schools before making his mark for Hammers' youth and reserve teams, Simon's first team experience was limited to three outings as sub. The tall, lean striker came on for the last minute of the Second Division match at Watford (12.1.91), was given the full second half at Manchester City (18.4.92) and played for the last 18 minutes at Millwall (15.11.92). Joined non-league Kettering Town on loan in Dec.1992 and was freed by Hammers in May 1993.

COKER, Ade   1971-73

Born: Lagos, Nigeria. 19.5.54
Lge apps: 10 (3 gls)
Cup apps: 1

■ A lively Nigerian striker whose first appearance for Hammers caused a sensation. A late replacement for the injured Geoff Hurst v Crystal Palace at Selhurst Park (30.10.71), he stunned the Glaziers with his close-ball skills and sent the fans into raptures, scoring a goal and being largely instrumental in a 3-0 victory. English winters were not conducive to his style, however, and he never fully recaptured the same scintillating form. His last outing was as sub v Leicester City at Upton Park (22.9.73) before gradually falling into obscurity after playing in the North American Soccer League for Boston Minutemen and being loaned to Lincoln City.

COLEMAN, Keith   1973-77

Born: Washington, Co. Durham. 24.5.51
Lge apps: 101
Cup apps: 16

■ A solid, competent full-back signed from Sunderland for £20,000 after a period on loan from the Roker club. Made his League debut v Burnley at Upton Park (6.10.73), but had to be content to share the full-back berths with McDowall and Lampard, often deputising when either were injured. Won European Cup Winners' Cup runners-up medal in 1976, and played his last game in 1-1 draw at Leeds (26.4.77). Signed a two-year contract with K.V. Mechelen of the Belgian Second Division. Later had a spell at Darlington. Now working at a sports centre in Brentwood, Essex.

COLLINS, Jimmy   1924-36

Born: Brentford, Middlesex. 1903
Lge apps: 311 (3 gls)
Cup apps: 25

■ Affectionately referred to by the fans as "Lottie" - after the famous music-hall artiste. One of the longest-serving players in the club's history, Jim first played at the Boleyn Ground in 1917 as captain of East Ham Boys, and the same year was chosen to represent England v Scotland; but as the game was cancelled, never received his School's cap. Modelling his game on his idol, Syd Puddefoot, he soon put that disappointment behind him, and after doing the rounds with Chelmsford, Clapton and Leyton, signed amateur forms for Hammers in 1921. Two years later he was elevated to full professional status, and the following season made his First Division debut v Spurs at Upton Park (9.2.24). Owing to the abundance of forward talent at West Ham in those days, his baptism was to be one of his few appearances in the front line, as he converted to wing-half to win a regular place. He made the switch well enough to make 160 consecutive appearances until a cartilage injury ended the run. A measure of his worth can be gleaned from the fact that he was one of the comparatively few professionals retained after Irons' disastrous relegation season of 1931/32; going on to appear in the gallant FA Cup semi-final defeat to Everton at Molineux the next season. When he finally retired from the game in 1936, he found plenty to occupy his time, following the example of Vic Watson before him by going into the nursery and growing trade. As well as being a keen motorist (he claimed to be the first West Ham player to own a car in 1921!), he also trained greyhounds in his spare time, owning kennels along with his brother Ted, who was himself an England amateur international, and won Amateur Cup Final medals with both

Leyton and Walthamstow Avenue, as well as playing for the Hammers as an amateur. The brothers' most famous canine "discovery" was the aptly-named Golden Hammer, who finished second in the Greyhound Derby and once beat the renowned Mick the Miller. Jim retained his allegiance to West Ham United throughout his life, and with his wife was a season ticket holder at Upton Park until his death in May 1977, at the age of 74.

Played	League		FAC		LC		Europe		Total	
	App	Gls	App	Gls	App	Gls	App	Gls	App	Gls
1923-24	5	1	0	0	0	0	0	0	5	1
1924-25	2	0	1	0	0	0	0	0	3	0
1925-26	24	0	1	0	0	0	0	0	25	0
1926-27	42	1	3	0	0	0	0	0	45	1
1927-28	42	0	2	0	0	0	0	0	44	0
1928-29	39	1	5	0	0	0	0	0	44	1
1929-30	21	0	4	0	0	0	0	0	25	0
1930-31	38	0	1	0	0	0	0	0	39	0
1931-32	35	0	2	0	0	0	0	0	37	0
1932-33	33	0	6	0	0	0	0	0	39	0
1933-34	17	0	0	0	0	0	0	0	17	0
1934-35	12	0	0	0	0	0	0	0	12	0
1935-36	1	0	0	0	0	0	0	0	1	0
TOTAL	311	3	25	0	0	0	0	0	336	3

CONWELL, Larry   1935-37

Born: Aberdeen, Scotland
Lge apps: 8 (1 gl)

■ A Scottish outside or inside-forward who had the unusual experience of representing the Irish League v Football League in Belfast while on Portadown's books in 1935. He crossed the Irish Sea to join Hammers on October 12 of the same year and made his Second Division debut later that month, against Bradford City at the Boleyn. At the end of that campaign he was a member of the West Ham United party which embarked on a close-season tour of Switzerland, but the following season managed only two senior outings before his transfer to Coventry (17.3.37).

CONWAY, Herman   1934-38

Born: Gainsborough, Lincolnshire. 11.10.1908
Lge apps: 121
Cup apps: 5

■ A big, dependable goalkeeper signed from Burnley, having previously made a name for himself with Midland League Gainsborough Trinity. A six-footer, he was inspired as a boy by Sam Hardy of Villa, Liverpool and England fame and joined Burnley on the recommendation of another ex-England 'keeper, Jerry Dawson, who spent 21 years between the sticks for the Clarets. With his safe handling inspiring confidence among his fellow defenders, Herman made 41 League appearances in the 1934/35 season, the end of which saw Irons just pipped for promotion to Division One by their old adversaries Bolton Wanderers - on goal average. After making over a century of senior appearances, he lost his

COOPER, Fred   1956-57

Born: West Ham, London. 18.11.34
Lge apps: 4

■ Ground-staff from school, 1949. Reserve team skipper who made his initial League appearance v Fulham at Craven Cottage in Aug. 1956. Had progressed through the junior ranks at Upton Park earning honours with West Ham, London and Essex Boys. Fred, incidentally, played in the first schoolboy international to be staged at Wembley, between England and Scotland; conceding a penalty in the opening minutes when he saved a "cert," by catching the ball on the goal-line. Luckily the incident didn't affect the final outcome too much, as England eventually won 8-2. He retired from the professional ranks after playing two games in the promotion season of 1957/58 to become the full-time licensee of the Essex Arms, Stratford. Fred died at the tragically early age of 38, in Apr. 1972.

COPE, Billy   1914-22

Born: Stoke-on-Trent, Staffs. 25.11.1884.
Lge apps: 137
Cup apps: 10

■ Exceptionally hard in the tackle, many reckoned the Hammers' skipper and full-back to be a better exponent of the offside trap than Newcastle United's famous Bill McCracken. Bill's first senior club was Burslem, Port Vale, joining them in 1904/05 and spending three seasons at the Athletic Ground before they resigned from the Football League Second Division. With Stanley Matthews still a twinkle in his dad's eye, he moved across the Potteries

Billy Cope

place to Harry Medhurst in Dec. 1938, but was to have one last moment of glory as a member of the Hammers' team which won the Football League War Cup at Wembley in 1940. Soon afterwards he began his war-time service, and rose through the ranks to become Commandant of a supply camp at Accrington as Adjutant-Quartermaster during the conflict. When his military commitments permitted he turned out for the losers of that 1940 final, Blackburn Rovers, and was invited to stay on at Ewood Park when the war ended. But he decided to return south to continue his building trade interests. The post-war season was played on a regionalised transitionary basis, and Southend United manager Harry Warren managed to persuade Herman to participate and end his career with the Essex club. Living at nearby Chadwell Heath, Herman and his wife were regular matchday visitors to Upton Park until his sad passing in Apr. 1983.

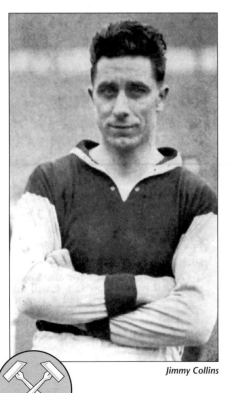

Jimmy Collins

to join Stoke for the 1907/08 season. playing 25 times before they also left the League. Not to be denied, Bill moved to Oldham Athletic, then beginning their second season as a League club, but failed to establish himself with The Latics. Signed from Oldham in 1914, Billy had a steadying influence on the West Ham rearguard during their first three seasons of League football following World War I and later continued his career with Wrexham. Known as a 'hard man' of his day, Bill was sent off more than once during his long career. A great disciple of the one-back game, Bill died at Stoke (18.2.37).

CORBETT, David   1936

Born: Falkirk, Scotland
SL apps: 4

■ Like his younger brother, Norman, Dave was a tough-tackling right-half in the true Scottish tradition. Making his debut in a 3-3 draw at Carrow Road against Norwich City (10.10.36), he made a further three Second Division appearances before Christmas, but that proved to be his sum total of senior outings.

CORBETT, Fred   1899-02

SL apps: 3 (1899/1900) TIW
Lge apps: 33 (13 gls) WHU
Cup apps: 2 (2 gls)

■ A leading light in Irons' first season under the new banner of West Ham United FC in the Southern League, Fred scored the only goal of the game in his initial appearance before the Memorial Ground crowd v Swindon Town (6.10.1900). He continued to be a vital source of goals during his season and a half in the first XI. His best display was in a re-arranged game against Wellingborough Town (30.9.01), after the first fixture was abandoned because of poor light due to the late arrival of the Northamptonshire club. Hammers won 4-2, with Fred scoring a hat-trick. Described as 'strong and determined', he later had successful spells with Bristol Rovers, Bristol City and Brentford.

CORBETT, Norman   1937-50

Born: Camelon, Falkirk, Scotland. 23.16.19
Lge apps: 166 (3 gls)

■ Long-throw expert and one of three footballing brothers associated with the club. Had it not been for the war it was generally thought that "Norrie" would have emulated his brother Willie (who guested for Hammers during hostilities and won full Scottish international honours). Represented the Football Combination against Belgian opposition and won a Football League War Cup medal - even though he did not appear in the 1940 Final v Blackburn Rovers at Wembley; having played in enough earlier rounds to qualify for the honour. While a youngster he had skippered Falkirk when they won the Scottish Schools Trophy, and also played for Scotland Boys and Scotland Juniors (while at Musselburgh). He signed pro for Hearts at the age of 15, then joined Hammers in Apr. 1937. His WW1 service as T.A. volunteer with the Essex Regt. in 1939 ended with the rank of Sergeant-Major PTI. He appeared as a guest for Southampton during the war, as did his brother Willie on one occasion. After 1950 he continued playing in the reserves and became an FA coach, later joining Clapton. Unfortunately, illness brought his eventual retirement from the game

COSHALL, John   1928-29

Born: London
Lge apps: 2

■ An adventurous full-back who was signed on pro forms along with his Erith club-mate Arthur Smith after impressing during Hammers' practice matches prior to the 1928-29 campaign. He was destined never to appear in a senior match at Upton Park, however, his first two first team appearances both being away from home in disastrous defeats at Bolton (1-4) and Derby (0-6).

COSTELLO, Frank   1908-09

Born: Birmingham. 1884.
Lge apps: 12 (3 gls)

■ A poor man's Ian Rush of the Edwardian era. West Ham never lost a match in which Frank scored. Although not a prolific scorer, his three counters in seperate matches were vital in a season which saw Hammers struggle to finish 17th in the SL in 1908/09 without recording a single win away from Upton Park. Normally an inside-left, he played one of his dozen senior appearances at centre-forward against Millwall at Cold Blow Lane. A midlander by birth, Frank was also known as Frederick, but seemed to prefer the former name. Beginning his football life with the risque named Soho Villa, he joined West Bromwich Albion as an amateur in Sept. 1904 before a brief spell with Halesowen prior to joining Southampton in May 1907. Scoring on his debut v Luton Town (14.9.07), he went on to make a total of 48 SL and cup appearances for Saints in which he scored 13 goals before joining Irons in March 1909, as a straight exchange for Jack Foster who went to the Dell. He left the Boleyn for Bolton Wanderers in June 1909 and later had spells with Nelson, Merthyr Town and Salisbury City. He returned to Hampshire to settle in the Southampton area but was killed in action in France serving his country at the beginning of WW1.

Tony Cottee

COTTEE, Tony   1983-88

Born: West Ham, London. 11.7.65
Lge apps: 212 (92 gls)
Cup apps: 43 (25 gls)

■ The most prolific West Ham striker since Geoff Hurst, Tony Cottee made Hammers' history when he joined Everton in July 1988 for £2.5 million - a British record at the time and the most West Ham have ever received for a player. Tony had an insatiable appetite for goals, catching the eye in his schooldays for Barking, Havering, East London and Essex before signing apprentice for Hammers (11.5.81). Turned pro 31.8.82 and on New Year's Day, 1983, aged 17, he exploded on to the first team scene by scoring in the 26th minute of his First Division debut v Tottenham at Upton Park."TC"scored five times in eight appearances that season but his well-preserved personal scrapbooks would be filled by many more headline-grabbing moments in the years to follow. In 1985/86 he established himself in the England Under-21 side and won PFA Young Player of the Year, Fiat Uno Young Player of the Year and Hammer of the Year awards. He was top scorer in four of his five full seasons with tallies of: 15, 17, 20, 22 and 13. His 20-goal haul in 1985/86 was bettered only by strike-partner Frank McAvennie, who hit 26 in a brilliant partnership that propelled West Ham to their best-ever First Division placing - third, behind Liverpool and Everton. Soon after the start of the following season, he made his full England debut, as a second half sub in

Stockholm, Sweden (10.9.86). Also appeared as sub in the next game, v Northern Ireland at Wembley (15.10.86). His only other England appearance while with West Ham was as sub v Hungary in Budapest (27.4.88). It was Tony's frustration at Hammers' failure to build on their success in 1986/87, and his belief that the club's ambitions did not match his own, that led to his unrest and inevitable transfer. He withdrew one transfer request but after the team narrowly avoided relegation at the end of 1987/88, it was only a matter of time before his big-money move went ahead. Arsenal and Everton led the chase for the pint-sized striker, who chose the long haul north from his Upminster home. It was some debut. TC celebrated his first goal for Everton after just 34 seconds and went on to score a hat-trick against Newcastle United at Goodison Park (27.8.88). Tony's first season on Merseyside under Colin Harvey brought him three more England caps as sub, before his first - and so far only - full appearance v Scotland at Hampden (27.5.89). Although Tony has maintained his formidable strike-rate at Everton, he was at times unsettled and found himself battling to prove his worth in a team struggling to recapture the glories of the mid-eighties.. At West Ham, however, there has never been any doubt about his value as a natural goalscorer, a poacher of half-chances who was lightning in the penalty box. It is these qualities that led Harry Redknapp to re-sign Cottee, in September 1994, in the swap deal that took David Burrows to Goodison Park. TC's return was typically explosive: he was sent off on his second debut, at Liverpool (10.9.94) and then scored the winner v Aston Villa (his 93rd in the League for Hammers) on his Upton Park homecoming a week later!

☆ **England caps:** *1986 v Sweden (sub), Northern Ireland; 1988 v Hungary. (3)*

Played	League		FAC		LC		Europe		Total	
	App	Gls	App	Gls	App	Gls	App	Gls	App	Gls
1982-83	8	5	1	0	0	0	0	0	9	5
1983-84	39	15	4	0	4	4	0	0	47	19
1984-85	41	17	5	4	4	3	0	0	50	24
1985-86	42	20	7	4	3	2	0	0	52	26
1986-87	42	22	5	1	6	5	0	0	53	28
1987-88	40	13	2	2	2	0	0	0	44	0
TOTAL	212	92	24	11	19	14	0	0	254	117

COTTON, Charles   1903-06

Born: Plymouth, Devon. 1882
SL apps: 18
Cup apps: 1

■ Signed from Reading along with Ernest Watts and Tommy Allison, Charlie began the 1903/04 season as first choice custodian, but lost his place after only eight matches to the more experienced Welsh international, Fred Griffiths. Later understudy to Matt Kingsley and George Kitchen, he failed to overcome their presence and although an able deputy, was allowed to seek pastures new in the close season of 1906. Somewhat short for a

goalkeeper at 5ft 8ins, he played for SL Sheppey United before Reading, where his record was second to none. He conceded the least goals of any goalkeeper in the SL during a three-season spell in which he missed just one match. He joined Liverpool from West Ham but was not long at Anfield, transferring to Southend United on that club's formation in 1906, after a brief return to West Ham. Only missed one match for Shrimpers up to 1909, when he was forced through illness to give up playing in Nov. 1909. He contracted Bright's disease and died in Jan. 1910.

COWELL, Herbert   1921

Lge apps: 1

■ Made his only League appearance from the inside-right berth against Rotherham County at Upton Park (9.4.21) when a Dick Leafe goal won the spoils for West Ham.

COWIE, George   1982-83

Born: Buckie, Scotland. 6.5.51
Lge apps: 8
Cup apps: 1

■ When George was appointed captain of the Scottish Youth XI in 1978, Hammers had the unique distinction of having the skippers of Scotland and England among their apprentice ranks - Paul Allen winning the equivalent honour for the latter. After gaining honours in schools football with North of Scotland, the young defender joined his local side Buckie Rovers from where he signed for West Ham United in July 1977. Made a full pro just over a year later, he had his First Division debut v Ipswich Town at Portman Road (13.4.82). Despite proving himself a valuable squad member, George was allowed to transfer to Hearts in 1983, where he was later joined by another former Hammer in striker Sandy Clark; and the pair became involved in the quest to bring the first Premier League Championship to Edinburgh but ended as runners-up. George was forced to retire from the game after sustaining an injury similar to the one that sidelined Alan Devonshire for so long after joining Dunfermline.

COWPER, Peter   1924

Born: Tyldesley, Lancs. 1.9.02

■ Right-wing flier whose two First Division outings were against Bury at Upton Park (11.10.24) and v Nottingham Forest at the City Ground the following Saturday. Signed from Rossendale. Before whom he played for Burns Celtic, Parkside Rangers, Atherton, Bolton Wanderers and Wigan Borough. His first XI opportunities were limited by the fine form of rival flankmen, Tommy Yews and Bill Edwards. He joined Grimsby on leaving Hammers and later played for Lancaster Town, New Brighton, Southampton,

Southport, Carlisle United, Wigan Athletic, Altrincham, and finally, Prescot Cables in 1936. His best spell was at New Brighton, where he scored 19 times in 70 League games. Died 26.9.62.

COX, Chas William   1927-32

Born: West Ham, London. 31.7.1905
Lge apps: 88

■ Bill played for the local Glico works club and also for Ilford in the Isthmian League. A wing-half, he came as understudy to Albert Cadwell in 1927. Bill made first team grade fairly quickly (playing 26 times that season), and by the end of the 1931/32 campaign totalled 88 League appearances. He was then granted a free transfer and joined Southend United. Bill was 73 at the time of his death in 1978. He lived in Albert Square, Stratford.

Note: Another half-back named Tom Cox signed for the Hammers in 1928. There appears to have been some confusion regarding the two Coxes, but there is no record of Tom Cox playing in the first team.

CRAIG, Charles   1899-02

Born: Dundee. 1863
SL apps (TIW): 17
SL apps (WHU): 53
Cup apps: 7

■ A Scotsman from Dundee, Charlie left the jute city to join Thames Ironworks and enter the ranks of professionalism in 1899. He began his career in ernest with "Our Boys," Dundee, played half-a-dozen matches and was promoted to the first team, which ultimately amalgamated with the East End Club and became Dundee FC. A member of the last Thames Ironworks side and the first under the West Ham United title at the turn of the century, he tried a number of positions before settling his 6ft 1in, 13st frame at left-back. One of the last links with the old Ironworks club was severed when Charles joined Nottingham Forest in the Football League. By a strange twist of fate, he passed away on the same day in 1933 as his former full-back partner and Hammers manager, Syd King. Described by a contemporary scribe as being a 'genial, good natured giant,' Charles was also a keen athlete and won a host of medals for his achievements on the track. He left Forest for Bradford Park Avenue, then moved on to Norwich City in 1908, but returned to Bradford P.A. at the end of 1908/09. Originally came south to work as a mechanic at Tate Sugar Refinery at Silvertown and then Thames Ironworks.

CRAWFORD, Ian 1961-63

Born: Edinburgh, Scotland. 14.7.34
Lge apps: 24 (5 gls)
Cup apps: 2 (2 gls)

■ Scotland Under-23 international signed from Hearts for £7,000 in July 1961 after he had won every possible club honour north of the border. Equally at home on either wing, Ian was unlucky not to have been given an extended run in the First Division, and surprisingly transferred to the then Second Division Scunthorpe United. Afterwards joined Peterborough United. Began his career in football administration as player/manager of Stamford in the Midland League towards the end of the 1969/70 season and later had coaching posts at Everton and Arsenal as youth coach. He also managed Norwegian Division One club, Hamkan, in the early eighties.

CRIPPS, Harry 1957-59

Born: East Dereham, Norfolk. 29.4.41

■ Ground-staff, 1956. Although he never played for the first team, this colourful character became something of a legend after leaving Hammers for Millwall and deserves a mention. A product of West Ham's youth policy, he was a member of the FA Youth Cup Final side narrowly defeated by Blackburn Rovers in 1959. Managed Barking after ending his League career at Charlton Athletic. Later became assistant to Bobby Moore at Southend. He was manager of London side Crown & Manor after leaving Roots Hall and was more recently coach to East Ham United. Now working as a broker by Royal London Assurance.

CROSS, David 1977-82

Born: Heywood, Lancashire. 8.12.50
Lge apps: 179 (77 gls)
Cup apps: 44 (20 gls)

■ Signed from West Bromwich Albion for the then record club fee of £180,000 (9.12.77), he made his League debut for Hammers a week later - against his old club! West Ham had tried, unsuccessfully, to sign David when he left Coventry City a year earlier, but he was well worth the wait. Nicknamed "Psycho" by the fans, this tall, lean, though very tough, striker was fearless and won many important aerial battles. He was the ideal target man alongside first Bryan Robosn and then Paul Goddard, playing a prominent part in the entertaining and successful side that romped to the Second Division championship in 1981. Bearded David's touch improved in his time under John Lyall and no one worked harder in the 1980 FA Cup Final triumph over Arsenal than the uncompromising number nine, who was asked to play up front as the lone striker on that sweltering afternoon. Formerly with Rochdale, Norwich City and Coventry City before going to The Hawthorns, he proved to

David Cross

be one of West Ham's best-ever buys, scoring regularly in the First and Second Divisions. Although his nine goals in 21 League games failed to keep Hammers in Division One in May 1978, he notched 18 goals in his first full season, 12 the next and 22 in the title-winning season, in which he also gained European experience and a League Cup Final runners-up medal. And when Hammers made it back into the First Division for 1981/82, David top-scored for the second consecutive season with 16 League goals - including the only one in his farewell game v Wolves at Molineux (15.5.82). He twice scored four in one game - at Grimsby (11.4.81) and, more memorably, at Spurs (on Ray Clemence's home debut! - 2.9.81). After leaving West Ham, Dave had spells with Manchester City and Oldham and was back with WBA in 1984/85 before joining Bolton Wanderers for the 1985/86 season. He ended his career on loan to Bury at the end of the 1985/86 campaign where he made 13 appearances.

CROSS, Roger 1968-69

Born: East Ham, London. 20.10.48
Lge apps: 7 (1 gl)
Cup apps: 1

■ AP 7/64. Top reserve team scorer for two consecutive seasons, this underrated striker was forced to drop into the lower echelons of the League with Brentford to find regular first team soccer. Joining the Upton Park staff in 1964 as an apprentice after schools football with East Ham and Essex, he was at one time taken on loan by Leyton Orient before making the move to Griffin Park for £12,000. He later went on a merry-go-round of the London clubs with Fulham (£30,000), Brentford again and Millwall (£8,000). Played in the USA with Seattle in 1977 and was appointed youth team manager at Millwall in 1979.

CROSSLEY, Charlie   1922-23

Born: Wolverhampton. 1892
Lge apps: 15 (1 gl)
Cup apps: 1

Chas Crossley

■ An experienced inside-right signed from Everton. Chas, as he was better known, made his first appearance for Hammers in a 2-1 defeat to Bradford City at Upton Park on the opening day of the eventful 1922/23 season. He was also in at the start of the dramatic FA Cup run that campaign, when he played in the 3-2 first round victory v Hull City at Boothferry Park. He later left Upton Park to join Swindon Town and from there joined Ebbw Vale as player/manager in Sept. 1925. During WW1 he guested for Clapton Orient, Huddersfield Town and Spurs whom he made one appearance for, at Portsmouth in Feb. 1917 while on leave from serving as a stoker on a U-boat Destroyer. When the conflict was over he returned to Sunderland whom he had joined from Walsall in Feb. 1914. Played for the North v England in an international trial game in Feb. 1920. He died in the Black Country (29.4.65).

CROWTHER, G.   1920

Born: Bishop Middleham

■ An inside-left who made his Second Division debut in a 1-0 victory over Wolves at Upton Park (6.9.20), he made another two League appearances, at home and away v London rivals Fulham, to complete a hat-trick of senior outings. Later played for Hartlepool.

CUMMINGS, James   1919-20

Lge apps: 20

■ An outside-right signed from Manchester City. Totalled 15 Second Division appearances during Hammers' first League season and a further five the following campaign without getting on the scoresheet.

CURBISHLEY Alan   1975-79

Born: Forest Gate, London. 8.11.54
Lge apps: 85 (5 gls)
Cup apps: 11

■ AP 7/74. Schoolboy prodigy who was reluctantly allowed to join Birmingham City for a huge fee in 1979 after a dispute over his role in the side. A stylish midfield play-maker who looked confident on the ball, Alan made his first team debut v Coventry City at Upton Park (19.4.75), two games from the end of the 1974/75 season, aged 21. Alan nevertheless found himself in the shadow of Trevor Brooking. And with another exciting, creative midfielder, Alan Devonshire, emerging in the late seventies, he was unfortunate to find himself squeezed out of the first team too often for his liking. Made his last appearance for Hammers as sub v Leicester City at Upton Park (26.3.79). In addition to starring at schoolboy level he also won six caps for England Youth and was a member of the Hammers' side which reached the FA Youth Cup Final in 1975. Joined Charlton Athletic after a spell with Aston Villa. Alan is now joint-manager of Charlton with Steve Gritt and one of their signings in 1993/94 was West Ham winger Mark Robson.

Alan Curbishley

CURTIS, F   1909-11

Lge apps: 6 (4 gls)

■ This centre-forward made his first appearance in the first team as deputy to Albert Scales in a 1-0 defeat at New Brompton (2.4. 09). He scored in both his other two outings that season - a 3-3 draw at Queens Park Rangers and a 1-2 reverse at home to Luton Town. His goals ratio was the same the following campaign thanks to a brace in the 3-0 Boleyn win v QPR (1.10.10), in his penultimate Hammers' appearance.

CUSHLEY, John   1967-70

Born: Blantyre, Scotland. 21.1.43
Lge apps: 38
Cup apps: 8

■ Given the unenviable task of filling the number five shirt vacated by Ken Brown from the Upton Park scene, the Glaswegian made his debut in the opening game of 1967/68, v Sheffield Wednesday (19.8.67) in a 2-0 home defeat. But after a run of 27 games alongside Bobby Moore, manager Ron Greenwood replaced him with Alan Stephenson from Crystal Palace. John made only a further 11 first team appearances, as cover for injuries, in the following two seasons before bowing out in a goalless draw v Ipswich Town at Upton Park (14.3.70). Signed from Glasgow Celtic for £25,000, the likeable Scot (nicknamed "Wilbur") made many friends during his three-year stay at the club before returning north of the border to Dunfermline Athletic for a smaller fee. Afterwards transferred to Dumbarton.

John Cushley

Billy Dare

DAWKINS, Trevor — 1964-66

Born: Rochford, Essex. 7.10.45
Lge apps: 6

■ AP 10/62. Great things were expected of this highly-talented and creative wing-half by his manager and mentor, Ron Greenwood, but the player failed to win a regular place in the first team. Transferred to Crystal Palace, where he met up with fellow ex-Hammers Dave Bickles and Eddie Presland, he ended his League life at Brentford.

DAWSON, C — 1908-10

Born: Barking, Essex. 1888.
Lge apps: 6

■ This goalkeeper made only half-a-dozen appearances for early century Irons, two of them against arch rivals Millwall. The first was one of four outings in 1908/09 in a 3-0 defeat at Cold Blow Lane, the inhospitable home of The Lions. The second came the following season, also at The Den, but with happier consequences as he kept a clean sheet in a 0-0 stalemate. His SL chances were impeded by the consistency of Irons' regular 'keeper, George Kitchen.

DAWSON, Harold — 1911-13

Born: Bolton, Lancashire.
SL apps: 22 (3 gls)

■ Outside-left who made his debut v Luton Town at Kenilworth Road (16.3.12) in a 1-2 defeat. He scored on his Boleyn bow the following week in the 6-2 thrashing of Bristol Rovers, his only goal in 10 outings that campaign. He scored again v Exeter City on the opening day of the 1912/13 season as Hammers romped home 4-0. His final goal for Hammers made it a hat-trick against West Country opposition when Plymouth Argyle were defeated 3-1 at Upton Park. Came from Croydon Common during 1911/12 but returned there in cs 1913.

DARE, Billy — 1955-59

Born: Willesden. 14.2.27
Lge apps: 111 (44 gls)
Cup apps: 8 (5 gls)

■ This popular forward made a major contribution to Hammers' Second Division triumph of 1958. Signed from Brentford for £5,000 to give extra strike power, he made a perfect foil for his more robust scoring partners, Johnny Dick and Vic Keeble. Unfortunately he was in the veteran stage when the club re-entered the First Division, and made only two appearances in the higher sphere. Joined Southern League Yiewsley where he came under the managership of Bill Dodgin (Snr.) and later the great Jackie Milburn. Bill passed away in Apr. 1994.

DAVIDSON, William — 1902-03

Born: Beith, Scotland. 1879.
SL apps: 9 (2 gls)

■ Previously with Third Lanark, Glossop, Manchester City and Reading, from where he joined Irons in 1902, he was "a fearless player but rather erratic." Wearing number nine, Bill was given that amount of first team appearances to make a name for himself at The Memorial Grounds. Making his debut in the 1-2 home defeat by Southampton on Christmas Day, 1902, he had to wait until his fourth game to open his account, when he scored in the 3-0 victory over Wellingborough Town (10.1.03). He scored again in a 3-2 win against Northampton Town but it proved to be his last for the club. Moved to Luton Town, then on to Fulham for 1903/04.

DAY, Mervyn — 1973-79

Born: Chelmsford, Essex. 26.6.55
Lge apps: 194
Cup apps: 39

■ AP 7/71. Such was the impact this brilliant young goalkeeper made on breaking into West Ham's first team that he prompted the normally reticent Ron Greenwood to declare: "This is the West Ham goalkeeper for the next 10 years." Alas, Mervyn never quite lived up to that heady expectation and his sad departure from Upton Park was not helped by media exposure, which seemed to blow up any little mistake out of all proportion. Made his first team debut as Bobby Ferguson's 18 year-old replacement v Ipswich Town on a rainy East London night (27.8.73). But during a period in the club's history when survival in the First Division was no mean achievement in itself, Mervyn was pleased to win an FA Cup medal in the 2-0 victory over

Fulham at Wembley in 1975. More seasons of struggle followed as Day shared the number one shirt with the recalled Ferguson in 1977/78 and 1978/79, before their respective Hammers' careers were ended by the arrival, in Feb. 1979, of QPR's Phil Parkes for a world record fee for a 'keeper. Just like his first senior game for West Ham, Mervyn's final appearance at Upton Park also resulted in a 3-3 draw v Sunderland (10.2.79). He rebuilt his shattered confidence at nearby Leyton Orient, who paid £100,000 for him in the summer of 1979. He performed with distinction for the O's and was chosen as the England 'B' sub goalkeeper v New Zealand at Leyton in Oct. 1979, in addition to being made club captain in 1982. He went to Leeds United after a spell in the First Division with Aston Villa and his fine displays were a major

influence on the club reaching the 1987 FA Cup semi-final and their return to the top flight. Honours: England Youth International, England Under-23 caps (4); FA Cup winner 1975; E.C.W.C. runner-up 1976. Also recipient of PFA Young Player of the Year award in 1975. Mervyn is now player/coach at Carlisle United after appearing in over 700 League and Cup matches.

DEACON, Bob 1932-33

Lge apps: 3

■ Signed from Wolverhampton Wanderers where he had made a fine left-wing partnership with Barraclough. Bob played his first game for

Hammers v Bradford City in the inside-left position (29.8.32) at Upton Park, and was later tried at inside-right and centre-forward to complete a trio of first team appearances in the claret and blue. He later played for Chelsea.

DEAR, Brian 1962-70

Born: West Ham, London. 18.9.43
Lge apps: 69 (33 gls)
Cup apps: 16 (6 gls)

■ Joined the club as a 15 year-old, this rumbustious striker is one of the few ex-Hammers who have enjoyed two spells with the club. A member of the victorious European Cup Winners' side of 1965. Brian holds the national record for the quickest-ever five goals in one match, achieving the feat in an incredible 20 minute spell - either side of half-time - v West Bromwich Albion at Upton Park (16.4.65). He also distinguished himself by scoring five times in seven matches while on loan to Brighton & Hove Albion, but decided against a permanent move to the south coast club. Transferred to Fulham for £20,000 in 1969, "Stag" rejoined his former colleagues after a short spell at Millwall in Oct. 1970, but only added a further four appearances to his previous total before being given a free transfer at the end of that campaign. His last game in claret and blue was in the number nine shirt at Chelsea (19.12.70), shortly before the much-publicised Blackpool nightclub affair - also involving players Moore, Greaves and Best and physio Rob Jenkins - that so concerned manager Ron Greenwood at the time. Brian later played for Woodford Town and was recently working as a social club steward at Southend after a succession of jobs as a publican in Essex.

Mervyn Day

Brian Dear

DEATH, Stephen — 1969

Born: Elmswell, Suffolk. 10.9.49
Lge apps: 1

■ AP 7/65. Another talented goal-keeper, Stephen was limited to just one senior game - as cover for Bobby Ferguson in the last match of the 1968/69 season v Manchester City at Maine Road (30.4.69) which was drawn 1-1. It cost Reading their then record fee of £20,000 to secure his transfer to Elm Park. One of the smallest 'keepers in the League, he went on to make over 450 appearances for the Berkshire club, where he had a testimonial match in 1979.

DELL, Fred — 1936-38

Born: Dartford, Kent
Lge apps: 4

■ A towering six-footer signed by Hammers from non-League Dartford in 1935, Fred made his initial Second Division appearance in a 0-2 defeat v Sheffield United at Bramall Lane in Sept. 1936. Making one more first team outing that season and a further two in 1937/38, he was transferred to Doncaster Rovers - where he met up with former Hammers, Albert Walker and Jackie Kirkaldie.

Fred Dell

DENYER, Albert — 1912-14

SL apps: 46 (16 gls)
Cup apps: 4 (1 gl)

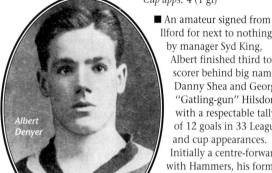

Albert Denyer

■ An amateur signed from Ilford for next to nothing by manager Syd King, Albert finished third top scorer behind big names Danny Shea and George "Gatling-gun" Hilsdon with a respectable tally of 12 goals in 33 League and cup appearances. Initially a centre-forward with Hammers, his form plummeted the following season when he played in several forward positions in an effort to rectify the situation. His strike rate was down to five from 17 SL showings. East End born and bred, Albert was the better-known of the two Denyer brothers and represented West Ham Boys in the final of the English Schools Shield in May 1907 at Sunderland. The Wearsiders won 2-0 before 25,000 fans. A pupil of Balham St. School, he and Frank were the first brothers to appear in the same team for Irons. He moved to Swindon Town in 1914 and had a long career with the Wiltshire club which extended into the 1920's. Albert holds the distinction of being the first London Schoolboy capped for England.

DENYER, Frank — 1913-14

Lge apps: 2

■ Defender Frank joined his more illustrious brother for Irons' away clashes at Cardiff and Southend at the tail-end of the 1913/14 season. He played at right-back in the 2-0 defeat at Ninian Park on Good Friday and turned out in the right-half position at Roots Hall on Easter Saturday. And so ended his West Ham career. Like his more famous brother, Frank also began his career with Ilford.

DEVLIN, Ernie — 1946-52

Born: Gateshead. 6.3.20
Lge apps: 70
Cup apps: 2

■ Affectionately nicknamed "Joe" by the Upton Park faithful, this whole-hearted full-back was immensely popular with the fans - mainly because of his never-say-die attitude. Making his League debut with the long-defunct Gateshead in his native North-East, he was transferred to Hammers in 1946, and had to wait a further two years before gaining a regular place in the senior side. A bad knee injury hampered his career and he ended his time at the Boleyn captaining the combination team before moving to Darlington in 1953/54. Passed away in 1976, aged 56.

DEVONSHIRE, Alan — 1976-90

Born: Park Royal, London. 13.4.1956
Lge apps: 358 (29 gls)
Cup apps: 88 (3 gls)

■ Became, arguably, West Ham's best-ever buy. Eddie Baily and Charlie Faulkner spotted 'Dev' playing for non-league Southall in the Isthmian League, and manager Ron Greenwood got him in Sept. 1976 for just £5,000. That was after Crystal Palace (where his father, Les, used to play on the left-wing) told Alan he was 'too small' at the age of 14. He returned to Selhurst Park two years later but after a handful of youth games, he was among a number of youngsters released by the manager, former West Ham star Malcolm Allison. Reading, Wimbledon, Southampton and another of his father's old clubs, Brentford, also showed interest, but could not tempt him away from Southall. But their loss was definitely Hammers' gain, as Dev - who starred for Ealing and Middlesex Schools as a kid - emerged from non-league obscurity (and his full-time job as a fork-lift truck driver at the Hoover factory!) to become one of the biggest favourites and most skilful players in the club's history. A down-to-earth character the fans have always found easy to relate to, Dev was a first team star at Upton Park while still travelling to home matches by tube train from his West London home! It was a rather frail-looking Dev, sporting his familiar dark moustache, who made his West Ham debut in a 2-0 League Cup defeat by QPR at Upton Park (27.10.76). His League debut came three days later (30.10.76) in a 3-0 defeat at West Bromwich Albion. Dev made 28 appearances in his first season, showing plenty of promise on the left side of midfield. Although Hammers just managed to avoid relegation from Division One in May 1977, they could not repeat their escape act a year later. But in the next three seasons, Alan enjoyed almost a telepathic understanding with fellow midfielder, Trevor Brooking, that formed the cornerstone of West Ham's successful return to the top flight as record-breaking Division Two champions in 1981. A year earlier Alan had played an outstanding part in Hammers' FA Cup success. In the semi-final replay at Elland Road, he scored a brilliant individual goal against Everton. And it was Alan's cross, following a typical shimmy and surging run to the by-line, that led to Brooking's headed winner against Arsenal in the final. Frank Lampard, at left-back, completed an irresistible left-sided trio that tore opposing defences to shreds, created so many goals and scoring chances and enthralled fans everywhere.
A few days after the 1-0 victory over Arsenal, Dev was back at Wembley to gain the first of his eight full England caps - in a 1-1- draw with Northern Ireland (20.5.80). Dev was 24 and in his prime. Season 1980/81 brought him European experience and another Wembley visit - for the League Cup Final v Liverpool. The first match was drawn 1-1

before the Reds came from behind to win the Villa Park replay 2-1. By then, though, Hammers were going flat out for the Second Division title and achieved it by losing only four matches. Dev was unlucky not to be included in Ron Greenwood's squad for the 1982 World Cup finals but the disappointement he felt then was nothing compared to the pain and heartbreak he suffered in a third round FA Cup tie at home to Wigan Athletic (7.1.84) . Dev snapped three ligaments in his right knee and - apart from making an abortive comeback bid in two FA Cup clashes with Wimbledon in Mar. 1985 - it was 19 months before he was fit enough to resume for the first team. The long rehabilitation was a test of mental, as well as physical, strength and Alan passed it with flying colours. Although he lost a yard or two of pace, his footballing brain was as sharp as ever. It was great credit to him that he not only beat the odds, proved utterly wrong the few who had written him off and came back to the First Division, but he did so playing some of the most stylish and effective football of his career. As creator and provider, Dev set up a large proportion of the goals scored by Cottee and McAvennie in Hammers' best-ever 1985/86 campaign, during which he made his 300th

League appearance v Spurs (31.3.86). Dev's first serious injury would have finished lesser men, yet he fought back from another serious blow. The first game of the 1987/88 term was just 15 minutes old when Alan snapped his Achilles tendon and faced another year on the sidelines. It was no happy return either, because Hammers were relegated at the end of 1988/89, with Dev playing in only 20 First Divison matches. His appearances were more infrequent under Lou Macari who picked him to start only two matches and used him as sub on 12 other occasions. Alan certainly won't recall his last game for the club with any relish - the 6-0 Littlewoods (League) Cup semi-final slaughter at Oldham Athletic (14.2.90) that also preceded Macari's departure the following weekend. Alan was given a free transfer by Billy Bonds in May 1990 but his Football League career was still not quite finished. He moved on to Second Division Watford, where former West Ham director Jack Petchey had taken over the chairmanship from Elton John. But after playing 24 League games in 1990/91, the classy midfielder was restricted to just one more sub appearance the following season before fading from the Vicarage Road scene. Now Dev is looking for a player/manager's role. If his team display even

half the flair he showed as a player with West Ham, they will be well worth a look! A loyal club servant, only 13 players in Hammers' history have made more League appearances than Alan Devonshire. Not bad for a skinny lad who cost a mere £5,000!

☆ **England caps:** *1980 v Northern Ireland, Australia (sub); 1982 v Holland, Iceland, West Germany; 1983 v Wales, Greece, Luxembourg (8).*

Played	League App	Gls	FAC App	Gls	LC App	Gls	Europe App	Gls	Total App	Gls
1976-77	28	0	0	0	1	0	0	0	29	0
1977/78	34	3	3	0	1	0	0	0	38	3
1978-79	41	5	1	0	1	0	0	0	43	5
1979-80	34	5	8	1	7	0	0	0	19	6
1980-81	39	6	3	0	9	0	4	0	55	6
1981-81	35	1	1	0	5	0	0	0	41	1
1982-83	39	3	1	0	6	0	0	0	46	3
1983-84	22	1	1	0	4	2	0	0	27	3
1984-85	0	0	2	0	0	0	0	0	2	0
1985-86	38	3	6	0	3	0	0	0	47	3
1986-87	20	2	3	0	4	0	0	0	27	2
1987-88	1	0	0	0	0	0	0	0	1	0
1988-89	20	0	7	0	4	0	0	0	31	0
1989-90	7	0	0	0	3	0	0	0	10	0
TOTAL	358	29	36	1	48	2	4	0	446	32

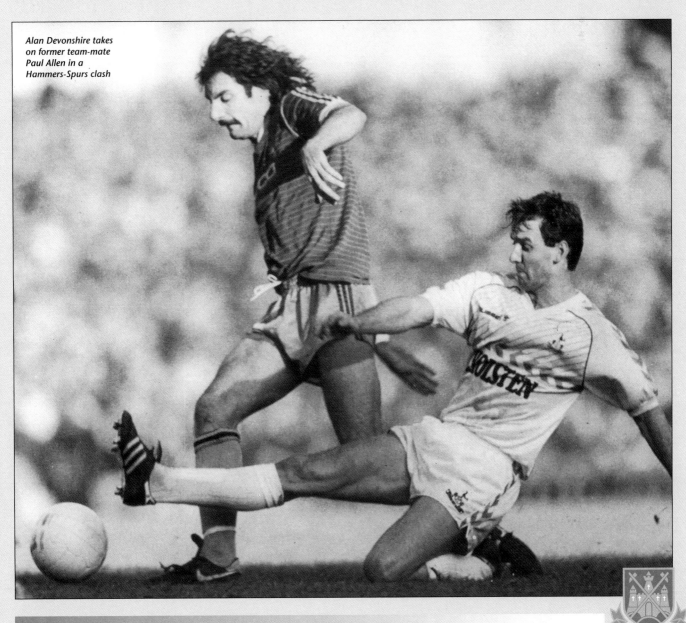

Alan Devonshire takes on former team-mate Paul Allen in a Hammers-Spurs clash

George Dick

DICK, George   1948-49

Born: Torphichen, Scotland. 12.6.21
Lge apps: 14 (1 gl)
Cup apps: 1

■ No relation to his namesake in the next item, George was signed by Charlie Paynter from the then star-studded Blackpool in an attempt to solve a goal-scoring problem. A member of the Tangerines' Cup Final side of 1948, he made his first appearance for Hammers v Luton Town at Upton Park in October the same year; went on to make 13 more that season, but the hoped for goals didn't materialise. He later regained his scoring touch on his travels with Carlisle, Stockport and Workington, and also coached on the continent. George died in tragic circumstances when he was involved in a motor accident at Carlisle in Sept. 1960.

DICK, Johnny   1953-62

Born: Govan, Scotland, 19.3.30
Lge apps: 326 (153 gls)
Cup apps: 25 (13 gls)

■ Previous clubs were Maryhill (Scotland) and Crittall Athletic (Essex). This tall, rangy Scot was West Ham's major source of goals for nearly a decade. Indeed, he still holds fourth place in the club's all-time highest scorers' list behind Vic Watson (306), Geoff Hurst (180) and Jimmy Ruffell (164). Four of his 153 total came in the record-breaking 8-0 home win over Rotherham during the promotion year of 1958. John was transferred to Brentford for £17,500 in Sept. 1962, and later returned to the club in the early seventies to help run the junior side after ending his playing career at Southern League Gravesend. John pursued full-time employment outside of football with the Inner London Education Authority in company with ex-Hammers

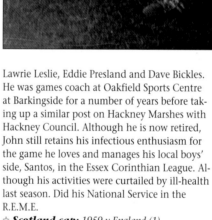

Johnny Dick

Lawrie Leslie, Eddie Presland and Dave Bickles. He was games coach at Oakfield Sports Centre at Barkingside for a number of years before taking up a similar post on Hackney Marshes with Hackney Council. Although he is now retired, John still retains his infectious enthusiasm for the game he loves and manages his local boys' side, Santos, in the Essex Corinthian League. Although his activities were curtailed by ill-health last season. Did his National Service in the R.E.M.E.
☆ *Scotland cap:* 1959 v England (1).

Played	League		FAC		LC		Europe		Total	
	App	Gls	App	Gls	App	Gls	App	Gls	App	Gls
1953-54	39	13	3	0	0	0	0	0	42	13
1954-55	39	26	2	0	0	0	0	0	41	26
1955-56	35	8	6	6	0	0	0	0	41	14
1956-57	36	8	2	1	0	0	0	0	38	9
1957-58	41	21	3	2	0	0	0	0	44	23
1958-59	41	27	1	0	0	0	0	0	42	27
1959-60	24	11	1	1	0	0	0	0	25	12
1960-61	34	16	2	1	2	2	0	0	38	19
1961-62	35	23	1	0	2	0	0	0	38	23
1962-63	2	0	0	0	0	0	0	0	2	0
TOTAL	326	153	21	11	4	2	0	0	351	166

DICKENS, Alan   1983-89

Born: Plaistow, East London. 3.9.64
Lge apps: 192 (23 gls)
Cup apps: 39 (6 gls)

■ The term 'local lad' can genuinely be applied to Alan Dickens, who was born a corner kick away from Upton Park and has continued to live at nearby Barking even since leaving the club, in June 1989, to try his luck across West London with Chelsea and then Brentford. Initially made his mark for Newham, Essex and London Schoolboys, "Dicko" signed apprentice for West Ham 14.7.81 after playing for Hammers' FA Youth Cup-winning side that beat Spurs (1981). Signed pro 2.8.82 and, at 18, made a memorable scoring League debut only four months later in a 2-1 win at Notts County (18.12.82). Having won four England Youth caps, Alan made the first of his two Under-21 international appearances as sub v Finland (16.10.84). A number of promising performances in central midfield earned Dicko rave reviews and when Trevor Brooking retired in May 1984, many regarded him as the player

equipped to fill his number 10 shirt. It was an enormous burden for any youngster to bear and the Upton Park crowd were, unfortunately, never slow to voice their dissatisfaction with young Alan in the games when he didn't measure up to those high expectations. Yet Dicko was a player in the club's best traditions: stylish, a good passer who could unlock the tightest defences with a perfectly-weighted through-ball. Or if there were no options available, he could score spectacular goals himself from long-range. For a player so tall (6ft 1ins), Alan possessed unusually good ball skills and neat control as well as awareness. And as he gained more experience, he learned to add more aggression to his game. A shy, unassuming man, Alan's confidence was affected as much as anyone's by relegation in May 1989 and within days of John Lyall's departure, and with West Ham still in turmoil, he made a £600,000 move

to Chelsea. It seemed, at the time, like the ideal transfer to enable Alan to finally fulfil his undoubted potential in the top flight. But after playing 22 League games in his first season at Stamford Bridge under Bobby Campbell, the classy midfielder made only a handful more appearances before being given a free by Ian Porterfield. A brief spell on loan to West Bromwich Albion, around Christmas 1992, was followed by a slightly longer stint at Brentford as the 1992/93 season closed. But when David Webb - the next Chelsea manager, who was technically loaning Alan to the Bees - arrived at Griffin Park as the new boss in May 1993, it was Dicko's cue to move on again. This time he joined Colchester United's bid to re-establish themselves in the Third Division of the Football League. He has since joined non league Chesham United while learning the 'knowledge' as a cabbie.

DICKIE, Alan

1962-66

Born: Charlton, London. 30.1.44
Lge apps: 12
Cup apps: 3

■ AP 7/60. Reliable, competent 'keeper. Travelled as 12th man during the victorious European Cup Winners' Cup campaign of 1964-65, after making one appearance in the preliminary round v La Gantoise of Belgium. Transferred to Coventry City after impressing the Midland club in a friendly against them. Later played for Aldershot and is now in the police force, for whom he works in coroner's office at Queen Mary's Hospital, Sidcup, Kent.

Alan Dickens (right) and another former Hammer, Ray Houghton, in action at Anfield.

DICKS, Julian   1988-93

Born: Bristol, Avon. 8.8.68.
Lge apps: 159 (29 gls)
Cup apps: 33 (7 gls)

■ One of the most popular players ever to wear the claret and blue, Julian Dicks was a cult hero to many modern-day Hammers' fans. And it is a measure of his enormous popularity that on his first appearance back at Upton Park, following his transfer to Liverpool (16.9.93), he received a tremendous ovation. West Ham fans had been dreading the departure of the tough-tackling, no-nonsense left-back for some time. He was the club's biggest asset and with Hammers struggling near the bottom of the Premiership after seven matches of the 1993/94 campaign, there was an inevitability about his move to Anfield - in the £2.5 million valued swap deal that brought David Burrows and Mike Marsh in the opposite direction. It was a deal that suited both clubs, as well as Julian, at the time, although the man they call "The Terminator" has not found it easy to win over the Anfield fans. He spent a number of weeks sidelined by a knee injury that led to a cartilage operation. And when he got back in the side, manager Graeme Souness was about to resign. Unlike some fans on Merseyside, the West Ham crowd have been in no doubt about Julian's qualities since he was signed by John Lyall from Birmingham City for £300,000 (24.3.88) and made his debut at Sheffield Wednesday (2.4.88). Ferocious in the tackle, with a thunderbolt shot to match, deadly Dicks terrorised the opposition with his surging runs deep into opposition territory. Sometimes, he tackled too recklessly, as in the 1992/93 First Division promotion-winning season when he was sent off three times (the most by any player at West Ham in one season) and missed 13 games due to suspension. So disillusioned by his disciplinary problems and the 'Bad Boy' reputation he was getting among referees, Julian said once during a moment of deep despair that he thought seriously about quitting the game. But his ample collection of yellow and red cards should not overshadow the natural talent he possesses. For all his 'hard man' image, as a rebellious character who wears his hair short and rides a Harley Davidson for fun, there is another, more subtle, side to the man who dotes on his young twin daughters. Julian has a sweet left foot and is comfortable on the ball. His biggest strengths are turning defence into attack, winning aerial battles, striking dead balls and spraying accurate passes with a subtlety not usually associated with many modern-day defenders. It's easy to see that he began his career playing left-midfield for Birmingham under Gary Pendrey and Ron Saunders, before settling at full-back. His direct pinpoint passing from one side of the field to the other, with almost effortless ease, changed the dimension of many attacks. And although a large proportion of his 36 goals were from the penalty spot, Julian contributed more than his fair share of others (often spectacularly) from varying range. Julian's fighting qualities were demonstrated most vividly when he snapped the cruciate ligament in his left knee in Oct. 1990. He missed most of that promotion-winning season and it was 14 months before he resumed in the first team, in Dec. 1992, in the midst of the First Division relegation struggle. Julian regained the captaincy from Ian Bishop and there was another big boost around the corner when he was called up by England manager Graham Taylor for the 'B' internationals against Czechoslovakia and the CIS in Eastern Europe. After returning from his long lay-off - Julian scored in his comeback game v Sheffield United (21.12.91) - no one did more than Dicksy to try and save Hammers from the drop in May 1992. His valiant efforts were rewarded with a new four-year contract in Feb. 1992 and the fans' vote as Hammer of the Year (even though he played only half that season!) three months later. In their heart of hearts, though, few at Upton Park expected Julian to see out his new contract. Despite his indiscretions on the field during the early part of 1992/93, Julian still contributed 11 vital goals in 34 League appearances as Hammers bounced straight back into the top flight. But once he learned of Liverpool's interest, and with Hammers languishing near the base of the Premiership, a parting of the ways was inevitable. Still, Julian Dicks certainly left his mark on West Ham United and will always be fondly remembered by his legion of fans.
Rejoined club in October '94.

DIXON, Robert   1928-33

Born: West Stanley, Durham
Lge apps: 65
Cup apps: 3

■ Mainly an understudy to Ted Hufton during his first two seasons at Upton Park, this former Stoke City goalkeeper had a good run in the First Division side during 1930/31 and 1931/32, proving himself a capable net-minder. However, the arrival of George Watson and the emergence of Pat McMahon as his deputy on West Ham's return to Division Two the following season limited Bob to just three more senior outings.

DIXON, Tommy   1952-54

Born: Newcastle-upon-Tyne. 8.6.29
Lge apps: 39 (21 gls)
Cup apps: 3 (2 gls)

■ Top scorer for Hammers with 19 League and Cup goals in season 1953-54, the likeable Geordie played only four times the following campaign. Was transferred to Third Division (South) Reading in Mar. 1955, where he topped the Biscuitmen's scoring charts for two consecutive seasons. His success at Elm Park drew the attention of Brighton & Hove Albion, and he subsequently joined up with former team mate Dave Sexton at the Goldstone Ground, before seeing out his playing career with Workington and finally Barrow.

Eamonn Dolan

DOVE, Charles   1895-01

Born: 1877.
SL apps (TIW): 29 (3 gls)
Lge apps (WHU): 13
Cup apps: 3

■ Attended Park School, East Ham, and later captained Plaistow Melville before having short spells with Upton Park and South West Ham. Joined the Thames Ironworks as a 16-year old in 1894. The longest-serving of all the Thames Ironworks players, popular Charlie also filled every position for Irons, including goal! Representing the home growth of local talent, he spent his early days with the Forest Swift Club before becoming a pro. His one game between the posts came when he deputised for Tommy Moore and kept a clean-sheet in a 4-0 victory at Maidenhead (31.12.1898); a win which kept Irons on course for the Southern League Second Divison championship that season. Believed to have been an apprentice at the Thames Ironworks factory, Charles transferred to those great rivals of the Edwardian era, Millwall, in Sept. 1901, but a knee injury in 1902/03 ended his first class career.

DOLAN, Eamonn   1987-91

Born: Romford, Essex. 20.9.67.
Lge apps: 15 (3 gls)
Cup apps: 4

■ Nicknamed "The Professor" for gaining 12 'O' levels and one 'A' at school in Chelmsford, Essex, the likeable Eamonn will perhaps consider that he deserved more than nine starts and six sub outings to prove his first team worth at Upton Park. Born in Romford of Irish parents, Eamonn was a product of Hammers' youth team, Scored a hat-trick for Republic of Ireland Under-17's against Northern Ireland in Jan. 1985 - three months before turning pro at Upton Park. He was also capped at Under-21 level while still 19. Eamonn made his senior Hammers debut as sub v Manchester City (9.5.87) on the final day of the 1986/87 season and, after a Simod Cup start v Millwall (10.11.87), started his first League match v Charlton Athletic at Selhurst Park (12.3.88). Scored his first senior goal after coming on as sub v West Bromwich Albion (30.9.89) but his most memorable match was against Sunderland (18.10.89) when he netted twice in a 5-0 victory. The tall striker's best run in the side was a nine-game stint under Lou Macari in 1989/90. In Feb. 1989 he went on loan to Bristol City (three matches) but West Ham manager John Lyall denied Eamonn the chance of playing for City in the League Cup semi-final against Nottingham Forest because Hammers were in the other semi, against Luton Town, and he would have been cup-tied if required for the final. Eamonn was set to sign for Birmingham City in the summer of 1990 but the initial deal fell through when he dislocated his shoulder in pre-season training. The move did eventually go ahead but

Eamonn made just 12 League appearances - most of them under Macari, who returned to football as Blues' boss following his shock resignation at West Ham - before moving on to Exeter City shortly after the start of 1991/92. After spending all of his career trying to establish a first team place, Eamonn faced his biggest battle in 1993 when he underwent treatment for a cancer growth. Eamonn's twin brother, Patrick, played centre-half for Walsall.

DONALD, Warren   1983-84

Born: Hillingdon, Middlesex. 7.10.64
Lge apps: 2

■ A battling midfield play-maker who made his initial senior appearance in the 1982-83 friendly clash with Scottish champions Dundee United. Had to wait until Boxing Day 1983 for his League baptism v Southampton at Upton Park, coming on as sub for the injured Frank Lampard in a 1-0 defeat. His only other senior game was the final match of that season (14.5.84. - Trevor Brooking's farewell) v Everton. Despite his limited first team opportunities at Upton Park, this former Berkshire and England schoolboy star looked set for a bright future in the game. "Wozzer" joined Fourth Division Northampton Town for a fee of £11,000 in Oct. 1985 and linked up with another ex-Hammer, Mark Schiavi, at the County Ground.

DOW, James   1902-03

Born: Dundee, Scotland. 1873.
SL apps: 13
Cup apps: 1

■ A well-built defender who could perform equally well at either right or left-back. Signed from Middlesbrough in time for the start of the 1902/03 season, he made his debut in the opening match v Reading at the Memorial Grounds, but by the end of the season he couldn't get past unlucky 13 in Southern League appearances when he was released. Before Middlesbrough, Dow had seen service with Newton Heath and Glossop North End. At the start of 1904/05 he was captain at Luton Town.

John Dowen

DOWEN, John Stewart   1936

Born: Wolverhampton. 1914

■ Prominent in junior football with Walsall Schools and Courtaulds, he went on to win schooboy caps v Scotland and Wales in 1929, and also represented the Birmingham FA v Scotland in 1934. This left-back was signed from Wolves and made one Second Division appearance for West Ham (2.5.36) in a 4-2 defeat v Sheffield United at Bramall Lane before returning to Molineux. Unable to win a regular spot in the Wolves side, his fortunes changed on his move to Hull City where he struck up a fine partnership with the redoubtable Cliff Woodhead at Anlaby Road and chalked up 39 appearances in 1938/39.

DOWIE, Iain   1991

Born: Hatfield, Herts. 9.1.65.
Lge apps: 12 (4 gls)

■ Fulfilled a life-time's ambition when Billy Bonds signed him from Luton Town in Mar. 1991 for £480,000 as cover for the injured Trevor Morley. But Iain's dream move - he supported Hammers as a kid and stood on the North Bank - turned sour five months later when he was sold to Southampton in a shock £500,000 move, having played only 12 matches in the 1990/91 Second Division promotion campaign. Tall, blond striker in the old-fashioned centre-forward mould, he had little time to win over the fans and show that he could settle into Hammers' style of play. Even so, Iain still contributed four important goals (including one on each of his first three outings at Upton Park) and showed his particular threat in the air. Made his West Ham debut at Hull City (23.3.91), having made his Football League bow for Luton v Spurs (28.3.89). Ironically, Southampton initially signed Iain as an associate schoolboy . . . but let him go

because he was 'too small'. Determined to prove Saints wrong, he made his mark in non-league circles for Cheshunt, St. Albans, Bishop's Stortford and Hendon. This also gave him the time to gain a Masters degree in mechanical engineering and he became a development engineer for British Aerospace. Signed by Luton for £30,000 in late 1988 and impressed by scoring 15 First Division goals in 53 starts. Now the six-foot striker is back at The Dell as a first team regular and an established Northern Ireland international. N.I. Caps 1991 v Yugoslavia, Faroes (2).

DOWSEY, John   1926

Lge apps: 1

■ Winger cum-inside-forward who started his career with Hunswick Villa and was secured from Newcastle United after scoring 54 goals for the Magpies' second string during two seasons in the North Eastern League. Found success hard to come by at Upton Park, making only one First Division appearance v Sheffield Wednesday at Hillsborough in Sept. 1926. John joined Carlisle when he left West Ham in Aug. 1927. He moved on to Sunderland in 1928, Notts County in 1929 and was with Northampton between 1931 and 1934.

DUNMORE, Dave   1960-61

Born: Whitehaven, Cumberland. 8.2.34
Lge apps: 36 (16 gls)
Cup apps: 3 (2 gls)

■ Experienced centre-forward who arrived at Upton Park in an exchange deal which took Johnny Smith to Spurs. He acquitted himself

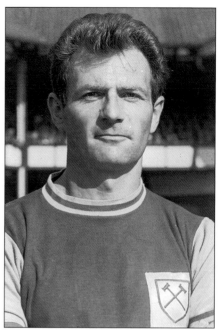

Dave Dunmore

well during his two years in the claret and blue, scoring some useful goals and beefing-up the forward line at a time when Hammers were struggling to consolidate their First Division status. Found himself involved in another exchange, this time with near-neighbours Leyton Orient, in a transfer which resulted in Alan Sealey joining the club. Dave top-scored for O's in their 1961/62 Second Division promotion season with 22 goals from 39 appearances and scored 58 times in 168 League and Cup matches during five seasons at Brisbane Road. Dave later returned to the team where he started his career - York City - and in

Iain Dowie

another two seasons there he scored 13 goals in a further 63 outings but could not prevent the Yorkshiremen from finishing bottom of Division Three in 1965/66 and third from botton in the Fourth the following year. After scoring 132 goals in a total of 369 League games Dave went into non-league soccer in 1967 with Wellington. He is now a sheet metal worker in his native York.

DUNN, Richard　　　　　1946-47

Born: Easington, Co. Durham. 23.12.19
Lge apps: 11 (2 gls)

■ An inside-forward who joined the club in 1937 from Ferryhill Athletic, he was one of many players who had their careers decimated by WW2, in which he served for over six years in the Essex Regt, and R.A. He made one guest appearance for Spurs during the conflict at Reading (9.9.44), when Spurs arrived for the match with only four men! Fortunately Dunn was at the game as a spectator and was able to turn out at the last minute at inside-left. He also played for Hartlepool United, Preston North End and York City in the war. Managed 10 Second Division appearances with the resumption of normal League activities in 1946-47, before transferring to Hartlepool. Later served as an officer in Durham Gaol. Passed away in Dec. 1985 at the age of 65.

DUNN, Thomas　　　　　1899-00 TIW

Born: Falkirk, Scotland. 1872.
SL apps: 35
Cup apps: 7

■ Thames Ironworks signed Tom from Chatham and he made his first appearance in a 4-1 win at Wycombe (14.1.1899). A member of the Wolves team which were defeated 2-1 in the 1896 FA Cup Final by The Wednesday at Crystal Palace, he was equally at home in either of the full-back berths and appeared in the final 13 matches of 1898/99. On duty for the opening match of the following season in a 0-1 defeat at Reading, he missed only six SL games that season and was also an ever-present in Irons' extended FA Cup run which ended in a 1-2 defeat by Millwall at the Memorial Grounds after disposing of Royal Engineers (6-0), Grays (4-0), Sheppey (4-2), Dartford (7-0), and New Brompton (2-0). Tom had left the club before the momentus decision to become West Ham United FC and fully embrace professionalism.

DURRELL, Joe　　　　　1971-72

Born: Stepney, London. 15.3.53
Lge apps: 6

■ AP 7/68. Diminutive, nippy winger who always showed up well on his rare first team appearances. Replacing Johnny Ayris, he made his debut in the 2-1 home win over Stoke City (25.9.71) and his remaining four full and one sub appearances all came in that 1971/72 season. His last outing came in the final match

Joe Durrell

v Southampton (1.5.72). Competition for places led to his transfer to Bristol City. He later played for Cardiff City and Gillingham before going out of the League.

DWYER, Noel　　　　　1959-60

Born: Dublin, Republic of Ireland. 30.10.34
Lge apps: 36
Cup apps: 2

■ Courageous Irish international goalkeeper, signed from Wolves in Dec. 1958. Could be brilliant one match and infuriating the next. It was this inconsistency which prompted his transfer to Swansea Town. Returned to Upton Park with the Swans for an FA Cup fourth round tie in Mar. 1963 and put up a fine display to limit

Hammers to a 1-0 passage in to the next round. He was not always as competent, however, and much of the blame for a 5-3 home defeat by Newcastle United (20.2.60) was attributed to him. Indeed, there were newspaper reports suggesting that the result of the match had been 'rigged', following the unusual amount of money being taken by bookmakers on the outcome of the game. One West Ham director was said to have walked out of the match in disgust at the result. But the rumours were never proven to be true and the scandal blew over. Noel Dwyer never played for Hammers again, however, joining Swans for a fee of £3,000. Capped 24 times by his country, he later had spells with Plymouth Argyle and Charlton Athletic. He sadly died in 1992.
☆ **Republic of Ireland caps:** 1959 v Sweden; 1960 v Chile, West Germany, Sweden. (4).

DYER, James　　　　　1908-09

Born: 1884
SL apps: 3

■ James threw in his lot with Hammers at the beginning of the same season that his former Manchester United colleagues brought the FA Cup back to their Bank Street headquarters. Making his debut in a 2-0 win over Queens Park Rangers at the Boleyn Ground, in the season's opening fixture, it proved to be the inside-forward's last taste of success as a Hammer - his other two appearances, v Brighton and Brentford respectively, ending in defeat.

Another goal goes past Noel Dwyer in the infamous 5-3 home defeat by Newcastle. Noel Cantwell and Ken Brown look on.

EADIE, Doug   1966-68

Born: Edinburgh, Scotland. 22.9.46
Lge apps: 2

■ Flying Scottish winger whose first team opportunities were extremely limited. In fact, he made only two League appearances, making his debut v Spurs at Upton Park in May 1967, and his final showing four days later v Manchester City in the last match of that campaign. Later moved to Leyton Orient where he had the same amount of matches. In 1970/71 he was at Bournemouth under the management of John Bond and Ken Brown with ex-Hammers Tony Scott, Trevor Hartley and Keith Miller, but couldn't break into the first team. Turned up to watch Hammers on a pre-season tour of Scotland at the beginning of the 1992/93 campaign.

EARL   1903-04

■ There is no doubt a story behind Earl's solitary appearance for Irons in the 4-1 Memorial Ground defeat inflicted by Bristol Rovers. He had deputised for Charlie Sattherwaite at outside-left but failed to do anything to grab the headlines and thus ensure a more lasting testimony than: Earl, SL apps. 1.

EARL, Alfred   1925-33

Born: Earlsfield, London. 19.3.1903
Lge apps: 181
Cup apps: 15

■ Tall, constructive defender who held the right-back position during his eight seasons at Upton Park, making close to 200 senior appearances in the process. Signed from Summerstown in 1925, he is remembered not only as a cool, thoughtful player but also for having ate four hot cross buns

Alfred Earl

one Good Friday before a match and collapsing on the field! A contender, if ever there was one, for the current fans' song 'Who ate all the pies?'. Later played for Streatham Town and played for a French team, Soucaux, in Paris. He died 17.8.51.

EASTMAN, George   1925-26

Lge apps: 2

■ A remarkable feature of George's two First Division outings for Hammers was that they were both against Everton in direct confrontation with the legendary Dixie Dean. He proved himself a more than capable understudy to George Kay and later Jim Barrett in the two Upton Park clashes with the Toffeemen which, incidentally, took place almost a year to the day of each other with West Ham victorious on both occasions. The first (18.4.25) ended 4-1 in favour of Irons, and the second (17.4.26), 1-0. Brother of a well-known Essex cricketer and no slouch at the bat-and-ball game himself, George was somewhat surprisingly overlooked after that. He later joined Clapton Orient. He played 48 matches for Essex as a wicket-keeper between 1926 and 1929 taking 29 catches and making 21 stumpings. George passed away at his Eastbourne home on March 16, 1991.

EASTWOOD, H   1908-09

Lge apps: 6

■ This right-winger made his Southern League debut v Portsmouth at the Boleyn (10.10.08), when centre-forward Jack Foster scored a hat-trick in the 3-1 win. It was the start of a five-match run in the first team which culminated in a 1-0 victory over Millwall at The Den with Foster again doing the goal-scoring honours. His Christmas Day appearance in the 1-0 Upton Park win over Southampton proved to be his last for Hammers, however.

ECCLES, George   1902-04

SL apps: 59
Cup apps: 5

■ George was a sturdy defender, equally at home in either of the full-back berths. The former Everton man made consistency his by-word during his two seasons at the Memorial Grounds, missing only five Southern League outings in that

EARLE, Stanley   1924-32

Lge apps: 258 (56 gls)
Cup apps: 15 (2 gls)
Born: Stratford, London. 6.9.1897

■ A superbly creative six foot-plus inside-right who followed his former Clapton FC colleague Vivian Gibbins in signing for Irons. He had played Division One football for Arsenal before coming to Upton Park. Stan won an FA Amateur Cup Winners' medal with Clapton in 1924 and was honoured with a full cap v Ireland in Belfast in 1927. Initially reluctant to relinquish his amateur status, he became a leading light in Hammers' attack and struck up a fine under-standing with Vic Watson. Often getting among the goalscorers, it was his ability to take as well as create chances which made him such a valued member of West Ham's team in the twenties and early thirties. He ended his career with Clapton Orient. Honours: England Amateur caps v Ireland 1922-23 and

1923-24; France 1923-24. Full cap v Ireland 1927. Essex cap. London cap. Represented FA XI v Army 1922-23 and 1923-24; also represented the Isthmian League. Later had spells as Walthamstow Avenue coach and Leyton manager. The son of Harry Earle, an 1890's centre-half with Clapton, Millwall and Nottingham Forest. Stan passed away in Sept. 1971 at Colchester after a long illness.
☆ *England cap:* 1927 v Ireland (1)

Played	League		FAC		LC		Europe		Total	
	App	Gls	App	Gls	App	Gls	App	Gls	App	Gls
1924-25	18	6	0	0	0	0	0	0	18	6
1925-26	37	9	1	0	0	0	0	0	39	9
1926-27	42	13	3	0	0	0	0	0	45	13
1927-28	31	11	1	0	0	0	0	0	32	11
1928-29	41	6	5	2	0	0	0	0	46	8
1929-30	36	3	4	0	0	0	0	0	40	3
1930-31	36	8	1	0	0	0	0	0	37	8
1931-32	17	0	0	0	0	0	0	0	17	0
TOTAL	258	56	15	2	0	0	0	0	273	58

time and being an ever-present in 1903/04. But even that proud record could not save him from the ruthless purge on the playing staff which saw only five players retained and a major influx of new faces to coincide with the move to Upton Park. But when one door closes another opens, and George joined Bolton Wanderers against doctors' advice that the Lancastrian climate would not agree with his health. He married the trainer's daughter and stayed at Burnden Park for 40 years as assistant and then trainer. Bolton's directors had a special medal struck for George in 1930 to commemorate his handling of three successful Wanderers' FA Cup Final XI's, including the 1923 Final against West Ham. Described as a player as being 'a grand tackler and an untiring worker,' George Eccles died just before Christmas, 1945. Had played for Burslem Port Vale, Wolverhampton Wanderers and Preston North End before Everton.

EDWARDS, Bill   1923-26

Lge apps: 37 (3 gls)
Cup apps: 2

■ Joining Irons from Newport County in an exchange deal which resulted in William Charlton signing for the Welsh club. Bill made his debut v Crystal Palace (1.3.23) and did well from the outside-right position. His best run in the first XI came in 1923/24 when he made 25 First Division appearances and two in the FA Cup. He later went back to Newport after spells with Shrewsbury Town, Llanelly and on retiring from soccer became a Licensee at Hereford. A very good bowls player, he was a leading light in the Hereford Bowls Club and a member of their team which won the English Bowling Association's triples championship in 1950. Bill died on June 4, 1952.

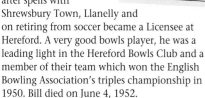

WM. F. EDWARDS WEST HAM

ENGLAND, Ernest   1930-31

Born: Shirebrook, Derbys. 3.2.01
Lge apps: 5

■ Ernie was a long-serving left-back with Sunderland, when they were a force in the land and could boast of such illustrious company as England international goalkeeper Albert McInroy and a trio of Scottish internationals in right-half Billy Clunas, Tommy McInally and Adam McLean (who joined the

Ernie England

Wearsiders as a complete left-wing from Glasgow Celtic). The experienced defender made his Hammers' debut in the amazing 5-5 home draw with Aston Villa (3.1.31) and later proved invaluable in passing on his wealth of knowledge to the younger players before joining Mansfield Town. Ernie passed away at Radcliffe-on-Trent. 22.2.82.

ETTE, Clifford   1934

Lge app: 1

■ Inside-right Cliff scored on his West Ham debut in the Second Division clash at Deepdale v Preston North End (3.2.34). Hammers lost 3-1 and, mysteriously, he never appeared for the first team again. Cliff began his career with Northampton Nomads and signed amateur forms for Hammers after being personally asked, in a letter by West Ham manager Charlie Paynter, to turn out in the match v. PNE. He later captained the London League Park Royal side which dumped Swindon out of the 1935/36 FA Cup before losing 3-1 at Cardiff in the Third Round. Represented the London League v. Paris League and scored a goal in his side's 3-1 victory at the famous Parc de Princes Stadium in the French capital. His team-mate in that match was Dick Walker, who also played for Royals. Later with Southall when the club took over Park Royal when they lost their ground in 1936. A bad knee injury ended his career and brought about the onset of arthritis which partially disabled Cliff in later life. In 1989 he was awarded the Arthritis and Rheumatism Council's Running Man trophy for his service to sport in collecting thousands of postage stamps to raise funds for ARC's cause over the years.

EUSTACE, Peter   1970-72

Born: Stocksbridge, Yorks. 31.7.44
Lge apps: 44 (6 gls)
Cup apps: 5 (1 gl)

■ Bought from Sheffield Wednesday for a then Hammers' record fee of £90,000 to replace Martin Peters, he never quite succeeded. A creative wing-half on the verge of full international honours with Wednesday, he could not reproduce the same form under Ron Greenwood at West Ham and was allowed to rejoin the Hillsborough club at a reduced fee after only two years at Upton Park (part of which he spent on loan to Rotherham United and his former club). Peter was manager of Sheffield Wednesday in the later 1980's after being assistant to Howard

Wilkinson prior to the latter's appointment as boss of Leeds United. Was youth team boss at Charlton before becoming assistant to Frank Clark at Leyton Orient. Took charge at Brisbane Road in 1991 but was dismissed in April 1994.

EVANS, Arthur   1930

Born: Barking, Essex, 1906
Lge apps: 1

■ Evans was a pupil of Creeksmouth School and developed the football skills he learned there in a local junior team before joining Barking Town in 1921. He spent four seasons in the Athenian League club's reserves before making the outside-right position his own. Described by the distinguished football reporter Norman Ackland as "Tremendously fast, at ball control he has few masters. He centres

Peter Eustace

splendidly, anticipates the run of play like a veteran, and converges in on goal from the outside-left." From the mid-20's onwards honours were bestowed on this lead-burner by trade, thick and fast. Among them an FA Amateur Cup Final medal, London Senior cap and badge and an Athenian League cap and badge. In 1925 he twice represented Essex County and was on two occasions picked for the Athenian League in memorable victories over the Isthmian League and Corinthians. Other honours included playing for London v Brussels (1927), London v Lancashire, for the FA XI v the Navy and against the Army (1928). After an impressive display in a trial for England v The Rest, Arthur became the first Barking Town player to be capped for England when he was selected for the match v Wales at Brighton 16.2.1928. But by May, 1933 Arthur had retired and was working for the Gas Light and Coke Co. In a newspaper article of that time he said: "Professional football is a full-time job if you have the ambition to progress and become a star player. My choice went to my job because I was married, but I had some great times touring the Continent and Europe with Middlesex Wanderers - as an amateur."

EVANS, Roger   1902-03

SL apps: 1

■ A centre-forward who played in the penultimate Southern League fixture of the 1902/03 season on the occasion of a 4-0 defeat by Luton Town at Dunstable Road. He failed to get on the scoresheet and consequently to make any more appearances in the claret and blue. An amateur with Clapton where he was a club-mate of W. Miecznikowski. Also appeared for Ilford, Queens Park Rangers and London Welsh.

FAIR, Aubrey   1901-07

SL apps: 31 (1 gl)
Cup apps: 2

■ Normally a left-back, although he sometimes switched to the right and on one occasion played at centre-forward (scoring at Brighton), Aubrey was sufficiently well thought of to survive a purge on the playing staff in the close season of 1904 which saw himself, Tom Allison, Billy Bridgeman, Charles Cotton and Len Jarvis the only survivors of the previous season's squad. Making his debut in an FA Cup tie at Leyton in Nov.1901 in his solitary appearance that season, he was by no means a first team regular and failed to appear during the entire 1905/06 season. His last outing was v Queen's Park Rangers when Hammers won 2-1 at Upton Park (25.2.1907).

FAIRMAN, Robert   1909-12

Born: Southampton, Hants. 1885.
SL apps: 90
Cup apps: 12

■ This left-back was signed from Birmingham in the close-season of 1909/10 and made his SL bow in the 2-1 home win over Exeter City on the opening day of the season when Danny Shea scored both goals. It was the first of 90 first team outings - quite a run for those days - and he showed his versatility by switching to right-back when the need arose in his final season of 1911/12. Played in the Football League with the Birmingham side relegated from Division One at the end of 1907/08. Stayed at St. Andrews for one season of Second Division football, when he scored one goal in 19 games, before moving south to Irons. Very dark skinned, he was most popular with the Upton Park patrons. Moved back to Brum in 1912, but was unable to command a regular place in the first XI, appearing only 16 times (Div. 2) between 1912/13 and 1913/14. Seems to have dropped out of senior soccer after this, as he was not registered with any FL or SL club for 1914/15. The 'Athletic News' described him as a 'cool, calculating defender.'

FARRELL, John   1902-03

Born: 1874
SL apps: 20 (3 gls)
Cup apps: 1

■ "Jack" Farrell made his name with Southampton when the Saints won the Southern League Championship for the third year running in 1899 and was also on duty when the south coast club lost 4-0 to Bury in the 1900 FA Cup Final at Crystal Palace. The following year the hard hitting centre-forward came under the guidance of the later to be legendary Herbert Chapman, then making his way as player-manager of little Northampton Town, and who with Jack's help, found success in only his second season by winning the Southern League. It was considered a major coup on West Ham's part when, as a relatively new club, they managed to sign such a well-known player for the commencement of the 1902/03 season. Duly making his Hammers' debut in the season's opening fixture v Reading at the Memorial Grounds, he went on to make 20 Southern League appearances, and although slightly past his best, proved that he could still hold the line together. He began his top class career with Stoke City in Oct. 1894 when the Potters signed him from Dresden United for £40 - a lot of money then. Prior to his move to Northampton, Jack spent a year with New Brighton Tower from June 1901 and actually had two spells with Stoke, returning there from Saints in cs 1898. He joined Southampton again for the 1899/1900 season and in his two spells at The Dell scored 54 goals in 97 SL and Cup games. He retired after his one season at the Memorial Grounds and became a publican in his home town of Tunstall. He died on February 22, 1947.

FASHANU, Justin   1989

Born: Hackney, East London. 19.2.61.
Lge apps: 2
Cup apps: 1

■ Controversial striker who spent just one month (Nov. 1989) on loan in which he started two Second Division matches and one League Cup tie under Lou Macari's management. The former Dr Barnardo's boy was struggling to re-establish himself in Britain at the time, having battled to overcome a serious knee injury that threatened his colourful career. He made his debut as a 76th minute sub v Wimbledon in the Littlewoods Cup at Upton Park (22.11.89), and also played the full 90 mins. at Blackburn Rovers and at home v Stoke City. An expensive £1 million signing by Nottingham Forest from Norwich City in Aug. 1981, "Fash" - the elder brother of Wimbledon striker John - also had brief spells with Southampton, Notts County, Brighton & Hove Albion, Manchester City, Leyton Orient, Torquay United and, in Scotland, for Hearts.

FEATHERSTONE, Arthur   1905-08

Born: Barking, Essex.
SL apps: 24 (1 gl)
Cup apps: 1

■ A right-winger whose forte was making, rather than scoring, goals, although he did score one during his two dozen outings in the claret and blue. It came during a 3-0 Upton Park win over Queens Park Rangers on Boxing Day, 1907. He made

PROMINENT FOOTBALLERS.

A. FEATHERSTONE,
WEST HAM UNITED.

only 5 SL appearances that season and his last for the club came in the penultimate fixture of the season, when Rangers got their revenge with a 4-0 victory at the Park Royal Ground. Won a number of medals as a youngster with the national school side, including a Glenny Shield award. Was a member of Barking St. Andrews, the winners of East Suburban League. Also won medals with Barking Victoria (London Junior Shield), Newportonians (Sth. Essex League) and Barking (London Junior Cup and Sth Essex League). A keen athlete of some repute, he won the 100-yard sprint event at the Barking Athletics meeting seven times out of eight. Affectionately known as "Moppy."

FENN, George   1958

Born: West Ham, London.

■ Although this former schoolboy prodigy never made a League appearance while at West Ham, he did play v Reading in a Southern Floodlight Cup match: a competition virtually regarded as a first team tournament in those days when floodlights were still a novelty and borne out by an attendance of over 13,000 at Elm Park. Equally at home at centre-forward or on the wing, George transferred to Southern League Bedford Town in cs 1959. A far cry from the days when, in Ted Fenton's words: "George Fenn is the most exciting prospect in the country" and was expected to be the 'cream of the crop' of a batch of starlets being nurtured by Malcolm Allison. When asked who he wanted to keep, Big Mal said: "I'll have the boy Scott, the boy Cartwright and the boy Moore." "But what about Fenn?" asked Fenton. "Every club in the country is after him." Mal replied prophetically: "I don't think he'll make it."

Ted Fenton

FENTON, Benny   1937-39

Born: West Ham. 28.10.18
Lge apps: 21 (9 gls)
Cup apps: 1

■ Brother of the famous former West Ham player and manager Ted Fenton, Ben followed in Ted's footsteps as a West Ham, Essex and London schoolboy representative player, and joined him in West Ham United's League side before WW2. Ben served in the same T.A. unit as his Hammers' colleagues, but had not been retained by the Hammers at the end of the 1938-39 season. Mainly playing at outside-left with Hammers, Ben converted to wing-half when football resumed in 1946 and served Millwall, Charlton and Colchester (where he played on loan before WW2) as a defender; he later managed all three in turn as well as Leyton Orient. Ben guested for Norwich City, Manchester City, Charlton Athletic, Crystal Palace and West Ham. Also an Essex County lawn bowler and keen cricketer.

FENTON, Frederick   1900-01

Born: Gainsborough, Lincs
SL apps: 14 (2 gls)
Cup apps: 1 (1 gl)

■ A product of Midlands football, Freddie was signed from a club later to become a sort of unofficial nursery for Hammers - Gainsborough Trinity. An extremely modest man, he filled the outside-left position with verve and flair in the opening 13 fixtures of the club's initial season, but managed only one further Southern League appearance before transferring to Swindon Town. He was also with West

Bromwich Albion. Although the Fenton name is more remembered in the annals of West Ham history by the exploits of Fred's more illustrious namesake, former Hammers' captain and manager, Ted Fenton, and to a lesser extent the latter's brother, Benny, our subject does have the honour of scoring the club's first FA Cup goal under the banner of West Ham United - v Olympic (3.11.1900).

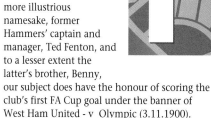

FENTON, Ted   1933-46

Born: Forest Gate, London. 1915
Lge apps: 163 (27 gls)
Cup apps: 13

■ Although he had already left Upton Park to become player/manager of little Colchester United when full League football was resumed for the 1946/47 season. Ted did in fact play for Hammers in their four FA Cup ties regarded as official the previous campaign. He guided the Essex club to the fifth round of the FA Cup in 1947/48, and it soon became apparent that their success was not solely due to the players thriving on the local speciality - oysters! Inundated with management offers from elsewhere, Ted plumped to return to his former club and was officially appointed manager in Aug. 1950 -taking over from the legendary Charlie Paynter. A schoolboy international as a forward, he made his League debut for Hammers in 1934 at centre-half, but it was at wing-half that he really made his mark: winning a Football League War Cup medal in 1940 and playing five times for England. His greatest achievement as manager was undoubtedly returning the team to the First Division in 1958 after an absence of 26 years. He later managed Southend United before going into the pub trade when he retired from the game. After that he opened a sports shop in Brentwood, Essex, passing on the business to his son Alan (who played for Hammers' "A" team in the fifties), when retiring to live in Gloucestershire where he was able to cultivate his love of golf. Ted died tragically in July 1992, aged 77, following a car crash near Peterborough.

FENWICK, Alfred   1914-19

Born: Hamsterley, Co. Durham. 26.3.1891
SL apps: 19 (1 gl)
FL apps: 2

■ Despite a tendency to neglect his defensive duties for frequent forays upfield, Alf was a fine utility player who filled all the rearguard positions (with the exeption of goalkeeper) for Hammers, as well as the two inside-forward positions in war-time matches. Beginning his career with Cragheart United in Co. Durham, he progressed to Football League status with Hull

City, making 16 appearances for the Tigers and scoring seven times while taking over the centre-forward role following the transfer of Hull's regular number nine, Tom Browell, to Everton. Joining Hammers in cs 1914, he made his SL debut v Gillingham in the opening game of the season at Upton Park in the right-half berth. The combative north-easterner totalled 19 appearances in the uncertain times of the initial war-time season, managing to get himself sent-off in one of them. But by 1918/19 he was guesting for Hartlepool United. Returning to Upton Park to make two appearances in the club's first Football League season, Alf was transferred to Coventry City in Dec. 1919 and had 53 games for the Bantams before returning "home" to join Blyth Spartans in 1921.

FERGUSON, Bobby   1967-80

Born: Ardrossan, Scotland. 1.3.45
Lge apps: 240
Cup: 36

■ Signed for the then record British fee (for a goalkeeper) of £65,000 from Kilmarnock, after winning a string of international caps with the Rugby Park club as well as being a member of the 'Killie' squad which won the Scottish First Division in 1964, and reached the Fairs Cup semi-final in 1967 v Leeds United. Making his debut v Sheffield Wednesday on the opening day of the 1967/68 season (19.8.67), Bobby managed to amass a surprisingly large total of appearances - considering he twice lost his first team spot for lengthy periods to Peter Grotier and later Mervyn Day. "Fergie" began the 1978/79 term between the sticks, but was initially replaced by Day and then the arrival of Phil Parkes, in Feb. 1979, effectively spelled the end of his Hammers' career. His last-ever game in the number one shirt for West Ham came in a 2-1 defeat at Chelsea (14.11.79). He also played five times for Sheffield Wednesday while on loan to the Yorkshire club in 1973. Went to Australia with his wife Greer and joined Adelaide City. He later owned a marine complex, but gave it up after a close friend was killed by a shark. He has now started a much safer business, selling carpets and floor tiles. Bobby received £20,000 from his testimonial v Southampton in 1981.

Played	League App	Gls	FAC App	Gls	LC App	Gls	Europe App	Gls	Total App	Gls
1967-68	39	0	3	0	2	0	0	0	44	0
1968-69	39	0	3	0	3	0	0	0	45	0
1969-70	30	0	1	0	2	0	0	0	33	0
1970-71	23	0	1	0	0	0	0	0	24	0
1971-72	36	0	4	0	10	0	0	0	50	0
1972-73	31	0	2	0	0	0	0	0	33	0
1973-74	9	0	0	0	0	0	0	0	9	0
1974-75	0	0	0	0	0	0	0	0	0	0
1975-76	1	0	0	0	0	0	0	0	1	0
1976-77	0	0	0	0	0	0	0	0	0	0
1977-78	19	0	3	0	0	0	0	0	22	0
1978-79	11	0	0	0	1	0	0	0	12	0
1979-80	2	0	0	0	1	0	0	0	3	0
TOTAL	240	0	17	0	19	0	0	0	276	0

Hammers v Sheffield United, FA Cup 5th round, March 1968. Bobby Ferguson punches clear.

Ian Feuer

FEUER, Ian   1994-

Born: Las Vegas, California, USA 20.5.70

■ Giant 6ft. 6in. American goalkeeper who signed from Los Angeles Salsa for £70,000 in May 1994 after 12 reserve team appearances at the end of 1993/94. Yet to make his first team debut but occupies a place on the subs' bench as cover for Ludek Miklosko. Likeable Ian left the States at the age of 16 to sample football European-style. Spent five years with FC Brugge in Belgium and also had a 35-match spell with RWD Molenbeek before going home to play for LA Salsa. Represented USA at the 1992 Barcelona Olympics.

FLETCHER, Albert   1923-24

Born: Wolverhampton
Lge apps: 8 (1 gl)

■ A regular member of Hammers' London Combination XI who could operate effectively in either of the inside-forward positions. Chosen to represent the London League on three occasions, he made his League debut during the exciting 1922/23 season, in a 2-0 win over Fulham at Craven Cottage. He was previously with Brentford.

FLETCHER, Jack   1904-05

SL apps: 25 (7 gls)
Cup apps: 1

■ Jack was an inside-right who also played at inside-left in his 25 appearances during Hammers' first season at the Boleyn Ground. He scored the first of his seven goals v arch-rivals Millwall in a 1-1 draw at The Den (17.9.1904). Signed from Reading in 1904, he joined Queens Park Rangers for 1905/06 and then transferred to Fulham.

FLYNN, Jack   1904-05

Born: 1875
SL apps: 20 (3 gls)
Cup apps: 1 (1 gl)

■ Jack Flynn is officially credited with scoring one of Hammers' goals when they defeated Millwall 3-0 in the first match at the Boleyn (1.9.1904). Some historians have listed Billy Bridgeman as netting all three - a fact unsubstatiated by contemporary newspaper reports. Jack served Bristol City in the Second Division of the Football League in 1901/02 and joined Reading CS 1902. Hammers signed him from the Biscuitmen in 1904.

FOAN, Albert   1950-56

Born: Rotherhithe, London. 30.10.23
Lge apps: 53 (6 gls)
Cup apps: 7 (3 gls)

■ A Londoner who escaped the attention of the capital's clubs until Hammers signed him from Norwich City. Equally at home on the wing or at inside-forward, his early honours were with London Boys. His finest hour at Upton Park came during the great Cup run of 1955/56, when he scored a hat-trick v Preston North End. The significance of that event can be gauged by glancing at his total League goals. Albert joined up with former Hammer Almer Hall at Kent League Margate when he left the club. Albert later enjoyed four seasons with Lowestoft where his former Hammers' team-mate Mike Grice was on the opposite wing, and for whom the pair were in action v Leyton Orient in an FA Cup first round tie in Nov. 1966, at Brisbane Road.

FORD, William   1905-06

Born: Scotland, 1881
SL apps: 7 (1 gl)

■ Bill Ford made seven SL appearances during West Ham's second year at the Boleyn Ground in 1905/06 . His initial outing came in the opening fixture v Swindon Town at inside-right but he played his remaining matches at outside-right, the final one in the penultimate game of the campaign in a 3-1 defeat at Brentford. Bill began his career in earnest with Scottish junior side The Rovers before signing for the then Scottish Northern League club, Arbroath. He later played for Hearts and Motherwell before moving south to join Portsmouth from where he transferred to Irons at the end of 1904/05.

FORDE, Steven   1948-51

Born: South Kirkby, Yorks. 29.8.14
Lge apps: 170 (1 gl)
Cup apps: 6

■ Yet another who had his playing career badly disrupted by WW2. Steve had seen service with Sheffield Wednesday, Wolves and Rotherham United before arriving at the Boleyn Ground in 1937. Making his debut v Tottenham in Apr. 1938, he looked set for a long run in the first XI, but circumstances decreed otherwise. He did, however, play in the victorious War Cup semi-final v Fulham which saw Hammers through to Wembley. It was after demobilisation that the tough Yorkshireman showed his true worth, turning in some sterling performances and being ever-present in 1947/48. One of the finest full-backs to appear for the club in the immediate post-war period. Steve retired from League soccer in 1951, later managing Penzance in the Western League.

FOREMAN, Alec George   1939-46

Born: West Ham, London. 1.3.14
Lge apps: 6 (1 gl)
Cup apps: 3 (1 gl)

■ Not to be confused with another pre-war Hammer of the same surname, this former England and Walthamstow amateur was shaping up well at centre-forward when WW2 broke out. The highlight of his fragmented time with the club must surely have been the Football League War Cup Final at Wembley in 1940. It was from a shot by George, which the Blackburn 'keeper fisted out, that Sam Small scored the only goal to take the cup to Upton Park. Transferred to Spurs, where he scored 15 goals in 37 matches in 1946-47, George died in June 1969. George's war-time playing record was second to none. He scored a staggering 154 goals in 156 Football League South and London League appearances and a further 34 goal haul in 46 various cup competitions.

FOREMAN, John
1934-36

Born: Tanfield, Newcastle-upon-Tyne. 1914
Lge apps: 49 (7 gls)
Cup apps: 2

■ A Durham schoolboy, previously with Sunderland, John made his first appearance for West Ham on the right-wing v Plymouth Argyle at Upton Park (29.9.34). He went on to make 21 Second Division outings that season and only one less the following campaign before being superceded by Stan Foxall in 1936/37. In order to obtain regular first team football the speedy flankman transferred to Bury (11.3.37).

FORSTER, Harry
1912-14

SL apps: 40
Cup apps: 4

■ This left-back was signed from Sunderland and made his Boleyn bow in the 4-0 win over Exeter City on the opening match of the 1912/13 season. He played in 25 SL games that campaign in addition to four FA Cup ties, but lost his place after appearing in a 0-1 home defeat to Southend United (6.12.14) when his place was taken by George Irvine.

FOSTER, Colin
1989-94

Born: Chislehurst, Kent. 16.7.64
Lge apps: 93 (4 gls)
Cup apps: 14 (2 gls)

■ Became Lou Macari's second signing, in Sept. 1989, when he moved from Nottingham Forest back to East London in a £750,000 deal. At 6ft 4ins, "Fozzie" is one of the tallest central defenders in the country. Made his debut at Upton Park v Watford (23.9.89) - the club he finally left Hammers for in Mar. 1994. Colin, who made his League debut for Leyton Orient at Grimsby (9.1.82) while still an apprentice, played 174 League matches for O's before his £50,000 transfer to Forest (May 1987). He made a further 72 League appearances under Brian Clough at the City Ground. Although Colin was Macari's most expensive signing, he failed to earn a regular first team place in his first season under the little Scot. Fozzie was, however, a regular during the 1990/91 Second Division promotion campaign, but a succession of niggly injuries limited his contribution in the next three seasons when he struggled to win a first team place. A projected £400,000 transfer back to Forest fell through when Colin failed to agree personal terms at the start of the 1992/93 season and he remained with Hammers on a weekly contract from then until his eventual move. Notts County looked likely to end Fozzie's spell in the wilderness of the Combination League when they took him on loan for two months from Jan. 1994. But West Ham finally cut their losses and accepted £100,000 for Colin from First Division Watford, just prior to the Mar. 1994 transfer deadline. The undoubted highlight of Fozzie's time at Upton Park was his volleyed goal in the 1991 FA Cup quarter-final victory v Everton that set up the semi-final showdown with his former club, Forest.

FOSTER, Jack
1908-09

Born: 1883
SL apps: 15 (9 gls)

■ Signed from Sunderland, centre-forward Jack made a scoring start in the first game of the season v Queens Park Rangers at Upton Park. His scoring-rate was a match for any, as he rifled home nine goals in 15 SL appearances, including a hat-trick in a 3-1 victory over Portsmouth at the Boleyn. But Jack's exploits had caught the attention of Southampton, and he was soon back in red and white stripes again, this time down on the south coast. He was ex-changed for Saints' Frank Costello and had begun his League career with Stockport, moving to Watford in 1906 where his goalscoring feats had tempted Sunderland to part with £800 to take him to Roker. After only one goal in six appearances at the Dell, Jack transferred back to his native Yorkshire with Huddersfield Town in May 1909. He joined Castleford Town in 1910. West Ham were well aware of Jack's goalscoring capabilities when they signed him from the Wearsiders as he had scored all three goals for Watford v Irons in the two SL fixtures in 1906/07 which ended 1-1 at Upton Park and 2-0 at Watford. One source has Jack joining the Herts club from Rotherham Town. He played at centre-forward in the Midland League's annual fixture for the Rest v The Champions.

Colin Foster (right) pictured with the other goalscorer, Stuart Slater, after Hammers memorable FA Cup quarter-final win against Everton in 1991.

Stan Foxall

FOXALL, Joseph Stanley   1934-39

Born: Crowle, Lincolnshire. 8.10.14
Lge apps: 106 (37 gls)
Cup apps: 7 (5 gls)

■ Equally as well known by both his first and second Christian names, Stan (or Joe) was yet another import from Gainsborough Trinity, partnering Johnny Morton in the latter's first game for the Midland League club against local rivals Lincoln St. Andrews; he had three seasons with the Midland club. Sometimes known as the "Mystery Man" because his unorthodox methods were baffling to opponents (and occasionally bewildering even to his team mates), he was nevertheless a fine player who could operate anywhere in the forward line. He was chosen to represent London Combination v Central League in Nov. 1936, and was a member of the West Ham team which won the Football League War Cup in 1940. In the season leading up to WW2 Stan was encouraged to adopt a more direct approach by manager Charlie Paynter, who switched him into the near-centre of attack. With Sam Small moving out to the wing, the results were devastating. In the 1938/39 season his name became a by-word for concern to rivals Spurs when, in four matches against the North Londoners, beginning with a League match at White Hart Lane on Oct. 29, he hit a nap-hand of goals. "He was in his own half when he received the ball," *The Times* reported, "but a combination of swerve and speed took him right through the defenders until he had only Hooper to beat and he equalised." West Ham lost 2-1, but it was a different story when the two sides were paired there in the fourth round of the FA Cup. *The Times* again: "On a pitch that was so generously covered in sand as to suggest spades and donkey rides rather than football, not only did Foxall score two brilliant goals but his mere presence in the centre - after a somewhat unprofitable time on the right wing until West Ham were two down - seemed to revitalise the team. Almost immediately he scored a magnificent goal after a long dribble, and when he did very much the same sort of thing again 10 minutes from the end, West Ham drew level." In the Upton Park replay Foxall and Small again switched roles. After Archie McCaulay had missed a penalty Spurs went in front after 29 minutes, but four minutes later Foxall equalised for the third time in three matches against Tottenham. In the second replay in front of a 50,000 crowd at Highbury, Spurs led again, but after 55 minutes the 'Fox' struck again. He latched on to a long clearance, held off the challenges of two defenders and beat Hooper with a stinging, low shot from outside the area. A crucial goal which led the way for McCaulay to hit the winner. Stan scored 63 goals in 156 League and Cup matches during WW2, but suffered a knee injury v Queens Park Rangers in Sept. 1944, which effectively ended his career.
Stan died at the age of 76 on August 12, 1991.

FROST, A. 1910-12

Born: 1888
SL apps: 4

■ This centre-forward-cum-inside-forward made his first team baptism in the 2-0 Upton Park win over Luton Town (18.2.1911) from the inside-right berth after joining Irons from Southend United. He was on duty again on the 18th of the following month, again at the Boleyn, in a 4-1 thrashing of Exeter City. His final game was in the last match of 1911/12 season at Coventry.

FROST, James 1907-08

Born: Wolverton. 1880
SL apps: 20 (4 gls)
Cup apps: 5

■ Jim made his first appearance in Hammers' colours on the right-wing in the 1-0 home win over Luton Town (25.1.08). It was the start of an uninterrupted 13-match run in the SL side which saw him get on the scoresheet against Portsmouth, Watford and Norwich City. Ironically, his last appearance for Hammers was also against Luton, but this time the scores were reversed, with the Hatters being victorious 1-0 at Kenilworth Road (20.1.09). Previously with Northampton Town and Chelsea, he transferred with colleague Bill Yenson to play for Croydon Common in that club's first season in the First Division of the SL in 1909/10. Played for his local Wolverton team as a 16-year-old and played against TIW in the Second Division of the SL in Jan. 1899. Chelsea paid Northampton £350 for his transfer in cs 1907, after he had spent six years with the Cobblers.

FRYATT, William 1931-32

Born: Matlock, Derbys
Lge apps: 3

■ Bill was a reserve left-back who played his first game in the League side v Derby County at Upton Park (28.3.31) in a match the Rams won 1-0. He failed to make any First Division appearances the following season, but had two more outings on Hammers' return to Division Two in 1932/33, again finishing on the losing side in successive defeats v Bury and Lincoln City. Bill had a novel experience (4.1.33) when, with team mates Bill Johnson and Jimmy Ruffell, he played in the first FA official floodlight match in England. The game was staged at the White City Stadium (as an experiment by the FA) using players picked from London's League clubs, the ball frequently being dipped in a bucket of whitewash before a curious crowd of 12,000!

FURNELL, George (1897-1898) TIW

■ Earlier with the Old Castle Swifts club, this goalkeeper played in all three of Thames Ironworks' FA Cup ties in 1897/98 and was a regular in the London League side. Transferred to Hammersmith Athletic in 1898/99.

Tony Gale

Proud Dad Tony Gale is joined on the pitch by son Anthony and daughter Alexandra before kick-off on the occasion of his Testimonial game against Republic of Ireland XI in May 1994.

GALE, Tony 1984-94

Born: Westminster, London. 19.12.59
Lge apps: 300 (5 gls)
Cup apps: 59 (2 gls)

■ One of the most stylish and accomplished central defenders in Hammers' history, Tony proved a real bargain when John Lyall signed him from Fulham for £200,000 - the fee decided by tribunal - in the summer of 1984. It is perhaps unfortunate that, despite giving Hammers sterling service in 359 League and cup games over a 10-year period, the one match fans will remember most is that fateful 1991 FA Cup semi-final when "Galey" was controversially sent off 26 minutes into the game v Nottingham Forest. Sheffield referee Keith Hackett must have been the only person inside Villa Park that afternoon who thought the West Ham number four deserved a red card - for an alleged professional foul, after clashing with Forest winger Gary Crosby. West Ham supporters - who saw their side tumble to a 4-0 defeat after Tony's dismissal - have never forgiven Hackett who did not officiate again at Upton Park between that black day (14.4.91) and his retirement from the League list in May 1994. Ironically, it was in this month that Tony's long and distinguished West Ham career also ended - he was given a free transfer on the day of his Testimonial game (v Republic of Ireland XI, 8.5.94), 24 hours after making his 300th, and final, League appearance for Hammers v Southampton. That sending-off - the only blemish in a career spanning 577 League appearances for two clubs - will haunt Tony forever, but it should not overshadow his immense contribution and loyalty to the club. He first caught the eye with London and Middlesex Schools and signed apprentice for Fulham in 1977. An outstanding teenage prospect, Tony made the first of 277 League appearances for the Cottagers v Charlton Athletic at Craven Cottage (20.8.77), although his first team debut came at Leyton Orient (Anglo-Italian Cup, 11.8.76) while he was still only 16-years-old. Tony was given the huge responsibility of trying to replace Bobby Moore, who had moved there from West Ham in 1973 and was nearing the end of his illustrious career. Although disappointed to play only one match alongside the legendary Moore - a reserve team game v Bristol City - Tony was, however, privileged to be a team-mate of another football superstar, George Best, seven times, as well as acting as 'boot boy' for Rodney Marsh during the most colourful era in the club's history. Manager Bobby Campbell appointed Galey captain of Fulham's first team at the age of 18 (a role he occasionally fulfilled at Upton Park in the absence of others) and, under Malcolm MacDonald in 1982, he led the team to promotion to Division Two. When Billy Bonds seemed set to retire at the end of the 1983/84 season, Hammers' boss John Layll turned to Tony for his replacement. Having followed in Moore's footsteps at Craven Cottage, this was another huge burden for the West Londoner to bear. Bonzo subsequently made several remarkable comebacks before finally retiring as a player in May 1988, but he did not prevent Galey from firmly establishing himself at the heart of West Ham's defence. In his second season in East London, Tony formed a formidable partnership with Alvin Martin that served Hammers so well as they achieved their highest-ever First Division placing - third - in 1985/86. Tony has seen it all in his time at Upton Park - two relegation and two promotion seasons - but he never compromised his own high standards and footballing principals. No one has ever seen Tony Gale aimlessly boot the ball into touch. He has always been comfortable on the ball - a talent underlined by the fact that he occasionally pushed forward into midfield. A classy player who epitomised the best traditions of West Ham United, Tony was a perceptive reader of the game who used the ball well. His effective execution of free-kicks was illustrated when he curled home the fourth goal in a memorable 4-1 1988 League Cup victory over Liverpool. His scoring efforts were few and far between, but Tony helped create a number of goals with his near-post flicks from corners. And although not a naturally aggressive defender, he added another dimension to his

game in his last two seasons at Upton Park, when he had to assume a more dominate role in the air, alongside his shorter partner, Steve Potts. A dressing room comic who was dubiously nicknamed "Reggie" (after notorious East End gangland boss Reggie Kray!) for his wicked sense of humour, Tony Gale was a true character and quality footballer who served the club with distinction.

Played	League		FAC		LC		Europe		Total	
	App	Gls	App	Gls	App	Gls	App	Gls	App	Gls
1984-85	37	0	0	0	3	0	0	0	40	0
1985-86	42	0	7	0	3	0	0	0	52	0
1986-87	32	2	4	1	4	0	0	0	40	3
1987-88	18	0	2	0	0	0	0	0	20	0
1988-89	31	0	5	0	6	1	0	0	42	1
1989-90	36	1	1	0	7	0	0	0	44	1
1990-91	24	1	7	0	1	0	0	0	32	1
1991-92	25	0	2	0	4	0	0	0	31	0
1992-93	23	1	0	0	0	0	0	0	23	1
1993-94	32	0	1	0	2	0	0	0	34	0
TOTAL	300	5	29	1	30	1	0	0	358	7

Tony Gale, controversially sent-off by referee Keith Hackett in the FA Cup semi-final with Nottingham Forest

In a sensational turnaround of his fortunes, Tony was called upon by Blackburn Rovers on the eve of the 1994/95 season to play in a prestige friendly v Celtic at Hampden Park and impressed Kenny Dalglish and his assistant Ray Harford sufficiently to earn a three-month contract and a Charity Shield appearance at Wembley - his first at the famous venue in 17 years as a pro!

GALL, Herbert   1935

Born: Glasgow, Scotland
Lge apps: 1

■ Tricky outside-left who made his only first team appearance in the 0-3 defeat v Newcastle United at St. James's Park (23.2.35). Signed from Aberdeen prior to the 1934/35 season, he returned north of the border the following summer to join St. Mirren.

GALLAGHER, Joe   1983

Born: Liverpool. 11.1.55
Lge apps: 9
Cup apps: 2

■ Emergency signing from Wolves, where he was at loggerheads with the Molineux management over a difference of opinion. Drafted into the side following the suspension of Alvin Martin during the 1982/83 season, he proved a capable deputy. An experienced professional, he was with Birmingham City before joining Wolves. Teamed up with former Hammer John Bond's multi-million pound Burnley squad in the summer of 1984.

GAMBLE, Frederick   1931

Born: Charing Cross, London. 29.5.05
Lge apps: 2 (2 gls)

■ Freddie was a magnificently-built centre-forward whose six-foot frame was capable of unsettling the strongest of defences. At Upton Park, however, Fred had the stiffest possible competition for the first team places in Vivian Gibbins and Victor Watson; and although he scored in both his First Division appearances, at Bolton and Leicester respectively, he was never given the opportunity to show the Boleyn fans his undoubted talent at the highest level. Starting his career with Southall, in common with former Hammers' favourite Alan Devonshire, he signed professional forms for Brentford before joining West Ham in 1931. Later returned to Griffin Park. Fred died 15.5.65.

GARDNER, David   1904-07

Born: Glasgow. 31.3.1873
SL apps: 77
Cup apps: 3

■ A Scotsman from Glasgow, David began his career with the local Third Lanark club as an amateur before turning pro in 1896. Transferred to Newcastle United in May 1899, he made his Football League debut for the Magpies in his usual left-back berth v West Bromwich Albion at Stoney Lane (2.9.1899). In all he made 80 appearances in the famous black and white stripes before his next move, to Grimsby Town for a reported fee of £250 in May 1902. A healthy 51 appearances were added to his growing record following his debut for the Mariners in Aug. 1902, and he was soon appointed captain of the team; an honour bestowed on him by every club he served. His move to West Ham coincided with the club's switch to the Boleyn Ground, being on duty there for the first Southern League match with Millwall (1.9.04). An ever-present for the 1905/06 season, he was described variously as "being a thoughtful player, as fast as most forwards and possessor of an excellent kick. A great favourite with the spectators, an intelligent and elegant player, a perfect gentleman too." Dave possessed a crowd-pleasing trick of back-heeling the ball to fool his opponent. Assisted Croydon Common when he left Hammers in 1907, he was Leicester City's trainer from 1919 until his death in 1931, which occurred while he was indulging in his second greatest sporting passion - golf.
Honours: Represented Glasgow in an inter-city match. One Scotland cap v Wales, 1887.

GATLAND, Bill   1921

■ A right-winger who made a solitary Second Division appearance in Hammers' penultimate fixture of 1920/21 - a 2-1 win over South Shields at Upton Park.

GAULT, James   1907-09

SL apps: 49
Cup apps: 2

■ A right-back of average height and weight, James joined Hammers from Aberdeen and made his first SL appearance in a 1-1 draw at Swindon (14.9.07), when West Ham fielded a club record six Scotsmen. Absent on only two occasions up to the end of that season, his appearances were greatly reduced the next campaign when he faced rivalry for the number two spot from Fred Shreeve, who eventually won the battle. The Aberdonian's fate being settled after taking part in an unfortunate 6-0 defeat at Northampton Town (27.2.09). Syd King had earlier acclaimed him as being: "The best full-back in Scotland." Spent his formative years with Victoria Thistle and Abergeldie north of the border.

GAZZARD, Gerry   1949-54

Born: Cinderford, Gloucestershire. 15.3.25
Lge apps: 119 (29 gls)
Cup apps: 7 (3 gls)

■ The original "Pirate of Penzance", this likeable West Countryman was discovered playing as an inside-forward for Penzance, but had turned out on 20 occasions as an orthodox winger for the County of Cornwall XI. Signing pro for Hammers in May 1949, he made his first team bow v Luton Town on the opening day of the following season. Gerry had 37 appearances in 1949/50, and was one game short of being an ever-present the next campaign. Troubled by a cartilage injury, he transferred to Brentford after losing his place to Johnny Dick, and finally played out the remainder of his career back at Penzance as a reinstated amateur with the Pirates.

GEGGUS, John   1909-12

Lge apps: 31

■ Jack, as he was better known, made his Hammers' debut between the posts in a 2-2 SL draw v New Brompton at Upton Park, but things didn't always go smoothly for the former Custom House custodian. In a SL match at Leyton in Apr. 1912 Jack walked off the field with the hump after being on the receiving end of some disparaging remarks by his team's supporters. He was coaxed back on to the pitch and Hammers lost 3-1. Significantly, he was not on duty for the next match when his place was taken by Joe Hughes. He played only one more game in the first team - a 2-0 defeat at Coventry on the last day of the 1911/12 season. He later joined Gravesend.

GIBBINS, Vivian   1923-32

Born: Forest Gate, London. 10.8.01
Lge apps: 129 (58 gls)
Cup: 9 (5 gls)

■ As an amateur, he appeared in the line-up as "V.W.T. Gibbins," to distinguish him from the pro's who were not then given Christian names

Gerry Gazzard

Gerry Gazzard, Harry Kinsell and Bert Hawkins sharing some of the groundman's duties.

in programme details. A pupil of Godwin Road School and like that other great West Ham United and England amateur international before him, Harry Stapley, Viv became a schoolmaster by profession and also a centre-forward for club and country. The last of the great amateurs imbued with the Corinthian spirit to serve the club, he became the first from the non-paid ranks since WW1 to head a League club's scoring lists by topping Hammers' goalscoring charts with 18 goals in 1930/31. Making his debut v Aston Villa on Boxing Day 1923, Viv found the pace of First Division soccer somewhat faster than that which he had experienced previously with local amateurs Clapton, but nevertheless laid on the only goal of the match for Billy Moore. His pen-picture in a 1925/26 Club Handbook gives some idea of the esteem in which he was held at the Boleyn: "The name of Gibbins is a household word in London football, and it is our great regret that he cannot assist us regularly, for we would always find a place for him." The writer of those notes must have been happy when Vivian decided to play permanently for West Ham United in 1927/28 while still retaining his amateur status, but not so pleased when he transferred to Brentford (19.2.32). Retiring from his post as headmaster at Harold Road School in the early 1970's, he kept his interest in the game alive by watching local schools' football and occasional visits to Upton Park. One of the last amateurs to gain full England recognition when he was capped while with Clapton v France in 1924 and 1925, he left an impression on the French by scoring three times in the two matches. He also won FA Amateur Cup winners' medals with Clapton in the same two years, and was a losing finalist with Leyton in 1934, whom he had joined following spells with Bristol Rovers and Southampton, after leaving Brentford in cs 1932. He joined his last club Catford Wanderers in 1934, retiring in 1939. Died at Herne Bay 21.11.79.

Vivian Gibbins

GLOVER, Horace   1911-12

Born: Ashford, Kent. 1883
SL apps: 29
Cup apps: 5

■ A sturdy left-back signed from Southampton, Horace made his first appearance for his new team in the fourth match of the 1911/12 season v Reading at Upton Park; the 5-0 win providing a perfect start. He managed to hold on to the number three shirt for most of the season in the SL matches and was an ever-present in Hammers' five-match FA Cup run that campaign. His main claim to fame while a Hammer came against the team which ended that run - Swindon - when he conceded two own goals in the replayed cup-tie at the County Ground, which was lost 4-0. An architect's assistant during his early career as an amateur with Ashford, Hastings and St. Leonards, he went to Saints on the recommendation of former player Jimmy Yates. He went straight into Southampton's SL side and made 174 SL and cup appearances and scored four goals between 1906/11. He was made team captain at The Dell in 1909 and played for Boscombe after leaving Irons in 1912. He lived within earshot of The Dell in later years and died at Winchester 28.1.67.

GODDARD, J.   1913-14

SL apps: 1

■ A left-back who played his solitary game in Hammers' SL side in the 4-1 defeat at Swindon (27.12.13) when Syd Puddefoot scored West Ham's goal. His place was taken the following match by Frank 'Bronco' Burton, who held the position to the end of the season.

GODDARD, Paul   1980-86

Born: Harlington, Middlesex. 12.10.59
Lge apps: 170 (54 gls)
Cup apps: 43 (17 gls)

■ Stocky striker who created a slice of history on his one and only full England international appearance v Iceland (2.6.82). Paul, who ran on to Glenn Hoddle's pass to net the 69th minute equaliser on a frozen pitch in the 1-1 draw in Reykjavik, became the only England player to score while playing less than a full match (he subbed for the injured Cyrille Regis). Paul was signed by John Lyall for a club record £800,000 from Queens Park Rangers in Aug. 1980. He had impressed the previous season by scoring 16 goals alongside Clive Allen, having made his First Division debut for Rangers as sub v Arsenal in Apr. 1978 (Phil Parkes was in goal for QPR

Paul Goddard

that day). Made his Hammers' debut v Liverpool in the Charity Shield at Wembley and went on to prove a valuable asset. In his first season with Hammers "Sarge" - as he was known to his team mates after his Boys' Brigade days - netted 17 goals in a formidable partnership with David Cross that proved the cutting edge to West Ham's record-breaking Second Division championship term. He also played a key role in the 1980/81 League Cup campaign, scoring in the semi-final second leg v Coventry City at Upton Park and in the final replay v Liverpool at Villa Park, which Hammers lost 2-1. The following season the muscular, diminutive, striker finished just one goal behind Cross, on 15, although he top-scored in 1982/83 with 10. It was midway through that season when Tony Cottee burst upon the scene and his sensational pairing with Frank McAvennie - who arrived in the summer of 1985 - severely restricted Sarge's first team chances. Injuries also took their toll and it was after dislocating his shoulder at Birmingham City in the opening game of the 1985/86 season that Paul lost his place to McAvennie, who maintained remarkable goalscoring form throughout Hammers' best-ever season. For Paul, there was only bench-warming duty. After his 31 minutes at St. Andrews, he did not start another League match all season, and made just five appearances as sub. His only goal came in a memorable 8-1 demolition of Newcastle United at Upton Park. Paul added just one more goal to his tally, at Norwich City (18.10.86), before his final appearance, in the live TV game v Everton at Upton Park (2.11.86). Paul then became West Ham's double record transfer-breaker when, frustrated at the lack of chances, he moved to Newcastle United (7.11.86) in a £415,000 deal - Hammers' biggest transfer receipt at that time. The blond, clean-cut Sarge spent only 15 months in the North-East before another big-money move to Derby County for £425,000. But, just a season-and-a-half-later, Paul was back in London with Millwall, who paid Derby £800,000 for his services in Dec. 1989. It was an expensive buy for the Lions, who released him on a free transfer to Ipswich Town a little over two years later having played only 20 League matches. John Lyall, who was criticised in some quarters at West Ham for allowing Paul to leave when he was pressurising Cottee and McAvennie for their places, was delighted to be reunited with him at Portman Road. And Sarge responded by helping Ipswich to win promotion to the Premier League in his second season in Suffolk. In the summer of 1994, he and another experienced pro, John Wark, were appointed by general manager Lyall as the new first team coaches at Ipswich.

☆ **England cap:** *1982 v Iceland (sub) (1)*

GOODACRE, Reg   1931-33

Born: Boston, Lincolnshire
Lge apps: 20

■ A Lincolnshire lad who had three seasons at Upton Park after signing from non-league Boston United. Usually employed in the right-back position, Reg was the cousin of a more famous pro, Eric Houghton, the Aston Villa left-winger, capped seven times by England. Making his debut v Manchester United at Old Trafford in Feb. 1931, Reg proved an invaluable deputy for Hammers' more experienced backs, and gave the club good service until his move to Mansfield Town.

GORDON, Dale   1993-

Born: Great Yarmouth, Norfolk. 9.1.67.
Lge apps: 8 (1 gl)
Cup apps: 1

■ Major £750,000 signing by Billy Bonds in the summer of 1993, Dale still has everything to prove to people at Upton Park after a dismal first year ravaged by injury. Scored Hammers' first-ever FA Carling Premiership goal in the 1-1 draw at Coventry City (21.8.93) but he was plagued by persistent knee problems and made only nine first team appearances. Dale, nicknamed "Flash" for his flamboyant dress-sense and ball trickery, made his name as a dazzling right-winger with his local club, Norwich City, and went on to represent England at Schoolboy, Youth, Under-21 and 'B' level. He was Player of the Year in Canaries'

Dale Gordon

successful 1988/89 campaign (fourth in Division One) but after 206 League (31 gls) and 40 cup (9 gls) appearances, he moved to Glasgow Rangers for £1.2 million in Nov. 1992. Celebrated his debut by scoring twice at Dunfermline Athletic (9.11.91) and was a first team regular (28 games, five gls) as Rangers romped to the Premier League title. But in a large Ibrox squad of proven internationals and big-name stars, Dale found it difficult to hold down a regular first team spot in his second season in Scotland. A recurrence of a shoulder injury, sustained during his Carrow Road days, didn't help his cause, limiting him to 22 League games in 1992/93 (1 gl) as the championship was retained in style. Competition for places was further intensified by the foreign player rule which restricted Dale to one European Cup game, at Leeds United. He jumped at the chance of moving back to England, making his West Ham debut in the opening game of 1993/94 v Wimbledon (14.8.93).

WILLS'S CIGARETTES

1. GOULDEN (WEST HAM UNITED)

GORE, Reg   1938-39

Born: Henthorne, Lancashire
Lge apps: 5 (1 gl)

■ Scoring on his debut against Bradford at Park Avenue, this useful left-winger won the right to keep his place for the remaining four fixtures of the 1938-39 season on the strength of that display. Big for a winger, he joined West Ham from his local works side, Frickley Colliery.

GOULD, Bobby   1973-75

Born: Coventry. 12.6.46
Lge apps: 51 (15 gls)
Cup apps: 7 (4 gls)

■ A great-hearted competitor whose signing from Bristol City coincided with a big uplift of team-spirit at Upton Park, culminating in the 1975 FA Cup Final triumph. A much-travelled striker, his list of clubs includes: Coventry City, Arsenal, Wolves, West Bromwich Albion, Bristol City, Hammers, Wolves again, Bristol Rovers, Hereford United, Chelsea, Wimbledon, Aldershot. Then manager of Coventry City, but went back in charge of Bristol Rovers before managing Wimbledon to their shock 1988 FA Cup Final success over Liverpool. Moved back to boss Coventry in 1992 after an unhappy spell in charge at West Bromwich Albion. Now a TV pundit.

Bobby Gould

GOULDEN, Len   1933-39

Born: Hackney, London. 16.7.12.
Lge apps: 239 (54 gls)
Cup apps: 14 (1 gl)

■ Although it is not necessarily the intention in this work to seek to determine Hammers all-time greats, the name of Len Goulden would inevitably figure high on any list of that nature. Born in Hackney, he moved a few miles nearer to the scene of his eventual triumphs when his family went to Plaistow three years later. One of the most revered of all manager Charlie Paynter's discoveries, he graduated through his school side to West Ham Boys and then to England Schoolboys, playing against Wales and Scotland in 1926. Len signed amateur forms for Hammers as early as 1931, but as there was no youth team in those days he was farmed out to Chelmsford, and later Leyton, to gain experience. During the summer months in this period Len worked on the redevelopment of Highbury Stadium which was being transformed into the finest football arena in the country at the time. As Len laboured concreting the terraces he was openly envious of the Arsenal players as they trained on the pitch. Little could he have realised then that his own son, Roy, would one day play for the famous Gunners, and later Southend. But back to dad. Returning to Upton Park towards the end of 1932/33 he went straight into the League side, after signing pro, against Charlton Athletic at The Valley to commence a much-talked about partnership with the legendary Jimmy Ruffell from the inside-left berth. He became an automatic choice and despite the fact that Hammers were in the Second Division, his impressive displays drew the attention of the England selectors, culminating in the first of his 20 appearances for his country (v Ireland in 1937). His ability to take as well as create chances was much in evidence during his outings for England in overseas internationals, getting him on the score-sheet in the 6-0 victory v Norway in Oslo in 1937; v Germany in Berlin in 1938 when the England team were duped into giving the Nazi salute before the match; and also v Romania, during the longest tour undertaken by England at that time. The nearest he got to a major honour with West Ham was a member of the side which won the Football League War Cup with a 1-0 victory over Blackburn Rovers at Wembley in 1940. During the conflict he joined the police force and continued to play for Irons and his country in what matches could be arranged. He also made guest appearances for Chelsea (winning a Football League South Cup winners' medal in 1945), which paved the way for his eventual transfer to Stamford Bridge after WW2. Although Hammers' management of that time were reluctant to part with their biggest star, they did not want to stand in the way of one who had served them so well. So Len stepped up to the First Division stage with the

Pensioners without any recriminations from either direction for a reported fee of £5,000. He joined the Blues in time to appear against the legendary Moscow Dynamos in 1945, and had five happy years with them as a player in the top flight, without, alas, winning any medals. He played 111 league and cup matches in which he scored 19 times. The nearest he came to appearing at Wembley again was when Chelsea were pipped by Arsenal in an FA Cup semi-final replay at White Hart Lane in 1950; a situation which was repeated two years later with Len in a non-playing role as coach to the West Londoners. In the summer of 1952 he took up the manager's job with Watford, remaining in that capacity until 1956. Then there followed a period of seven years out of full-time football when he worked as a postmaster; but the lure of the game proved too strong and Hammers' former star subseqeuntly took off to North Africa for two years to fulfil a coaching commitment. When he returned to England he was appointed manager to little Banbury Town for a similar period, and then coached Oxford United reserves until 1969. After that he worked at a U.S.A.F. base in Northamptonshire while living at nearby Fritwell in Oxfordshire. He still retained his allegiance to Hammers, however, watching his old team whenever he could when they played in the Midlands. It must have seemed strange to Len when he moved to Cornwall to retire... a county without a single Football League club. In his hey-day he played with the outstanding players of London football. Men of the calibre of Vic Watson, Jimmy Ruffell, Jackie Morton and Archie Macaulay at Upton Park... at Chelsea, the two Tommies, Walker and Lawton. With his midfield mastery and ability to change the point of attack with devastatingly accurate crossfield passes to the opposite flank, he was well at home in such esteemed company. Still living just a short distance from the Upton Park ground, you could safely say Len Goulden was one of the "Greats".

☆ **England caps:** *1937 v Sweden, Norway, Wales, Northern Ireland, Czechoslovakia; 1938 v Germany, Switzerland, France, Wales, Rest of Europe; 1939 v Italy, Scotland, Romania, Yugoslavia (14).*

Played	League		FAC		LC		Europe		Total	
	App	Gls	App	Gls	App	Gls	App	Gls	App	Gls
1932-33	7	1	0	0	0	0	0	0	7	1
1933-34	40	7	2	1	0	0	0	0	42	7
1934-35	40	3	2	0	0	0	0	0	42	3
1935-36	38	15	2	0	0	0	0	0	40	15
1936-37	42	15	2	0	0	0	0	0	44	15
1937-38	35	9	1	0	0	0	0	0	36	9
1938-39	37	4	5	0	0	0	0	0	42	4
TOTAL	**239**	**54**	**14**	**1**	**0**	**0**	**0**	**0**	**253**	**55**

GRASSAM, William   1900-1910

Born: Larbert, Scotland. 20.11.1880
SL apps: 169 (65 gls)
Cup apps: 10 (3 gls)

Len Goulden

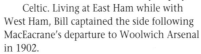

W. GRASSAM,
WEST HAM UNITED.

■ Billy began his career in Glasgow junior soccer with Redcliffe Thistle before joining Maryhill in 1897, where his early enthusiasm for the game was rewarded by the latter club with a medal for "regular training." After playing in county matches and an international trial for Scotland, he came south to join Burslem Port Vale in 1899, staying a year in the Potteries before signing for the newly-formed West Ham United at the turn of the century. A goal-scoring in-side-right, Bill scored four goals in a Southern League match v Gravesend on his debut (1.9.1900), thus becoming the first Hammer to score a hat-trick. He was also the first Hammer to score three goals in an FA Cup tie, a feat he achieved against Clapton in Dec. 1900. After three seasons at the Memorial Grounds he signed for Manchester United but by 1905/06 was back in East London after spells at Glasgow Celtic and Leyton. It is believed that he went back to his home city to play for Celtic. Living at East Ham while with West Ham, Bill captained the side following MacEacrane's departure to Woolwich Arsenal in 1902.

GREAVES, Jimmy   1970-71

Born: East Ham, London. 20.2.40
Lge apps: 38 (13 gls)
Cup apps: 2

■ Already a living legend when he arrived at Upton Park as a £54,000 make-weight in the deal that took Martin Peters to Tottenham, Jimmy was, quite simply, the greatest goalscorer in the world. The fact that he had performed his finest feats and was past his best when he came to West Ham didn't really matter; it was almost enough for many fans just to see him in a claret-and-blue shirt. He characteristically kept up his record of scoring on every debut by giving Manchester City a double dose of the old 'Greavesie' magic when making his first appearance for Hammers at

Maine Road in Mar. 1970. West Ham won 5-1 that day, typical of the effect Jimmy had on new team-mates. Although his performances the next season fell short of the very high standard he had set earlier with Chelsea, AC Milan and Spurs, one can't help feeling, with the benefit of hindsight, that he retired too soon. An England Youth International, Jimmy made his League debut for Chelsea at the age of 17. He scored in the first match of the season, a 1-1 draw against Tottenham, to begin a habit of scoring on his debut for every club he played for. It was the first of 357 goals he scored in the Football League, all of them in the First Division. His 41 in 1960-61 still stands as Blues' League record. Capped 11 times at England Under-23 level, Jimmy earned his first full cap in Peru (17.5.59). He stayed with Chelsea until June 1961 when he joined A.C. Milan in Italy. Despite the notoriously tough Italian defences, Jimmy still netted on his debut and went on to score nine goals in 14 matches. But this effervescent cockney character soon tired of the strict disciplines of Italian football life and was delighted to make a rapid return to England in Dec. 1961, when he joined Spurs for £99,999 (Bill Nicholson denying him the distinction of becoming the first £100,000 British footballer!). The North London club (Jimmy's favourite team as a boy) certainly got their money's worth from the naturally gifted marksman. Greavsie celebrated his debut with a hat-trick and quickly turned the talented Tottenham double side into one of the most exciting in Europe. A member of Spurs' FA Cup-winning teams of 1962 (scoring the first goal) and 1967, he also scored twice in the European Cup Winners' Cup triumph of 1963. His 37 League goals in 1962/63 still remains a Spurs' club record, as do his totals of 220 League and 32 FA Cup goals. When he topped the First Division scoring chart in 1964/65 Jimmy became the first player to do so in three consecutive seasons. And he also holds the record of top-scoring in the First Division on six occasions. In his time at White Hart Lane, Jimmy gained 42 full England caps (28 goals) but, unfortunately, hepatitis caused him to miss England's greatest victory. He played in the early stages of the 1966 World Cup Finals but had not fully recovered from illness and Geoff Hurst replaced him for the later stages. In Mar. 1970 Jimmy and Geoff became team-mates at Upton Park, as Greavsie moved back to East London. But despite scoring twice on his debut for the Hammers at Manchester City, and netting another 11 in 38 games, he retired at the end of the 1970/71 season at the age of only 31. It is a measure of Jimmy Greaves' greatness that a crowd of 45,799 turned out to pay tribute at his testimonial game v Feyenoord at White Hart Lane in October 1972. Jimmy found it very difficult to cope soon after his playing days were finished, but he successfully beat the threat of alcoholism and now, football fans everywhere know Jimmy as the cheeky soccer pundit who has established a successful career for himself as a leading TV personality and after-dinner speaker.

GREEN, Bill

1976-78

Born: Newcastle-upon-Tyne. 22.12.50
Lge apps: 35 (1 gl)
Cup apps: 5

■ A £100,000 signing from Carlisle United who had a promising First Division career badly disrupted by injuries. A giant centre-half, he joined the Brunton Park club from unfashionable Hartlepool and played a major role in the Cumbrians' promotion to Division One in 1974. The unlucky Geordie was sold to Peterborough United for £90,000 in 1978 and later played for Chesterfield. Appointed manager of non-league Buxton in October 1994.

GREEN, Tommy

1919

Lge apps: 3

■ A left-winger signed by manager Syd King from Southport, Tom was an unfortunate debutant in the record 7-0 hammering at Barnsley (1.9.19), but switched to inside-left for his other two Second Division outings, at Rotherham County and v Stoke City at Upton Park.

GREEN, Tommy

1936-39

Born: Droitwich, Worcestershire. 1913
Lge apps: 40 (6 gls)
Cup apps: 4

■ A scheming inside-foward, Tommy made his Hammers' debut v Bradford City (5.12.36) in the shadow of the Main Stand at Valley Parade which burnt down with such tragic conse-quences in 1985. Signed from West Bromwich Albion, he returned to Bradford on Christmas Day to do battle with the City's other foot-balling denizens, the now defunct Park Avenue, scoring his first goal for West Ham in a 2-1 defeat. Providing invaluable cover for both the inside-forward berths, Tom remained at Upton Park until 1938, when he joined Coventry, scoring two goals in nine games in the Third Division South. He began his career with Droitwich Spa and then Droitwich Comrades before joining WBA whom he also guested for during WW2. Won junior international honours in 1932. Tom was living in the pleasant Herefordshire town of Bromyard in the early 90's.

Tommy Green

GREGORY, Ernie

1946-60

Born: Stratford, London. 10.11.21
Lge apps: 382
Cup apps: 24

■ The longest-serving member on the Upton Park staff, Ernie actually joined the ground-staff in 1936 - one year before that other great club servant, Eddie Chapman. Catching the attention of Charlie Paynter when he appeared for the West Ham Boys team which met Preston in the English Trophy Final at the Boleyn Ground (the Northerners had Tom Finney as 12th man!), it proved to be the beginning of an association that lasted a record-breaking 50 years. Winner of an Isthmian League Championship medal as an amateur with Leytonstone, this great goalkeeper first appeared for Hammers in their Midweek League team in 1938. It was another eight years before he made his League debut v Plymouth Argyle at Upton Park in Dec. 1946, due to serving in the Essex Regt. and RA during WW2. A regular member of the 1958 promotion side, he received the Football League Long-service statuette when he retired. He then became coach to the reserves and later first team, specialising in the art of goalkeeping. Also helped with general coaching and team administration, and received a special award for 50 years' service. Ernie could have transferred to Arsenal in the mid-fifties and would surely have added full international recognition to his solitary England 'B' cap, v France in 1952, in the higher profile of the First Division, but he decided to remain loyal to Hammers. Making his final West Ham appearance v Leeds United at the Boleyn in Sept. 1959, he was awarded a fully deserved testimonial match the following year, v the LDA club of Costa Rica. Ernie officially 'retired' in May 1987, after completing 51 years exceptional service to his one and only club. Still a regular visitor to Upton Park and often to be seen at the training ground putting today's young 'keepers through their paces!.

Played	League		FAC		LC		Europe		Total	
	App	Gls	App	Gls	App	Gls	App	Gls	App	Gls
1946-47	9	0	0	0	0	0	0	0	9	0
1947-48	42	0	2	0	0	0	0	0	44	0
1948-49	27	0	1	0	0	0	0	0	28	0
1949-50	42	0	2	0	0	0	0	0	44	0
1950-51	30	0	2	0	0	0	0	0	32	0
1951-52	28	0	3	0	0	0	0	0	31	0
1952-53	42	0	1	0	0	0	0	0	43	0
1953-54	27	0	3	0	0	0	0	0	30	0
1954-55	0	0	0	0	0	0	0	0	0	0
1955-56	36	0	6	0	0	0	0	0	42	0
1956-57	29	0	0	0	0	0	0	0	29	0
1957-58	37	0	3	0	0	0	0	0	40	0
1958-59	32	0	1	0	0	0	0	0	33	0
1959-60	1	0	0	0	0	0	0	0	1	0
TOTAL	**382**	**0**	**24**	**0**	**0**	**0**	**0**	**0**	**406**	**0**

Ernie Gregory saves at the feet of Fulham's Roy Dwight

GREGORY, John 1951-53

Born: Shoreditch, London. 24.9.26
Lge apps: 24 (6 gls)
Cup apps: 1

■ A former England amateur international who played his early soccer with Hackney and Middlesex Boys before progressing to senior amateur status with Bromley, and later Hayes. Remained an amateur when joining the Boleyn club for the 1950/51 season, but signed full pro the following campaign when he made the first of 24 League appearances. Transferred to Scunthorpe United, he scored a lot of goals for the other Irons, before moving on to Aldershot. He later became player/coach to St. Neots Town.

GRESHAM, George 1895-98

Born: 1875
SL apps: (TIW) 15

■ An inside-forward, George was the first of many players to join Thames Ironworks/West Ham United from Gainsborough Trinity. In addition to appearing at least 15 times in the Ironworks' first season, he also turned out in three FA Cup ties in 1897/98. Scored twice v Arsenal XI in a friendly (16.3.1896).

GRICE, Mike 1955-61

Born: Woking, Surrey. 3.11.31
Lge apps: 142 (17 gls)
Cup apps: 8 (1 gl)

■ Another member of the 1958 promotion-winning side, this blond-haired flying winger made a big contribution to that success. A maker, rather than a taker, of goals, he provided the perfect complement to his opposite flankman, Mal Musgrove. Signed from Colchester United for £10,000, he moved to Coventry City for the 1961/62 season where he scored six goals in 38 Third Division games before falling out with Jimmy Hill and returning to Layer Road the following year to end his League days with the Essex club. Mike was still scoring regularly for Lowestoft in the Eastern Counties League in 1966, where he had fellow ex-Hammer Albert Foan on the opposite flank.

GRIFFITHS, Frederick 1902-04

Born: Presteigne, South Wales. 1876.
SL apps: 48
Cup apps: 4

■ The son of a Presteigne coal merchant, Fred commenced his career in Welsh junior football but began at senior level with South Shore in 1894, then Clitheroe in 1896 before returning to South Shore in 1887 and was with them when they amalgamated with Blackpool in 1899. In an age when big goalkeepers were fashionable, Fred's towering 6ft 2in frame

Michael Grice

and 15st bulk must have provided a daunting sight for opposing forwards. Capped at full international level by Wales in 1900 on three occasions v England and Scotland (twice) while with Blackpool. He was the first Blackpool player to win an international cap, an honour he held for 20 years, and also served Stalybridge, Millwall, Preston North End and Tottenham before joining Hammers. Managing only nine Southern League appearances with Spurs in 1901/02, Fred fared far better upon his move to the Memorial Grounds, when, after taking over from William Biggar following a disastrous 5-1 reverse at Wellingborough Town, he made the first team spot more or less his own for the next two seasons before moving on to New Brompton cs 1904 and Middlesex in 1906. Fred later worked as a coalminer at Shirebrook where he trained the Central Alliance team. He fell in France on October 30, 1917 fighting for his country in the Great War while serving with Sherwood Foresters.

Peter Grotier

Billy Guest

GROTIER, Peter   1969-74

Born: Stratford, London. 18.10.50
Lge apps: 50
Cup apps: 4

■ So great was the impression this capable 'keeper made when transferred on loan to Lincoln City that the Imps' fans whipped round to raise the £16,666 necessary for his permanent transfer! Always a useful contender for Bobby Ferguson's first team place at Hammers, he had earlier been loaned to Cardiff City before moving to Sincil Bank. As reserve-team coach at Grimsby, he made a sensational return between the posts when he turned out for the Mariners' home FA Cup tie v Watford in 1985 - at the age of 36!

GUEST, Billy   1936-37

Born: Denaby, Yorks. 8.2.13
Lge apps: 3 (1 gl)

■ A collier who played part-time for Denaby United, Bill joined Hammers as a left-winger from the Yorkshire club in Mar. 1936. In an era when the club had such luminaries as Jimmy Ruffell, Stan Foxall and Johnny Morton available as flank players, he found it difficult to hold down a regular Second Division place and had only a brief sojourn at Upton Park before transferring to Birmingham FC. He joined Blackburn Rovers in 1938 and was on duty for Rovers v Hammers in the 1940 League War Cup Final at Wembley. After WW2 he saw service with Blackburn and Walsall. Bill passed away in Nov. 1973, aged 60. Not to be confused with the player of the same name who also played for Brum and Warwickshire C.C.

GUNNING, Harry   1952-53

Born: Leigh-on-Sea, Essex. 8.2.32
Lge apps: 1

■ This outside-left made only one appearance in the first team, away to Lincoln City in May 1953. Signed from Gravesend, he later made 62 League outings for Crystal Palace, whom he joined from Hammers. Had one season with Reading before signing for Guildford City in the Southern League.

GURKIN, John   1921

Born: Murton, Co. Durham. 9.9.1895

■ Signed from South Hetton Rovers, this centre-half was given only one first team outing - in a 0-2 reverse at the Victoria Ground v Stoke City - before transferring to Norwich City. In 1923 he transferred to Stalybridge Celtic and the following season joined Durham City. In Aug. 1928 he rejoined Stalybridge. From May 1929 to Sept. 1932 he was with Jarrow and ended his playing days with his home town team, Murton.

HALES, Derek 1977-78

Born: Lower Halstow. 15.12.51
Lge apps: 24 (10 gls)
Cup apps: 3

■ Striker with an insatiable appetite for scoring goals, he was snapped up by Charlton Athletic from Luton Town for a bargain fee and later transferred to Derby County for £300,000 - the highest ever paid for a Second Division player at that time. Hammers got him for a third of that price, but the player found it hard to settle at the Boleyn and he returned to The Valley the following year. Then moved to Gillingham. Character-wise he was an extrovert, who had a happy-go-lucky out-look on life. The son of former Gillingham centre-forward William Hales.

HALL, Almeric George 1946-49

Born: Hove, Sussex. 12.11.12
Lge apps: 50 (11 gls)
Cup apps: 6 (3 gls)

■ A clever inside-forward who had seen service with Brighton, Spurs, Southend and Bradford City before the war. Formerly a prodigy with Southwick, Brighton and England Schools, Almer signed for West Ham in Dec. 1945 from the Bradford club whom he had also served during WW2. He made his official Hammers' debut at Plymouth Argyle on the day that League soccer got back to normal on 31.8.46. But he had also appeared in 44 war-time League

Almeric Hall

and Cup matches, scoring 25 goals. He scored twice on his Spurs debut v Grimsby Town on Boxing Day, 1934, but the win was Spurs' last before a fateful run of 16 matches without another victory that saw Hall dropped and the North Londoners relegated at the end of the season. He played just four matches the next campaign, but remained at White Hart Lane until Apr. 1937 when he moved to Southend United after scoring eight times in 24 League and Cup games for Spurs. He hit 10 goals in 41 League Division South and cup games for the Shrimpers.

HALLAS, Geoff 1954-55

Born: Lydgate, Lancashire. 8.12.30
Lge apps: 4

■ Promising young full-back who had his career tragically terminated when he developed eye trouble. Signed from Warminster in March 1954, he was granted a joint testimonal by the club along with Brian Moore, who suffered a similar fate.

HAMILTON, John 1904-05

Born: Glasgow, Scotland. 1880
Lge apps: 5

■ This right-winger was one of two forward-line changes imposed by manager Syd King in an abortive attempt to halt a mid-season slump. Coming into the side v Portsmouth at Fratton Park, along with centre-forward John Blackwood, on Boxing Day 1904, Hammers presented Pompey with a post-Christmas gift in the form of a 4-1 scoreline, although his co-debutant scored Hammers' goal. He was in for the next three matches, all 1-0 defeats, one playing at inside-right. His West Ham career ended on a happier note, though, in a 3-0 victory over Watford at Vicarage Road. John was with London rivals Millwall (1902/03) and Queen's Park Rangers (1903/04).

HAMMOND, Syd 1904-08

Born: Woolwich, London
Lge apps: 32
Cup apps: 2

■ Right or left-back, Syd made his 34 first team appearances thinly spread over four seasons - quite a long stint at a time when the club were operating a 'revolving door' policy. A debutant in the 1-0 defeat at Tottenham (21.1.05), his final appearance came in another away defeat, 0-3 at manager Syd King's former club, New Brompton (7.4.08). A commercial clerk by profession, Syd joined Irons as an amateur after learning the game with Leyton National School, Leyton Ashville, Leyton Rovers, Leyton and Woodford. Occasionally playing at centre-forward in his early career, he played for Woodford v Clapton in the final of the West Ham Charity Cup in 1902.

HAMPSON, Tommy 1920-25

Born: Bury, Lancashire. 20.5.1898
Lge apps: 70
Cup: 9

Tommy Hampson

■ Signed from South Shields to understudy Ted Hufton, he proved to be a shrewd capture and an able deputy when the great man suffered a serious knee injury in 1923/24. Showing form far superior to his performances in the reserves, Tommy took his chance, literally, with both hands, with the result that Ted was hardly missed. Later joined Blackburn Rovers.

HARRIS, Jimmy 1930-32

Born: Tunbridge Wells, Kent. 1907
Lge apps: 7 (1 gl)

■ Normally a left-winger, Jimmy made his West Ham debut in the inside-left position in a 4-3 victory over Portsmouth on Christmas Day 1930 at Upton Park. Signed from Kent League Folkestone, he made a further four First Division appearances that season and two more the next before moving on to Southampton in July 1932, for whom he made his debut at Millwall (27/8/1932). He only made one more first team appearance and after playing 44 combination games and scoring eight goals, he was given a free transfer.

HARRISON, Fred 1910-13

Born: Winchester, Hants. 2.7.1880
SL apps: 54 (19 gls)
Cup apps: 8 (4 gls)

■ Signed from Fulham with team-mate George Redwood, Fred got off to a flying start in Hammers' colours by scoring on his debut on Good Friday, 1911 against one of his former clubs, Southampton, in a 4-1 win at the Boleyn. Also played several games at centre-half for Hammers, notably the 1913 FA Cup tie v Aston Villa. Discovered by a famous Saints player, Joe Turner, when he spotted Fred playing on Southampton Common, "Buzzy", as he was known by his adoring Dell public, was soon knocking in the goals. A product of local Hampshire clubs Fitzhugh Rovers and Bitterne Guild, Fred scored five goals in consecutive SL games v Wellingborough Town and Northampton Town at the Dell in 1902/03 and ended the season with 17 goals from just 13 matches. The following campaign he netted 27 times in 32 games as Saints clinched the Southern League Championship and he earned an England trial. Altogether he scored 88 goals in 166 SL and Cup appearances for Saints. In 1907 Fulham offered the the huge sum of £1,000 to take him and a team mate to Craven Cottage which was duly accepted. He had two- and-a-half seasons at Hammers before transferring to Bristol City in Aug. 1913. After being gassed during action in WW1, he set up a master plasterers business in Southampton. He died in 1969, aged 89.

HART, J.   1921

Born: Bulwell, Notts

■ This right-back made only one League appearance - in a 1-1 draw v Port Vale at the Boleyn during Hammers' second season as a Football League club in 1921. Later with Millwall.

HARTLEY, Trevor   1966-68

Born: Doncaster, Yorkshire. 16.3.47
Lge apps: 5

■ Joined from Holloway School 1.7.64. Speedy, fair-haired winger who made a handful of First Division appearances. Was granted a move to Bournemouth for a small fee to enable him to pursue regular first team soccer. A brother-in-law, incidentally, of fellow former Hammer - Bobby Howe. Trevor later managed the Cherries for a short time in 1974 (when he took over from John Bond) and at the age of 27, was the youngest manager in the Football League until his departure after a year at Dean Court. Became assistant to David Pleat at Luton Town, subsequently moving with David to Tottenham Hotspur in May 1986. Recently appointed coach at Sunderland.

PROMINENT FOOTBALLERS.

A. HARWOOD,
WEST HAM UNITED.

HARWOOD, Alfred   1907-09

Born: Bishop Auckland. 16.5.1881
SL apps: 12

■ Alf was a centre-forward with Fulham before transferring to the fore-runners of Leeds United - Leeds City - in May 1906, but stayed at the Old Peacock Ground (now Elland Road) for just one season before joining Hammers in the 1907 cs. With only one Second Division appearance, albeit a scoring one, to show for his time in Yorkshire (although he had scored over 40 times for City's reserves), he fared better at Upton Park after being converted to left-back and making his debut in that position in a 1-0 victory at Reading (23.11.07). Alf began his career with famous amateurs Crook Town, winning an FA Amateur Cup winners' medal in 1900/01. He then moved to Bishop Auckland with whom he gained a losers medal in the same competition in 1901/02. Represented the Northern League; Southern League (Div. 2), two London League and West Yorkshire Cup medals. Alf was one of several Hammers' players affected by a wholesale clear-out of playing staff in the cs of 1909.

HAWKINS, Bert   1951-53

Born: Bristol. 29.9.23
Lge apps: 34 (16 gls)
Cup: 3

■ Enjoyed a brief, but spectacular, stay at Upton Park following his transfer from Southern League Bath City, where he was on loan from Bristol City. He scored on his debut

for Hammers in a 1-1 draw v Hull City at Boothferry Park, and went on to net 15 goals in 32 Second Division appearances during that 1951-52 campaign. Not bad for a player plucked from the obscurity of non-league football. He sustained an injury in a pre-season practice match, however, and failed to regain a regular place; moving on instead to London rivals QPR where he met with further success.

HAY, Sam   TIW

Born: Renfrewshire, Scotland

■ Strongly-built inside-right. Played in the Ironworks' first season at Hermit Road in 1895/96 when he was a regular choice after joining from Victoria.

HAYNES, Vincent   1909-10

Born: 1887
Lge apps: 15 (5 gls)

■ A six-foot centre-forward signed from Crewe Alexander, Vince scored in his second match for Hammers in a 3-1 win at Norwich in September 1909. His five goals in 15 SL outings were a fair return, but he had George Webb to contend with as a rival for the number nine shirt. He

Trevor Hartley

Bert Hawkins

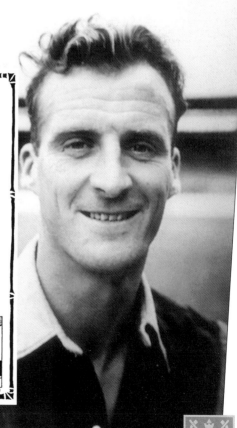

subseqeuntly lost the battle and after making his last appearance in a 5-0 defeat at Swindon on the final Saturday of the 1909/10 season, he transferred to West Bromwich Albion.

HEATH, Robert   1897-98 TIW

■ Goalkeeper signed from West Ham Garfield after assisting that club in winning the West Ham Charity Cup against TIW in Apr. 1897.

HEBDEN, Jack   1921-27

Born: Castleford, Yorkshire
Lge apps: 110
Cup apps: 6

■ This strong-tackling full-back joined Hammers from Bradford City in May 1921 in time to make his debut against South Shields as partner to Billy Cope on the last day of the season. After recovering from a bad injury sustained during the following campaign, Jack settled down to figure consistently in the First Division side during the mid-twenties and was appointed skipper in 1926/27. Leaving West Ham for Fulham in 1928, along with fellow full-back George Horler, for a combined fee of £850, he later captained Thames FC, who played at the old West Ham Stadium in Prince Regent Lane. Disbanded in 1933 because of crippling debts, Thames' problems were evident as early as 6.12.30. when they sent out the smallest cheque ever received as a share of an away gate to Luton Town. The attendance for the Third Division South fixture was 469 and Luton's cheque was for 1s 8d. But back to Jack. The demise of the Thames club saw him continue his League career with Clapton Orient and then Halifax Town. He continued to play in local soccer and found employment at the Electricity Works in Nelson Street, East Ham. He lived originally at 210 Central Park Road and later in Hatherley Gardens, East Ham. Jack was a good friend of George Robson (who later joined Hammers' coaching staff).

Jack Hebden

HEFFER, Paul   1967-69

Born: Upton Park, London. 21.12.47
Lge apps: 15
Cup apps: 2

■ Born within earshot of the "Upton Park Roar," this tall, commanding centre-half had his promising career cut short by injury. Paul, signed as a pro in Aug. 1965, made his senior debut v Nottingham Forest in Mar. 1967 and was given a testimonial by the club when it became clear he had to give up the game. Was recently back at Chadwell Heath training the youngsters. His son, Steve, played for West Ham youth before moving on to Southend United.

HENDERSON, William   1922-28

Born: Whitburn, County Durham. 5.1.1900
Lge apps: 162
Cup apps: 21 (1 gl)

■ Like his full-back partner Jack Young, Billy was a native of Whitburn; sadly the comparison between the two players does not end there, as Billy, too, was affected by poor health and died of tuberculosis at a tragically early age in 1930. Joining Hammers from Welsh club Aberdare (then in the Second Division of the Football League) to replace the injured Jack Hebden in Jan. 1922, the well-built defender went on to win a place in the first Wembley Cup Final the following season, playing in every match leading to that famous confrontation with Bolton Wanderers. An ever-present in 1923/24,

Billy Henderson

and only one short the next campaign, he was selected for the FA v The Army and for the Professionals v Amateurs during those seasons. On the verge of international honours until a bad knee injury forced him to miss half the 1925/26 season and the whole of the next, he was given the following tribute in a club history published in 1947: "Willie was a stylist and recognised as the greatest right-back the Hammers ever had." An amazing coincidence surrounded Bill's only goal in 183 first team appearances for West Ham United. It was scored in an FA Cup-tie against his former club, Aberdare!

HILSDON, George   1904-05/1912-15

Born: Bromley-by-Bow, London. August, 1885
SL apps: 85 (31 gls)
Cup apps: 7 (4 gls)

■ "Gatling Gun" George's early career was unusual in that he was transferred from West Ham to London rivals Chelsea even though he was obviously a great prospect and had scored seven times in 16 SL appearances. A pupil of Marner St. School, with Billy Bridgeman, who later became his colleague at West Ham and Chelsea, the Hilsdon family moved to East Ham where George switched to Plashet Lane School and captained East Ham Boys to victory in the 1900/01 Corinthian Shield. Played as an amateur for Clapton Orient and Luton Town cs 1902 before Hammers after learning his trade with South West Ham and Castle Swifts. Spotted by Irons' manager Syd King playing in a Sunday League match on the eve of the 1904/05 season, the club duly signed the slimly-built 18-year-old who promptly scored four goals against Bristol Rovers in a Western League fixture. After suffering a foot injury he was seen playing for Hammers' second string by the shrewd Chelsea player/manager, John Tait Robertson, who had turned up to watch another player. In his official report on his mission the canny Scot enthused at the time: "I never even set eyes on the player I went specially to see. They were glued all the time to the inside-left, a cockney lad 19 years of age." Added to this was an amazingly accurate prophesy: "If I get him he'll be our first team centre-forward next season." And so he was. In his initial appearance for his new club, v Glossop in a Second Division fixture at Stamford Bridge, George made a sensational start by scoring five of Chelsea's nine goals. His old colleagues at West Ham showed their delight at his success when the whole team turned out to see the young sharp-shooter play for the South v the North in a trial for the England team. Within six weeks he was selected to lead the Football League attack v Irish League, scoring a hat-trick. His 26 goals for Chelsea that campaign made a major contribution to their promotion to the First Division in only their second League season. But after winning eight full England caps and once bagging six of the Pensioners' nine goals in a 1908 FA Cup romp over Worksop, George almost inevitably suffered a loss of form. His plight at this stage of his career is best summed up in an extract from Reg Groves' Official History of West Ham United in the Famous Football Clubs series, published in 1947: "After several great seasons with Chelsea, 'Gatling Gun' George had fallen on bad times. He had been too sociable, too careless with his strength and vitality and had lost his place in the Chelsea first team during season 1911/12. A sad falling off, but West Ham found a place for their former player, resigning him for season 1912/13." It proved a good move: George, who was only 26, brought a skill and experience in first-class football which proved invaluable to many up-and-coming youngsters - and his lively, jesting and good-natured humour helped a lot to keep a good team spirit. It seems there were temptations to distract top footballers from their profession even in those austere

George Hilsdon

days. But if Chelsea thought George was finished, they had made a big mistake...as their former star was to prove when he returned to neutral Stamford Bridge in January 1913 to do battle for Hammers v First Division West Bromwich Albion in an FA Cup first round play-off. Southern League Irons thrashed the Thostles 3-1, with George scoring twice on his old stamping ground to give Chelsea a timely reminder that they may have been too hasty in letting him go. As well as proving he was far from finished on the playing field, he was also spending more and more time developing the skills of the club's younger players. One he particularly helped was later to become a West Ham legend... Sydney Puddefoot. Charlie Paynter once recalled: "Yes, you could say George Hilsdon was the making of Syd." Even after the Great War (in which George was badly affected by mustard gas poisoning) the two former England centre-forwards remained close friends. Syd often popping in to the Hilsdon family home in Westbury Road (off Green Street) when he, too, returned to Upton Park in 1932. So, one way or another, George Hilsdon was responsible for the making of quite a few legends in his lifetime. He ended his

career with Gillingham, and Kent League Chatham in 1919. In 1924 George went into another brand of entertainment when he joined Fred Karno's Troup, a famous vaudeville act. George died 10.9.41.

HILSDON, Jack   1903-04

Lge apps: 1

■ The brother of George, he made a solitary appearance in an uninspiring 0-0 Memorial Ground stalemate with Luton Town (24.9.03) at inside-right. Earlier in his career his scoring exploits had rivalled those of his brother, as he scored both goals in Clapton Orient's first London League match v Barnet in Sept. 1898. He won a West Ham Charity Cup Winners' Medal with O's in Apr. 1902 when Clapton were defeated 1-0 at the Spotted Dog Ground. A month later he was in the O's side which defeated Ealing 1-0 to annexe the Middlesex Charity Cup. It set the seal on a successful last season with O's for Jack, as he joined Luton after scoring 50-plus goals for Hammers' near neighbours, including a 26 goal haul in 1901/02.

HILTON, Paul   1983-89

Born: Oldham, Lancashire. 8.10.59
Lge apps: 60 (7 gls)
Cup apps: 5

■ It was a case of: "If you can't beat 'em, join 'em!" for this tall central defender. On the receiving end of Hammers' record 10-0 League Cup thrashing of Bury in 1984, Paul made the transition from Fourth to First Division with

Tony Cottee and Paul Ince join the celebrations after a goal from Paul Hilton (left) against Tottenham

relative ease. A former England Schoolboy international in the centre-forward position ("Hilts" once scored 70 goals in a season at schoolboy level), he was snapped up by Bury after scoring a first-half hat-trick in a trial game v Newcastle United in 1977, having earlier been rejected by Lancashire rivals Blackpool. Made his League debut at Wrexham (12.8.78) and went on to make 136 League appearances for the Shakers. Transferred to West Ham in Feb. 1984 for £100,000 and made his debut v Watford (21.2.84) at Upton Park. His debut was delayed due to a freak training injury when, two days after signing, he twisted his knee and lost a tooth! Initially, Paul played in midfield to ease Hammers' injury problems, but centre-back was his more familiar role. Although he was used mainly as cover for first team regulars Alvin Martin and Tony Gale, Hilts still had plenty of senior outings, including a crucial end-of-season clash with Chelsea at Upton Park in 1987//88. His goal in the 4-1 victory proved vital in avoiding relegation. Unfortunately, Hammers could not avoid the drop a year later when big Paul's career ended. A series of cartilage and knee injuries had taken their toll and after months of battling for fitness, he received the sad news in Oct. 1989 that he would have to quit playing at the age of 31. The heartbreak was eased, however, when he was appointed youth team coach by Billy Bonds, after Bonzo stepped up from that position to first team boss in Feb. 1990, and in May 1991 he was awarded a testimonial by the club. After two seasons managing the youngsters, Hilts took charge of the reserves in 1992/93.

HINDLE, Harry   1905-06

Born: Blackburn, Lancashire. 1882
SL apps: 3

■ Harold had not made the first team in two seasons with Blackburn Rovers, but fared slightly better at the Boleyn, playing in the opening two matches of the 1905/06 season, v Swindon and away to Millwall, at right-half. But he played only once more, at centre-half v Reading in a 3-2 defeat at Elm Park (28.10.05). A mill worker by trade, he had spent his pre-professional years with a Blackburn junior side, St. James Road FC. He then progressed to the Lancashire Combination with Oswaldwistle Rovers, and from there on to Ewood Park, where he teamed up with Fred Blackburn and his left-wing partner Lionel Watson, who both joined him at the Boleyn and played with him in the aforementioned opening games of 1905/06. Harry actually joined Hammers from Lancashire Combination team Nelson, where he had gone after failing to break into Rovers' First Division side. He was also approached to join Second Division Grimsby Town, but Blackburn demanded a £75 transfer fee and the deal fell through. He was able to join Irons on a 'free' because their SL status put them outside the jurisdiction of the Football League.

HITCHENS, J.   1901-02

Lge apps: 1
Cup apps: 1

■ Formerly with Old St. Lukes, this inside-left played one SL and one FA Cup tie in Hammers' colours. His first outing was in a 0-0 stalemate at Watford (19.10.01) and the second came in a 1-0 FA Cup victory at Leyton the following month.

HODGES, Harry   1923-24

Born: Dagenham, Essex. 1897
Lge apps: 2 (1 gl)

■ Made an auspicious First Division scoring debut v Arsenal at Highbury (10.9.23) in the centre-forward berth, but spent most of his time as understudy to the great Vic Watson. Made only one more first XI appearance, v Spurs at Upton Park, the same season. Harry joined Hammers from the same Essex club that also provided fellow striker Les Robinson - Stirling Athletic. His brother, John, played for Hammers as an amateur and was nicknamed "Digger." Played for Lincoln for a time after leaving West Ham. An enthusiastic member of the former Old Players' Association, Harry died 12.12.66 at the age of 69.

HODGSON, Tommy   1922-29

Born: Hetton, Co. Durham. 1902
Lge apps: 87 (1 gl)
Cup apps: 5

Tommy Hodgson

■ A former coal miner, this rugged full-back served West Ham United throughout the 1920's and would have totalled many more first team appearances had illness and injury not interrupted his career. Signed from Hetton Colliery in 1921. Made his Hammers' debut v Blackpool at Bloomfield Road in the final match of the 1921/22 season. Became one of the renowned Hammers' "5-H" quintet of defenders: Hufton, Hebden, Henderson, Hodgson and Horler. Transferred to Third Division South Luton Town in 1930, teaming up with his old Hammers' colleague George Kay, who was then manager at Kenilworth Road. After making 67 League appearances, injury ended his career. Tommy went on to create a unique record with the Bedfordshire club by becoming the only man in soccer to be player, captain, director, managing director, chairman and president of one Football League club. He also had the honour of leading out the Hatters at Wembley for the 1959 FA Cup Final v Nottingham Forest, when Town were without a manager.

HODSON, J   1916-18

Born: Horwich, Lancashire
Apps: 49

■ All Hodson's 48 games for West Ham took place during the 1914/18 War, in a good many of which he partnered his former Oldham Atheltic colleague Bill Cope. He was with Oldham when they won the Lancashire Combination in 1906/07. Oldham joined the FL for 1907/08 and between then and 1914/15 Hodson played in 252 FL matches including 32 in Div. Two (1909/10) when Latics finished runners-up and won promotion. He also won a First Division runners-up medal in 1914/15 with the Lancastrians. After the Armistice he joined Brentford in the SL for 1919/20 and was with the Bees for their first season in the FL. Hodson made 68 apps with Brentford in the first two peace-time seasons of 1919/20 and 1920/21. He joined new SL club Guildford United for 1921/22.

HOLLAND, Pat   1969-81

Born: Poplar, London. 13.9.50
Lge apps: 245 (23 gls)
Cup apps: 51 (9 gls)

■ Full pro. 21.4.69. One of the unsung heroes of Upton Park who, nevertheless, played his part in the side that beat Fulham in the 1975 FA Cup Final and lost to Anderlecht in the European Cup Winners Cup Final a year later. Indeed, Patsy scored in the 4-2 defeat in front of 58,000 fans in Belgium's Heysel Stadium. A 90-minute grafter who never gave less than 100 per cent effort and to whom fate was not particularly kind. Patsy sustained the knee injury which ended his career in typical fashion - going in where it hurts and scoring a vital promotion goal in the process. That happened at Notts County (17.1.81) and although he made a comeback in the reserves, he couldn't win back his first team place. Curly-haired Pat,

Pat Holland

who played mostly on the right wing, had been plagued with knee problems for some time and it was this which cruelly forced him to miss the 1980 FA Cup Final v Arsenal - the team he supported as a boy! Pat remained at Upton Park for a while in a coaching capacity before being given a free transfer in 1984. He joined up with near-neighbours Orient in a player/coach capacity and enjoyed a fond farewell to Upton Park during his testimonial match with Spurs. Pat was later appointed reserve team coach at Queens Park Rangers and youth team coach at Orient. In 1988 he joined Spurs to coach their youth and reserve teams. Ironically, Tottenham wanted to sign Pat way back in 1965, but Hammers' chief scout Wally St. Pier got in before Bill Nicholson to snap up the East London Schools star who was then on his way to the English Schools Final. Pat combines his duties at White Hart Lane with the running of his wine bar at Shenfield, Essex.

Played	League App Gls	FAC App Gls	LC App Gls	Europe App Gls	Total App Gls
1968-69	1 0	0 0	0 0	0 0	1 0
1969-70	8 1	0 0	0 0	0 0	8 1
1970-71	3 0	0 0	0 0	0 0	3 0
1971-72	4 0	0 0	0 0	0 0	4 0
1972-73	32 1	2 1	2 0	0 0	36 2
1973-74	23 2	2 1	2 0	0 0	27 3
1974-75	22 4	7 2	2 0	0 0	31 6
1975-76	35 2	1 0	5 0	7 2	48 4
1976-77	6 0	0 0	1 2	0 0	7 2
1977-78	21 3	1 0	0 0	0 0	22 3
1978-79	39 3	0 0	1 0	0 0	40 3
1979-80	26 4	1 0	8 1	0 0	35 5
1980-81	25 3	2 0	4 0	3 0	34 3
TOTAL	245 23	16 4	25 3	10 2	296 32

HOLMES, Jim   1936

Born: Skelmersdale, Lancashire.
Lge apps: 2

■ A powerful pivot signed from Sheffield United, both his Second Division appearances took place in away matches v Blackpool, in a 1-0 reverse (5.9.36), and in a 5-3 defeat at Newcastle four days later. He began with Sutton Schools as a right-winger, then Sutton Commercial and Sutton Parish. Joined Liverpool as an amateur, Wigan Borough, Prescot Cables and Chesterfield before joining the Blades. Found himself on the "not retained" list at the end of the season and joined Reading.

HOLMES, Matthew   1992-

Born: Luton, Beds. 1.8.69.
Lge apps: 52 (4 gls)
Cup apps: 8

■ The first of several ex-Bournemouth players assistant manager Harry Redknapp brought with him to Upton Park. Matt cost Hammers an initial fee of £40,000 in Aug. 1992, with a further £60,000 due to the south coast club after his 60th League appearance for Hammers. This diminutive, shy midfielder made an eventful debut at Newcastle (29.8.92), where he suffered a broken nose after just 20 minutes! Mattie,

Matt Holmes

who has a sweet left foot, close control and excellent ball skills, was unlucky to start only six League matches in the 1992/93 Second Division promotion campaign, although he did feature 12 times as sub. But, despite dislocating his finger in the opening game of the 1993/94 Premiership season v Wimbledon, he held down a regular place on the left side of midfield with a number of promising performances. His efforts did not go unnoticed by the fans, who voted him runner-up (to Trevor Morley) in their Hammer of the Year poll. Supported Luton Town as a kid but was rejected by Hatters who told him he was too small to make the grade. Likeable Matt finally proved himself on the south coast, but it was during a loan period with Cardiff City that he made his League debut as sub. v Aldershot (25.3.89). Matt's brother, Danny, plays for non-league Farnborough Town.

HORLER, George   1922-27

Born: Frome, Somerset, 1895
Lge apps: 45
Cup apps: 5

■ His full-back partnership with Jack Hebden in the old London Combination was reckoned to be the finest in the Reserve League, and led to the pair being chosen to represent the competition before progressing to the First XI. Signed from Reading, he had several seasons with the Biscuitmen before donning the claret and blue, and continued to reside in Berkshire while a Hammer. George was also an accomplished singer and often formed a duet with pianist Tommy Yews to entertain at social gatherings, both at home and on tour. He joined Fulham on leaving the club in Sept. 1927, and also had a spell at Aldershot.

HORN, George   1906-08

SL apps: 8
Cup apps: 1

■ Better known as "Johnny," he'd played for Army and Navy (Anchor FC) and joined Hammers from Tunbridge Wells in 1906. Said to be a "terror for his size," half-back George transferred to Chelsea in 1909.

HOUGHTON, Ray   1982

Born: Glasgow, Scotland. 9.1.62
Lge apps: 1

■ Due to intense competition for midfield places (Trevor Brooking and Alan Devonshire played the starring roles then), John Lyall allowed this talented young Scot to join Fulham in 1982. He held the unique record for the least amount of playing time for West Ham's first team - coming on as sub (for fellow Scot George Cowie) for the last half-hour v Arsenal at Highbury (1.5.82). That sole appearance puts him some way behind Billy Bonds in the record books, but he made the First Division grade with Oxford United following a £147,000 transfer from the West Londoners in Sept. 1985. He then moved on to Liverpool in 1987 for £825,000 and after winning two championship and one FA Cup winners medal, he moved to Aston Villa in July 1992 for £900,000. The dynamic little midfielder helped them to a shock League Cup Final victory, which denied Manchester United the treble, in Mar, 1994. Three months later he was the toast of Republic of Ireland as he scored the winning goal in their opening World Cup game v Italy at USA '94. Although born in Glasgow, he was first capped for the Republic of Ireland in 1986, through family qualification, and has now won over 60 caps for his country. His first international goal was v England at Stuttgart in the 1988 European Championship finals. in addition to playing in over 500 League and Cup matches for his various clubs. A far cry from that one substitute appearance as a Hammer!

HOWE, Bobby   1966-71

Born: Chadwell St. Mary, Essex. 22.12.45
Lge apps: 75 (4 gls)
Cup apps: 7

■ A model professional and fine wing-half, Bobby served the club well during his five years in first team contention. A former Essex Schools star, he signed full pro. in Dec. 1962 and was a member of the club's Youth Cup-winning side the following year. He made his League bow as sub. v Southampton in Sept. 1966, and joined up with former Hammer and then Bournemouth manager - John Bond - when he left the Boleyn. Now manager of USA Under-18 side.

HOOPER, Harry   1950-56

Born: Pittingdon, Co. Durham. 14.6.33
Lge apps: 119 (39 gls)
Cup apps: 11 (5 gls)

■ The son of Hammers' trainer, Harry Hooper Snr., this dashing, goal-scoring winger from Hylton Colliery, was the star attraction at the Boleyn during his reign. While with the Hammers he represented the Football League v Irish League (1954) and the Scottish League (1955). When Wolves came dangling an open cheque book, there was little the club could do to stop their England Under-23 international from joining the then most famous club in the land for £25,000. However, the game turned sour on him at Molineux and after scoring 19 times in 39 matches, he moved on to Birmingham City. In 105 League games with Brum he plundered another 34 goals but in Sept. 1960 he moved to his home-town club, Sunderland, where he ended his career with 65 games and another 16 goals. One wonders, in retrospect, whether he would have been better off staying with the "Homely Hammers."

HUBBARD, Cliff   1939

Born: Woksop, Nottinghamshire. 1911
Lge apps: 1 (1 gl)

■ Previously with Scunthorpe United (1932-33), after spending his formative years with Worksop Schools, Notts Schools and Manton Colliery, this centre-forward was signed from Hull City towards the end of the 1938/39 season for £3,000 after scoring 62 goals in 182 League appearances for the Tigers. He emulated the feat of Dick Bell before him by scoring on his solitary Second Division appearance for the Hammers. He earned his one-game, one-goal distinction with a brilliant display v Manchester City at Upton Park in the final match of 1938/39. An extremely

Cliff Hubbard

versatile player who had appeared in every position (including goal for Hull), he was strongly tipped for a regular place in the first team when League Football was suspended in Sept. 1939. After WW2 he played for Ransom & Marles (Newark), Goole Town and Worksop Town, where he was trainer/coach from 1960 till his death in Nov. 1962.

HUFTON, Edward 1919-32

Born: Southwell, Notts. 25.11.1892
Lge apps: 370
Cup apps: 31

■ Rivals Ernie Gregory, Phil Parkes and Ludo Miklosko for the title of West Ham's greatest-ever goalkeeper. The meteoric rise of his early career with Sheffield United was almost matched by the suddenness of its temporary decline, following a bizarre chain of events in his first season with the Yorkshiremen. Signed by the Blades from local works side Atlas & Norfolk in 1913, Ted soon seized the first team spot and acquitted himself well enough to prompt United to transfer their regular goalkeeper. However, they did obtain the services of another young 'keeper as cover, one Harold Gough from Castleford, and when Hammers' hero-to-be broke his nose in a practice match, the situation reversed itself; Gough going on to play for Blades in the 1915 FA Cup Final and later gain England honours. Ted, meanwhile, joined the Coldstream Guards and was swept up in the horrors of WW1, being wounded in action in France. If fate had been unkind to Ted Hufton, it certainly wasn't the case as far as West Ham United were concerned. For it was after he had been on sick leave and recovered from his shrapnel wounds that he made the first of 64 war-time guest appearances for the club, paving the way for his eventual transfer when hostilities ceased. Once again it was a fellow goalkeeper who had a big hand in Ted's future fate - best illustrated in a story traditionally handed down over the years at Upton Park. Legend has it that during that last war-time season, Joe Hughes, then Hammers' regular 'keeper, saw the young Ted Hufton keeping goal in a practice match. After a while Joe turned to manager Syd King and asked to be put on the transfer list. "Why?" came the reply, for Joe, too, was a fine player. Joe allegedly pointed to his rival: "He's my governor - let me go. He's a better goalie than I'll ever be." And so it was. Joe Hughes transferred to Bolton Wanderers, later joining Chelsea; and Ted joined Hammers for a £350 fee! Irons' first season in the newly-formed Second Division were memorable ones for Ted, and it was around this time that he acquired the nickname "Penalty King", by saving 11 out of 18 spot-kicks against him in two seasons. During the 1920/21 season he had two former Sheffield United men for company in the first team: Dick Leafe (who was later appointed the club's assistant secretary) and another forward, Jimmy Simmons (who had scored for the Blades in the aforementioned FA Cup Final of 1915). Jim, incidentally, has often been confused with another ex-Hammer of the same surname, who was signed from West Bromwich Albion in 1904 and was with the club for four seasons, "Chippy" Simmons. The 1920/21 campaign also saw Ted scale new heights of excellence when he received the notable record of not conceding more than two goals in any of the 38 League matches he played - the best goals-against record in the country that year. International recognition followed in the Cup Final and promotion year of 1923, but Ted had to decline joining fellow West Ham team-mates Jack Tresadern and Billy Moore in action for England v Sweden in Stockholm due to injury. So his debut was delayed to the following year, when he won the first of his six caps v Belgium - and another record which still stands to this day, being the only goalkeeper to play for England while with West Ham. He played against the immortal "Wembley Wizards" in 1928, when Alex James & co. ran amok for the Scots. But even in defeat Ted was magnificent, his display preventing a greater debacle. The case was the same when Hammers lost a vital League match v Everton at Goodison Park nearing the end of the club's relegation season in 1931/32. The Toffeemen ran out 6-1 victors, virtually assuring themselves of the League championship with the help of a hat-trick from the legendary Dixie Dean. A subsequent match report in an Everton programme of that period exonerated the Hammers' 'keeper of blame for the reverse. We quote it verbatim: "The display against the Londoners was brimful of interest, and though there was but a narrow margin at the interval there could be no mistaking our superiority during the second portion. Dunn was the star artist in the forward-line, though not among the scorers because of the brilliance of the West Ham goalkeeper Hufton, but for whom a double score might have been established." West Ham's return to the Second Division saw the by now veteran 'keeper lose his place to George Watson, and he was granted a free transfer at the end of the 1932/33 season, joining Watford for a brief spell. On retiring from the game he went into the motor trade as a rep. while still living locally at Manor Park. After WW2 he returned to Upton Park to take up the position of press-room steward on match days. Ted's later life was beset by ill-health, however, and a tragic traffic accident further compounded his problems. Deciding to move to Swansea to convalesce, his health deteriorated still further, failing eyesight leaving him with only radio reports to keep him in touch with soccer. On Feb. 2, 1967 a great Englishman died in Wales... and left behind a lasting legend.

☆ *England caps:* 1923 v Belgium; 1927 v Northern Ireland; 1928 v Scotland; 1929 v France, Belgium, Spain (6).

Played	League		FAC		LC		Europe		Total	
	App	Gls	App	Gls	App	Gls	App	Gls	App	Gls
1919-20	38	0	4	0	0	0	0	0	42	0
1920-21	38	0	1	0	0	0	0	0	39	0
1921-22	33	0	3	0	0	0	0	0	36	0
1922-23	39	0	9	0	0	0	0	0	48	0
1923-24	15	0	0	0	0	0	0	0	15	0
1924-25	7	0	0	0	0	0	0	0	7	0
1925-26	38	0	1	0	0	0	0	0	39	0
1926-27	40	0	3	0	0	0	0	0	43	0
1927-28	25	0	2	0	0	0	0	0	27	0
1928-29	31	0	4	0	0	0	0	0	35	0
1929-30	30	0	4	0	0	0	0	0	34	0
1930-31	14	0	0	0	0	0	0	0	14	0
1931-32	22	0	0	0	0	0	0	0	22	0
TOTAL	**370**	**0**	**31**	**0**	**0**	**0**	**0**	**0**	**401**	**0**

HUGHES, Joseph   1911-15

Born: London. 1892
Lge apps: 90
Cup apps: 15

■ A whole succession of rival goalkeepers laid claim to Joe Hughes' jealously guarded position as the last line of Hammers' defence. The able custodian saw them all off with the exeption of Ted Hufton, as is told in the previous entry. Joe was transferred to Chelsea, who he played for in WW1, but later transferred to Bolton and played over 50 matches for the Trotters until the famous Dick Pym took over between the posts for the Lancastrians. He then returned to London to join fellow former Hammers Bailey, Burton and Lane at Charlton Athletic, who were about to embark on their first season (1921/22) as a FL club. Hughes (and Bailey) were at Clapton Orient at the start of 1923/24, but neither made a League showing. He began with Tufnell Park and then South Weald, from where Hammers signed him in 1911

Joe Hughes

HUGHTON, Chris   1990-92

Born: Forest Gate, London. 11.12.58
Lge apps: 33
Cup apps: 7

■ Returned to East London as cover for injured left-back Julian Dicks in Nov. 1990, this popular Republic of Ireland international proved a solid, dependable member of the 1990/91 Second Division promotion-winning side. Made his debut at Notts County (3.11.90) and following a two-month loan spell, Billy Bonds signed him from Tottenham on a free transfer in Dec. 1990. Played in every game, including the ill-fated FA Cup semi-final defeat by Nottingham Forest, as Hammers returned to the top flight. An articulate pro, Chris brought a wealth of experience to the back four, having previously made 297 League appearances for Spurs and gained 53 full Irish caps. The arrival, in Aug. 1992, of his former White Hart Lane team mate Mitchell Thomas left Chris out in the cold at Upton Park. He made only one appearance that season - as sub at home to Notts County, which turned out to be his last for the club. How many players made their first and last League appearances against the same team? At that stage of his career Chris, understandably, wanted first team

football and, after a spell on the transfer list, joined Brentford on a free for the last 13 games of the 1992/93 term. Unfortunately a recurrence of a knee injury, midway through the following season forced the likeable Chris into retirement at the age of 34. At Spurs, Chris won UEFA Cup, FA Cup and League Cup winners' medals, and in the summer of 1993 he returned to White Hart Lane as coach to their Under-21 team. Appointed manager of the reserves in July 1994.
☆ *Republic of Ireland caps:*
1991 v Chile; 1992 v Turkey (twice).

HUGO, Roger   1964

Born: Woking, Surrey. 6.9.42
Lge apps: 3 (2 gls)

■ A fine inside-forward whose opportunities were restricted by a surplus of candidates for the inside-berths during his time with the club. Scored in two of his first three First Division appearances in 1963/64 - all away from home, v Leicester City, Stoke City and WBA respectively - so he was unable to show the Upton Park crowd his undoubted skill at senior level. Transferred to Watford in the summer of 1965.

HULL, Archie   1928

Born: East Ham, London. 8.8.1902
Lge apps: 2

■ Rated the best amateur centre-half in London when his club side Ilford were sweeping all before them in the late twenties, he was unable to assist West Ham on a regular basis due to his commitment to the Isthmian League outfit. A team-mate of a later West Ham centre-half at Ilford, Wally St. Pier - Archie made his debut v WBA (19.2.27) and had one more First Division outing with Hammers in a 0-4 defeat v Huddersfield Town (22.12.28). A Chemist in private life, he was well known as a fine singer at concerts and banquets in the East London and Essex area, and later joined Clapton Orient with whom he made one appearance, in 1931. Died 6.3.78.

HUNT, Fergus   1900-02

Born: 1876
SL apps: 42 (9 gls)
Cup apps: 6 (1 gl)

■ "Fergie" Hunt was a fast-raiding outside-right who came from Woolwich Arsenal and missed only one match in the club's first season as West Ham United. Beginning his career with Mexborough in Yorkshire and later playing for Middlesboro' Ironopolis and Darwen, he switched to centre-forward during the later stages of his career at the Memorial Grounds and gained a reputation for scoring late, match-winning goals. Returned to Woolwich for 1902/03, where he made three appearances in 1903/04 and was with Fulham, making 19 appearances. In 1905/06 he joined Burton United.

HUTTON, E.G.   1896-98 TIW

■ An inside-right signed from Reading in Aug. 1896, he played in a disastrous 8-0 first qualifying round FA Cup defeat at Sheppey United (10.10.1896) and also three further FA Cup ties the following season. Played in an unspecified number of League fixtures over the same period.

Chris Hughton

Geoff Hurst scores Hammers second goal past Liverpool's Tommy Lawrence in the FA Charity Shield match at Anfield in 1964.

HURST, Geoff   1960-72

Born: Ashton-under-Lyne, Lancs. 8.12.41
Lge apps: 411 (180 gls)
Cup apps: 91 (72 gls)

■ Blossomed from a competent wing-half who by sheer determination and hard work became one of the most feared and revered strikers in world football. Of course, he had some help on the way to achieving that goal. Notably from his father, former professional with Oldham, Bristol Rovers and Rochdale, Charles Hurst, who came south to play for Chelmsford City; from family friend Jack Redfern, who recommended Geoff to Hammers; and most of all, Ron Greenwood, who converted him to striker. Geoff made his first senior appearance v Fulham in a Floodlight Cup tie in Dec. 1958, signed pro forms four months later and made his First Division baptism at Nottingham Forest (27.2.60). After that his goal-scoring exploits became legend. His World Cup Final hat-trick v West Germany at Wembley in 1966 and six goals v Sunderland (19.10.68) two years later, have been woven into the fabric of football folklore. Geoff is still the only player to score three goals in a World Cup Final, while his six-of-the-best for Hammers is a club record he shares with Vic Watson, who first managed the feat nearly 40 years earlier. The second-highest Hammers' marksman of all-time, behind Watson, with 180 League goals, (but easily the best cup goalscorer with 68); holder of 49 full England caps (24 gls); winner of FA Cup (1964), and ECWC (1965) medals; World Cup winners' medal and Football League Cup runners-up medals (1966). These are the landmarks the fans remember most. Geoff's first-ever senior goal for West Ham came in a 4-2 win over Wolves at Upton Park (18.12.61) - he was wearing the unfamiliar number four shirt that day. Despite the challenge from the young Bobby Moore, Eddie Bovington, Bill Lansdowne and Malcolm Pike, Geoff was delighted to start the 1962/63 season at wing-half. But he was dropped for the next match and played the following five games in the reserves. When Greenwood summoned him to his office, Geoff expected a rocket for his poor form. Instead, Greenwood was looking for "someone big and strong and not afraid to work", to play inside-left for him at home to Liverpool. Geoff agreed, Hammers won 1-0 and the rest is history. His first season as a regular first-teamer was 1963/64, which netted him 26 League and cup goals including West Ham's second in the 3-2 FA Cup Final triumph over Preston North End. By then he had made the number 10 shirt his own and truly arrived as a first class striker, developing alongside the more naturally-gifted Johnny Byrne. In his book, The World Game, Geoff wrote: "The coming of 'Budgie' Byrne was a great thing in my career. He and I worked up a great partnership, and as the team began winning I was perfectly happy to be the bread-and-butter part of the partnership. I rate Budgie as the best player I have ever played alongside." Geoff totalled 40 goals in the season before he became England's World Cup-winning hero, which meant he was the First Division's leading scorer. But his best-ever haul was the 41 he amassed in 1966/67. Only four goals by Southampton's Ron Davies, on the last day of that season, prevented Geoff from emulating his previous success as Division One's leading hot-shot. Along with West Ham and England team mates Bobby Moore and Martin Peters, Geoff enjoyed world-wide fame. But Geoff was most respected by his fellow-pro's for his unselfish running. He perfected the near-post run that produced so many great goals under Greenwood and his strength in the penalty area was renowned. He took a lot of punishment from close-marking opponents, but remained brave and strong, always so good at shielding the ball and laying off passes with the use of his chest. That memorable sunny afternoon at Wembley in July 1966 provided a clear illustration of Geoff's all-round qualities. His first goal in the 4-2 victory over the Germans came from his head; the second with his right foot; and the third with his left foot. The powerful hat-trick-clinching strike into the roof of the net, just seconds from the end of extra-time, prompted those immortal words from BBC commentator, Ken Wolstenholme: "Some people are on the pitch... they think it's all over... IT IS NOW!" It was an incredible end to a tournament that began with Geoff on the subs' bench and Jimmy Greaves leading the England attack. Moore admitted his surprise that Hurst had successfully switched from wing-half to striker: "Ron (Greenwood) turned Geoff from a bit of a cart-horse at wing-half into a truly great forward. None of us thought Geoff was going to make the switch. It took him years of hard work and patience. He was so willing he ran himself into the ground. He ran and ran and ran and was always just short of everything. I don't know how he put up with the abuse but it was worth it because in the mid-sixties he became, for a few seasons, a genuine world class player." Indeed, Geoff's life has been full of turning points. Even before he made his name with West Ham, he might have emerged as a useful county cricketer. He played in the same Essex Schools XI as Bobby Moore, turned out for Essex Seconds for three summers and did in fact appear in one championship match for the county - v Lancashire at Liverpool in 1962, although without scoring in either innings! Geoff's final season for West Ham earned him 16 League and cup goals and only the great Gordon Banks denied him a 17th. The epic League Cup semi-final clashes with Stoke City produced many memorable moments spanning the first two legs and both replays, but they still talk now of the great save Banks made to block Geoff's thunderbolt penalty in extra-time of the second leg at Upton Park. Ironically, after his final Hammers' appearance, v Liverpool (15.4.72), Geoff joined Stoke City the following season in a £80,000 deal. He made over 100 appearances for the Potters (30 gls) in three

Geoff Hurst

years before moving on to end his League career at West Bromwich Albion, where he played 10 games and scored two more goals, before spending a season in the USA with Seattle Sounders. He then became player/manager of non-League Telford before moving into full League management with Chelsea. He later assisted Ron Greenwood in the running of the England side. Joined forces with former team mate Peters as director of a motor insurance company, but in recent years has become

increasingly involved in promotions work. Notably with former club sponsors BAC and as host to the '66 Club' in the Bobby Moore Stand at Upton Park. A footballing legend in his own right, Geoff Hurst lies ninth in the list of Hammers' all-time League appearance-makers. Perhaps only the inimitable Moore enjoyed more world-wide fame and acclaim than this Golden Great.

☆ ***England caps:*** *1966 v West Germany (twice), Scotland, Yugoslavia, Finland, Denmark, Argentina, Portugal, Northern Ireland, Czechoslovakia, Wales; 1967 v Scotland, Spain, Austria, Wales, Northern Ireland, Russia; 1968 v Scotland, Sweden (sub), West Germany, USSR, Romania, Bulgaria; 1969 v Romania, France, Northern Ireland, Scotland, Mexico, Uruguay, Brazil, Holland; 1970 v Holland (sub), Belgium, Wales, Northern Ireland, Scotland, Colombia, Ecuador, Romania, Brazil, West Germany, East Germany; 1971 v Greece (twice), Wales, Scotland, Switzerland (twice); 1972 v West Germany (49).*

Played	League		FAC		LC		Europe		Total	
	App	Gls	App	Gls	App	Gls	App	Gls	App	Gls
1959-60	3	0	0	0	0	0	0	0	3	0
1960-61	6	0	0	0	0	0	0	0	6	0
1961-62	24	1	1	0	2	0	0	0	27	1
1962-63	27	13	0	0	2	2	0	0	29	15
1963-64	37	14	7	7	6	5	0	0	50	26
1964-65	42	17	1	2	1	0	9	0	53	19
1965-66	39	23	4	4	10	11	6	2	59	40
1966-67	41	29	2	3	6	9	0	0	49	41
1967-68	38	19	3	1	3	5	0	0	44	25
1968-69	42	25	3	2	3	4	0	0	48	31
1969-70	39	16	1	0	2	2	0	0	42	18
1970-71	39	15	0	0	2	1	0	0	41	16
1971-72	34	8	4	4	10	4	0	0	48	16
TOTAL	411	180	26	23	47	43	15	2	499	248

HUTCHISON, Don

Born: Gateshead. 9.5.71.

■ Attacking midfielder who became the club's record signing when he moved from Liverpool soon after the start of the 1994/95 season for a £1.5 million fee. "Hutch" scored on his debut at Upton Park v Newcastle United (31.8.94) - the club he supported as a boy. Don first caught the eye while playing for Paul Gascoigne's former club, Redheugh Boys, but he made the breakthrough to league status for Hartlepool United. The gangling Hutch was used either as a striker or central defender before settling into his now familiar attacking midfield role. But struggling 'Pool were eager to cash in on their promising youngster and attempted to sell their prized asset by sending a video of him in action to all First and Second Division clubs. It was as a result of this unusual marketing ploy that Liverpool boss Kenny Dalglish signed Don for £300,000 in November 1990, after he had made just 24 league appearances for the north-east minnows. At Anfield, where he scored seven goals in 45 league outings, Hutch more than justified that fee. And despite some controversial off-the-field antics which earned him a somewhat dubious reputation, it was with great reluctance that Roy Evans finally agreed to make him Harry Redknapp's first signing as manager at Upton Park.

Don Hutchison

INCE, Paul
1986-89

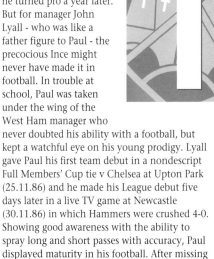

Born: Ilford, Essex. 21.10.67.
Lge apps: 72 (7 gls)
Cup apps: 19 (1 gl)

■ Despite whatever his many Upton Park critics say, Paul is one of the most talented young players ever produced by West Ham and currently worth more than any other on the transfer market. Midfielder Paul has established himself as a firm favourite at Manchester United, where, after a subdued start (he even found himself filling in at full-back for a while!), he has developed into a leading Premiership star and England regular. In five hugely successful seasons at Old Trafford, "Incey" has collected medals for winning two Premiership championships (1993, when he was voted player of the year, and 1994), two FA Cups (1990 and 1994) and one League Cup (1992).´Despite his suspect temperament, which has landed him in trouble with many referees, Paul also became the first black player to captain England, during the US Cup matches under Graham Taylor in the summer of 1993.

Not many unforgiving West Ham fans would have shared in his pride that day, for the circumstances surrounding Paul's controversial transfer to United, in Sept. 1989, provoked a stormy reaction from supporters. They were understandably incensed by Paul's somewhat naive appearance in a national newspaper wearing a Man. Utd shirt - three months before he left Upton Park! And when the player hit back in print after receiving a hostile reception from the terraces in the opening game of the 1989/90 season, at Stoke City (10.8.89), it was obvious that Ince and West Ham would soon part company. New manager Lou Macari was looking to cash in on Paul's undisputed talent but the big transfer deal almost fell through at the eleventh hour, when Paul failed his Old Trafford medical. An old hernia injury showed up on X-rays and Alex Ferguson only agreed to sign Paul for £800,000, with the balance payable in instalments. In a unique pay-as-you-play deal, West Ham collected £5,000 for each first team appearance Paul made, up to a total of £1.5 million. United certainly got good value for a player who first showed promise for Essex Schoolboys. He joined Hammers on the YTS

scheme in July 1984 and made such rapid progress, he turned pro a year later. But for manager John Lyall - who was like a father figure to Paul - the precocious Ince might never have made it in football. In trouble at school, Paul was taken under the wing of the West Ham manager who never doubted his ability with a football, but kept a watchful eye on his young prodigy. Lyall gave Paul his first team debut in a nondescript Full Members' Cup tie v Chelsea at Upton Park (25.11.86) and he made his League debut five days later in a live TV game at Newcastle (30.11.86) in which Hammers were crushed 4-0. Showing good awareness with the ability to spray long and short passes with accuracy, Paul displayed maturity in his football. After missing an opening game defeat by QPR in 1987/88, he was recalled to the side in the role of sweeper. He could also fill in at full-back, although his best position was as a hard-running mid-fielder

January 1989, and Paul Ince evades a tackle by Bryan Robson at Upton Park. Before the end of the year Ince had joined Robbo at Old Trafford, where he has now taken over his mid-field mantle.

who liked the ball at his feet. Yet it was only in his third, and last, season at Upton Park that he retained a regular first team place. The 1988/89 season was a miserable one in general, culminating in relegation, but one amazing night will forever remain in the memory of West Ham fans, and Paul Ince in particular. Mighty Liverpool were crushed 4-1 in the Littlewoods (League) Cup (30.11.88) - Reds' biggest cup defeat since 1939 - and Paul emerged from nowhere to score the two sensational first half goals that set up this famous victory and projected him into the football limelight. United, and the rest of the big guns, were suddenly alerted to his talent and it was not long before Paul was on his way. His desire for fame and glory only increased with the departure, in July 1989, of his long-time mentor, Lyall. Four-and-a-half years had passed when Paul returned to Upton Park with title-chasing Man Utd in Feb. 1994. This time Ince denied Hammers a memorable victory with the last-gasp equaliser in a 2-2 classic, but the main media talking point surrounded the torrent of abuse he received from large sections of the crowd. For all his undoubted ability as a footballer, the fans in claret and blue made it abundantly clear that it will be some time yet before they are ready to forgive and forget.

INGHAM, William   1903-04

Born: 1882
SL apps: 2

■ In an age when goals were the demanded pre-requisite of centre-forwards, Billy's failure to get on the score sheet in the two opportunities afforded to him makes his demise self-explanatory. Making his first appearance on the season's opening day at Millwall, he was given another chance to shine in a 1-1 home draw with Reading in Sept. 1904, which proved to be his last SL outing with Hammers. He was signed from Aberdare Athletic who were finalists in that season's Welsh Cup, and again in 1905. He played for Bristol City in Division Two of the FL in 1905/ 06 and moved further west to join Plymouth Argyle for 1908/09. The following season saw him at Accrington Stanley.

INNS, Tommy   1933-34

Born: Plaistow, London. 30.1.1911
Lge apps: 4

■ A tough-tackling full-back signed from local amateurs Clapton, Tom made his first appearance in West Ham's colours v Swansea Town at Vetch Field on Boxing Day, 1933. Making three more Second Division outings that season, Tom remained a reserve thereafter and transferred to London rivals Millwall in the summer of 1936 ,along with team-mate Dave Mangnall, where he built up a fine reputation as an accomplished defender and formed a successful partnership with his fellow full-back Ted Smith. Played 36 matches when Millwall won the Third Division South Championship in 1938 and became the first Third Division side to reach the semi-finals of the FA Cup. Repre-sented Essex County and West Ham Schoolboys in addition to being an Essex Senior Cup finalist with Clapton, the famous London amateur side. A commercial artist by profession, he designed the front cover of the Millwall Supporters' Club publications, Focus on the Lions. A relative, L. Inns, also played for Clapton.

IRVINE, George   1912-14

SL apps: 21

■ This tough defender could perform equally well at either right or left-back and made his debut alongside another new signing, left-back Harry Forster, in the 4-0 win over Exeter City on the opening day of the 1912/13 season. Signed from Barrow, he made his last appearance in the 6-0 defeat at Watford (1.4.14)

George Irvine

JACKMAN, Derek   1948-50

Born: Colchester, Essex. 20.8.27
Lge apps: 8

■ Yet another player with Hammers/Palace con-nections, having played for the Glaziers before the war. An uncompromising wing-half, his League appearances were sparsely spread over three seasons, making his first outing in a 2-1 win over Blackburn at Upton Park in the number 10 shirt. His last was in a 2-1 home defeat v. Brentford (2.9.50) at half time.

JACKSON, James   1905-06

Born: Cambuslang, Scotland. 1880
SL apps: 24

■ James was a major capture for West Ham when they signed him following his resignation as player/manager to Leyton. A big name with Woolwich Arsenal, whom he captained for four of the five seasons he was with them, he was a strong, forceful defender who formed a fabled full-back partnership with another Scot, Dave Gardner, at Upton Park. His family had emigrated to Australia when he was but two years of age, leaving young "Jemmy" to the mercy of Australian Association (a mixture of soccer and rugby) and Australian rules football. He nevertheless proved capable enough to play for Scottish side Newton Thistle when he returned to his native country in 1898, as a centre-half. A strict teetotaler, his displays soon drew the attentions of Glasgow Rangers and he duly signed for the Ibrox club the same year. At the end of his first season with the Light Blues Jackson came south to join Newcastle United, who he helped to promotion to the First Division of the FL in his first season with the Magpies. His fame spread further south culminating in his move to the Woolwich Arsenal "Reds." "Rambler," of the East Ham Echo, drafted an interesting report following his move to Hammers, part of which read: "While with Arsenal Jackson was regarded as one of the finest backs in the South, and it was with great regret that the Woolwich club's supporters learned that the skipper was leaving to take up the position of player/manager to Leyton. A few days ago the sporting public were greatly surprised to read in the London papers that Jackson had tendered his resignation, which had been accepted by the Leyton directorate. This was indeed a sensation, and was quickly followed by the startling, but welcome, news that he had been signed on for West Ham. True, the news appeared in the London press a day before the signature had really been obtained, but, nevertheless, no great harm was done by that, for Jackson is now the wearer of the red, white and blue colours." In addition to participating in North v South and Anglo-Scots v The Scots representative matches, it is also recorded that the footloose Scot also played for Newton Heath and Cambuslang before he joined Newcastle although the exact dates are a bit hazy.

JACKSON, Tom
1921-22

Lge apps: 3 (1 gl)

■ At home in either of the inside-forward positions, Tom made a scoring debut in a 3-0 victory over Stoke City at Upton Park (3.9.21) and went on to make a further two Second Division outings that campaign.

JACKSON, William
1927

Lge apps: 2

■ Secured from Leeds United, where he had made 40 League appearances, Bill came into the West Ham side for the Christmas holiday matches v Sheffield United, making his debut in a 6-2 defeat at Bramall Lane on Boxing Day, and playing against the Yorkshiremen again the following day in the return fixture at Upton Park which ended 1-1. Signed as an understudy to Jimmy Ruffell, they were his only League appearances with Hammers and he subsequently moved to Chelsea.

JAMES, Wilf
1930-32

Born: Cross Keys, Monmouthshire, Wales. 19.2.1907
SL apps: 40 (7 gls)
Cup apps: 1

■ Wilf was a fine inside-left and a great character who had a deep affection for his bowler hat. In fact, it was the first article of clothing he would put on when he changed after a match, often standing stark naked in the dressing room wearing only his titfer! Wilf began his career with Cross Keys School just after WW1 and graduated to local Welsh sides Abercarn Welfare and Ynysddu Crusaders before signing for Newport County in 1925, where he had a reputation for "good distributive work" and scored eight goals in 20 League appearances between 1925 and 1927. Went to Yorkshire works team Thorne Colliery before moving on to Owston Park Rangers for 1927/28. He re-entered League football with Notts County in Oct. 1928 where he scored six goals in 16 appearances up to his transfer to Hammers in May 1930. Transferring to Charlton Athletic for £600 in Feb. 1932, he scored three times in 28 League games at the Valley but decided to move to Workington in the 1933 cs but found it hard to hold down a first team place. Carlisle offered him a trial period in Sept. 1935 and he signed on six weeks later. Wilf played most of his football for the Cumbrians with the reserves in the North Eastern League but at the end of season 1936/37 was given a free transfer.
☆ *Wales caps:* 1931 v Northern Ireland; 1932 v Northern Ireland (2).

James Jackson

JAMES, William 1920-22

Lge apps: 54 (7 gls)
Cup apps: 3

■ Bill came from Portsmouth for the 1920/21 season, making 18 League appearances, and played in 36 matches the following campaign before leaving the club. An inside or outside-right, he was succeeded by Jimmy Ruffell.

JARVIS, Len 1903-09

Born: Grays, Essex
SL apps: 133 (5 gls)
Cup apps: 7

■ With his never say die attitude to the game, Dick - as he was popularly known - was one of Irons' most consistent performers in the transitory years following the move from the Memorial Grounds at Canning Town to the Boleyn. His spirit was typified in a match v Brighton when he was kicked in the face and sustained a deep cut which required several stitches. He was soon back in the fray, however, heavily bandaged but making light of his injuries, a la Billy Bonds. Employed at a Grays cement works, Dick was spotted by a Hammers' director playing in local Essex soccer and brought to the Memorial Grounds. His whole-hearted approach sometimes got him in trouble with referees and he was suspended for 14 days in late 1906 arising from an incident in a Western League game v Millwall at Upton Park (17.9.06). Equally at home in any of the half-back positions, he eventually made the number six shirt his own. Dick made his last appearance for Irons in a SL fixture at Reading on the final day of the 1908/09 season, playing at centre-half. Transferring to First Division Bury, he played 22 FL matches in 1909/10, 13 in 1910/11 and 20 in 1911/12 when the Shakers were relegated.

PROMINENT FOOTBALLERS.

L. JARVIS,
WEST HAM UNITED.

JENKINSON, William 1901-02

Born: Chesterfield, Derbys. 1877
SL apps: 19 (2 gls)

■ Bill did not get off to the best of starts with Hammers, as he was tried in three different positions in the consecutive defeats. Formerly with Burnley, where he spent four years, he eventually settled down at inside-left as the side finished the season on a brighter note by going the last 11 matches unbeaten. Later returned to Burnley.

JENNINGS, Billy 1974-79

Born: Hackney, London. 20.2.52
Lge apps: 99 (34 gls)
Cup apps: 25 (5 gls)

■ Quick-silver striker whose £110,000 arrival from Watford coincided with a distinct revival of fortunes for Hammers, culminating in the 1975 Cup Final win over Fulham. That victory put Hammers back in Europe, and

after a disastrous start to the quarter-final of the Cup Winners' Cup v Den Haag of Holland when they trailed 4-0, Billy's two second half goals kept his team in with a chance for the return leg at Upton Park. A serious Achilles tendon injury threatened to end Billy's career in 1977 and he struggled to hold a regular place from then on. A former England Youth international, Billy played just short of a 100 League games and scored many vital goals before taking the well-worn transfer trail between Upton Park and Brisbane Road in 1979 where he made 70 senior appearances for O's before leaving for Luton. He made only two sub. appearances in the Second Division (scoring once) for the Hatters, however, before deciding to retire in 1981. Bill spent three years running the Fleet Street wine bar and was later the proprietor of a Brentwood brasserie. In between, he had made an ill-fated comeback with non-league Dagenham. In 1993 Bill had a spell working for former club sponsors BAC. but is now back running a restaurant in the City

JENNINGS, Samuel 1924-25

Born: Cinderhill. 18.12.1898
Lge apps: 9 (3 gls)

■ A fine centre-forward who joined West Ham from Reading, and he was also on Middlesbrough's books at one time. With Victor Watson in such good fettle in the middle of Hammers' attack, Sam played his first League game at inside-left - scoring the only goal of the

Sam Jennings

game v Preston North End on the opening day of the 1924-25 season at Upton Park. On other occasions he switched to inside-right with equal effect. Left Hammers for Brighton and Hove Albion. Died Battle, Sussex 26.8.1944.

JOHNS, Stan 1950-51

Born: Liverpool. 28.6.24
Lge apps: 6 (2 gls)

■ Signed from under the noses of Liverpool and Everton in Aug. 1950, from those well-known providers of football talent, South Liverpool. Stan's career at Upton Park was short and sweet - the striker making half-a-dozen Second Division appearances in 1950/51.

JOHNSON, W Joseph 1927

Born: Wednesbury, Staffs.
Lge apps: 15 (7 gls)

■ A sharp-shooting inside-foward who achieved the obligatory goal-every-other-game for strikers of those days during his 15 First Division appearances in the 1926/27 season. Born in the Black Country, Joe's first professional club was Talbot Stead in the Birmingham Combination, whom he joined from Bradley United in 1920/21. From then on it was very much a case of "have goals, will travel," with Cannock Town his next point of call. Then he joined Crystal Palace for his first taste of League football, moved on to Barnsley and transferred to Hammers from the Yorkshire club in 1927. Joe made a scoring debut v Huddersfield Town at Upton Park (5.2.27). Switching to the outside-left position on occasions, he held his place to the end of the season. Despite his promising beginning at the Boleyn, Joe made only one first XI appearance the following season, and faded from the picture after moving to Southend.

JOHNSON, William 1919

Lge apps: 2

■ A Scotsman from Aberdeen, Bill made his first appearance in Hammers' colours in a cracking 4-1 win against Lincoln City at Sincil Bank (6.9.19), and was on duty at right-half again two days later v Barnsley at the Boleyn - when the Yorkshiremen spoiled his second, and what was to prove to be his last League outing, by winning 2-0.

JOHNSON, William 1932

Born: Leigh-on-Sea, Essex
Lge apps: 5

■ Bill made the first of his handful of Second Division appearances at centre-half for Hammers in the 5-2 victory over Oldham at Upton Park (15.10.32). After coming to prominence in the Southend Schools XI and later Leigh Amateurs, the tall defender followed the natural progression by signing for his local League club - Southend United - then playing at the Kursaal Ground. A public-spirited individual, who was a member of Southend Fire Brigade and also drove the police ambulance, he found his first team opportunities limited after his transfer to Hammers due to the fine form of Jim Barrett and Wally St. Pier.

JOHNSTONE, Robert Gordon 1956-57

Born: Edinburgh, Scotland. 19.11.34
Lge apps: 2

■ A fine wing-half in the best Scottish tradition, Gordon played his early soccer with Edinburgh Schoolboys and East of Scotland Select while with junior side Ormiston Primrose. Came to the Boleyn for a trial, and impressed sufficiently to sign pro forms in Apr. 1953. National service commitments interrupted his soccer career - delaying his initial senior appearance until Nov. 1956, when he played at Doncaster Rovers. He made only one more Second Division showing before being transferred to Ipswich Town. Served the Suffolk club well until 1959, when he gave up the game to embark on a professional singing career in Canada.

JONES, Steve 1992-

Born: Cambridge, Cambs. 17.3.70
Lge apps: 14 (4 gls)
Cup apps: 4 (1 gl)

■ Tall, pacy striker who lived in a caravan and was made redundant from the Yardley soap factory at Basildon, shortly before he joined Hammers from non-league Billericay Town in Nov. 1992 for £22,500. Steve made his debut for the club in the reserves v Southampton (17.11.92) but his senior bow came in the Anglo-Italian Cup at Cosenza (8.12.92). On a waterlogged pitch, Steve set up Clive Allen's winning goal but he had to wait until the visit of Barnsley for his full First Division debut (6.2.93), having played only the last two minutes as sub in the previous match at Leicester. Replacing the injured Clive Allen, Stevie was only 10 minutes into his full debut when he scored his first goal for the club. Then he followed it by netting in the next game v Peterborough United. But Steve, who began his non-league career with Basildon United before becoming Billericay's goal machine in the Diadora League, is still striving to prove himself at Upton Park. Although very popular with the fans, who appreciate his wholehearted

endeavour, "Jonah" has been described as 'raw' by the management, who gave him just three starts in the 1993/94 Premiership. In October 1994, Steve was put out on loan to Harry Redknapp's old club, Bournemouth.

JONES, William 1901-02

Born: Penrhiwceiber, Wales
SL apps: 15

■ Bill Jones became the first West Ham player to be capped for his country when he played for Wales v England and Scotland in 1902, adding to the two caps already won with Aberdare against the same countries the previous year. Although a bit on the slow side, Bill was a sound tackler adept at supplying his wingers from the half-back berth. Captain of Aberdare, it was a great loss to the Welsh club when he embarked on a disastrous move to SL Kettering Town in Sept. 1901. Unable to settle with the Poppies, his fortunes improved considerably when he was transferred - in a straight swap for West Ham's Peter Kyle - in Dec. 1901, as he went on to complete 15 SL appearances at centre-half before returning to the valleys at the season's end to join Aberamen whom he helped steer to the final of the Welsh Cup in 1903. They lost 8-0 to Wrexham, but became the first club from South Wales to reach the final. He left Aberamen to join a club named Rogerstone in 1904 and stayed until 1906. Bill Jones is believed to have been killed in action in Serbia in May 1918 while serving with the Royal Welsh Fusiliers.
☆ **Wales caps:** *1902 v England, Scotland (2).*

JOYCE, Bill TIW 1899-1900

SL apps: 28 (11 gls)

■ Bill joined Thames Ironworks for their last season of existence from Spurs after scoring 26 goals in 38 matches for the North Londoners. A centre-forward typical of the Victorian era, he achieved a more modest total with Hammers, although there were some vital strikes among them: and none more so than his celebrated hat-trick on his return to neutral Tottenham - along with fellow-former Tottenham man Ken McKay - in Ironworks' 5-1 Test match victory v London rivals Fulham which preserved their jealously guarded senior status. At the turn of the century Bill left Irons to join Portsmouth as replacement for Sandy Brown, who had ironically joined Spurs. A year later he moved to Burton United where he played for another two seasons and appeared in 29 matches. He had begun his career with Greenock Morton in his native Scotland before transferring to Bolton Wanderers (cs 1894), where he sustained a broken leg in 1896.

Steve Jones

KANE, Alex — 1926-27

Lge apps: 2

■ Often confused with fellow goalkeeper William Kaine and vice-versa, Alex played just two First Division matches for Hammers - at home, v Liverpool (16.1.26) and Derby County on New Year's Day, 1927, both of which ended in 2-1 defeats.

KAINE, William — 1924-25

Born: East Ham, London. 27.6.1900
Lge apps: 7

■ A member of the Hammers' reserve team which carried off the London Combination championship in the big goalkeeper's first season at Upton Park. Bill followed that success by being selected to represent London Combination v London League. After touring Germany with Hammers in the summer of 1924 the popular cockney returned to England to share the task of deputising for the injured Ted Hufton in the League side with Tommy Hampson. He moved across London to join Spurs in 1925 (playing 11 times in the League and one cup game) and later went to Luton Town and moved on to Bradford City in Mar. 1928. Bill joined Hammers from the Stirling Athletic club of Dageham. He died 3.1.1968.

KAY, George — 1919-26

Born: Manchester. 21.9.1891
Lge apps: 237 (15 gls)
Cup apps: 22 (2 gls)

■ This fine centre-half was one of the first former West Ham players to make a mark in football management and could justifiably lay claim to be the pioneer behind the famous West Ham managerial "Academy." Formerly with Bolton, George recorded another first when he became the only Englishman ever to captain an Irish League team during his spell with Belfast Celtic. Served with the Royal Garrison Artillery in the Great War and signed for Hammers in 1919, making his debut v Barnsley in September of that year. Taking over the team captaincy from Billy Cope for the 1922/23 season, he led Irons to Wembley and promotion to the First Division during his initial campaign as skipper. One of the few members of Hammers' Cup Final side not to win an international cap, he nevertheless became the first Hammer to play more than 200 League games for the club. He picked up the managerial reins with Southampton, when he retired from playing after a spell with Stockport, and did sufficiently well during his five years with the Saints to attract an offer from Liverpool to fill the manager's job at Anfield. Appointed in 1936, he had to wait until after the war for his first success with the Liverpudlians. Under his guidance the Reds won the first post-war First Division championship in 1946/47, and were narrowly defeated by Burnley in a replayed FA Cup semi-final at Maine Road. George was affected by ill health in the

George Kay

late forties, and was a sick man when the 'Pool reached their first Wembley Final v Arsenal in 1950. Although confined to his sick-bed during the two days prior to the game, he still proudly led his players on to the Wembley turf for presentation to His Majesty The King. George Kay retired from football in Feb. 1951 on medical advice, and sadly passed away in Apr. 1954.

Played	League		FAC		LC		Europe		Total	
	App	Gls	App	Gls	App	Gls	App	Gls	App	Gls
1919-20	27	3	4	0	0	0	0	0	31	3
1920-21	36	1	1	0	0	0	0	0	37	1
1921-22	39	5	3	0	0	0	0	0	42	5
1922-23	36	0	5	0	0	0	0	0	41	0
1923-24	40	3	3	1	0	0	0	0	43	4
1924-25	41	2	6	1	0	0	0	0	47	3
1925-26	18	1	0	0	0	0	0	0	18	1
TOTAL	237	15	22	2	0	0	0	0	259	17

Vic Keeble

KAYE, Albert   1900-01

Born: Stavely, Derbys. 1875
SL apps: 14 (2 gls)
Cup apps: 6 (3 gls)

■ Bert's football education began when his school days ended with his local village side, Stavely. Spotted by a Sheffield Wednesday scout, he subsequently spent four years with the Yorkshire club before coming south to join Chatham. West Ham United signed him in time for their first season, during which he made the majority of his senior appearances at inside-left, although he did appear once at centre-forward and on two occasions the left-wing. He later crossed the Irish Sea to play for a club in Belfast in company with Walter Tranter, a former TIW player.

KEARNS, Fred   1949-54

Born: Dublin, Republic of Ireland. 8.11.27
Lge apps: 43 (14 gls)
Cup apps: 2 (1 gl)

■ This likeable Irishman enjoyed a chequered career at Upton Park. Signed from Shamrock Rovers as a full-back, he found brief fame and international recognition when switched to the centre-forward berth! He was transferred to Norwich City in the summer of 1954, shortly after winning his first international cap.
☆ ***Republic of Ireland cap:*** *1954 v Luxembourg (1)*

KEEBLE, Vic   1957-59

Born: Colchester, Essex. 25.6.30
Lge apps: 76 (45 gls)
Cup apps: 4 (4 gls)

■ Hammers had gained a mere 12 points from the same amount of games when this great centre-forward joined them from Newcastle United in Oct. 1957 for £10,000. At the end of that campaign West Ham were back in the First Division, and Vic had grabbed 19 precious goals and much of the credit for getting them there. Originally signed for Colchester United by Ted Fenton when he was manager there in 1950, he moved to Tyneside for £15,000 and played for the Geordies in the 1955 Cup Final at Wembley. Ted remembered his protege and brought him to Upton Park just in the nick of time! Vic's career was brought to a sadly premature conclusion at the age of 29, due to worsening injury problems. He later worked as a football reporter and became general manager of Southern League Chelmsford City where he is now club secretary. The Essex club gave him a testimonial match in 1985/86 for which the Hammers provided some players in the opposing team

KEEN, Kevin   1986-93

Born: Amersham, Bucks. 25.2.67
Lge apps: 219 (21)
Cup apps: 44 (6)

■ Another home-grown product who made it through the youth ranks to become a first team regular. Kevin battled hard over several seasons to establish himself in the side, often appearing as sub under John Lyall. But Billy Bonds used him regularly and Kevin repaid that faith by playing a key role in the promotion-winning campaigns of 1990/91 and 1992/93. Ironically, many believed that Kevin's last season - in which he was ever-present, scored seven goals and made countless others for team mates - was his best at the club. Yet within weeks of reaching the Premiership with Hammers, "Keenie" was on the move to free-spending Wolves in a £600,000 deal that suited all parties. Although Wanderers were still only mid-table in Division One, the ambitious Midlands club were spending freely on new players and made Kevin an offer he could not refuse. The transfer ended his 10-year association with West Ham, which began when he signed apprentice 1.7.83, after playing three games for Wycombe Wanderers in 1982/83. Turned pro 6.3.84 and six months later he made his League debut at Upton Park v Liverpool (6.9.86) in a 5-2 defeat. Capped 15 times by England at Youth level and eight times as a Schoolboy, Kevin scored his first senior goal v Leyton Orient in the FA Cup (31.1.87) - his only goal in that competition. Scoring goals was never Kevin's main strength, although he still managed one or two spectacular efforts. He was essentially a very hard-working winger or midfielder, who chased up and down either the right or left flank to support the attack and, when required, assist his full-back. His pace and willingness to run at defenders unsettled the opposition, even though he was somewhat lightweight. Kevin set up many goal chances for team mates, but never forgot his defensive duties and was a good team man, appreciated by fellow players. Ironically, it was not until he showed consistently brilliant form in 1992/93 that Kevin, a shy, unassuming lad, finally won over the majority of the Upton Park crowd, who had, at times, treated him harshly in the past. His father, Mike, won a League Cup winners' medal with QPR in the first final to be played at Wembley, in 1967, and also played for Luton Town and Watford in the sixties. An intelligent man who once said it was his ambition to become a schoolteacher when he gives up the game, Kevin was not only missed by his team mates on the field when he left for Molineux. For it was invariably Keenie who supplied the board games that kept everybody entertained on the long coach trips to away games! In October 1994, Kevin joined former West Ham manager Lou Macari at Stoke City for a fee of £300,000.

Kevin Keen

Played	League		FAC		LC		Europe		Total	
	App	Gls	App	Gls	App	Gls	App	Gls	App	Gls
1986-87	13	0	2	1	2	0	0	0	17	1
1987-88	23	1	0	0	1	1	0	0	26	2
1988-89	24	3	5	0	2	1	0	0	31	4
1989-90	44	10	1	0	10	0	0	0	55	11
1990-91	40	0	7	0	3	1	0	0	50	1
1991-92	29	0	5	0	2	1	0	0	36	1
1992-93	46	7	2	0	2	0	0	0	50	7
TOTAL	219	21	22	1	22	5	0	0	263	27

KELLY, David   1988-90

Born: Birmingham. 25.11.65
Lge apps: 41 (7 gls)
Cup apps: 20 (5 gls)

■ Snapped up by John Lyall for £600,000 in the summer of 1988 despite competition from Tottenham, Paris St. Germain and Bayern Munich, who were all impressed by his scoring record for Walsall, where he netted 70 goals in two seasons. But "Ned" found the transition from Third to First Division quite difficult and, in a side that was struggling badly at the time, he (and Allen McKnight) quickly came under fire from supporters who expected much more from Tony Cottee's replacement. David's ordeal began on his debut when Hammers were crushed 4-0 at Southampton on the opening day of the season (27.8.88). He managed six goals in his first 21 League outings but his partnership with Leroy Rosenior was floundering and David found himself replaced by Stuart Slater early in 1989. Hammers could not avoid relegation that season and David's misery continued under new manager Lou Macari, who started him in only eight Second Division games. Playing for his third manager in 10 months, David managed to score in Billy Bonds' third match in charge, but his next game (v Portsmouth, 10.3.90) was his last for the club. The arrival of Trevor Morley and Jimmy Quinn again left him out in the cold and shortly before the end of the 1989/90 season David was on his way to Leicester City for £300,000, making a swift return to Upton Park for their visit on 2.5.90. Made 66 appearances for the Foxes before joining promotion-chasing Newcastle United in Dec. 1991 for £250,000. Helped the Magpies to win the First Division (at Hammers' expense) in May 1993 before joining Kevin Keen at Wolves in a £750,000 transfer a month later. So the striker who struggled at Upton Park has now been involved in almost £2 milllion pounds worth of transfer deals. A regular member of the Republic of Ireland squad, David scored a hat-trick on his full debut v Israel (10.11.87) and appeared as sub v Norway in the 1994 World Cup Finals in America.
☆ ***Republic of Ireland cap:*** *1989 v Tunisia (sub) (1)*

KELLY, Gary 1994

Born: Preston, Lancs. 3.8.66

■ Former Newcastle United goalkeeper who was signed on loan from Bury in Mar. 1994 after regular reserve team 'keeper Gerry Peyton suddenly left for Japan. West Ham needed cover for Ludek Miklosko in the season in which Premiership clubs had to name a sub. 'keeper for the first time. The Republic of Ireland Under-21 international watched 18 first team matches from the bench before returning to Gigg Lane without making a senior appearance. His father, Alan, played for Preston against West Ham in the 1964 FA Cup Final.

KELLY, Paul 1990

Born: Bexley, Kent. 12.10.69
Lge apps: 1

■ Starred for England at Schoolboy and Youth level and spent two years at the FA's National School of Excellence before returning to Hammers' apprentice ranks in 1986. This diminutive midfielder/right-back was a reserve team regular, but featured in only one League game - as second half sub for Steve Potts v Hull City at Upton Park (20.1.90). Paul's only full outing at senior level came in a 5-1 ZDSC defeat at Luton (19.12.90). He was given a free transfer by West Ham in May 1991 and another free, by Fulham, in the summer of 1994.

KELLY, William 1900-03

SL apps: 33
Cup apps: 4

■ This Scottish Junior international was signed from Everton at the beginning of the century and played in the club's first three seasons under the new banner of West Ham United. A centre-half, he made his debut in a 2-0 defeat at Bristol Rovers (24.11.1900). Transferred to Notts County in 1903, he was with Brighton for 1904/ 05.

KEMP, Fred 1906-07

Born: Tottenham, London. 1887
SL apps 11

■ Fred played for his school team in North London before his family moved to Barking and he took up with Ethelburgas and Barking St. Andrews. He spent one season with Newportonians before moving on to the Barking Victoria Club. Kemp made the big time with Woolwich Arsenal playing at inside-left. He made his initial appearance in Irons' SL side in a 3-1 Boleyn Victory over Brentford (6.10.06) in the outside-left position. He later reverted to the left-wing berth where he made his last appearance at Bristol Rovers (9.11.07).

KENNEDY, William 1910-12

Born: Grays, Essex
SL apps: 21 (10 gls)
Cup apps: 2

■ Bill came to West Ham from the club which was later to become known as Spurs' "nursery", Northfleet and had also played for Grays. A schoolteacher by profession, he marked his debut in the 3-1 Guy Fawkes day demolition of Brighton at Upton Park with a goal, and completed 10 SL appearances with four goals to his credit in that 1910/11 season. Looking likely to greatly overhaul those totals in the following campaign, all was well until he sustained a knee injury in a third round FA Cup replay with Middlesbrough, which effectively ended his first-class football career. Although not considered fit enough for the rigours of pro soccer, he was, however, given the all-clear to participate in the greatest conflict ever known to man - World War One - and subsequently lost his life serving the London Scottish Regiment in France.

David Kelly

Syd King (right) and Charlie Paynter - two great West Ham servants

KING, Syd
1899-03

SL apps: (TIW) 16
SL apps: (WHU) 59
Cup apps: 7

■ Anything that E.S. (Syd) King achieved in his playing career was destined to be eclipsed by his success as the first manager of West Ham United FC. Beginning his career as a full-back with Northfleet, grammar school-educated Syd once claimed to have conceded a hat-trick of own goals for that club v Swindon Town. Transferring to New Brompton (now Gillingham) in 1897, he spent two seasons with the Kent club before joining TIW in cs 1899. King was considered to be the best full-back in the SL and as if to underline the fact, TIW immediately received an application for his transfer from Derby County before he had kicked a ball for the Irons. He suffered a bad ankle injury in a match v Spurs at the Memorial Grounds (10.3.1899), however, which ruled him out for the rest of the term and although he recovered sufficiently to continue playing for the new West Ham United club the following season, he was never quite the same player. He still managed to form a formidable full-back pairing with Scotsman Charlie Craig but the fact that he was appointed club secretary in 1902, while still continuing to play, suggested that he saw his future in administration. Syd made his last SL appearance in Irons' 1-1 draw at Ketttering (15.4.03) and although he still played the occasional match in the London or Western League, his retirement heralded a new era which saw him successfully oversee the club's embrace of professionalism, the move to the Boleyn Grounds and the eventual elevation to Football League membership in 1919. The latter was achieved by skilful manipulation of the media over many years, King having long since realised the power of the press. Ably assisted by Charlie Paynter, Syd gradually improved the team's performances in their first three League seasons, until 1922/23 when he really hit the jackpot, leading the team to the first-ever FA Cup Final at Wembley and out of the Second Division wilderness. After nine long and hard seasons in the First Division, West Ham were relegated at the end of 1931/32 and Syd King's world fell apart. Despite West Ham's fall back to Division Two, his position was not under threat because of it. However, during a board meeting (7.11.32), when team matters were being discussed, King was drunk and insubordinate and insulted at least one director. At an emergency board meeting the following night (only the third in the history of the club) it was decided that 'Mr E.S. King be suspended for three calender months from 9 November 1932 without salary and further stipulate that he shall not visit the ground during this period.' The terse statement sounded the death knell for the man who had done so much for West Ham, but was now strictly persona non grata. The board had also expressed concern about King's honesty in the day-to-day business of running the club and in a further meeting (3.1.33), concluded that it could not re-engage him in any capacity. The new secretary, Alan Searles (himself sacked for defalcation in 1940), advised King of the decision and informed him of the board's offer of an ex-gratia payment of £3·per week. But King saved them their money by taking an alcoholic drink laced with a corrosive liquid and committing suicide less than a month after his dismissal.

KINGSLEY, Matthew
1904-05

Born: Turton, Lancashire, 1879.
SL apps: 29
Cup apps: 1

■ Already established as one of the country's top goalkeepers when he joined Hammers at the age of 29 from Newcastle United in the summer of 1904, Matt was on duty between the posts in the unaugural Southern League match v Millwall at Upton Park on Sept. 1, that year. Starting his career amid humble surroundings with his village side Turton, and then Darwen, he signed for Newcastle in 1898. He made his Magpies' debut in the club's first-ever First

Harry Kinsell leads out Hammers at Upton Park followed by Ernie Gregory and Tommy Moroney. There are some well-known faces in the player's enclosure also, including Ernie Devlin (front, second from right) and Bill Robinson (holding paper).

Division fixture v Wolves (3.9.1898) at St. James's Park, and three years later experienced the thrill of keeping goal for England v Wales at the same venue, thus becoming Newcastle's first bona fide English international. After making 189 Football League appearances for the Tynesiders, his Hammers' career began promisingly enough, but was destined for a premature end following a fracas with former West Ham player Herbert Lyon, in an SL clash with Brighton in Mar. 1905. It was to be Kingsley's last game in the claret and blue and, after his suspension, he joined London rivals Queens Park Rangers in the close season. One season with Rangers was followed by a year out of football before he made a comeback with

Rochdale, whom he served until retiring to settle in the Blackburn area.

KINSELL, Thomas Harry 1951-56

Born: Cannock, Staffs. 3.5.21
Lge apps: 101 (2 gls)
Cup apps: 4

■ Already an experienced England international defender when he arrived at the Boleyn from Reading for £5,250. Harry had also seen service with West Bromich Albion (who he helped to promotion to Division One in 1949) and Bolton Wanderers, as well as guesting during war-time

with Grimsby Town, Middlesbrough and Blackpool (where he had won Football League and North Cup medals). His signing was another shrewd venture into the transfer market by manager Ted Fenton, who had been a colleague in the England team. He gave Hammers five seasons' yeoman service, often captaining the side, before being given a free transfer to Southern League Bedford Town. He was mine host of the Alma Arms public house at Stratford in 1981, and later took over at an off-licence. Harry had returned to his roots and was living in the heart of the Black Country, at Brierley Hill, in 1990.

KIRBY, William 1903-04

Born: Preston, Lancashire. 1882
SL apps: 33 (gls 10)
Cup apps: 3 (1 gl)

■ An outside-right who liked a crack at goal, Bill was given a spell at centre-forward in an attempt to further encourage his goal-scoring inclinations, but only one goal resulted from his three appearances in the number nine shirt, although he still continued to deliver the goods when returned to his natural position. Formerly with Swindon Town, he scored on his opening-day-of-the-season debut v Millwall, and missed only one match throughout the campaign - funnily enough, the last fixture of the season v Swindon at the Memorial Grounds. Nicknamed "Sunny Jim" by colleagues and fans alike, Bill returned to Swindon for 1904/05 and then commenced (1905) a seven-year stay at Portsmouth. His wanderings were far from over, however, the 1912/13 season seeing him with his home town club, Preston North End. He then had spells with Merthyr Tydfil and Exeter City up to the outbreak of WW1, during which he assisted Croydon Common and Brentford. He joined the Royal Engineers early in the war but was invalided out of the service. He then worked in munitions at the Woolwich Arsenal but found the confined conditions did not agree with him and re-enlisted with his old regiment in 1917.

Joe Kirkup in action against Olympiakos

KIRKALDIE, Jack 1937-39

Born: Coventry. 2.8.1917
Lge apps: 11 (1 gl)
Cup apps: 1

■ A former rugby player, Jack was discovered in Warwickshire junior football by Southend United scout Syd Gibson after converting to soccer. When Syd joined the Upton Park ground-staff he subsequently recommended the speedy winger to Hammers, who in turn promptly signed him from the Shrimpers. Although facing stiff opposition from Johnny Morton and Stan Foxall, he made his Second Division baptism at the Boleyn in the 4-0 victory over Southampton (27.3.37). His solitary goal during his Hammers' career came against those other distinguished wearers of the claret and blue, Aston Villa, at Villa Park the following month. Only six first team appearances in 1937/38 and a paltry two the next campaign made him unsettled, with the result that he transferred to Doncaster Rovers in Apr. 1939, after his 18 goals for Irons' reserves had alerted the Yorkshire club to his potential. Alas, after participating in the false start of the truncated 1939/40 season, Jack found himself playing war-time football along with fellow ex-Hammers Albert Walker and Fred Dell at Belle Vue. He returned to Rovers with the resumption of normal football in 1946, and made his mark with 16 goals in 51 appearances during the immediate post-war period.

KIRKUP, Joe 1958-66

Born: Hexham, Northumberland. 17.12.39
Lge apps: 165 (6 gls)
Cup apps: 22

■ A constructive, resourceful full-back, the popular North-Easterner was a product of the club's ground-staff and signed pro when he was 17, making his First Division debut v Manchester City at Maine Road in Dec. 1958. His highlight with Hammers must have been playing at Wembley in the 1965 European Cup Winners' Cup Final v TSV Munich, after gaining Youth and Under-23 honours. Hammers made a killing when they sold Joe for £27,000 to London rivals Chelsea in Mar. 1966, but although Joe played 53 First Division games for the Blues, just as he had missed the 1964 Cup final versus PNE in '64, he was again unlucky when passed over for Chelsea's 1967 Wembley meeting with Spurs. It was in that year another sizeable fee took him to his last port of call as a player, Southampton. He amassed a further 169 First Division appearances with the Saints which, added to his 165 Division One games for Hammers, made a grand total of 388 League appearances - and not one of them outside the First Division. In 1975 he emigrated with his family to become player/manager at Durban City in South Africa, taking over the post vacated by his old Hammers team-mate Budgie Byrne, who is still out in S.A. managing Hellenic. But it was a shorter stay for Joe who couldn't settle there. Especially when the club

chairman began meddling in team affairs. So he returned to England during that scorching summer of 1976 and left football for good when he joined Byfleet Machine & Tool Co. Ltd. as a progress manager, in the employ of his old M.D. at Chelsea, George Thomson. After three years as a 'trouble-shooter' Joe fancied another change and dispensed hospitality as mine host of the Rose & Crown at Upper Farringdon in Hampshire. With his children Tony and Nick growing up Joe decided to leave the pub trade so he could spend more time with his sons and wife Jill and went back to engineering. As Hammers were winning the Cup in 1980, Joe made another career change when he took over a sports shop in Cranleigh, near Guildford. Now Joe sells the news instead of helping to make the headlines, as he did as a player, from behind the counter of J & J Kirkup Newsagents at Ewell, Surrey. But he's still running a team - his 12 paper boys and girls at the crack of dawn every morning!

KITCHEN, George 1905-11

Born: Fairfield, Derbys. 1876
SL apps: 184 (5 gls)
Cup apps: 21 (1 gl)

■ Many players have marked their debut for West Ham by scoring one goal or more, but to George Kitchen goes the distinction of being the only goalkeeper to do so! The unique event in Hammers' history occurred when George fired the ball past his opposite number in the Swindon Town goal from the penalty-spot in the opening fixture of the 1905/06 season at Upton Park. By the end of that winter his successful conversions had become a major talking-point among fans up and down the country, as had his equally successful efforts in keeping his own goal intact. Considered one of the finest uncapped 'keepers in the country when with Everton, George had begun has career with Buxton and then Stockport County in the Lancashire League in 1897, and won a Manchester Cup Winners' medal with them. Awarded a benefit at Goodison, his services were similarly recognised at the Boleyn Ground when he was given joint-share of the receipts for a match with Coventry, along with Fred Blackburn. Seriously injured in a cup match at Newcastle in Feb. 1908, he bounced back to earn his cash reward and founder membership of Hammers' goalkeeping "Hall of Fame." Signed to replace the equally high-profile Matt Kingsley, who had transferred to QPR, George was a first-class golfer and became a professional at the age of 14. He made a good living at that sport but eventually decided to concentrate on soccer. He was also a fine cricketer and acted as coach to the Dulwich College team. Asked for his views on the new

PROMINENT FOOTBALLERS.

G. KITCHEN,
WEST HAM UNITED.

ruling in 1905, that stipulated that goalkeepers must remain under their cross-bar when facing penalty kicks, Kitchen laughingly observed: "It won't make it easier for the goalkeeper; I should say that there will not be many penalty kicks stopped." It was a rule that both helped and hindered him in his almost unique role of penalty-stopper and taker! Transferred to Southampton in 1912, he served Saints for two years and made 39 SL and Cup appearances (but no goals!) before retiring from football to become a golf pro. George was "still alive and kicking" and working as a doorman at Lee Green Working Man's Club in 1969.

KITCHENER, Bill   1966-67

Born: Arlesley, Beds. 3.11.46
Lge apps: 11

■ Tall, skilful full-back who signed pro forms in Nov. 1963, after playing in the Youth Cup-winning team of that year. Returned from a six-month loan period at Torquay United (where he played under ex-Hammer Frank O'Farrell) to make his initial First Division appearance v Nottingham Forest at the City Ground in Mar. 1967. He won an extended run in the first team, being a member of the Hammers' side that gained maximum points from their three Easter engagements that year. Permanently transferred to Torquay in Dec. 1967, he later moved along the coast to end his League days at Bournemouth, before joining the Devon and Cornwall Constabulary; later stationed in Bournemouth. He is now stationed at Burley in the New Forest, Hants.

KYLE, Peter   1901-02

Born: Glasgow, Scotland. Sept. 1880
Lge apps: 1
Cup apps: 2

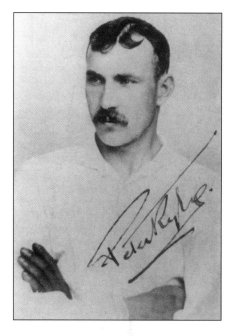

■ A larger than life character who learnt his football with Glasgow and District schools and his first club Glasgow Parkhead, Peter was rejected after trial periods with Clyde, Hearts and Hammers. A state of affairs which led to the player returning to Scotland briefly to play for junior club Larkhall Thistle.
The trepidation of his earlier potential employers proved to be well-founded when the extrovert centre-forward was suspended, and then sacked, by Spurs after scoring 19 goals in 41 appearances for the North London club in the spring of 1905, for "a breach of the club's training rules" along with team-mate Chris Carrick, who also played for West Ham.
It seemed there was little doubt over his footballing ability but a big question mark over his temperament. His sole SL appearance for Irons came in an unremarkable 2-1 defeat at Queens Park Rangers (9.11.01), after which he was involved in a straight swap for Welsh international full-back Bill Jones from Kettering Town. A month after falling foul of the Spurs' management, Kyle was transferred to Woolwich Arsenal, in Apr. 1906, who then played at Manor Road. He scored 22 goals in 60 senior outings for Arsenal, and joined the last club he played against for Gunners - Aston Villa - in Mar. 1908. By October the wayward star was on the move again, to Sheffield United, but once again his old failing came to the fore when he failed to train properly with the Blades and returned to Scotland to join Royal Albert FC.
He did return to SL football with Watford in Nov. 1909, but soon returned home again north of the border. A sad decline for a player who had taken part in a trial match for his country in 1907.

Bill Kitchener

Frank Lampard

LAMPARD, Frank 1967-85

Born: East Ham, London. 20.9.48
Lge apps: 551 (17 gls)
Cup apps: 114 (4 gls)

■ When Frank's outstanding career as a West Ham full-back finally came to an end, he went down in the history books as one of the greats, of the post-war era. Signing apprentice forms in 1964 and full professional a year later, he twice fought off serious injury to continue his advancement. He made his League debut v Manchester City at Upton Park (18.11.67) - six months and 19 senior outings later he suffered his first set-back...breaking a leg v Sheffield United at Bramall Lane. Slowly, and with a great deal of sweat and toil, Frank recovered to regain his confidence and with it his first team place. International recognition followed with four Under-23 appearances and then the first of his two senior England caps, v Yugoslavia (11.10.72). Alf Ramsey also gave Wembley debuts that night to Mick Mills, Jeff Blockley and Mick Channon, but England - led by Bobby Moore - were fortunate to salvage a 1-1 draw and Frank had to wait another eight years for his other cap. This time under Ron Greenwood - the man who brought him to West Ham - Frank played in the 2-1 victory over Australia in Sydney (31.5.80 - Alan Devonshire made a sub. appearance), although he can consider himself very unlucky not to have been selected more often. But the sweet and sour intermingled in 1972/73, with Hammers' heart-breaking knock-out in the League Cup semi-final marathon by Stoke City. Frank duly got to Wembley in 1975, however, picking up a winners' medal in the 2-0 victory over Fulham. Frank experienced the thrill of European competition the following season and contributed a vital goal in the 3-1 quarter-final home win over Den Haag, after Hammers' had lost the first leg in Holland 4-2. But, typical of Frank's roller-coaster career, the European Cup Winners' Cup Final in Brussels v Anderlecht brought about the biggest disappointment of his soccer life. A goal ahead with only minutes to go to half-time, Hammers were playing like world-beaters and seemed to be cruising to victory, when Frank went to play a ball that - 99 times out of 100 - he would have got safely back to 'keeper Mervyn Day. But on this occasion his studs caught in the turf, causing him to sustain an excruciating stomach injury. To make matters worse the Belgians scored from the incident and went on to win 4-2. Frank was flown home immediately after the game for an emergency operation. Once again he fought back to fitness, although at one time there was talk of a transfer to Norwich City. It must have been particularly gratifying for him when he scored the semi-final winner v Everton in the epic replay at Elland Road to take Hammers to Wembley for the victorious FA Cup Final v Arsenal in 1980. Frank's celebratory dance of delight around the Leeds corner-flag will be remembered probably as much as his timely headed winner! Frank was now at the peak of his illustrious career and in the season after gaining his second full cap, he won League Cup runnners-up and Second Division championship medals (1980/81). In September the following year he joined the exclusive band of West Ham players who have played 500 or more League games for the club. Frank was awarded a free transfer after playing in the final fixture of 1984/85 v Liverpool (20.5.85). He joined Southend United, pairing up with his old mate Bobby Moore who was managing the Shrimpers. It was like a Hammers' mini reunion, with central defender Kevin Lock in the side and Harry Cripps on the coaching staff. But after 38 League and cup appearances for Southend in Division Three, Frank hung up his boots at the same time Mooro resigned as manager. And now a new Lampard has emerged on the Upton Park scene, for his son, Frank junior, is a star in the youth team. Young Frank has a very tough act to follow. His dad, quietly spoken off the field, was as hard as nails on it. But he played with brain, not brawn. His fierce tackles visibly shook many opponents, but Frank was much more than a solid full-back. Comfortable in possession, he made himself available to receive passes from fellow defender Moore and would begin many attacks himself from deep within his own half. His triangular link up with those two other gifted left-sided players, Trevor Brooking and Alan Devonshire, proved the cornerstone of so many victories over a period of six years. At times in the 1980/81 Second Division promotion-winning campaign, they were unstoppable. Frank also packed a ferocious shot and claimed his fair share of spectacular goals from long-range. And only Billy Bonds made more League appearances for West Ham United than fearless Frank. Despite pursuing a number of business ventures outside the game, West Ham have remained close to Frank's heart. He regularly worked for the club in a part-time scouting and coaching capacity before being appointed assistant to his brother-in-law, Harry Redknapp, when 'H' stepped up to take over from Billy Bonds in August 1994.
☆ *England caps:* 1972 v Yugoslavia; 1980 v Australia (2)

Played	League		FAC		LC		Europe		Total	
	App	Gls	App	Gls	App	Gls	App	Gls	App	Gls
1968-68	19	0	3	0	0	0	0	0	22	0
1968-69	1	0	0	0	0	0	0	0	1	0
1969-70	30	0	1	0	2	1	0	0	33	1
1970-71	41	1	1	0	2	0	0	0	44	1
1972-73	38	0	2	0	2	0	0	0	42	0
1973-74	42	2	2	0	2	0	0	0	46	2
1974-75	40	4	8	1	3	0	0	0	51	5
1975-76	37	3	1	0	4	0	9	1	51	4
1976-77	36	1	2	0	1	0	0	0	39	1
1977-78	40	0	3	0	1	0	0	0	44	0
1978-79	29	3	1	0	1	0	0	0	31	3
1979-80	36	0	7	1	6	0	0	0	49	1
1980-81	39	1	2	0	8	0	6	0	55	1
1981-82	28	0	2	0	5	0	0	0	35	0
1982-83	37	2	1	0	4	0	0	0	42	2
1983-84	18	0	3	0	3	0	0	0	24	0
1984-85	1	0	0	0	0	0	0	0	1	0
TOTAL	551	17	43	2	54	1	15	1	660	22

LANDELLS, Jack — 1933-34

Born: Gateshead 11.11.1904
Lge apps: 12 (3 gls)
Cup apps: 1

■ Although he was born in the North-East, Jack played all his football in the south after his family moved to Essex. He spent his formative years in that county and gained experience with local sides Thames Board Mills, Jurgens, Grays Athletic and Grays Thurrock. He then joined Millwall and had eight years at The Den, winning FA honours. Making the short journey across the Thames to sign for Irons in the summer of 1932, he made his Second Division bow v Bolton Wanderers on the opening day of the 1933/34 season at Upton Park. A scheming inside-forward, Jack transferred to Bristol City in 1934. In June 1935, he moved on to Carlisle United and the following summer joined Walsall. He was back in London with Clapton Orient in June 1937. He was selected for a Test match appearance v South Africa in July 1929 and also represented The Rest v England in March of the same year. He and Millwall colleague John Page were known as the 'Grays Twins,' a reference to their earlier association with the Essex club. John was responsible for 33 of Lions' 127-goal haul when they won the Championship of the Third Division South in 1929. A former clerk, he went into the motor trade after hanging up his boots. Also acted as Midlands scout for Arsenal. His brother, George Landells, was a player with Tunbridge Wells Rangers in 1933.

Billy Lansdowne, Snr

LANDSDOWNE, Bill, Snr. — 1956-62

Born: Shoreditch, London.
Lge apps: 57 (5 gls)
Cup apps: 3

■ Signing pro after his demobilisation from the RAF in Apr. 1956, this consistent wing-half made his League debut later the same month v Lincoln City at Upton Park and was a frequent member of the Second Division championship side in 1958. He was appointed coach to the juniors in 1965, but left a year later to become manager of Eastbourne United (where Ron Greenwood served his managerial apprenticeship) after qualifying for his FA coaching badge. Bill returned in 1967, however, to take charge of Hammers' youth squad, later moving up to coach the reserves. He then became connected with Dagenham FC.

LANSDOWNE, Billy, Jnr. — 1978-81

Born: Epping, Essex. 28.4.59
Lge apps: 9 (1 gl)
Cup apps: 5 (3 gls)

■ A live-wire young striker who was well-schooled by his above-mentioned father. Scored a celebrated hat-trick to end the League Cup marathon with Southend United in 1979 and made his League debut when he came on as sub v Wrexham the previous season. Transferred to Charlton Athletic in 1981, Bill later had a spell in Sweden but returned home to feature in Dagenham's great FA Cup run in 1984/85.

LANE, Harry — 1919-21

Born: Hinckley, Leicestershire. 23.10.1894
Lge apps: 19

■ A schoolmaster signed from Sutton, Harry made his Second Division bow as a right-half and later showed his versatility by switching to the centre-forward position and then right-back. He transferred to London rivals Charlton Athletic in 1921. Joined QPR in July 1922.

Billy Lansdowne, Jnr

LA RONDE, Everald   1982-83

Born: Forest Gate, London. 24.1.63
Lge apps: 7

■ A promising young coloured defender who appeared to have a bright future at Upton Park. Captained the 1981 Youth Cup-winning side and showed up well when drafted into the senior side, making his League debut v Coventry City in Apr. 1982. Then joined up with former Hammer Harry Redknapp at Bournemouth, but after a spell he returned to local junior soccer.

LAVERY, William   1909-11

Born: Fleetwood, Lancashire. 1887
SL apps: 17
Cup apps: 2

■ Bill was a right-back who made his SL debut for Irons in a 4-2 defeat at Luton (11.12.09). His next appearance was at left-back in a 0-0 draw at Brentford (22.1.10) and was his last outing that season. The second game of the following season, at Coventry, saw him embark on an uninterrupted 14-match sequence back at his favourite right-back position - in the SL side. He was to make just one more appearance, however, in a 6-0 win at Southend (31.12.10), when Danny Shea scored four. Transferred from Preston North End in 1909 where he had appeared in 14 First Division matches in 1906/07, none in 1907/08 and eight in 1908/09. Mostly a reserve at the Boleyn Ground due to the fine displays of Fairman and Shreeve, he later played in Ireland.

LEAFE A. Richard   1913-22

Born: Boston, Lincs. 1891.
SL apps: 63 (33 gls)
Cup apps: 6 (4 gls)

■ Dick Leafe began his career with Boston Town and along with his elder brother Tom, a wing-half, signed amateur forms for Grimsby Town in May 1909. He made one appearance for the Mariners before returning to his home town club in 1910, but then signed for Sheffield United in Nov. 1910. Dick joined Hammers from the Blades in 1913 during the club's Southern League days, and quickly made his impact as a goal-scoring forward, ending up leading marksman in 1914/15. Making only a handful of appearances in war-time competitions, he returned to the first team following the election of the club to Division Two of the Football League in 1919, his versatility proving an asset in the higher grade. Appointed assistant secretary when he retired from playing in 1922, he held the post up to the outbreak of WW2, when the management was forced to reduce the staff. Also had an interest in a pre-war bookmaker's business.

Dick Leafe

LEE, James   1919-21

Born: Rotherham, Yorkshire, 1892.
Lge apps: 26

■ Began his career with Rotherham County. Transferred from Grimsby Town in time to participate in Hammers' first-ever Football League match v Lincoln City on the opening day of the 1919/20 season, he understudied regular full-backs Billy Cope and Frank "Bronco" Burton. Moved on to Newport County in 1921. Described as "a deceptive player in that he might give an impression of lacking concentration and then found difficult to outwit. His speciality, a clean kick. Could also play half-back."

LEE, Thomas   1907-08

SL apps: 6

■ Tommy showed his versatility when he played in three different positions in his first three games for West Ham, at outside-right, inside-left and outside-right. Previously with Woolwich Arsenal, he made six Southern League appearances that season, his final outing coming in the last fixture of the campaign at Plymouth. Transferred to Coventry City, Lee played in the same side as E (Patsy) Hendren, the well-known England and Middlesex cricketer, but only had six outings with the Bantams.

PROMINENT FOOTBALLERS.

T. LEE,
WEST HAM UNITED.

LEONARD, Patrick   1898-99

SL apps: 12 (8 gls) TIW

■ This former Manchester City winger caused a sensation when he scored a hat-trick in his first outing for Irons in a friendly against Upton Park. He also scored twice on his second SL showing in a 4-3 win at Wolverton which was just one of a run of 16 consecutive victories in the SL Second Division. He hit four in the 10-0 win over Maidenhead in the last match of the season at the Memorial Grounds and also scored in the 3-1 championship decider at Millwall v Isle of Wight team Cowes, who had won a low-profile six-club section of the SL representing the South-West. But they were not pleased with the choice of venue which was 100 miles from the Solent and only three from the Memorial Grounds. By the following season he had returned to Manchester City after only five months at Canning Town.

LESLIE, Lawrie   1961-63

Born: Edinburgh, Scotland. 17.3.35
Lge apps: 57
Cup apps: 4

■ One of the most popular goalkeepers ever to appear for West Ham. Played his first competitive football with Hawkhill Amateurs from where he graduated to Newton Grange Star and part-time pro status in the early 1950's. Joining the army in 1956, Lawrie was stationed at Oswestry in the Artillery and played for the Regimental side, progressing to command trial with the great Duncan Edwards and Bobby Charlton of Manchester United. Midway through his service he met one of the Hibs' players, Jock Buchan, who persuaded him to write to Easter Road for a trial. After a test for the reserves he duly signed pro forms and in 1958 he was in the Hibs side which lost to Clyde in the Scottish FA Cup Final. He transferred to Airdrie in November, 1959 for £4,475 and was appointed captain at Broomfield Park where he also won five international caps for Scotland. Courageous almost to a fault, this daring Scot had broken almost evey bone in his body before arriving at Upton Park, from Airdrie for £14,000. He was run over by a truck as a small boy and told he would be lucky to walk again, but confounded the doctors to reach the pinnacle of his profession. His worst playing injury occurred at the Boleyn Ground (3.11.62) when he sustained a broken leg while repelling a

Lawrie Leslie

Bolton Wanderers' attack. Although he made a remarkable recovery to regain his place in the first XI for the final four matches of the season, he was passed over for the start of 1963/64 and asked for a transfer. He did not have to wait long for Stoke City to offer him a regular First Division spot and a move to the Victoria Ground for a fee of £15,000. After three successful seasons with the Potters, Lawrie returned to the East End with Millwall and earned great respect at The Den as a trainer/coach after he had ended his playing career at Southend United. Lawrie represented the Scottish League on three occasions. After finishing his playing days at Southend, he then sought a career outside the game and began working on a part-time basis for the council in North London and now has a dual role of Head of Centre at the Cardinal Pole School in Homerton and youth centre organiser for Hackney Borough Council. When pressure of work permits, he likes a round of golf at Bexley Heath Golf Club.

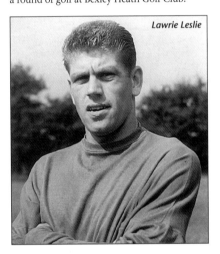

Lawrie Leslie

LEWIS, Eddie   1956-58

Born: Manchester. 3.1.35
Lge apps: 31 (12 gls)
Cup apps: 5 (3 gls)

■ A former "Busby Babe," Eddie joined Hammers from Preston North End in an exchange deal which resulted in Frank O'Farrell going to Deepdale. Originally a centre-forward, he was successfully converted to the full-back berth when he joined Leyton Orient. He had previously turned in some useful performances during Hammers' promotion season, and later did the same for the O's when they too were elevated to the First Division in 1962. He later played for Folkestone Town and went on to manage Ford Sports in the Greater London League. Eddie emigrated to South Africa in the late sixties and has become a well known figure in the S.A. game, making up a quartet of former Hammers living there - Johnny Byrne, Johnny Sissons, Andy Malcolm and Ed.

LEWIS, Harry   1935-36

Born: Abergavenny, Wales. 25.10.1910
Lge apps: 4 (4 gls)

■ A Welsh schoolboy international, he joined Arsenal after a spell with Rochdale, and then played for Southend United and Notts County making his Hammers' debut in a 3-0 drubbing at the hands of Bury at Gigg Lane (28.9.35). He had ample revenge in the return fixture at Upton Park the following February, when he blasted a hat-trick in a 6-0 win against the Shakers. It was the highlight of the versatile Welshman's contribution to a season which saw West Ham narrowly miss promotion back to the First Division.

LILL, Mickey

Born: Romford, Essex. 3.8.36

■ A brilliant youth team winger who was lured away to Wolves, in 1954, before he had a chance to play for Hammers' League side. Sold to Everton six years later for a big fee, he had the satisfaction of scoring a goal against his former Hammers' team-mates at Goodison Park in Sept. 1960. An England Youth international, he played his early football with Storey Athletic, and later had spells with Plymouth Argyle and Portsmouth after he left the Merseysiders. He then went out of the League to play for Guildford City, later coaching in South Africa.

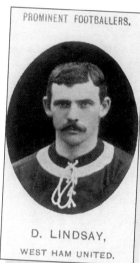

PROMINENT FOOTBALLERS.

D. LINDSAY,
WEST HAM UNITED.

Harry Lewis

LINDSAY, David   1906-08

SL apps: 50 (4 gls)
Cup apps: 2

■ Came to Hammers from Heart of Midlothian cs 1906. Formerly with St. Mirren, he was capped for Scotland v Ireland in 1903. Dave missed only one match on the right-wing in 1906/07 and his accurate crosses led to many goals for his inside men, Stapley, Grassam and Watson.

LINDSAY, J   TIW

■ An inside or centre-forward from the Old Castle Swifts club who played in a number of early games for the Irons and probably in the very first fixture v Royal Ordnance (7.9.1895).

LINDSAY, Jimmy   1968-70

Born: Hamilton, Scotland. 12.7.49
Lge apps: 39 (2 gls)
Cup apps: 6

■ A scheming midfield motivator, plucked from Scottish junior football where he had gained considerable respect playing for Glasgow Boys. Signing pro forms in the summer of 1966, he won a Scottish Youth cap the following year and made his initial First Division appearance as sub v. Burnley in Oct. 1968. Transferred to Watford in 1971, later playing for Colchester United, Hereford United and Shrewsbury Town.

Jimmy Lindsay

LINWARD, William 1901-02

Born: 1878
SL apps: 40 (3 gls)
Cup apps: 2 (1 gl)

■ Bill's photograph in a 1902 club handbook portrays a fine example of fashionable Edwardian manhood, resplendent in a polkadot crevat and stiff-starched collar, setting off his moustachioed features just right for the times. He was no slouch on the field either, appearing in 40 consecutive Southern League fixtures following his transfer from Doncaster Rovers. An ever-present n 1901-02, he made all his appearances at outside-left. Billy joined London rivals Woolwich Arsenal in Dec. 1902 and moved on to Norwich City for 1905/06.

LIVETT, Simon 1990-91

Born: Plaistow, London. 8.1.69
Lge apps: 1
Cup apps: 1

■ Creative midfielder whose patience was finally rewarded when he was given his League debut v Wolves at Upton Park (15.9.90). Wore the number nine shirt as a replacement for the injured Stuart Slater but, unfortunately, Simon, too, was struck by the injury jinx and was forced out of the 1-1 draw at half-time due to a knee problem. His only other competitive senior appearance was as half-time sub. for Colin Foster v Aldershot in the FA Cup third round tie at Upton Park (5.1.91). Also played the full ZDSC game at Luton (19.12.90) and appeared in other first team friendlies. A mainstay of Hammers' reserves from 1985 until he left on a free transfer to neighbours Leyton Orient in 1992/93. Unable to command a regular place at Brisbane Road, Simon had a short spell on loan to Cambridge United and joined them on a full transfer for 1993/94. Spent the latter part of that season on loan to his local GM Vauxhall Conference League club, Dagenham & Redbridge. A West Ham lad through and through, Simon's brother, Richard, used to work as assistant manager in the Upton Park ticket office.

Simon Livett

LLEWELYN, David 1969-71

Born: Cardiff, Wales. 9.8.49
Lge apps: 6

■ Former Cardiff Boys star who attracted the attention of the Welsh Under-23 selectors with his prolific goal-scoring exploits in Hammers' reserve side. Despite this success he was unable to win a regular place in the first team pool and was reluctantly allowed to join ex-Hammer Noel Cantwell at Peterborough United (then manager at London Road). Welsh Under-23 cap v Scotland (1972).

LLOYD, David 1898/99 TIW

Born: 1874
SL apps: 13 (14 gls)
Cup apps: 3

■ Standing at 6ft 4ins and tipping the scales at 13st, David must have been an imposing sight for opponents. Signed from the Third Grenadier Guards, he played his first two TIW matches as full-back, but caused a sensation when he scored three times on his debut at centre-forward v St. Albans. He scored 14 goals in 11 matches as a forward, including a vital opening goal in a SL championship decider in a 3-1 victory over Cowes (Isle of Wight) at neutral Millwall. He also scored Irons' goal in a Test match v Sheppey United who had finished 12th out of 13 clubs in the First Division of the SL, enabling them to draw 1-1 at Chatham. In the end it was all academic, as the senior division was enlarged for 1899/1900 so the four Test match combatants, plus QPR and Bristol Rovers from outside the League, were admitted. Irons were in the SL First Division, but David Lloyd had moved on before they played the first match at Reading.

Kevin Lock

LOCK, Kevin 1972-78

Born: Plaistow, London. 27.12.53
Lge apps: 132 (2 gls)
Cup apps: 29

■ First-class defender, given the unenviable task of filling Bobby Moore's number six shirt after Hammers' skipper had taken the road to Craven Cottage, he did well. Indeed, Kevin took the opportunity to show how well he had learned from the old maestro in the unique 1975 Cup Final confrontation, making a major contribution to West Ham's 2-0 victory. Hammers then made a £60,000 profit when Kevin joined the Cottagers, having paid out no more than the statutory signing-on fee in 1969. Kevin won three England Under-23 caps in 1973. Ironically, his link with Moore was rekindled in 1985 when he moved to Southend United on a free transfer and played 10 League games under the management of his former mentor, as well as alongside another ex-Hammer Frank Lampard. Fair-haired Kevin, a tall, lean central defender, stayed at Roots Hall in a coaching capacity after his playing days were over.

LONSDALE, Thomas 1913-14

Born: Bishop Auckland. 21.9.1882
SL apps: 21

■ After making his way with North-Eastern amateur clubs, West Auckland and the more famous Bishop Auckland, Tom entered League football with Grimsby Town in 1908. A safe, reliable goalkeeper, he made his Mariners' debut 5.12.08, and went on to make 87 Second Division appearances for the Humberside club and won a Midland League Championship medal with them in 1910/11, before joining Hammers in Oct. 1913. Taking over the first team spot from Joe Hughes, he made his first appearance v Crystal Palace at Upton Park (25.10.13) and all was well until January 14, 1914, when Tommy was reported at a board meeting for "being absent without leave." The board's reaction was to fine the player a week's wages and demote him to the reserve team. With the senior side in the middle of a seven-match winning run, it was some weeks before he regained his place, which he retained until the end of the season, when he transferred to Southend United and played 28 games in 1914/15. He saw service with Stalybridge Celtic (in Division Three North) and Port Vale after WW1, and in the early seventies proved there was no lingering animosity between himself and West Ham over the 1914 incident when he sent a nice letter to Jack Helliar. In it he gave details of both himself and Hammers' 1923 Cup final inside-right, Billy Brown, who lived near him at Fence Houses, Houghton-le-Spring, Co. Durham. An extract from Doug Lamming's Who's Who of Grimsby Town gives a further insight into the former Hammers' playing style: "Singularly elusive once he had gathered the ball, in the days when 'keepers could be bundled over the line. One writer couldn't remember Tommy ever being so treated. Thoroughly capable in other respects too, not least in the divining of opponents' intentions. Sold to West Ham to finance Willis Rippon's transfer." Originally a centre-half. Died 17.3.73.

LOUGHLIN, James 1927-28

Born: Darlington. 9.10.1905
Lge apps: 10 (4 gls)

■ A goal-scoring centre or inside-forward signed from Newcastle United to supplement the fire-power of Vic Watson and Vivian Gibbins. A prolific marksman with the Magpies, he scored in his first appearance in Hammers' colours v Huddersfield Town. After a pleasant introduction on West Ham's tour of Scandinavia during the close-season, he found it difficult to hold down a regular place in the first team once league action got under way. So the former blacksmith made only 10 First Division outings before moving on to join Coventry City (2.1.29), where he scored 39 goals in 65 games for the Bantams. Joined the Magpies from Darlington Railway Athletic. Transferred from Coventry to Northwich Victoria cs 1931. James joined his home town club, Darlington, in 1933.

John Lyall the player

LUTTON, Bertie
1973-74

Born: Banbridge, Northern Ireland. 13.7.50
Lge apps: 12 (1 gl)
Cup apps: 1

■ Despite his brief sojourn at Upton Park, this midfield man holds the distinction of being the first West Ham player to be capped at full international level by Northern Ireland. Signed from Brighton & Hove Albion after proving his ability on a month's loan from the Seasiders, Bertie made his Hammers' debut v Norwich City at Carrow Road in Feb. 1973. He began his career with Wolves, where he won the first two of his six appearances for his country. Northern Ireland caps: 1973 v Cyprus (sub), Scotland (sub), Wales (sub), Portugal (4).

LYALL, John
1960-63

Born: Ilford, Essex. 24.2.40
Lge apps: 30
Cup apps: 4

■ As player, office assistant, first team coach and ultimately manager, John Lyall features prominently in Hammers' history having served the club in various capacities for 33 years. A solid, capable full-back who had won England Youth honours, John had an unusual beginning to a playing career beset with injury problems. Like secretary Eddie Chapman before him, the young Hammer doubled as office-boy-cum-apprentice professional. It was a grounding to stand him in good stead in the years ahead. A member of the team which reached the Final of the FA Youth Cup in 1957, he made his League debut v Chelsea in Feb. 1960. Then followed a three-year fight against persistent injuries,

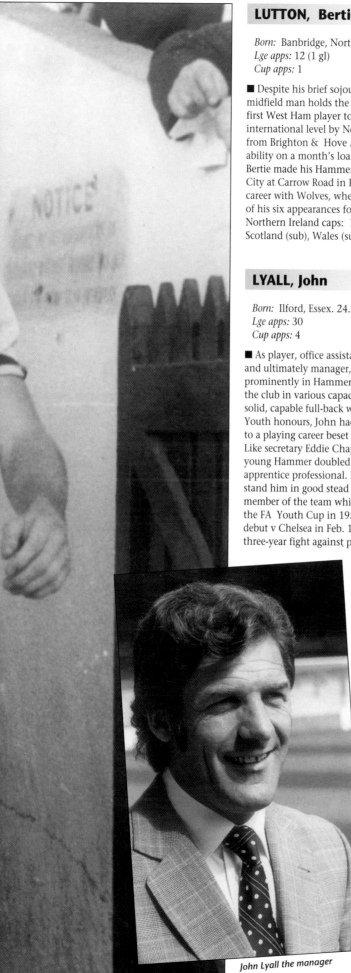
John Lyall the manager

during which time he first showed the qualities of character, now so well known. Finally succumbing to defeat, he was given a testimonial match on the eve of the 1964 FA Cup Final, and then began his long haul up the managerial ladder where his record with West Ham remains second to none. Taking over as team manager from his mentor Ron Greenwood in 1974, the FA Cup was on the Upton Park sideboard by the following year. His 1976 team is still the last to represent West Ham in a major European Final (the Cup Winners' Cup), and although he couldn't prevent a fall from grace in 1978, with relegation from the First Division, the winning of the cup against over Arsenal in 1980 and the Second Division Championship and League Cup final season of 1980/81, amply compensated. Under his management West Ham became one of the most feared cup-fighting teams in the country, twice reaching the sixth round of the FA Cup and semi-finals of the League Cup in 1989. In 1985/86 he guided the team to their highest-ever position in the First Division, when they finished third (behind champions Liverpool and Everton) and kept hopes of a first-ever First Division championship alive to the final Saturday of the season. Relegation at the end of 1988/89 led to his controversial dismissal but John was not short of job offers. After assisting Spurs and Bobby Robson's England on a part-time basis, he was appointed manager of Ipswich Town whom he quickly elevated back to the top flight. John has since 'moved upstairs' at Portman Road as board member and general manager.

A man of honesty and integrity, John learned much about the game from his mentor, Greenwood, and he did as much as anyone to establish West Ham's reputation for attempting to play open, attractive football, even in the face of adversity.

LYON, Herbert
1903-04

Born: 1877
SL apps: 29 (4 gls)
Cup apps: 4 (5 gls)

■ Previously with Leicester Fosse (1898/1900), Nelson (1900/01), and Watford (1901/02), Herbert was one of four players signed from fellow Southern League Reading, mostly recognised as an inside-right, but was also tried at number nine during Hammers' last season at the Memorial Grounds. Indeed, he scored two goals against Kettering Town in his first appearance at centre-forward in the second fixture of the 1903/04 campaign, an event which may have persuaded the management to persevere with him in that position until seven goal-less outings saw him revert to the number eight shirt. A victim of the major clear-out of players at the season's end, Herbert transferred to Brighton & Hove Albion in cs 1904, and in a match v Hammers at the Goldstone Ground in Mar. 1905, was involved in an unsavoury incident with goalkeeper Matt Kingsley which led to the custodian being sent-off and suspended. Herbert later served Swindon Town, Carlisle United, Swindon Town again and Blackpool before WW1.

Frank McAvennie

McALISTER, Tom
1981-89

Born: Clydebank, Scotland. 10.12.52
Lge apps: 85
Cup apps: 14

■ A once underrated 'keeper who was on the verge of breaking into the Scottish squad to go to Munich for the 1974 World Cup Finals, when he had to cry off with a broken leg. Disaster struck once more when he tried to come back too soon and broke the leg again. All this happened with Sheffield United, in their First Division days. He then moved to Rotherham (Jan. 1976) and Blackpool (July 1979). Signed for Hammers on a free transfer in May 1981 from Bristol Rovers, where he was on loan from Swindon Town. The experienced Scot

was understudy to Phil Parkes and made his senior debut at Birmingham City (3.10.81). But it was not until 1984/85 that he had a reasonable run in the side, playing 32 League matches before suffering a broken rib and punctured lung at QPR at the end of that season. The stocky Scot was helping out at Chadwell Heath training goalkeepers in 1993.

McATEER, T
1902-03

SL apps: 13

■ In common with team mate James Dow, this centre-half's Southern League appearances for Hammers got stuck on the number least liked by the superstitious - 13 - and stayed there. The

former Bolton man made one of his outings at outside-right, but with little apparent success as the team crashed 6-0 at Southampton. 'A big strapping fellow who brought a big reputation from Burnden Park, but it never materialised at the Memorial Grounds.' He joined Brighton for 1903/04.

McAVENNIE, Frank
1985-92

Born: Glasgow, Scotland. 22.11.60
Lge apps: 153 (49 gls)
Cup apps: 33 (8 gls)

■ Hugely popular striker and charismatic character who is fondly remembered by his many fans at Upton Park. Frank was relatively unknown when he signed from Scottish League St. Mirren for £340,000 in cs 1985, having first made his mark for St. Johnstone Boys' Club in the early eighties. But he made an immediate impact in the English First Division. After making his debut in midfield at Birmingham City (17.8.85), injury to Paul Goddard meant John Lyall pushed Frank up front to partner Tony Cottee on his home debut, v QPR, three days later and he scored twice in a 3-1 victory. "Super Mac" had arrived and there was no stopping the new goal-scoring sensation with the bleached-blond hair and dazzling skills to match. A remarkable spell of 12 goals in 11 matches earned him his first full Scottish cap, in Australia. Frank's goal in the return World Cup qualifying clash with the Aussies at Hampden Park helped the Scots to clinch their place in the 1986 finals in Mexico. Frank became the idol of East London football and his celebrity status brought him a number of TV appearances as people clamoured for a look at the new West Ham idol (no matches were screened this season due to a dispute between ITV and the Football League). Pictured regularly attending West End nightspots with Page 3 beauties on his arm, Frank was enjoying himself to the full. His partnership with Cottee was among the most formidable in the country. It was a strong team, but their goals (Frank scored 26 in the League - bettered only by Everton's Gary Lineker - while Tony netted an equally impressive 20) stole the limelight and ensured Hammers enjoyed their highest-ever placing in Division One - third behind champions Liverpool and Everton. It seemed everything Frank touched turned to gold, although he worked hard for his rewards. He was an unselfish striker, who chased for 90 minutes in the team's cause. He would regularly feature in the build-up to goals that he himself finished off. Indeed, Frank has always maintained that he is not a natural striker, more an attacking midfielder. After the disappointment of missing out on the title, there was a big feeling of anti-climax around Upton Park in 1986/87. Although Cottee maintained his high standards with 22 goals in the League, Frank's contribution slipped to seven. And he had not found the net once in the

Tom McAlister

first eight League matches of 1987/88 when Celtic - the team he supported as a boy - came in with a £750,000 offer that neither he nor Lyall could refuse. Frank soon recaptured his scoring touch in his home city, spearheading Celtic to the Scottish League and Cup double in his first season, but before the end of the following season he was back in London to try and save Hammers from relegation. Lyall, coming under increasing pressure, splashed out a club record £1.25 million to re-sign Frank, who turned down the chance to join Arsenal. The return of the Scottish favourite lifted everyone associated with West Ham but an injury - Frank broke his arm at Celtic shortly before returning south - limited the number eight to just eight games as Hammers bowed out of Division One in May 1989. There was another disaster awaiting Frank three months later when, on the opening day of the season at Stoke, he broke his leg in a tackle by Chris Kamara. By the time Frank declared himself fit again, Lou Macari had been replaced by Billy Bonds, who gave him four sub outings in the closing weeks of 1989/90. The good times returned to Upton Park in 1990/91 but Frank had difficulty winning a regular first team place in the face of competition from Morley, Quinn and Rosenior. His frustration boiled over in a home game v Bristol City, a sending off that cost him a place in the FA Cup semi-final v Nottingham Forest. Yet he still managed 10 vital goals despite starting only 24 matches in the promotion campaign. Forest were not immune from Frank's deadly touch in front of goal, though. After managing just three goals in 15 First Division starts in 1991/92, Frank doubled his tally with a sensational hat-trick in his farewell game against Brian Clough's boys. His army of Upton Park admirers were in full cry. "There's Only One McAVEN-E-E-E-E-E!" reverberated around the ground as Frank appeared from the subs' bench and proceeded to take Des Walker (playing his last game before his big money move to Sampdoria) and the rest of the Nottingham defence apart with a performance that was straight from the script of Roy of the Rovers. Frank McAvennie left Upton Park as he arrived - with a bang. At 31, he was given a free transfer but has yet to settle at a new base. A month on trial with Aston Villa, at the start of 1992/93, came to nothing when they signed Dean Saunders instead. A spell in Hong Kong with South China FC was followed by another stint with Celtic (where his old boss, Lou Macari, later resurfaced) and then, in 1993/94, he was given another run in the Premiership with struggling Swindon Town. Frank returned to Scotland for 1994/95 to join ex-Hammer Tony Parks at Premier League Falkirk. His career turned full circle when he returned to his first club St. Mirren for whom he made his second debut at Love Street in a 0-1 defeat v Airdrie (15.10.94).

❏ **Scotland caps:** 1985 v Australia; 1986 v Australia, Denmark (sub), West Germany (sub) (4).

McCARTNEY, Alex   1905-06

Born: Belfast 1882
Lge apps: 6 (0 gls)
Cup apps: 0

■ Signed from Everton, right-back Alex made his first appearance in a West Ham shirt in the opening fixture of 1905/06 in a 1-0 win over Swindon Town at Boleyn Castle. His last outing was in a 3-1 reverse at Watford (4.11.05). Alex played in the Irish league with Belfast Celtic in 1907/08. Capped six times for Ireland, against Scotland (3), Wales (2) and England. He also played for the Rosetta National School in Ireland and later for Ferndale, a team which competed in the North Belfast Alliance League. On leaving that team he played for Hatfield who won the Woodville Alliance Cup. He progressed to Distillery, Ulster and then Linfield. Joined Hammers with George Kitchen from Everton.

McCARTNEY, William   1904-05

Lge apps: 28 (3 gls)
Cup apps: 1 (0 gls)

■ Bill missed only six matches during 1904-05 on the right-wing for Irons after spending the previous campaign with Manchester United whom he'd joined from Edinburgh Hibs. Two of his three goals were scored in home and away fixtures with Southampton, the other coming in a 5-1 Boleyn thrashing of Northampton Town (15.4.05).

McCRAE, James   1919-21

Lge apps: 50 (0 gls)
Cup apps: 4 (0 gls)

■ Hammers signed this stubborn Scottish defender from Clyde, and he settled down to claim a regular place during the 1919-20 season, totalling 35 League and four FA Cup outings in the club's first campaign as a Football League outfit. Usually employed at left-half, he made another 15 Second Division appearances the following season before moving on to Bury.

James McCrae

McDONALD, Alex   1901-02

Born: Greenock, Scotland, 1878
Lge apps: 4 (2 gls)
Cup apps: 0

■ A top-class goalscorer, centre-forward Alex began his career with Jarrow before joining Everton in February 1900. He made an explosive start at his next port of call, Southampton, whom he joined in May 1901, scoring five goals in five starts. Transferring to Hammers in December the same year, he was true to his nature on his debut v Bristol Rovers,

scoring both goals in a 2-0 win. Curiously, he failed to score in his three other SL appearances and headed back to the more temperate climes of the south coast when he joined Portsmouth in March 1902. But he continued to move around, to Luton Town in 1905, Croydon Common 1907 and back to Luton in 1910.

McDONALD, Terry

Born: Plaistow, London, 12.11.38

■ A product of West Ham's youth policy, this fast, tricky winger was a member of the Hammers' team that reached the 1957 FA Youth Cup final against Manchester United. Although he only played one match for the first XI, against Sparta Prague of Czechoslovakia in a friendly game, he was obviously too good for reserve team soccer. He benefited from a move to Second Division Leyton Orient, scoring on his debut for O's and helping them into the top flight in 1961-62. He later moved to Reading and then out of the Football League with Wimbledon and Folke-stone Town. In recent years has coached in USA and back at his old club, Orient.

McDOWELL, John   1969-79

Born: East Ham, 7.9.51
Lge apps: 249 (8 gls)
Cup apps: 47 (1 gl)

■ Versatile, talented defender who operated mainly at right-back after Billy Bonds moved into midfield. Made his League debut against Blackburn Rovers in October 1969, and was picked 12 times for England under-23 side after gaining a Youth cap. John had ten years as a first teamer, but missed the entire 1976-77 season through injury. Honours: FA Cup Winners' medal 1975, European Cup Winners Cup runners-up medal 1976. Transferred to Norwich City in 1979, where he joined up with ex-Hammers John Bond and Ken Brown, then bossing the City outfit.

Played	League		FAC		LC		Europe		Total	
	App	Gls	App	Gls	App	Gls	App	Gls	App	Gls
1970-71	25	0	0	0	0	0	0	0	25	0
1971-72	40	0	4	0	10	0	0	0	54	0
1972-73	38	2	2	0	2	1	0	0	42	3
1973-74	33	2	1	0	2	0	0	0	36	2
1974-75	34	1	8	0	2	0	0	0	44	1
1975-76	37	0	0	0	5	0	7	0	49	0
1976-77	0	0	0	0	0	0	0	0	0	0
1977-78	14	1	3	0	0	0	0	0	17	1
1978-79	28	2	1	0	0	0	0	0	29	2
TOTAL	249	8	19	0	21	1	7	0	296	9

McEACHRANE, Roderick   1898-02

Born: Inverness, Scotland, 1878
SL apps (TIW): 53 (1 gl)
SL apps (WHU): 53 (5 gls)
Cup apps: 7 (0 gls)

■ Roddy made the long journey from Inverness in northern Scotland to Orchard Yard, Black-well, London to work at the Thames Ironworks

TACKLED! *John McDowell (right) on the receiving end of a rather unorthodox challenge from Norwich's Jimmy Bone in September 1972. McDowell was later to join the Canaries.*

and continue his football career with the works side. Having already earned a considerable reputation as a hard-tackling half-back with Inverness Thistle, he set about making a name for himself in the bigger spotlight of Southern League soccer and succeeded to the extent of being an ever-present in 1898-99 and 1899-1900. The metamorphosis from the old works team into the new West Ham United Football Club was also marked by his 100 per cent presence, and it was becoming obvious that future fame was beckoning, although not with the Hammers. Another fine season in 1901-02 (in which he missed only five Southern League outings) followed and prompted Woolwich Arsenal to offer him the opportunity of Football League status. If his form with Hammers had been outstanding, it was even more so at Plumstead; being a major factor in the Gunners' promotion to the First Division in 1903-04. But despite the merits of his transfer, major honours continued to elude Rod, his witty sense of humour probably helping him to overcome the disappointments, especially when the Gunners fell at the semi final stages of the FA Cup in 1906 and 1907. He made his last appearance for Arsenal in 1913-14, just after the move to Highbury and the dropping of the Woolwich prefix. His place in the team went to another Scot, Angus McKinnon, who, according to an extract from an Arsenal club history by Bernard Joy, "was bigger and more robust but lacking McEachrane's constructive ability." Roderick McEachrane passed away in 1952.

McGEORGE, Robert   1901-02

■ A right-half who came from amateurs Leytonstone, Bob played in Irons' two FA Cup ties in 1901/02, but strangely, no SL fixtures. His cup outings were against Leyton (1-0) and Grays (1-2).

McGIVEN, Mick   1973-77

Born: Newcastle-onTyne. 7.2.51
Lge apps: 48
Cup apps: 7

■ Geordie who was burdened with the responsibility of trying to replace Bobby Moore in the number six shirt after the legend left in 1973 for Fulham. Signed from Sunderland for £20,000 after a period on loan from the Wearsiders, with whom he had 107 League games. He had the toughest possible debut baptism v Liverpool at Anfield in Dec. 1973, but came through with flying colours. Later joined the senior coaching staff at the club. Followed John Lyall to Ipswich Town and succeeded him as manager at Portman Road. He is now Football Development Officer with the East Anglians.

McGOWAN, Danny   1948-54

Born: Dublin, Republic of Ireland. 8.11.24
Lge apps: 81 (8 gls)
Cup apps: 2 (1 gl)

■ Skilful Republic of Ireland international inside-forward, who converted to wing-half when competition for the inside-berths increased. Signed from League of Ireland club Shelbourne, after being recommended by their manager and pre-war Hammer, Charlie Turner. Danny arrived at Upton Park at the same time as two of his fellow countrymen, John Carroll and Fred Kearns. Completed six seasons at the Boleyn until his transfer to Southern League Chelmsford City in 1954. A year later he joined Folkestone Town in the Kent League before re-tiring from football and embarking on a 22-year career with the London Electricity Board. Danny sadly died in March 1994 after a long fight against Parkinson's Disease. West Ham sent a floral tribute to Dan's funeral at

St. Margaret's Church, Canning Town, which was attended by his former team mate, Scottish International John Dick.
☆ *Republic of Ireland caps:* 1949 v Portugal, Sweden, Spain (3).

McKAY, Ken   1899-00

SL apps: 27 (8 gls) TIW
Cup apps: 10 (1 gl)

■ Inside-forward Kenny won a First Division Championship medal in his one season with Sheffield United - 1897/98. The subject of a surprise transfer to Spurs for the following season, he made a scoring debut for the North Londoners v TIW on September 3, 1898 in common with Tom Bradshaw who joined him at the Memorial Grounds along with fellow former Spur, Bill Joyce the following season. Joyce benefited greatly from McKay's presence at both Northumberland Park and Irons, the latter laying on many scoring opportunities for the centre-forward, most of which he gratefully accepted. McKay scored eight SL goals in 28 appearances himself in 1899/1900 for Irons as well as five in seven FA Cup ties. Ken moved on to Fulham before TIW changed to West Ham United FC in July 1900, helping the Cottagers to win the Second Division of the Southern League in 1901-02. Ken scored in his first matches of three different competitions for Spurs, but had to wait until his second outing for Irons before scoring twice in a 4-0 SL victory over Chatham on September 18, 1900 at the Memorial Grounds.

McKNIGHT, Allen   1988-90

Born: Antrim, Northern Ireland. 27.1.64
Lge apps: 23
Cup apps: 10

■ Northern Ireland international goalkeeper signed from Celtic in the summer of 1988 for £250,000. Kept a clean sheet on his League debut at Wimbledon (10.9.88) in the third game of 1988/89, after taking over from Tom McAlister. But Allen endured an alarming spell (described in big tabloid headlines as a "McKnightmare!") in which Hammers lost 12 of their next 20 League games. After 33 consecutive matches, which culminated with a dismal 3-0 home defeat in the first leg of the Littlewoods (League) Cup semi-final v Luton Town in Feb. 1989, he was finally dropped by John Lyall, who turned again to the veteran Phil Parkes to try and save Hammers' First Division bacon. His confidence shattered by bad publicity and sustained abuse from the Upton Park terraces, Allen was recalled for the last two games of the season. The last of his 23 senior League appearances came on that emotional night at Anfield (23.5.89) when Hammers lost their fight for survival in a 5-1 defeat by Liverpool. Lyall's succesor Lou Macari did not give Allen even a single League outing after taking over for season 1989/90 and his brief, though eventful, Hammers' career ended

Mick McGiven

ignominiously with a 5-1 thrashing at Luton in the Zenith Data Systems Cup and a diabolical 11-0 crushing by Crystal Palace Reserves. Allen started his career with Distillery before crossing the Irish Sea to sign for Glasgow Celtic. Spent a year on loan to Albion Rovers in the Second Division before making 12 appearances for Celtic in their Championship winning campaign of 1987-88. Also won a Scotish Cup winners medal. After a period in the wilderness following his ordeal at Upton Park, Allen returned to play, with little success, for Exeter City late in the 1993/94 season. But he was turning out in the Diadora League Division Three, for Collier Row, at the start of the next season.

☆ **Northern Ireland caps:** 1989 v Republic of Ireland, Hungary, Spain (twice), (4).

McMAHON, Patrick   1933

Born: Glasgow, Scotland
Lge apps: 16
Cup apps: 1

■ His sensational debut between the posts against Birmingham in the FA Cup sixth round at Upton Park in March 1933 played a major part in Hammers' progress to that year's semi-finals. With regular goalkeeper George Watson sidelined by injuries received in a car crash, young Pat stepped in and kept a clean sheet as West Ham thrashed their First Division opponents 4-0. Although he lost his place v. Everton in the next round at neutral Molineux, he went on to total 13 Second Division outings that season. After leaving school in his native Scotland, the capable 'keeper had joined his local junior club Pollokshaws Hibernians - and from there went to those famous star-finders, St. Anthony's. In addition to providing Hammers with Pat McMahon, the Saints later supplied Hughie Mills and Arthur Tonner to the Upton Park payroll, Pat eventually returned to Scotland to join St. Mirren and then moved to Wrexham during the end of the 1934/35 season.

McPHERSON, Keith   1985-86

Born: Greenwich, London.
Lge apps: 1

■ This young defender was thrown in at the deep end, along with Football Combination colleague George Parris, in Hammers' last fixture of 1984/85 v League Champions Liverpool at Upton Park, and did enough to justify his selection. Joining West Ham as an apprentice in the summer of 1980 after representing Blackheath and Inner London at schools level, Keith was a member of the team which won the FA Youth Cup in 1981. A regular member of the Reserves, he had spells on loan to Cambridge United and Northampton Town before signing for the Cobblers at a reputed fee of £10,000. Made 182 League appearances (8 gls) before joining Reading in August, 1990.

Allen McKnight

MEDHURST, Harry   1938-46

Born: Byfleet, Surrey. 5.2.16
Lge apps: 24
Cup apps: 9

■ Although he became a Hammers' pro in 1936, this capable custodian had to wait a further two years before making his League debut v Fulham in Dec. 1938. He finished that season with 21 League games under his cap and started the next as first choice 'keeper, only for war to interrupt his promising start. Harry reached the rank of Sergeant P.T.I., having served with the Essex and R.A. from 1939 to 1946. When things had returned to normal and full League soccer resumed at Upton Park in 1946, the club found itself with a glut of goalkeepers, so Harry was transferred to Chelsea in exchange for "Ten-Goal" Joe Payne, after making a further three Second Division appearances. Harry enjoyed great success at Stamford Bridge and returned there after his playing days as trainer and, eventually, head coach to the first team. He was also a capable batsman, playing at county level for Surrey II. Harry died in April 1984.

McMANUS, Peter   1899/1900 TIW

Born: Edinburgh, Scotland. 1873
SL apps: 10
Cup apps: 5

■ Somewhat short for a centre-half, standing just 5ft 7ins in height, Pete made his name with Edinburgh St. Bernards whom he helped to annexe the Scottish FA Cup in 1895, when they defeated the redoubtable Renton team at Ibrox Park. Previously with West Bromwich Albion, the stocky defender joined Irons from Bristol side Warmley in 1899 and was said to "Play a cautious and waiting game." He was on the winning side in his first five games for Irons, beginning with his debut in a 1-0 win v St. Albans and culminating in a club record 10-0 Memorial Ground rout of Maidenhead in the last SL match of the season.

McQUEEN, Tommy   1987-90

Born: Bells Hill, Scotland. 1.4.63
Lge apps: 30
Cup apps: 6

■ Mild-mannered left-back signed by John Lyall in March 1987 to help solve an injury crisis. Cost £150,000 from Aberdeen, where he made 44 appearances and won a Scottish Premier League championship (1985) and Scottish Cup winners' medal (1986). Began his career with Clyde in 1981 and was ever-present in their Second Division title-winning side in his first season. The slightly-built McQueen made his Hammers' debut v Watford at Upton Park (28.3.87) but his hopes of establishing himself as a first team regular disappeared a year later when Julian Dicks arrived from Birmingham. After being released by Hammers, McQueen returned to Scotland to join Falkirk.

Archie Macaulay

MACAULAY, Archibald Renwick   1937-46

Born: Falkirk, Scotland. 30.7.15
Lge apps: 83 (29 gls)
Cup apps: 7 (2 gls)

■ Charlie Paynter signed this volatile red-haired Scot from Glasgow Rangers, and he soon made his presence felt at the Boleyn Ground. Like so many other players of this period. Archie had his career interrupted by the war, although he did win a Football League War Cup medal in 1940. After he had seen service with the Essex Regiment Territorials and hostilities had ceased, the former Sergeant-Major PTI found it difficult to settle, and was transferred to the then more glamorous Brentford in the First Division. He then moved on to Arsenal, winning a string of Scottish caps and playing for Great Britain v Rest of the World in 1947. Archie finished his playing days with Fulham, later going into management, first with Guildford and then guiding Norwich City to the FA Cup semi-finals when they were still a Third Division club in 1959. He was one of the first managers to implement the 4-3-3 system and generally regarded as being tactically ahead of his time. After leaving the Canaries he joined Scottish First Division club Dundee in an administrative capacity and was connected with Liverpool in 1970. Retired from the game after taking charge of West Bromwich Albion and Brighton & Hove Albion, respectively. He was working as a traffic warden in Chelsea in the '70's.

Tommy McQueen

MACDOUGALL, Ted   1973

Born: Inverness, Scotland. 8.1.47
Lge apps: 24 (5 gls)
Cup apps: 1 (1 gl)

■ Big-money signing, who never settled at Upton Park. Signed from Manchester United to cure a goalscoring problem, he had previously seen service with Liverpool, York City and

Continued on page 120

MALCOLM, Andy 1953-62

Born: Upton Park, London. 4.5.33
Lge apps: 283 (4 gls)
Cup apps: 23

■ Feared by the leading inside-forwards of his day because of his ability to close-mark and block his opponents out of the game. Jimmy Greaves, Johnny Haynes and Denis Law all gave testimony to his prowess. A tough-tackling, unassuming character, Andy must rank as one of the finest wing-halves the club ever employed. There was to be no room for Malcolm's uncompromising style of play at Ron Greenwood's West Ham, however. And although he was only one season away from qualifying for a testimonial match, Andy left Hammers for London rivals Chelsea in Nov. 1962 in return for £10,000 and centre-forward Ron Tindall in part-exchange. It was good business for West Ham to receive a player plus cash for someone who'd cost them only a £10 signing on fee in 1950. Especially as they had a ready-made replacement in Eddie Bovington, ironically a very similar type of player. Tindall was later sold to Reading for £12,000 so the deal eventually realised £23,000 profit for the club. Although he was on better money at Chelsea, Andy couldn't see eye to eye with boss Tommy Docherty and it turned out to be a bad move for him. Not only were Chelsea relegated at the end of that 1961-62 season, Andy was on the move again - to Third Division Queens Park Rangers for another £10,000 fee. Managed by Alec Stock, Rangers had just finalised negotiations for moving to the plush White City Stadium and were looking for players worthy of their new surroundings. Football became fun again under the genial Stock until an eye injury threatened to end Andy's career. But characteristically, he fought back to fitness to end the 1964-65 season as strongly as ever and complete a total of 84 Division Three appearances for Rangers before emigrating with his family to South Africa to join Greek Port Elizabeth side Apollen FC, and later Port Elizabeth. He had two enjoyable seasons in S.A. before returning to the UK for the 1967-68 season, and joined up with Southern League Brentwood Town. When he retired from playing at the end of the 60's, he joined Lyons, the ice cream people and he worked for them until 1977 when he took over the Ship & Anchor public house in Maldon, Essex. Later he had another pub, The Lion at Latchendon, but in 1986 decided to give it another go in S.A. where he still lives at Port Elizabeth. Although he was West Ham's first-ever England Youth international, Andy never won a full cap for his country, having to content himself with his selection (along with team-mate John Bond) for the Football League v Scottish League in 1959, as his sole senior representative honour. But if honours were awarded for wholehearted endeavour and 100 per cent commitment, Andy Malcolm would have had few peers.

Played	League		FAC		LC		Europe		Total	
	App	Gls	App	Gls	App	Gls	App	Gls	App	Gls
1953-54	14	0	3	0	0	0	0	0	17	0
1954-55	38	0	2	0	0	0	0	0	40	0
1955-56	22	0	6	0	0	0	0	0	28	0
1956-57	37	0	2	0	0	0	0	0	39	0
1957-58	42	3	3	0	0	0	0	0	45	3
1958-59	42	0	1	0	0	0	0	0	43	0
1959-60	40	0	2	0	0	0	0	0	42	0
1960-61	40	1	2	0	2	0	0	0	44	1
1961-62	8	0	0	0	0	0	0	0	8	0
TOTAL	**283**	**4**	**21**	**0**	**2**	**0**	**0**	**0**	**306**	**4**

Bournemouth (where he had been under the managership of ex-Hammer John Bond). Re-joined his former boss at Norwich City, for a £140,000 fee, after being a West Ham player for just 10 months, and then went on to Southampton, Bournemouth and Blackpool where he was player-coach and assistant manager from March 1980 to October the same year, before concentrating on his south coast sports shop. He later became a licensee, coming out of retirement to occasionally play for Salisbury, Poole Town and Gosport Borough. Ted won seven Scotland caps and can lay claim to being the 15th post-war player to score 250 League goals. Once scored a record nine goals for Bournemouth v Margate in an FA Cup tie.

MACKESY, Jack   1910-23

SL apps: 10 (2 gls)
Lge apps: 10

■ Evergreen stalwart who gave the Hammers unstinting service from the old Southern League days right through to the club's entry into League football. He scored 10 goals in 33 war-time appearances. Originally an inside-forward, Jack dropped back to half-back in later years, captaining the Reserves in the London Combination. Always hungry for the ball, he was awarded two benefits during his 13 seasons at Upton Park.

Jack Mackesy

MACKIE, Charles   1905-06

Born: Peterhead, Scotland. 1882.
SL apps: 10 (3 gls)

■ An inside-right or centre-forward, Chas, as he was better known, joined Manchester United from Aberdeen cs 1904, but had only one season with the Reds, playing in five Second Division matches, before joining Irons cs 1905. He made his West Ham debut in the first match of 1905-06 in a 1-0 win v Swindon Town at Upton Park, but had to wait until his fifth match before opening his goalscoring account in a 2-1 home win v Plymouth Argyle. Scored again in a 2-0 Boleyn victory against Brighton and also in the next match, a 1-2 defeat at Northampton (18.11.1905) - his last for the club.

MACKLEWORTH, Colin   1966-67

Born: Bow, London. 24.3.47
Lge apps: 3

■ Served Hammers well after signing apprentice professional in 1962 and full pro two years later. Winner of a Youth Cup Final

medal in 1963, he had to wait until 1966 to make the first of only three senior appearances (against Blackpool). Transferred to Leicester City in Nov. 1967, where he provided cover for Peter Shilton and made six First Division appearances before joining Southern League Kettering Town in 1970. Entered the Police force when he packed in playing and is now stationed at Bow, often being on duty at Upton Park.

MANGALL, David   1935-36

Lge apps: 35 (28 gls)
Cup apps: 2 (1 gl)

■ A former coal-miner at Maltby Colliery. After service with Leeds United (1927-30), Huddersfield Town (1930) and Birmingham (1934-35), this bustling centre-forward was signed as a replacement for Vic Watson. Dave set the Second Division alight in his second season at Upton Park when he scored 22 goals in 25 outings and numbered two hat-tricks among his harvest of net-finding efforts. Somewhat surprisingly transferred to Millwall the following season, the lad from Wigan Pier territory continued his happy goalscoring trend with Lions and later Queens Park Rangers whom he managed after the war. The highlight of his career came with Millwall in 1937, when he led the Third Division side's attack in the FA Cup semi-final against Sunderland at Leeds Road. Re-signed by the Lions after a spell running a Sutton Coldfield cafe and grocery business, he joined Queens Park Rangers in May 1939, where he was manager from 1944 to 1952 - taking the R's into Division Two for the first time in 1948. A guest player for Southend, Fulham and Millwall in WW2, the latter for whom he'd won a Division III (South) Championship medal in 1938, when he scored 18 goals in 25 League games. Once scored 10 goals for Leeds v Stockport County in a Northern Midweek League match. He began his career with Maltby New Church, Maltby Colliery and had trials with Rotherham United, Huddersfield Town and Doncaster Rovers before making the grade at Elland Road. Dave died at Penzance, Cornwall, in April 1962.

MAPLEY, Percy   1903-04

Born: 24.11.1882
SL apps: 13
Cup apps:: 4

■ It was a case of unlucky 13 in SL matches for left-back Percy who also managed four FA Cup appearances in his season at the Memorial Grounds. Making his debut in a 0-0 home stalemate v Luton Town on September 24, 1903, he missed the next match and then had a straight run of 12 matches, the last being in the 4-1 win over Wellingborough Town in East London. Transferred to Spurs in Feb.1904, he made his bow for them in a London League

match the same month. He spent most of his time at White Hart Lane in the reserves, but he did manage 10 senior appearances for the Lillywhites before being put on the not retained list at the season's end.

MARJERAM, Arthur   TIW

Born: 1877

■ A former Aston Villa amateur, Arthur joined Irons from Swanscombe and played at left-back in the first TIW pro XI v Sheppey United (1.9.1898) and the inaugural SL fixture (Div. II) nine days later v. Shepherds Bush.

MARSH, Mike   1993-

Born: Liverpool. 21.7.69.
Lge apps: 33 (1 gl)
Cup apps: 9 (1 gl)

■ True Scouser who suddenly found himself miles from home when Liverpool swapped him and David Burrows for Julian Dicks in a shock £2.5 million deal in Sept. 1993. Mike joined the Reds from local non-league side Kirby Town on a free transfer in 1987 and impressed with his creative midfield flair. Played well at right-back for Liverpool in the goalless draw at Upton Park in Nov. 1991 and Billy Bonds had long been an admirer of "Marshie" before he made his Hammers' debut - along with Burrows and Lee Chapman - in the number 34 shirt at Blackburn Rovers (18.9.93). Mike showed all his clever, deft touches and good passing skills that afternoon in the 2-0 victory that transformed Hammers' Premiership season. He struck up an excellent understanding with midfield partner Ian Bishop and played an influential role in many matches, although his talent seemed rather wasted when asked to play wide on the right. Marshie's first goal for West Ham was a late FA Cup third round match-winner v Watford (8.1.94), while his only League goal of his first season capped a brilliant 4-1 victory at Tottenham (4.4.94). Unfortunately, within days of the 1993/94 season ending, it was revealed that his family were unsettled and wanted to move back to Merseyside, where Mike's five sisters and a brother all still live. He was placed on the transfer list at his own request but was still a Hammer when the 1994-95 season began.

MARSHALL, Dr. James   1935-37

Born: Avonbridge, Stirlingshire. 3.1.1908
Lge apps: 57 (14 gls)
Cup apps: 2

■ The career of this famous thrice-capped Scottish international inside-forward followed a remarkably similar path to another wearer of the claret-and-blue, Archie Macaulay. The latter was understudy to Doctor Jim at Glasgow Rangers in the early '30's, and didn't win a regular place at Ibrox until Jimmy (a medical practitioner) transferred in July 1934 to Arsenal, with whom

Mike Marsh

MARTIN, Alvin   1978-

Born: Walton, Liverpool. 29.7.58
Lge apps: 431 (27 gls)
Cup apps: 110 (6 gls)

■ One of West Ham United's all-time greats who rose to seventh place in the club's list of League appearance-makers early on in the 1994-95 season and to fifth place with League and Cup appearances combined. Capped 17 times by England at full international level, Alvin became one of the most outstanding central defenders in Britain. Not only strong in the air, but a very classy performer who is equally comfortable in possession of the ball. Alvin arrived at Upton Park as a schoolboy in cs 1974, the year after Bobby Moore left for Fulham. He had impressed for Bootle and Lancashire Schoolboys but after being turned down by his local club, Everton, Alvin made his mark at West Ham. Played in the side that reached the FA Youth Cup Final in 1975 and signed pro 29.7.76. His first team debut came in a 4-1 defeat at Aston Villa (18. 3.78) but despite scoring in his first full game, at Leeds (8.4.78), and starting all of the last five matches, West Ham could not avoid relegation that season. Not that Second Division football hampered young Alvin's development. On the contrary, he took over Tommy Taylor's number five shirt in Feb. of the following season and went on to establish himself as regular partner to Billy Bonds in the centre of the back four. In May 1980 Alvin won an FA Cup winners' medal. A year later he missed just one League game as Hammers romped to the Second Division title and returned to Wembley to face Liverpool in the League Cup Final. It was Alvin's header - handled on the line by Terry McDermott - that led to Ray Stewart's dramatic penalty equaliser. Six European Cup Winners' Cup ties provided further education for Alvin, who was heading for international recognition. Made his full England debut v Brazil at Wembley (12.5.81) and emerged with credit from a tough baptism against Reinaldo and Zico, who netted the 12th minute winner. England manager Ron Greenwood (who signed Alvin as a kid at Upton Park) recalled him as sub v Scotland in the next game at Wembley and Alvin was back in the starting line up - alongside Phil Thompson - the following Nov. when England beat Hungary 1-0 to book their ticket to the 1992 World Cup Finals. Unfortunately, Alvin's long and distinguished career has been punctuated by injuries, which is why he did not go to Spain with the England World Cup party in 1982. However, Alvin was back to full fitness in 1982-83 and as well as helping Hammers to a creditable eighth place in Division One, he soon gained the recognition of Greenwood's successor, Bobby Robson, who included Alvin in most of his squads over the next few seasons. When Billy Bonds indicated that he would be retiring at the end of 1983-84, Alvin took over the club captaincy and formed a new formidable partnership with Tony Gale. As a central defensive pairing, they were probably the most accomplished in the First Division - rarely can a club have paired such footballing centre-backs together in the same side. It was a formula that was to provide the backbone to West Ham's most successful

Archie also played later in his career. Joining the 'Gers in 1925 from junior side Shettleston, "Doc" Marshall, as he was mostly known, won six Scottish League Championship medals (1927, 29, 30, 31, 33 and 34) and three Scottish Cup winners' medals (1930, 32 and 34) with the Light Blues. His three appearances for Scotland were all against England, also represented Scottish League. Hammers signed Jimmy from the Gunners in March 1936 and he played in the Second Division side at the inside-right position fairly regularly up to the commencement of 1937-38, when he was once again succeeded by Archie who had been purchased from Glasgow Rangers for a reported fee of £3,500. Later an employee of Bermondsey Borough Council, James passed away in Dec. 1977.

ever season, 1985-86, when they challenged Liverpool and Everton for the title before having to settle for third spot. Alvin missed only two of the 50 senior matches that season and was also involved in one of the most bizarre matches ever seen at Upton Park, v Newcastle United (21.4.86). It was that night when Alvin scored a hat-trick against THREE DIFFERENT 'keepers - Thomas, Hedworth and Peter Beardsley - in an 8-1 thrashing of the Magpies! Alvin was playing at his peak and the highlight of his international career came in the 1986 World Cup tournament in Mexico. England had begun the finals none too impressively but Alvin got his chance in the second round match v Paraguay in Mexico City (18.6.86) and played his part in a 3-0 victory. To this day, Alvin finds it difficult to understand why Robson inexplicably dropped him for the quarter-final v Argentina and brought in Terry Fenwick to face Diego Maradona and that 'Hand of God' in the match that ended England's hopes. Significantly, Alvin was recalled for the first international of the following season (v Sweden, when Tony Cottee made his debut as sub), but that was to prove his last game for his country before injuries took their toll. Problems with his instep resulted in a series of operations and further setbacks that have restricted Alvin's appearances since the winter of 1986. The 42 games he managed following Lou Macari's appointment in 1989 represented his best run in the side for four seasons. Alvin was still playing some of the best football of his career when an Achilles injury, in Dec. 1990, ruled him out midway through that promotion term. Missing from the first team for 16 months, and given a free transfer by Billy Bonds, many had written off Alvin . . . until he re-emerged to play in the last seven games of 1991-92 in a brave, though vain, attempt to save the club from relegation. His heroics earned him a new one-year contract. Alvin started 1992-93 at the heart of defence but a serious Achilles tendon injury, sustained in Feb. 1993, resulted in another long lay-off. Once again, though, he confounded the sceptics who said he was finished. Almost 10 months after bowing out at Derby, the big Scouser was back in the top flight, boosting Hammers' Premiership challenge. He made 11 first team appearances and was warmly welcomed back by the fans, who chanted: "Alvin, Alvin Martin . . . he's got no hair, but we don't care!" Nor did Billy Bonds and Harry Redknapp, who decided Alvin had done enough to earn yet another Premiership contract, at the age of 36. When Alvin does decide the time is right to hang up his boots, he would like to stay in the game as a coach or manager. With a wealth of top class experience to hand, he has plenty to offer.

❏ *England caps:* 1981 v Brazil, Scotland (sub), Hungary; 1982 v Finland, Greece, Luxembourg (twice); 1983 v Wales, Greece, Hungary (twice); 1984 v Wales; 1985 v Northern Ireland; 1986 v Israel, Canada, Paraguay, Sweden (17).

Alvin Martin receives one of his three Hammer of the Year trophies from John Lyall in 1980.

Total

Played	App	Gls	App	Gls	App	Gls	App	Gls	App	Gls
1977-78	7	1	0	0	0	0	0	0	7	1
1978-79	22	1	1	0	0	0	0	0	23	1
1979-80	40	2	7	0	8	1	0	0	55	3
1980-81	41	1	3	0	9	1	6	0	59	2
1981-82	28	4	2	0	5	0	0	0	35	4
1982-83	38	3	0	0	7	0	0	0	45	3
1983-84	29	3	1	0	5	1	0	0	35	4
1984-85	40	1	5	0	4	0	0	0	49	1
1985-86	40	4	7	0	3	0	0	0	50	4
1986-87	16	2	1	0	3	0	0	0	20	2
1987-88	15	0	0	0	2	0	0	0	17	0
1988-89	27	1	5	0	5	2	0	0	37	3
1989-90	31	0	1	0	10	1	0	0	42	1
1990-91	20	1	0	0	3	0	0	0	23	1
1991-92	7	0	0	0	0	0	0	0	7	0
1992-93	23	1	1	0	2	0	0	0	26	1
1993-94	7	2	3	0	1	0	0	0	11	2
TOTAL	**431**	**27**	**37**	**0**	**67**	**6**	**6**	**0**	**541**	**33**

League   FAC   LC   Europe

MARTIN, Dean   1991-92

Born: North London. 31.8.72
Lge apps: 2
Cup apps: 1

■ Diminutive, blond striker who quit his job installing air conditioning units to join Hammers from non-league Fisher Athletic for £25,000 in May 1991. His first senior outing was v Panathinaikos (Greece) in the Makita Tournament at Highbury in Aug. 1991. Came on as sub in the FA Cup at Wrexham (4.2.92) and was booked within seconds of coming on for his League debut at Coventry (25.4.92). Played his only full game in the final match of 1991/92 v Nottingham Forest at Upton Park (2.5.92). Dean went on loan to GM Vauxhall Conference League side Kettering Town in Dec. 1992 and later joined Colchester United on a free transfer.

MARTIN, Tudor James   1936-37

Born: Caerau, Wales. 20.4.1904
Lge apps: 119 (7 gls)

■ A former coal miner, Tudor had the amazing experience of scoring a hat-trick on his debut for Hammers at St. James's Park v Newcastle United (9.9.36) and ending up on the losing side, Magpies winning the encounter 5-3. At home in the centre-forward position or at inside-left, Hammers signed the goalscoring Welshman from Swansea Town where he had scored 45 goals in 116 League outings and rarely has a West Ham player made such a sensational start. Goalscorers then were not at the premium they are today, and on Feb. 16, 1937 Tudor was allowed to join Southend United. Beginning his career with Bridgend Town, he made a giant leap to join West Bromwich Albion in 1926. He won his solitary Welsh cap v Ireland in 1930 during his year with Newport County when he scored 34 goals in 27 Third Division South matches and drew the attention of Wolves manager Major Frank Buckley. He signed for the Midlanders and scored nine times in 15 First Division appearances between 1930/32. He also scored a mammoth 60 times for Wolves Reserves when they won the Central League Championship in 1932. Tudor died at Newport 6.9.1979.

MARQUIS, Paul   1994

Born: Enfield, Middlesex. 29.8.72
Lge apps: 1

■ Central defender who played just 60 seconds of League football for West Ham - as a 90th minute sub for Mike Marsh at Manchester City (12.2.94). But tall Paul did at least manage a touch as Hammers cleared a corner in the goalless draw! His only other senior experience came in the Ray Stewart testimonial v Ipswich Town (6.5.92). Joined Hammers' youth ranks after a spell with Cheshunt in cs 1989 and showed plenty of promise as he graduated to the reserves. A Combination League regular,

Paul's hopes of making the breakthrough in 1993/94 suffered a setback when he dislocated his shoulder in a pre-season friendly. Later joined GM Vauxhall League Dagenham & Redbridge on loan. Given a free transfer by West Ham in March 1994 and signed for Doncaster Rovers.

MASSEY, Frederick   1909-12

Born: East Ham, London. 2.11.1883

■ Originally with Leyton, Fred played one SL game for Tottenham in 1909 before transferring to West Ham where he was successfully converted to wing-half. Making his Hammers' debut at left-half in a 2-2 Upton Park draw with Swindon Town on Dec. 18, 1909, he eventually went on to fill all three half-back positions and gave three seasons sterling service. He'd played two seasons at the then professional Leyton club before his move to Spurs in the summer of 1907. He spent a similar period with Tottenham, but made only five senior outings, three in the secondary Western League, one in a friendly and that solitary SL appearance. Fred died at Watford, Herts, on January 26, 1953.

MATTHEWS, ("Terry"), George   1955

Born: Leyton, London. 25.2.36
Lge apps: 9 (1 gl)

■ A former Hackney and Middlesex Schools inside-forward, he signed pro forms in Aug. 1952 after junior service. Winning a first team spot in 1956, he transferred to Aldershot and later Gillingham before becoming a well-known figure in local non-league soccer as manager of Aveley and then Tilbury. His son, David, was given a free transfer at the end of the 1983/84 season after making his way through the junior ranks at Upton Park.

MERCER, Frederick   1903-04

SL apps: 8 (1 gl)

■ Fred made his Irons debut in the volatile atmosphere of a West Ham/Millwall London derby meeting at the Memorial Grounds on Jan. 2 1904. Lions won 1-0, and left-winger Mercer went back to the reserves. He was back in the team for another 1-0 defeat at Luton, however, on Mar. 26, 1904, which signalled the start of a seven-match run in the first team. His solitary goal came in a 3-1 win at Northampton on Apr. 7.

MIECZNIKOWSKI, W.L   1902-03

Born: Paddington, London. 1877
SL apps: 3

■ A prominent East End amateur with Pemberton and Clapton, who had played for and against West Ham at intervals. Also played for Portsmouth, but still retained his amateur status. He won innumerable county honours. In Dec. 1899 the "morning leader" announced that due to so many wrong spellings of this player's name it would in future refer to him simply as "Kowski." A winger of East European descent, he was happy on either flank.

MIELLEAR, J   1910-12

SL apps: 3
Cup apps: 1

■ An outside-right signed from leading amateur club Bromley prior to the start of the 1910/11 season, he was listed under the heading of "Promising youngster," in that year's handbook. He made his debut in a 2-1 reverse v Northampton Town at Upton Park on March 4, 1911 - his only appearance that campaign. He

'Ludo' Miklosko

MIKLOSKO, Ludek   1990

Born: Protesov, Ostrava, Czechoslovakia
Lge apps: 188
Cup apps: 31

■ Affectionately known as "Ludo", the giant 6ft 4in Czech goalkeeper will probably go down as Lou Macari's most telling contribution during his brief seven-month stay as manager. Macari gave Ludo trials in December 1989 although it was some two months later before he received work permit clearance to play in Britain, having made his name back home for First Division Banik Ostrava. Ludo spent 12 years with the club from northern Czechoslovakia and helped them win the Czech title before joining Hammers in 1989. Yet, ironically, Macari suddenly quit Hammers just hours before Miklosko made his debut in the Second Division at Swindon Town (18.2.90)! Thankfully for West Ham, Ludo stayed much longer than the man who signed him. His outstanding performances in England earned him a recall to the Czech national side in 1990 and he was in the World Cup for Italia '90 without getting a game. In his first full season, under Billy Bonds, he kept 22 clean sheets - equalling the club record set by Phil Parkes - and his popularity was underlined as he was voted Hammer of the Year by the fans on the day Hammers clinched promotion. Ludo's consistent contribution in 1990/91 was crucial because as many as 16 League matches were won by a single goal margin, while the club also enjoyed an FA Cup run all the way to the semi-finals. When Hammers were relegated a year later, Ludo missed six matches - and four of them were lost. Significantly, he was ever-present again the following season when Hammers bounced back to the top flight at the first attempt. Ludo retired from the international scene in December '92 - his 40th, and last, full cap came against England at Wembley (25.4.90). Happily settled in Essex with his wife and son, Ludo plans to underline his long-term intention to live in England by adopting British citizenship in 1995. It's a far cry from that winter when Macari's 'Mystery Czech' bounced into Upton Park, speaking barely any words of English and facing an agonising wait for a work permit. At a transfer fee of just £266,430, Ludek Miklosko proved a tremendous bargain.

☆ *Czechoslovakian caps:* 1990 v Spain, England; 1991 v Albania (twice), Iceland, France; 1992 v England (7).

Played	League		FAC		LC		Europe		Total	
	App	Gls	App	Gls	App	Gls	App	Gls	App	Gls
1989-90	18	0	0	0	1	0	0	0	19	0
1990-91	46	0	7	0	3	0	0	0	56	0
1991-92	36	0	3	0	4	0	0	0	43	0
1992-93	46	0	2	0	2	0	0	0	50	0
1993-94	42	0	6	0	3	0	0	0	50	0
TOTAL	188	0	18	0	13	0	0	0	219	0

John Moncur

doubled his Southern League outings the next season, being involved in fine wins at New Brompton and at home to Exeter City in Feb. 1912, but he was also in the side which crashed out of that season's FA Cup following a 4-0 third round replay defeat at Swindon, never to be heard of again at senior level.

MILLER, Keith 1968-70

Born: Lewisham, London. 26.1.48
Lge apps: 3

■ A tough-tackling wing-half signed from Walthamstow Avenue, his first team opportunities were extremely limited. First appeared in the senior side when coming on as a sub. v Ipswich Town at Portman Road in Nov. 1968. It was not until his move to Fourth Division Bournemouth that he was guaranteed regular League football and with whom he won promotion to Div. 3 under the management duo of John Bond and Ken Brown, in the company of ex-Hammers Tony Scott, Pat Holland (on loan) and Trevor Hartley, in 1970/71.

MILLER, Walter 1908-09

Born: 1885
SL apps: 11 (5 gls)
Cup apps: 6 (1 gl)

■ Walter joined Hammers as a 23-year-old centre-forward from Sheffield Wednesday in the 1908-09 close season and scored in his second Southern League appearance at New Brompton. His best performance came in a 4-1 Upton Park victory over Exeter City, to which he contributed two goals and he was also an ever-present in Hammers' fine FA Cup run that season, which ended with a third round replay defeat at Newcastle. Left to join Blackpool for the 1909/10 season and scored 14 goals in 31 outings for the Seasiders.

MILLS, Hugh 1932-35

Born: Bonhill, Scotland. 1912
SL apps: 21 (15 gls)
Cup apps: 2 (1 gl)

■ Alerted by his prolific goalscoring feats in Scottish junior football for St. Anthony's and Bridgetown Waverley of the Scottish Central League, Hammers brought the sharp-shooting centre-forward south along with his brother George during the summer of 1932. An athlete of some renown in his native Scotland, his ability to run 100 yards in 11 seconds made him a difficult proposition for opposing centre-halves, and stood him in good stead in the scoring stakes. Netted on his debut on the opening day of the 1932/33 season against Bradford City at the Boleyn, he managed an amazing goal-a-game scoring ratio in the 12 first XI appearances in 1934/35, scoring in 10 successive games. Hughie was transferred to Celtic in June 1935.

MILNE, Ralph 1990

Born: Dundee, Scotland. 13.5.1961
Cup apps: 1

■ Former Dundee United, Bristol City and Manchester United midfielder who made just one brief appearance for Hammers while on loan - as sub. in the goalless League Cup fifth round replay at Derby County (24.1.90).

MILNES, Frederick 1904-06

Born: Wortley. January 1878
SL apps: 2
Cup apps: 2

■ One of the most famous amateurs of his day, full-back Fred resisted the overtures of a host of top clubs who wanted him to turn pro. He steadfastly refused to relinquish his jealously-guarded amateur status, however, preferring instead to keep his allegiance to his first love, Sheffield FC, the oldest football club in the world and with whom he won an FA Amateur Cup winners medal in 1904. As an amateur he was free to play for any club he wished, but chose not to sign for any of them. Beginning his career with Sheffield Wycliffe before the turn of the century, he graduated to Sheffield FC and by 1902 had turned out for three steel city teams by virtue of his appearances for First Division Sheffield United. Fred played two SL matches for West Ham United in the right-back position in 1904/5 v. Wellingborough Town (4-0) and Southampton (2-2) at The Dell. In Sept. 1905 he was a member of the Pilgrims, virtually footballing missionaries selected from England's best amateur players, who voyaged to North America for a tour which was one of the first efforts to popularise the game over there. On returning Fred signed Southern League forms for Spurs on the recommendation of that other great amateur, Vivian Woodward, but made only two Western League games for Spurs. In March, 1906 he joined Manchester United and in 1907 had spells with Leicester Fosse, Reading and Ilford. He also played for Norwich City in 1908. He eventually emigrated to the USA and was reportedly still playing out there in 1912.

MITCHELL, Paul 1993-

Born: Bournemouth, Dorset. 20.10.71
Lge apps: 1

■ Joined Hammers for just £40,000 in August 1993 in the deal that also saw Keith Rowland switch from Bournemouth, where they had both previously played under Harry Redknapp. Paul made just 12 first team appearances for the Cherries, having made his league bow at Chester in Division Two (7.9.91). Can play either full-back or midfield. Paul was hampered by injury soon after arriving in East London, although he was non-playing sub. at Oldham and soon afterwards managed to make his Premiership debut as sub. - six minutes from time - in the home game v Blackburn Rovers (27.4.94).

MONCUR, John 1994-

Born: Mile End, East London. 22.9.66

■ It was just like coming home for East Ender John when he moved from relegated Swindon Town to West Ham for £1 million in the summer of 1994. This talented midfield creator first impressed for Harlow, South-West Essex and London Schools before joining Tottenham as an apprentice in April 1983, turning pro a year later. John trained with Arsenal, Orient and the Hammers as a youngster but was no doubt influenced by his father, John senior, who is Spurs' youth development officer. "Moncs" made his debut at Everton (11.5.87), in what was virtually a reserve side, five days before the 1987 FA Cup Final. He already had some league experience, though, having played four times while on loan to Doncaster Rovers in September 1986. John made his league debut v York City (27.9.86) but his spell there ended when he broke a leg. With talented flair players like Paul Gascoigne and Vinny Samways at Tottenham, John was always on the fringe of the first team but unable to command a regular place. He spent much of his time on loan and as well as Doncaster, he also had spells with Cambridge United, Portsmouth, Brentford, Ipswich Town and Nottingham Forest. He did make 21 senior games, scoring one goal, before his £75,000 transfer to Swindon in March 1992. Under the management of former Spurs favourite Glenn Hoddle, the blond Moncur emerged as a vital member of the Robins side that earned promotion to the top flight at the end of his first full season with the club. In fact, he scored in the crucial play-off semi-final at Tranmere that helped Swindon towards an epic 4-3 victory over Leicester City at Wembley in May 1993. Although the west country club finished bottom of the Premiership a year later, John had impressed a number of people and, indeed, Hoddle was keen to re-sign him after he took over at Chelsea. But John, who played 58 league

Paul Mitchell

matches for Swindon, chose Hammers instead. Classy and composed in possession with good vision , he is naturally left-footed although can perform well with both feet and has the knack of losing opponents with rapid change of direction. Missed the start of the 1994/95 season due to an ankle injury but soon established himself as a favourite after making his debut at Norwich City (27.8.94). Ironically his first, match-winning, goal for West Ham came at . . . Chelsea! (2.10.94)

MONTEITH, Hugh 1900-02

Born: Newcomnock, Ayrshire, Scotland. 1875
SL apps: 53
Cup apps: 7

■ Hughie began his career with one of Glasgow Celtic's nursery sides, Parkhead Juniors, and subsequently joined the famous Glasgow club. Staying at Celtic Park for just one season, he then moved south to join Loughboro Corinthians, and from there transferred to Bristol City for their first season as professionals, where he was regarded as one of the finest net-minders in the country. It was from the West Country club that the able custodian joined Hammers in the dawn of the Edwardian era, and at the very beginning of their existence under the banner of West Ham United FC. The goals against column totalled a miserly 28 in the club's first season seven of which were conceded during Hugh's five absences that campaign. The following season saw the well-built Scotsman miss only one match, and again the debit account stayed on 28. A fine record, and one which Football League clubs were quick to notice. His growing reputation led to his transfer to Bury - then a force to be reckoned with - and his appearance for the Shakers in the 1903 FA Cup Final at Crystal Palace v. Derby County. The 6-0 scoreline in favour of the Lancastrians remains as a record margin of victory in a final.

MOORE, Brian 1954-55

Born: Belfast, Northern Ireland. 29.12.33
Lge apps: 9 (1 gl)

■ Ball-playing Northern Irish inside-forward, who had his promising career tragically terminated by injury. Signed from Glentoran in Feb. 1955, he was granted a joint testimonial along with team-mate Geoff Hallas, who suffered a similar fate.

For BOBBY MOORE see pages 145-150

MOORE, Tommy 1898-01

SL apps (TIW): 48
Cup apps: 10
SL apps (WHU): 4

■ A sort of Bruce Grobbelaar character of his day, Tom was nicknamed the "Dancing Dervish" because of his unorthodox methods in evading challenging forwards. Despite having his critics, he managed to attain fair level of consistency during Hammers' last two seasons as Thames Ironworks, missing only two Southern League matches in that time. Although called up for the second match of the 1900/01 season against his former club Millwall, a 3-1 mauling from the Lions did little to help him wrest the first team spot away from the more experienced Hughie Monteith, and a 4-1 home defeat inflicted by London rivals Spurs on Feb. 16, 1901, signalled the end of his tenure at the Memorial Grounds. Dispatched to little Essex side Grays, Tommy seemed destined for obscurity, but football, and the FA Cup in particular, has a habit of throwing up opportunities to prove past masters wrong. Tom got, and took, his chance the very next season, when his inspired display of goalkeeping was largely responsible for the Essex village team's shock 2-1 Second qualifying round win, on a foggy November afternoon at the Memorial Grounds.

MOORE, William ("Billy") 1922-29

Born: Newcastle-upon-Tyne. 6.10.1894
Lge apps: 181 (42 gls)
Cup apps: 21 (6 gls)

Billy Moore

■ Another famous Moore from an earlier era, Billy joined Hammers from Sunderland in 1922, where he'd struck up a renowned left-wing partnership with England international H. Martin after joining from Seaton Dalaval. His arrival at Upton Park heralded the beginning of an even more famous liaison with the immortal Jimmy Ruffell, and in an age when exceptional inside-forwards were commonplace, Billy shone as brightly as any of his contemporaries. After winning amateur caps against Belgium, Denmark and Sweden, he gained full England international honours versus the latter country scoring twice, shortly after appearing in the first Wembley Cup Final in 1923, and further distinguished himself as an ever-present in West Ham's promotion side in his eventful first season at the Boleyn. Although recognised as a maker rather than taker of goals during his eight seasons as a West Ham player, Billy was not one to pass up scoring opportunities when they arose, as amply confirmed by his near half-century of goals whilst in the claret and blue. Appointed assistant trainer when he retired from

playing in 1929, he was promoted to trainer-in-chief in 1932 and remained in that capacity until his full retirement in 1960. Two years earlier he'd realised his greatest personal ambition in seeing Hammers return to the First Division after an absence of 25 years. Living in nearby Plashet Road, Billy and his wife were regular visitors to Upton Park throughout the sixties and indeed journeyed on many away trips, in which Bill often acted as unofficial courier, making sure everyone was accounted for on the coach which carried club officials and guests. It was a sad day for West Ham United, and football in general, when Billy Moore passed away on September 26, 1968 at the age of 73.
☆ *England cap:* 1923 v Sweden (1).

Nicky Morgan

MORGAN, Nicky 1979-83

Born: Eltham, London. 30.10.59
Lge apps: 21 (2 gls)
Cup apps: 4

■ Useful striker, who was unable to win a regular place in the first team. Signed apprentice professional in July 1976, full pro in October 1977. Made his League bow against Luton Town in April 1979. Gained invaluable experience on the Continent when loaned out to Hammers' 1976 Cup Winners' Cup opponents - Den Haag - during 1981/82, scoring seven goals in 16 appearances for the Dutch club. Returned to England to play for Portsmouth where he scored 32 times in 95 games between 1982 and '86 before transferring to Stoke City where he made 88 appearances and scored 20 goals. He joined Bristol City in 1989 and continued his strike rate in the West Country where he has made well over 100 League matches and teamed up with ex-Hammer, Leroy Rosenior.

Gallaher's Cigarettes.

ARTHUR E. HUFTON
WEST HAM UNITED

CHURCHMANS CIGARETTES.

T. RANDALL.

GALLAHER'S CIGARETTES.

GEORGE KITCHEN
WEST HAM UNITED, 1909-10

VICTOR WATSON
WEST HAM UNITED

J. COCKROFT

WILLS'S CIGARETTES

L. GOULDEN (WEST HAM UNITED)

WM. G. B. MOORE
WEST HAM UNITED

PLAYER'S CIGARETTES

S. EARLE
WEST HAM UNITED

OGDEN'S CIGARETTES.

G. KAY,
WEST HAM UNITED.

PLAYER'S CIGARETTES

T. H. YEWS
WEST HAM UNITED

PLAYER'S CIGARETTES

JAMES RUFFELL

J. BARRETT

DR. J. MARSHALL

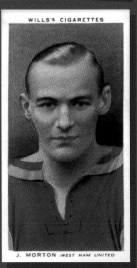

WILLS'S CIGARETTES

J. MORTON (WEST HAM UNITED)

W. THIRLAWAY

129

SECOND DIVISION CHAMPIONS 1958

Back row (left to right): Malcolm, Brown, Bond, Gregory, Cantwell, Lansdowne. *Front row:* Grice, Smith, Keeble, Dick, Musgrove.

**1964/65
FA CUP &
EUROPEAN CUP
WINNERS' CUP
WINNERS**

Back row (left to right): Malcolm Allison, John Bond, Ken Brown, Martin Peters, Peter Brabrook, Jim Standen, Johnny Byrne, Alan Sealey, Jack Burkett, Geoff Hurst, Noel Cantwell.
Front row (left to right): Ron Boyce, Joe Kirkup, John Sissons, Eddie Bovington, Brian Dear

KEN BROWN

JOHN BYRNE

RON
BOYCE

PHIL WOOSNAM

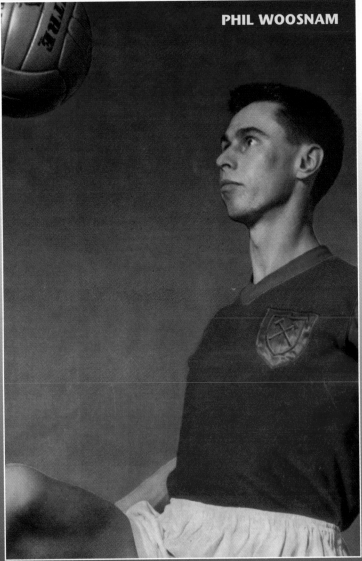

BOBBY MOORE

GEOFF HURST

MARTIN PETERS

BILLY BONDS

BILLY BONDS

FRANK LAMPARD

ALAN DEVONSHIRE

Hall of Fame

PHIL PARKES
& ALAN
DEVONSHIRE

RAY
STEWART

ALVIN
MARTIN

TONY GALE

FRANK McAVENNIE
& MARK WARD

TONY COTTEE

STEVE POTTS

LIAM BRADY

IAN BISHOP

JULIAN DICKS

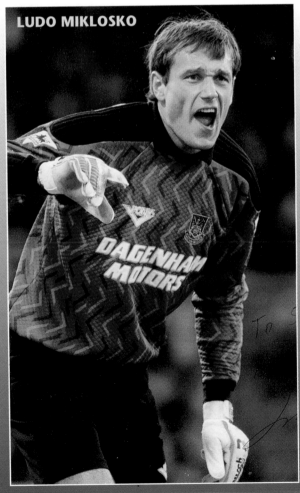

LUDO MIKLOSKO

TREVOR MORLEY

MOORE, Bobby   1958-1973

Born: Barking, East London. 12.4.41
Lge apps: 544 (24 gls)
Cup apps: 98 (3 gls)

■ **Without question, the greatest Hammer of all-time and, at his peak, the finest defender in the world. No British footballer was more revered or loved by the nation than the legendary Bobby Moore. As captain, he led Hammers to FA Cup victory in 1964 and, their biggest triumph, the European Cup Winners' Cup a year later. But on a hot summer's day in 1966, Bobby was back at Wembley - an arena he graced with such distinction so many times - for his finest achievement . . . leading England to their first, and only, World Cup Final victory over West Germany. It was a measure of the great man's immense stature, not only in football but in life itself, that his tragic and untimely death in February 1993, aged only 51, was mourned by millions all over the world. Quite simply, Moore, capped 108 times by his country, was a sporting hero, a player of incomparable style and grace both on and off the pitch. Yet he achieved every major honour - apart from a league championship medal - despite not being particularly naturally gifted. He reached the pinnacle and earned the respect and admiration of the people through sheer hard work and dedication...**

Bobby Moore captained Hammers to FA Cup success in 1964

Robert Frederick Chelsea Moore was born at 43 Waverley Gardens, Barking, on April 12, 1941, the only child of Robert Edward and Doris. He attended nearby Westbury School and began to play for a local Saturday morning side, South Park Boys, in the Ilford League. Rather short and a little on the tubby side, young Bobby did well enough in his centre-half role without, at that stage, showing signs of greatness. His first notable honour was winning the Crisp Shield as captain of Barking Primary Schools and he went on to represent Leyton Schools, while a pupil at Leyton's Tom Hood High School, and Essex. Bobby, typically, was usually successful at whatever he attempted, and he might have gone on to become a top cricketer rather than develop in football. Although Ted Fenton was manager at the time and Wally St. Pier chief scout, it is understood that a local scout, Jack Turner (who would later become involved in some of Moore's earliest business dealings), filed the first report on the blond youngster after being alerted by sports master, Tom Russell. It went something like: 'He looks fairly useful but won't set the world alight'. He was duly invited along to West Ham who had founded a

new youth policy to challenge the likes of Chelsea and Spurs. Under the watchful eye of influential senior pro Malcolm Allison, Moore attended coaching sessions at Upton Park on Tuesday and Thursday evenings. He was not the most outstanding kid around. But Moore, a quiet, modest boy, listened and learned under Mal. His thirst for greater knowledge of the game impressed the senior pro's. He might have lacked pace but even at that young age, Bobby perfected the art of reading the game, positioning himself so that any weaknesses he had were rarely exposed. His awareness of team mates and opponents alike was uncanny, even then. It was easy to see why Bobby had such great respect for that other footballing visionary, Fulham's Johnny Haynes. Bobby made his debut for England Youth against Holland in Amsterdam (2.10.57) whilst continuing to develop in Hammers' Metropolitan League side. West Ham had created its own highly acclaimed youth academy and Moore was rapidly becoming head boy. Ironically, his big chance came at the expense of his mentor, Allison, who, in Nov. 1957, was diagnosed as having tuberculosis. West Ham went on to win

promotion to Division One at the end of that season and the big time beckoned for Moore. With Allison still struggling to find a way back via the reserves, and fellow half-backs Bill Lansdowne and Andy Nelson both injured, Bobby was thrust into the spotlight for the first time when Manchester United visited Upton Park on the night of Monday, September 8, 1958. Noel Cantwell, the senior member of the team, was consulted by manager Fenton about who to pick at left-half to face United. The choice was between the vastly experienced, but still not fully fit, Allison, or the up and coming Moore. Cantwell jeapordized his long-time close friendship with Allison by recommending the kid. At the age of 17, Bobby had arrived on the big stage, playing his part in a 3-2 win in front of 35,672 fans. He wore the number six shirt, the one he later made famous, on just four more occasions that season, as first Nelson and then Johnny Smith reclaimed it. Bobby had to wait until the 13th league match of 1959/60 before being called upon and only 12 more appearances followed that term. But after Smith was transferred to Tottenham, Bobby started the 1960/61 campaign and never looked back. When Ron Greenwood arrived in 1961 to take over from Fenton, it was the start of the most golden era in West Ham's history. Greenwood wanted to build his side around Moore and did so to great effect in the mid-60's. Although never in serious contention for the championship, West Ham won many new friends away from East London with their exciting brand of attacking football. They beat Preston North End 3-2 in the final of the 1964 FA Cup, although it was perhaps the 3-1 semi-final victory over Manchester United, on a rain-soaked Hillsborough pitch, that really signalled West Ham's emergence as a major force that decade. Moore played at his immaculate best to outwit a star-studded United side boasting superstars such as Charlton, Law and Best. The victory over Preston, although not a vintage Hammers' performance, put the seal on a remarkable season for Bobby who, 48 hours before the final, was named Footballer of the Year. At 23, he was the youngest-ever recipient of the annual football writers' award. A year later and he was back at Wembley to lead West Ham to a glorious 2-0 win over TSV Munich 1860 in the European Cup Winners'

Cup Final. That performance against the Germans is ranked by many as West Ham's finest ever, and they became only the second English club (after Tottenham in 1963) to lift the coveted trophy. Greenwood also helped Moore progress along the international ladder in his early years, as coach of England youth and under-23 teams. Bobby earned a surprise late call-up to England's World Cup squad for the 1962 tournament in Chile. It was in the last friendly game in the build-up to the finals, in Lima, Peru on Sunday, May 20, that manager Walter Winterbottom gave the 21 year-old West Ham defender his full international debut, in a half-back line that also included another debutant, Maurice Norman, and Ron Flowers. Despite his inexperience, Moore gave his customary assured performance in a fine 4-0 victory in which his old mate Jimmy Greaves scored a hat-trick after Flowers had given England the lead from the penalty spot. It was the launch of a glittering international career for Bobby, who played in all four of England's World Cup matches in '62.

Winterbottom gave Moore his first taste of top class international football, but it was obviously Alf Ramsey - appointed in Feb. 1963 - who reaped the richest reward of having such a quality defender and leader at his disposal. Bobby, who had married Tina by this time, flourished under Ramsey - two men, both calm and sometimes detatched from the pack, who came from neighbouring towns, Barking and Dagenham. Together, they would conquer the world. Ramsey immediately identified Moore's leadership qualities and when Jimmy Armfield was injured, he had no qualms about handing

the captaincy to Moore for the game against Czechoslovakia in Bratislava on May 20, 1963. It was only his 12th senior international but he was well equipped for the task of his leading his country He always did so with immense pride and dignity. The notable victory over the 1962 losing World Cup finalists was England's first under the Ramsey regime - and note the scoreline . . . 4-2. A similiar result, on July 30, 1966, would catapult Moore and Ramsey to legendary status in world football. For that was the afternoon on which England defeated West Germany in extra-time of the 1966 World Cup Final. Moore set up the first and third goals for his West Ham team mate Geoff Hurst, who claimed a unique hat-trick, while the other goal was netted by the third member of Hammers' heroic trio, Martin Peters. So Moore led the red-shirted England team up the steps to collect the Jules Rimet trophy from Her Majesty the Queen. And typical of the gentleman of football, after all the drama of the occasion, he still had the presence of mind to wipe mud from his hands before accepting football's ultimate prize! But then Moore was always unflappable. In fact, while he was heading for immortality as

England's World Cup captain, he played every game of the '66 tournament against a background of unrest at West Ham, where his future was far from settled. In his authorised biography, 'Bobby Moore, The Life and Times of a Sporting Hero', by Jeff Powell, Bobby revealed that he was at loggerheads with Greenwood over his contract and refused to sign a new one. So for seven days, between June 30 and the start of the World Cup finals on July 7, he was unregistered to an English club! As Powell put it: 'Legally, he did not exist as a player in the eyes of the Football Association, whose team he was about to lead into the World Cup finals'. Moore actually signed a temporary one-month agreement so that he was eligible to play in soccer's showpiece event. More importantly for Hammers, Greenwood refused to sanction a possible move to Spurs, who were keen to sign him. But the professional manner in which he coped with the distraction of his contract dispute in '66 was nothing compared to the personal crisis which threatened his preparations for the 1970 finals in Mexico. Bobby was falsely accused of stealing a bracelet while in Bogota, Colombia with the England

party and was held under house arrest, just days before the tournament began. Once cleared of all charges, Bobby proceeded to produce one of his classic defensive performances against the brilliant Brazilians, who went on to win the final after Ramsey's title defence had ended at the hands of West Germany in the quarter-finals. The only other time Moore came close to leaving Upton Park, before his eventual departure to Fulham in 1974, was a year earlier than that. Controversial Derby County manager Brian Clough tabled a bid for Moore and Trevor Brooking, but a mooted £400,000 deal was again blocked by Greenwood - much to Moore's dismay at the time. Many people inside the game were surprised that he spent so long with Hammers who, after losing the 1966 European Cup Winners' Cup semi-final, slid into decline and a long period of under-achievement. They possessed England's famous World Cup trio but, for all their flair and entertaining football, were often regarded as a soft touch by opponents and failed to mount a serious bid for the First Division championship. Moore was the supreme individual during a golden era for English football - he became an overnight superstar, rubbing shoulders with famous film stars, politicians and other big name celebrities. Yet the club he captained were never in contention for the title, and the highest they finished under him was sixth, in season 1972/73. Ironically, it was "Mooro's" last full season in the claret and blue number six shirt.

*Bobby won
108 England caps*

He was ever-present, but the team was in a period of transition. Many of the old favourites had already gone - Peters to Spurs and Hurst to Stoke City, who had prevented West Ham from reaching the League Cup Final in 1972. That dramatic semi-final marathon with the Potters was memorable for Hurst's penalty miss (or rather a stunning Gordon Banks save) and Moore's decision to take over the goalkeeper's shirt after Bobby Ferguson was injured in the third game at Old Trafford. He even managed to push out Mike Bernard's penalty, who luckily hit home the rebound!

Yet Hammers followed their promising 1972/73 campaign with a more typical battle against relegation the following season. Bobby played in 22 league and two cup matches in 1973/74 but his career at West Ham and for England was drawing to a close. His errors were so rare that the mistake which proved costly in Poland, in the World Cup qualifier of 1973, was magnified and he was dropped for the first time by Ramsey for the decisive return clash at Wembley later that year. Then, ironically, it was a blunder by Bobby's replacement, Norman Hunter, which finally ended England's bid to reach the 1974 finals in Germany. Bobby's 108th - and last - England cap was a friendly v Italy at Wembley (14.11.73). It was a record haul - still is for an outfield player - and was bettered only by goalkeeper Peter Shilton's 125. Bobby's last-ever first team appearance for West Ham was against little Hereford United in the FA Cup third round at Upton Park on Saturday, January 5, 1974. Bobby sustained the worst injury of his illustrious career - twisted knee ligaments that forced him out of the reckoning for eight weeks. The relatively unknown Mick McGiven took over the celebrated number six shirt and a series of good performances by the Geordie helped Hammers to avoid the drop. Bobby's dispute with Greenwood over his chance to join Cloughie at Derby dragged on into the early weeks of 1974 a period when Ron decided to take more of a back seat and hand first team responsibilities to John Lyall. Moore had no problem with Lyall but he knew that his days were numbered at West Ham. He was "angered" by the Board's refusal to grant him a free transfer at the end of the season and to seek a fee of £25,000 instead. There was no shortage of interest in Bobby from the Second Division, including Norwich City, who were then managed by former West Ham team-mate John Bond, and Portsmouth. Bobby hoped that Crystal Palace, managed by his old mentor Malcolm Allison, would come in for him, but it was Fulham boss Alec Stock who eventually signed the Upton Park collosus on the March 14 transfer deadline day. After 16 years and a remarkable record of 642 first team games, 544 in the top flight, and 98 in various cups, Moore's final game for the club was a nondescript reserve fixture against Plymouth Argyle at Upton Park. Bobby's first appearance for Fulham doubled the Craven Cottage crowd to 18,000 for the visit of Middlesbrough (19.3.74). A disastrous debut (4-0 home defeat) was soon forgotten, though, as the following season Moore and another vastly experienced former England international, Alan Mullery, inspired revitalised Fulham to their first FA Cup Final appearance. Their Wembley opponents on

Saturday, May 3, 1975? Who else but West Ham! Fulham won the support of the neutrals with their flair and ambition, but the dream was ruined by Hammers' two-goal hero Alan Taylor. Moore could cope with the disappointment probably better than any other player in white. After all, Wembley was his second home and he had been there often enough and done it more often than the rest. They were happy days at Craven Cottage, enjoying the twilight of his playing career alongside Mullery and, later, two of the game's great entertainers, George Best and Rodney Marsh. The last of Bobby's 124 league and 26 cup appearances for the West London club, over a four-season period, came at Blackburn Rovers (14.5.77). It was his 668th in the Football League and, including England, West Ham and Fulham appearances, his 1000th in all competitions. Incidentally, Bobby was only once used by Hammers in the role of substitute - when he replaced Bobby Howe in a home game v Derby County (6.2.71). Bobby knew his own value to West Ham and fought hard for what he believed he was worth, even during his younger days after Hammers lifted the FA Cup in 1964 when he held out for improved contract terms for the first time. He was estimated to be earning around £60 per week at that time, although he was among the country's most highly paid players at an estimated £200 per week by 1972. He tried to lay the foundations for his future by pursuing a number of wide-ranging business interests, including ownership of a sports shop right opposite the Boleyn Ground in the 60's. Commercially, he was a very attractive commodity and, with the help of trusted agent Jack Turner, he virtually earned as much from advertising and product endorsement, newspaper and magazine columns, as he did playing football for club and country. Not all of his business ventures were a success, though, and after some costly investments turned sour, he reverted again to football for a fresh challenge. In the summer of 1976, aged 35, Bobby joined other greats, such as Pele, in the rich North American Soccer League. He spent one season with Texas-based San Antonio Thunder, and returned in 1978 for a spell with Seattle Sounders. In between, he returned to England for one more season with Fulham. When his playing days were finally ended at the age of 36, Moore wanted desperately to stay in football. But, for all his incredible talent and experience, Bobby received few offers. He had to settle for a brief managerial stint in tandem with former West Ham team mate Harry Redknapp at non-league Oxford City between 1979 and 1981. With nothing on offer at home, Mooro went to Hong Kong for six months in 1983 to coach Eastern Athletic. Between June 1984 and April '86 he tried in vain to make a go of management at Southend United, but presided over relegation in his first year and 20th position in the Fourth Division in his second, although a boardroom battle did

Upton Park became a shrine following the shock news of Bobby's death in 1993, its main gates covered in scarves, hats, mascots, mementoes and flowers.

Bobby's widow, Stephanie, unveils a bust in his honour

nothing to help matters. Despite having the backing of the directors, and with two years of his contract still to run, he decided to resign three games from the end of 1985/86 and turn instead to promotions work as well as reporting for the controversial new Sunday Sport newspaper. His Roots Hall connections were not entirely severed, though, because he agreed to serve on the board and was still club president right up until his death. Divorced from Tina early in 1986, Bobby found true love again with the new lady in his life, air stewardess Stephanie Parlane-Moore, whom he had met several years earlier on a flight to South Africa. Bobby's football interests were rekindled in 1990 when he joined London radio station Capital Gold as their match analyst for the World Cup finals in Italy. Bobby was back but his career behind the microphone would be cruelly cut short. In the spring of 1991 came the news that he was suffering cancer of the colon, which had spread to his liver. It was terminal. But Bobby Moore had never resisted a battle and he wouldn't this time either. He kept the tragic news a secret from all but his closest family, daughter Roberta and son Dean, and friends. He continued to cope with chemotherapy and radiotherapy, enjoy a round of golf, swim and live as normally as possible. He didn't want pity, only as much enjoyment of life as possible in the short time he knew he had left. In Dec. 1991 Bobby married Stephanie at a private ceremony at Chelsea Register Office. On Feb. 15, 1993 came the first public announcement of his illness. Two days later he attended Wembley Stadium for the last time, commentating for Capital Gold on England's 6-0 World Cup qualifying victory over San Marino. Exactly a week later, early on Wednesday, February 24, 1993, Bobby died peacefully, surrounded by his family, at home in Battersea. A private funeral service was held at Putney Vale Crematorium on Mar. 2 but a much bigger memorium was happening in East London and right across the globe. West Ham supporters had lost their favourite son and the tributes came flooding in. Upton Park, its main gates covered in scarves, hats, mascots, mementoes and flowers, became a shrine. Some kept a vigil at the main entrance, where men, women and children wept in memory and respect for the greatest player the club had

ever seen. Many made the pilgrimage to Sunderland for Hammers' next match, and West Ham's next home game against Wolves (6.3.93) became a tearful occasion. Fans came on to the pitch to lay flowers on the centre-spot, while Greenwood, Hurst and Peters carried a giant wreath designed in the form of the number six shirt, which was not worn by a West Ham player that day. The West Ham directors, criticised in some quarters for ignoring Moore's immense contribution to the club after he left 20 years earlier, were eager to make amends. They announced that the new South Stand would be named after him and prior to the home game v Chelsea (2.10.93), Stephanie Moore sealed a time capsule, containing items of memorabilia relating to her husband's career, in the foundations of the new two-tier all-seater stand. And Hammers turned the clock back again (7.3.94) when the stand's official opening ceremony was performed by Bobby's team mates from the cup-winning sides of 1964 and '65, prior to the memorial match between West Ham and a Premier League XI.

❏ *England caps: 1962 v Peru, Hungary, Argentina, Bulgaria, Brazil, France, Northern Ireland, Wales; 1963 v France, Scotland, Brazil, Czechoslovakia, East Germany, Switzerland, Wales, Rest of the World, Northern Ireland; 1964 v*

Scotland, Uruguay, Portugal (twice), Republic of Ireland, Brazil, Argentina, Northern Ireland, Belgium, 1965 v Scotland, Hungary, Yugoslavia, West Germany, Sweden, Wales, Austria, Northern Ireland, Spain; 1966 v Poland (twice), West Germany (twice), Scotland, Norway, Denmark, Uruguay, Mexico, France, Argentina, Portugal, Northern Ireland, Czechoslovakia, Wales; 1967 v Scotland, Spain, Austria, Wales, Northern Ireland, USSR; 1968 v Scotland, Spain (twice), Sweden, West Germany, Yugoslavia, USSR, Romania, Bulgaria; 1969 v France, Northern Ireland, Wales, Scotland, Mexcio, Uruguay, Brazil, Holland, Portugal; 1970 v Belgium, Wales, Northern Ireland, Scotland, Colombia, Ecuador, Romania, Brazil, Czechoslovakia, West Germany, East Germany; 1971 v Greece (twice), Malta, Northern Ireland, Scotland, Switzerland (twice); 1972 v West Germany (twice), Wales (twice), Scotland, Yugoslavia; 1973 v Northern Ireland, Wales (twice), Scotland (twice), Czechoslovakia, Poland, USSR, Italy (twice). (108)

Played	League App	Gls	FAC App	Gls	LC App	Gls	Europe App	Gls	Total App	Gls
1958-59	5	0	0	0	0	0	0	0	5	0
1959-60	13	0	0	0	0	0	0	0	13	0
1960-61	38	1	2	0	2	1	0	0	42	2
1961-62	41	3	1	0	2	0	0	0	44	3
1962-63	41	3	5	0	1	0	0	0	47	3
1963-64	37	2	7	0	6	0	0	0	50	2
1964-65	28	1	0	0	0	0	7	0	35	1
1965-66	37	0	4	0	9	2	6	0	56	2
1966-67	40	2	2	0	6	0	0	0	48	2
1967-68	40	4	3	0	3	0	0	0	46	4
1968-69	41	2	3	0	3	0	0	0	47	2
1969-70	40	0	1	0	2	0	0	0	43	0
1970-71	39	2	1	0	2	0	0	0	42	2
1971-72	40	1	4	0	10	0	0	0	54	1
1972-73	42	3	2	0	2	0	0	0	46	3
1973-74	22	0	1	0	1	0	0	0	24	0
TOTAL	544	24	36	0	49	3	13	0	341	27

Martin Peters, Geoff Hurst and Ron Greenwood carry a giant wreath onto the pitch, designed in the shape of Bobby's number six shirt

Trevor Morley

MORLEY, Trevor 1989-

Born: Nottingham, Notts. 20.3.61
Lge apps: 164 (57 gls)
Cup apps: 28 (12 gls)

■ Hard-working, bustling striker who proved a shrewd signing by Lou Macari when he swapped Mark Ward for Manchester City's Morley and Ian Bishop in December 1989. Apart from 1991/92, when he was often out of favour and started only 13 matches of the First Division relegation campaign, Morley has registered double figures each season and was leading scorer in 1990/91, 1992/93 and 1993/94 with 12, 20 and 13 goals respectively. A target man who relishes a physical battle, Morley's unstinting efforts were recognised by the fans who voted him Hammer of the Year for 1993/94. The son of a former Nottingham Forest player, Trevor was rejected by Derby County as a youngster and forced to prove himself in non-league circles with Corby Town and Nuneaton Borough (where he won a Southern League championship medal in 1982), while also running a fruit and veg market stall. He gained League status initially with

Northampton Town, who signed him for £20,000 in the summer of 1985. Made his debut at Burnley (17.8.85) and helped Cobblers to win the Fourth Division championship in 1986/87 - the second of his three seasons with the Midlands club. After scoring 39 League goals in 107 appearances for Northampton, Morley was signed by Manchester City manager Mel Machin for £175,000 in January 1988 and he contributed 12 vital goals in just 15 games to boost City's promotion from Division Two that season. Scored a dozen League goals in the top flight and added two more in the opening 17 games of 1989/90 before he was involved in the shock swap deal. Machin became one of chairman Peter Swales' many managerial casualties and his replacement at Maine Road, Howard Kendall, saw no place for either Morley or Bishop in his new set-up. West Ham should be pleased that he didn't, because both of the former City crowd favourites have been a big success for the East London club. Morley and Bishop both made their Hammers' debut at Leicester City (30.12.89), although were ineligible for the Littlewoods Cup run that was ended agonisingly at the semi-final stage by Oldham Athletic. Morley's goals played a large

part in the promotion campaigns of 1990/91 and 1992/93 and it is a measure of his resillience that he won his place back despite the subsequent arrival of fellow strikers Iain Dowie, Mike Small and Clive Allen. It seemed at one stage that Morley would be leaving to join Watford in a £100,000 deal, but he stayed at Upton Park, reclaimed a regular first team place and went on to make a mockery of that proposed fee by leading the scorechart on West Ham's return to the top flight in 1993/94. Indeed, it was a big blow when he had to undergo a cartilage operation soon after the start of the 1994/95 Premiership season. Strong and ever-willing to work hard for the team cause, Morley is a striker whose goals are scored from all angles and varying distances. His ability to 'hold the ball up', often under extreme pressure from close-marking defenders, led Billy Bonds and Harry Redknapp to play Morley in a lone striker's role on numerous occasions. Married to a Norwegian girl, Morley has previously spent the English close season playing in Norway for Brann.

Tommy Moroney

MORONEY, Tommy — 1947-53

Born: Cork, Republic of Ireland. 10.11.23
Lge apps: 148 (8 gls)
Cup apps: 3

■ Another member of the considerable Irish contingent assembled at Upton Park in the immediate post-WW2 period, Tommy was signed by manager Charlie Paynter from Cork United whilst still an amateur. Although an established wing-half, he also played in the forward-line occasionally before injury problems began to erode his first team outings. Moved back to Ireland with Evergreen United, later becoming manager of the other major club of his native city - Cork Hibs.
❏ *Republic of Ireland caps: 1948 v Spain; 1949 v Portugal, Sweden, Spain, Finland (2), England; 1950 v Belgium, Norway; 1951 v Norway; 1952 v West Germany; 1953 v France. (12).*

MORRIS, Robert — 1919-20

Lge apps: 3

■ After making his debut in Hammers' first-ever League match v Lincoln City at Upton Park on August 30, 1919, he made two more appearances that season - in a 7-0 thrashing at Barnsley and a 1-0 defeat against Bury at Gigg Lane (where George Kay was given his marching orders). Had originally joined West Ham from Preston North End.

MORRISON, J — 1911-12

SL apps: 15 (1 gl)

■ This left-winger played his first match for West Ham in a 0-0 draw at Plymouth (16.9.1911) but may have played for the old Thames Ironworks, as a player of the same name and position played in the first London League match v Vampires (19.9.1896). His only goal in the claret and blue came against Northampton (2.12.1911) in a 3-2 defeat at the County Ground.

MOYES, James — 1919

Lge apps: 2 (1 gl)

■ Earned himself an eternal place in Hammers' history when he scored the club's first-ever League goal on his debut against Lincoln City in the opening game of the 1919/20 season at Upton Park. Signed from Dundee, he made only one other League appearance, also at the Boleyn, against Rotherham County in a match West Ham won 2-1 (and had Jack Tresadern sent off).

MURRAY, F. — 1919

Lge apps: 2

■ Shared in the delight of Hammers' first-ever League victory, against Lincoln City at Sincil Bank on Sept. 6, 1919. Turned out again in the inside-left position two days later in a match which saw Barnsley triumph 2-0 at Upton Park.

MUSGRAVE, Joe — 1931-36

Born: Durham
Lge apps: 29
Cup apps: 4 (1 gl)

■ Formerly with non-leaguers Spennymoor United, Joe made his Hammers' debut in a 1-1 home draw with mighty Arsenal on Mar. 26, 1932. Two days later he was again in the side at left-half in a disastrous 1-6 defeat at Sheffield Wednesday. Although mainly a Reserve, Joe nevertheless managed a fair total of appearances during his six seasons at the Boleyn - despite having no League games in 1934-35 and 1936-37. On Jan. 27, 1937 he joined Swindon Town. 'A hard worker with a good sense of position.'

Joe Musgrave

MORTON, John — 1931-39

Born: Sheffield, Yorkshire. 1914
Lge apps: 258 (54 gls)
Cup apps: 17 (3 gls)

■ The first of Hammers' many successful signings from Midland League Gainsborough Trinity for £600, he became a pro at the age of 17 after learning the ropes with Woodburn Council School and Woodhouse Alliance before joining Trinity. Jackie went on to win international recognition when he partnered club-mate Len Goulden on England's left-wing against Czechoslovakia at White Hart Lane in 1937. Scorer of one of his country's goals in a thrilling 5-4 victory (Stanley Matthews contributed a hat-trick from the opposite flank), Johnny would have surely won more caps but for an untimely injury which resulted in Arsenal's Cliff Bastin taking his place. Although only a handful of his total appearances were in the First Division - during the ill-fated 1931/32 season the speedy Yorkshireman became an automatic choice throughout the thirties up to the outbreak of WW2 during which he served in the Royal Air Force. In 1935 John had the honour of being chosen for the Anglo-Scots XI in that year's Jubilee match, but overall could count himself unlucky not to have won more recognition. "Frail-looking winger. Fast, possessed a multitude of tricks and a good shot." Once worked in a Sheffield Steel mill. Died in March 1986 at the age of 72, having worked in a bookmaker's business.
☆ *England cap: 1937 v Czechoslovakia.*

Played	League App Gls	FAC App Gls	LC App Gls	Europe App Gls	Total App Gls
1931-32	5 1	0 0	0 0	0 0	5 1
1932-33	36 11	6 2	0 0	0 0	42 13
1933-34	42 6	2 0	0 0	0 0	44 6
1934-35	40 7	2 0	0 0	0 0	42 7
1935-36	26 5	0 0	0 0	0 0	26 5
1936-37	39 14	2 0	0 0	0 0	41 14
1937-38	39 3	1 0	0 0	0 0	40 3
1938-39	31 7	4 1	0 0	0 0	35 8
TOTAL	**258 54**	**17 3**	**0 0**	**0 0**	**275 57**

MUSGROVE, Malcolm — 1954-62

Born: Newcastle-upon-Tyne. 8.7.33
Lge apps: 282 (85 gls)
Cup apps: 16 (4 gls)

■ Direct, goal-scoring winger who didn't win the acclaim he fully deserved in 10 seasons at the Boleyn. Second only to the legendary Jimmy Ruffell (164) as the highest scoring Hammers' winger of all time with 85 goals, he was signed by manager Ted Fenton from Lynemouth Colliery following his demob from the R.A.F. in 1953. A member of the Second Division Championship team of 1958, he enjoyed four seasons in the top grade before joining Leyton Orient for a fee of £11,000 in 1962. Later became coach at Brisbane Road under fellow ex-Hammer Dave Sexton, after a spell as Chairman of the Professional Footballers' Association. Afterwards assisted Frank O'Farrell at Leicester City and Manchester United. Mal chose a much less glamorous United for his first job as boss, at Torquay. He took the Plainmoor post after nearly joining up again with Bob Stokoe at Sunderland and so missed the opportunity of the Wearsiders'1973 FA Cup Final win over Leeds. Malcolm held the helm at Torquay from 1973 to 1976 when, between jobs, he met up with his old West Ham boss Ron Greenwood. Ron asked him if he'd like to go over to the States for a week to help select a team franchise in the North American Soccer League for Connecticut Bi-Contennials. When he got there his old West Ham colleague Phil Woosnam persuaded him to join Connecticut on a pre-season tour to Portugal where they met Benfica and Sporting Lisbon. He helped manager Bobby Thomson, the former Wolves full-back, with training and the whole trip turned into a marvellous adventure. On his return he was offered a coaching post with Chicago Stings who had a really cosmopolitan playing staff including Americans, Scots, a Yugoslav, Germans, two Haitians and a young Dutchman named Dick Advocaat, whose tremendous training and tactical techniques led Holland to the 1994 World Cup Finals in the States. The one-week invite turned into a two-year stay in the USA. When he returned to the UK he had one of his rare spells out of the game selling insurance but one day, while selling policies at Exeter City, was asked by the Grecians' manager, ex-Villa star Brian Godfrey, to come back into the game as physiotherapist at St. James Park. He spent three happy years there before being made redundant. Then he was off on his travels again, accepting a physiotherapist post in oil-rich Qatar in the Gulf. He accompanied the national side to the Asian games and the Under 16's to the junior World Cup in China. Returning from the Gulf in 1984, he was lucky enough to land a job under Dave Smith at Plymouth Argyle as reserve team manager, coach and physio. Then his West Ham buddie Ken Brown took over the reins and Mal had five wonderful years at Home Park. Being a founder member of the West Ham Academy he was delighted when another of the 'old school', John Bond, rang and asked him to join him at Shrewsbury Town. Mal is still physio at Gay Meadow.

Played	League		FAC		LC		Europe		Total	
	App	Gls	App	Gls	App	Gls	App	Gls	App	Gls
1953-54	4	0	0	0	0	0	0	0	4	0
1954-55	21	8	1	0	0	0	0	0	22	8
1955-56	8	0	1	0	0	0	0	0	9	0
1956-57	39	8	2	1	0	0	0	0	41	9
1957-58	39	9	3	0	0	0	0	0	42	9
1958-59	40	7	1	0	0	0	0	0	41	7
1959-60	41	15	2	1	0	0	0	0	43	16
1960-61	40	17	2	0	2	1	0	0	44	18
1961-62	36	13	1	0	1	1	0	0	38	14
1962-63	15	7	0	0	2	1	0	0	17	80
TOTAL	283	84	13	2	5	3	0	0	301	89

Malcolm Musgrove

Frank Neary

NEIGHBOUR, Jimmy   1979-83

Born: Chingford, Essex. 15.11.50
Lge apps: 79 (5 gls)
Cup: 23 (1 gl)

■ Another winger not always given the credit he deserved. An experienced professional, he had seen service with Spurs and Norwich City before joining Hammers from the Norfolk club in 1979. Scorer of the goal that clinched a League Cup Final appearance for the club in 1981, he made his League debut v Sunderland in Sept. 1979. Jim had spent several years as Youth Development Officer with Hammers, but resigned in May 1994 and joined Doncaster Rovers as first team coach in Oct. of the same year.

NEILL, George   1897-1899

Born: 1875
SL apps (TIW): 2
SL Apps (WHU) (1900): 1

■ A wing-half or full-back, George probably played more than the two appearances credited to him above, but records were very sketchy at the time of his arrival from West Norwood in 1897. It is known that he first appeared in a TIW XI in Oct. 1897 v Leyton in the London League and played regularly until the club turned pro in 1898.

NELSON, Andy
1956-58

Born: Custom House, London. 5.7.35
Lge apps: 15 (1 gl)

■ Following in the footsteps of his brother Bill, who later played for Queens Park Rangers, Andy joined the Upton Park staff in Dec. 1953 as a junior. Although on the retained list for the 1958/59 season, an approach from Ipswich Town manager Alf Ramsey led to his transfer to the Suffolk side, where he gained Second and First Division championship medals in 1961 and 1962, and skippered the Suffolk club. Now lives in Alicante, Spain.

NELSON, Bill   1954-55

Born: Silvertown, London. 20.9.29
Lge apps: 2

■ Although he made only two Second Division appearances for Hammers, one of them was as a member of the team which recorded a rare victory v Liverpool in their Anfield fortress in Sept. 1954. Transferred to London rivals Queens Park Rangers in 1955, he later moved to Southern League Guildford.

NEVILLE, Billy   1957

Born: Cork, Republic of Ireland. 15.5.35
Lge apps: 3

■ Centre-forward who played for Wembley Town before graduating through the reserve ranks to first team contention in 1957/58, when he played three Second Division matches in the promotion year. Making his initial senior appearance v Sheffield United in Sept. 1957, Bill was forced to give up the game on doctor's advice following continued illness.

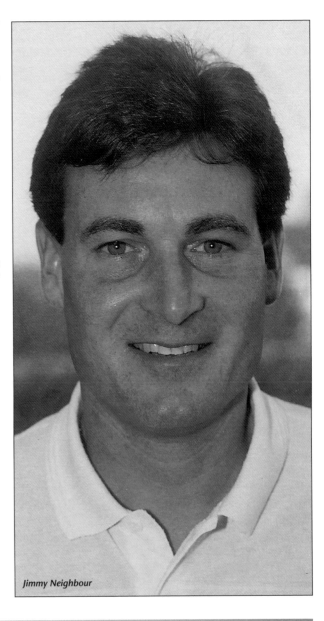

Jimmy Neighbour

NEARY, Frank   1946-47

Born: Aldershot, Hampshire. 6.3.1921
Lge apps: 17 (15 gls)

■ Signed from Queens Park Rangers to replace Joe Payne, Frank scored 15 times in only 14 Second Division appearances in 1946/47. Possessor of a fearsome shot, he went on a tour of the London clubs after playing only three times for Hammers the following season, moving to Leyton Orient, QPR, again, and finally Millwall. He began his career with Finchley and was nicknamed 'The Brown Bomber.'

Mick Newman

amateur, Cyril was also an accomplished billiards player, representing West Ham United in the Evening News Cup Competition. He made his First Division debut in the 2-0 victory over FA Cup winners Cardiff City at Upton Park (12.11.27). Joined Coventry City when he left Upton Park.

NORRIS, Fred 1928-33

Born: Birmingham
Lge apps: 65 (6 gls)

■ A man of many parts, Fred occupied all the outfield positions for Hammers, with the exception of inside and outside-left, with equal success. Initially making his mark as an inside-right with Adelaide in the Birmingham Victorian League, his next move was to sign professional forms for Halesowen. He transferred to Midland giants Aston Villa in 1925 and after three seasons at Villa Park changed his club (but not his colours) when he joined Irons. Despite his versatility, West Ham considered right-half to be Fred's best position, although his appearances there were restricted by the presence of the great Jimmy Collins. Not to be denied, Fred scored a celebrated hat-trick while playing in the forward-line v Oldham Athletic at Upton Park in Oct. 1932, and later continued his career with Crystal Palace.

NEWMAN, H. Mick 1957-58

Born: Canada. 2.4.32
Lge apps: 7 (2 gls)

■ The last amateur player to appear in Hammers' first XI. Made his Second Division debut v Doncaster Rovers at Upton Park in Mar. 1957, going on to total four appearances that campaign. Scored two goals during his three outings in the promotion season, he had previously been well known in local amateur soccer with Dagenham, Romford, Leytonstone and Rainham. Joined Dartford from Hammers. Now runs a business in Dagenham, Essex.

NORRINGTON, Cyril 1927-29

Born: Kensal Rise, London. 3.6.1896
Lge apps: 27

■ West Ham beat Leicester City to the signature of this stylish left-half or left-back, who settled down in the latter position for Hammers to prove a useful acquisition. Previously with Leytonstone and Barking Town as an

Andy Nelson

OAKES, William 1903-04

SL apps: 14

■ A left-back with the Leyton club, Bill made his first appearance for Irons in a 2-0 win over Northampton Town at the Memorial Grounds (27.2.04). It was the start of a 14-match run in the SL side which ended on the final day of the campaign v. Swindon. He transferred to Second Division Leicester Fossee (now City) for 1904/05. Died: 8.9.27.

OBENEY, Harry 1959-61

Born: Bethnal Green, London. 9.3.38
Lge apps: 25 (12 gls)
Cup apps: 2

■ Originally a half-back, this whole-hearted player was converted to centre-forward when Hammers were looking for a replacement for Vic Keeble. He met with a measure of success in his new role, having waited some three years for senior recognitition since signing full pro in May 1956 after playing for Briggs Sports. Harry was allowed to join Millwall after receiving a benefit from the club in 1961, making 75 League appearances for the Lions before a brief spell with Colchester. He later had a season at Southern League Dover, before settling down with Romford, for whom he made over 400 first-team appearances. Later joined Essex side Aveley.

ORHAN, Yilmaz 1976-77

Born: Nicosia, Cyprus. 13.3.55
Lge apps: 8
Cup apps: 1

■ Discovered by ex Hammer Terry Matthews at Aveley, who recommended him to his former club. Made his First Division debut v Queens Park Rangers in Jan. 1976, but failed to get on the scoring-list in nine senior outings. Left Hammers for Hawaii of the North Amercian Soccer League in Apr. 1977.

ORR, Neil 1982-87

Born: Greenock, Scotland. 13.5.59
Lge apps: 146 (4 gls)
Cup apps: 29 (1 gl)

■ Son of the late Scottish international and Greenock Morton player, Tommy Orr, Neil followed his father to Cappielow Park from where Hammers signed him in Jan. 1982 for £400,000 and made his debut at Manchester United (9.1.82). Recommended to the club by fellow team-mate Ray Stewart, Neil was capped seven times for Scotland Under-23's. One of the unsung heroes of Hammers' most successful league side, making 36 first team appearances in the 1985/86 campaign. A hard-running midfielder or defender, the versatile Neil went back north of the border to join Hibernian in 1987.

OTULAKOWSKI, Anton 1976-78

Born: Dewsbury, West Yorkshire. 29.1.56
Lge apps: 17

■ Signed from Barnsley on the strength of his performance against Hammers in a League Cup-tie in Sept. 1976, the promising midfielder of Polish extraction didn't quite live up to expectations and was subsequently transferred to Southend United in Apr. 1979. Then moved to Millwall where he made a considerable impression which led to his transfer to Crystal Palace in May 1986.

O'FARRELL, Frank 1950-56

Born: Cork, Republic of Ireland. 9.10.27
Lge apps: 197 (6 gls)
Cup apps: 13 (1 gl)

■ Replaced Tommy Moroney in the Cork United side when the latter joined Hammers in 1947, and later followed him to Upton Park. Became a regular in the senior side after playing over 50 reserve matches and won full international recognition for his country. One of the founder members of the famous West Ham managerial Academy, in company with Malcolm Allison, Dave Sexton, John Bond, Noel Cantwell, Ken Brown and Malcolm Musgrove, it was Hammers' longest-serving manager, Charlie Paynter, who gave Frank his first team debut in

Neil Orr (right of picture) celebrates a goal at Sheffield Wednesday with Ray Stewart and Alvin Martin

a Second Division match at Notts County in Dec. 1950. Transferred to Preston North End in a straight exchange deal for Eddie Lewis in 1956, he continued to make 118 First Division appearances at Deepdale. Went into football management when he hung up his boots, serving Torquay United, Leicester City (whom he took to the 1969 FA Cup Final and Second Division championship), Manchester United and Cardiff City after starting off with Southern League Weymouth. Vacated the Cardiff post to go to Iran. Seven Republic of Ireland caps between 1952 and 1956, then won two more with Preston.Frank has now retired from the game after assisting Everton and Bolton Wanderers in a scouting capacity in 1993.

❑ *Republic of Ireland caps:* 1952 v Austria, France; 1955 v Holland, Norway, Yugoslavia; 1956 v Holland. (7).

Frank O'Farrell

PADDON, Graham   1973-76

Born: Manchester. 24.8.50
Lge apps: 115 (11 gls)
Cup apps: 35 (4 gls)

■ Signed from Norwich City as part of an ex-change deal that resulted in Ted MacDougall going in the opposite direction, this fine midfielder was a great success at Upton Park. Originally bought from Coventry City for £25,000 by the Carnaries, in Oct. 1969, he was valued at £170,000 in the transaction which took him to Hammers. Blond, bearded Paddon formed a formidable midfield link with Billy Bonds and Trevor Brooking in the mid-70's. He won an FA Cup winners' medal in 1975 and European Cup Winners' Cup runners-up the following year, before returning to Carrow Road for £110,000 in Nov. 1976. Had a spell with Tampa Bay Rowdies before returning to UK for a brief spell at Millwall. A member of the Norwich promotion side of 1972 and also a League Cup finalist 1973. Later a licensee, running the South Walsham Country Club and squash courts. Returned to football as a member of the Portsmouth coaching staff in Aug. 1985.

Graham Paddon

Derek Parker

PALMER, James   1919-20

Lge apps: 13 (1 gl)

■ This left-wing flier made his debut in the claret and blue in a fine 4-1 win at Lincoln (6.9.19) and went on to make a dozen Second Division appearances that season. Jim scored his only goal as a Hammer v Grimsby Town (18.10.19) to win the match. He had only one more League outing the next season before transferring to Workington.

PARKER, Derek   1946-57

Born: Colchester, Essex. 23.6.26
Lge apps: 199 (9 gls)
Cup apps: 8

■ This popular player just failed to qualify for the exclusive "200 Club" with Hammers - his

appearances adding up to 199 in the League. Joining Hammers from Grays Athletic in Oct. 1944, he was originally an inside-forward but later converted to half-back. Also made over 250 Combination appearances for the reserves. He was chosen to tour Australia with an FA XI in 1951. Derek returned to his home town in Mar. 1957 to play for Colchester United when Ben Fenton (then manager at Layer Road) persuaded his brother Ted to release him to assist in the Essex club's eventually unsuccessful promotion drive from the old Third Division South. Derek went on to make 130 League appearances at Layer Road.

Played	League		FAC		LC		Europe		Total	
	App	Gls	App	Gls	App	Gls	App	Gls	App	Gls
1946-47	10	1	0	0	0	0	0	0	10	1
1947-48	2	0	0	0	0	0	0	0	2	0
1949-50	32	2	2	0	0	0	0	0	34	2
1950-51	38	1	2	0	0	0	0	0	40	1
1951-52	30	3	3	0	0	0	0	0	33	3
1952-53	39	0	1	0	0	0	0	0	40	0
1953-54	28	1	0	0	0	0	0	0	28	1
1954-55	7	0	0	0	0	0	0	0	7	0
1955-56	8	0	0	0	0	0	0	0	8	0
1956-57	5	1	0	0	0	0	0	0	5	1
TOTAL	199	9	8	0	0	0	0	0	207	9

PARKER, Reginald William   1935

Born: Reading, Berkshire. 1913
Lge apps: 2

■ This tall Berkshire-born left-back tasted both the sweet and sour of victory and defeat in his two Second Division appearances for West Ham in Sept. 1935. A member of Hammers' side which defeated Bradford Park Avenue 1-0 with a Len Goulden goal at Upton Park on the ninth of that month, he was also on duty when West Ham crashed 4-1 to Blackpool at Bloomfield Road five days later. Formerly with Bournemouth and Boscombe Athletic.

PARKES, Phil   1978-1990

Born: Sedgley, West Midlands. 8.8.50.
Lge apps: 344
Cup apps: 92

■ Undoubtedly the finest goalkeeper in Hammers' history, this genuine giant of the game was the backbone of the club's success under John Lyall in the early 80's. and it was a measure of his stature and durability that he was still earning a first team place in Division One at the age of 39. A former carpenter by trade, "Parkesy" progressed from non-league Brierley Hill to make his League debut for another local club, Walsall, v Mansfield Town (1.4.69), but after just 52 league matches he became a bargain £15,000 signing by Queens Park Rangers in 1970. In nine seasons at Loftus Road, Parkes established himself as one of the top 'keepers in the country. He helped the 'Super Hoops' climb from the Second to the First Division and to within a point of the Division One championship in 1975/76, only to be pipped at the post by Liverpool. At least that gave him UEFA Cup experience the following

season. Ever-dependable Parkes was dominant in the air and lightning reflexes on the six-yard line where he formed a human brick wall to defy the best attackers in the business. He kept the clean sheets while the flair players like Stan Bowles, Dave Thomas and skipper Gerry Francis did their stuff in an entertaining side. Phil was always on the verge of the England team, but unable to break the Peter Shilton/Ray Clemence monopoly under Alf Ramsey. His solitary senior international cap came under Don Revie, who named Parkes among six new caps for the visit to Lisbon to face Portugal on April 3, 1974 (Martin Peters and Trevor Brooking were also in the side that day). With the No.,1 position being dominated by two great 'keepers, he was never bitter about his lack of opportunity and still savours the one cap they can't take away - a quiet, goalless debut, too! QPR had declined and were regularly involved in relegation struggles when, with a testimonial looming, he jumped at the chance to join West Ham in Feb. 1979 for £565,000 - a then world record for a goalkeeper. Bobby Ferguson and Mervyn Day had shared the green jersey that season, but Lyall wanted to reconstruct his team from the back and Phil's signing proved a masterstroke. The fair-haired giant with the familiar moustache put his faith in Lyall and West Ham by dropping down a division and made his Hammers debut in a 3-0 home win v Oldham Athletic (24.2.79). After finishing fifth at the end of that Second Division season, the quest for honours was really on. In May 1980, although missing out on promotion, Hammers defeated London rivals Arsenal 1-0 in the FA Cup Final, and Phil was back at Wembley the next March to face Liverpool in the League Cup Final. Reds eventually won the replay at Villa Park, but Hammers made amends by continuing their surge towards the Second Division title. Lyall's new boys, Alvin Martin, Ray Stewart, Paul Allen, Paul Goddard and Parkesy, had gelled well with the established stars like Bonds, Brooking and Alan Devonshire. Everyone played their part, none more so than Phil who set a club record by keeping 22 clean sheets in the victorious 1980/81 campaign. Regular supporters at the time believed that the team had never played better, in terms of results and entertainment value. They underlined their appreciation of his goalkeeping skills by voting him Hammer of the Year (1980/81). But Parkes was at the heart of another splendid West Ham side in 1985/86, when they challenged strongly for the championship before having to settle for a best-ever third, behind Liverpool and Everton. It was a season to remember for Phil, in particular, because, at the age of 36, he was again a first team regular after injury had forced him to miss all but the last two months of the previous campaign. It was not the last time he would come back to prove himself as he entered the final phase of his illustrious career. People sometimes joked about Phil's infamous 'dodgy knees' but a career spanning more than 800 league and cup games speaks for itself. Even after Hammers brought Allen McKnight down from Scotland as Phil's supposed replacement, after a serious elbow infection and the form of his long-time understudy Tom McAllister restricted him to just one senior game in

1987/88, Parkes rescued the club from their 'McKnightmare'. His recall in Feb. 1989, aged 39, helped Hammers win an FA Cup fifth round tie v Charlton Athletic . . . but came a week too late to spare them a bad League Cup semi-final home defeat by Luton Town when McKnight conceded three. Too late also to avoid relegation and manager John Lyall - axed in July 1989 - could only wonder what might have been had he recalled the 'Old Man' sooner. The fact is that only five of the 13 end-of-season matches Parkes played in were lost, whereas only four of the previous 21 league games were won with the hapless McKnight in the No.1 shirt. Although Parkes kept his place for the first half of Lou Macari's seven-month reign, he eventually made way for 'mystery' Czech signing Ludek Miklosko, who came in for his debut in Feb. 1990. Phil won't recall his last game (14.2.90) for the Hammers with any satisfaction - an abysmal 6-0 defeat on Oldham's plastic pitch that shattered League Cup hopes at the semi-final stage for the second time in a year. Coincidentally, it was also Phil's good friend, Alan Devonshire's, last-ever appearance for the club, while Macari bowed out, too, before Ludo made his debut at Swindon a week later! But Phil Parkes can look back on a long career with immense satisfaction. One of the dressing room characters, he had an endearing personality that made him popular with players and fans alike. By a statistical quirk, he made exactly 344 league appearances for both QPR and Hammers before retiring as a player to be reunited with Lyall as part-time goalkeeping coach at Ipswich Town.

Played	League		FAC		LC		Europe		Total	
	App	Gls	App	Gls	App	Gls	App	Gls	App	Gls
1978-79	18	0	0	0	0	0	0	0	18	0
1979-80	40	0	8	0	8	0	0	0	56	0
1980-81	42	0	3	0	9	0	6	0	60	0
1981-82	39	0	2	0	4	0	0	0	45	0
1982-83	41	0	2	0	7	0	0	0	50	0
1983-84	42	0	4	0	5	0	0	0	51	0
1984-85	10	0	0	0	0	0	0	0	10	0
1985-86	42	0	7	0	3	0	0	0	52	0
1986-87	33	0	5	0	6	0	0	0	44	0
1987-88	1	0	0	0	0	0	0	0	1	0
1988-89	13	0	3	0	1	0	0	0	17	0
1989-90	22	0	1	0	9	0	0	0	32	0
TOTAL	344	0	34	0	52	0	6	0	436	0

PARKINSON, Harry   1902-03

SL apps: 2

■ Harry made his first appearance for Irons in a 1-1 SL draw at Kettering Town (15.4.03) in the left-half position and his second and last showing in the 1-2 reverse at Millwall in the final match of the season playing at right-half.

160

PARKS, Tony

1991-92

Born: Hackney, East London. 28.1.63
Lge apps: 6
Cup apps: 3

■ Smallish goalkeeper who was a big favourite with the fans on the handful of occasions that he came in as cover for regular first choice Ludek Miklosko. A chirpy cockney, Parks never fulfilled his early promise at Tottenham where, between 1981 and 1987, he played only 37 league games. There was one outstanding highlight, though, when, aged only 21, his dramatic penalty shootout save earned Spurs victory over Anderlecht in the 1984 UEFA Cup Final at White Hart Lane. Tony admitted later that he let that early success go to his head a little, although after spells on loan to Oxford United, Gillingham, Brentford (where he played 71 games) and Fulham, he appreciated being offered a fresh start at Upton Park. He never let Hammers down or lacked confidence in his nine appearances, screaming instructions to fellow defenders and generally fighting as hard as anyone in what was a traumatic relegation-haunted season, on and off the field. Disappointed to be offered only a

Tony Parks

new one-year contract by the club, Parks dropped out of the picture, although he did return to Chadwell Heath later to join in training sessions before moving from Essex to Scottish Premier League club Falkirk, where his team mates have included other ex-Hammers Tommy McQueen and Frank McAvennie.

.

PARRIS, George

1985-1993

Born: Ilford, Essex
Lge apps: 239 (12 gls)
Cup apps: 51 (5 gls)

■ A schoolboy star with Redbridge, Essex, London and England, George joined Hammers as an apprentice professional in July 1981, and signed full pro the following year. Made his First Division debut in the last game of the 1984/85 season v Liverpool at Upton Park (20.5.85), and was unlucky not to score. A regular member of the Football Combination side for two seasons, George made a considerable impact soon after the start of the 1985/86 campaign, and gained a regular first team spot at the expense of Steve Walford. Although not the most naturally gifted players, George certainly worked hard to prove himself. The arrival of Julian Dicks in 1988 cost George the number three shirt, but this strong-running, powerful utility player went on to make his mark in a bustling midfield role. Solid in the tackle, he bounced back from breaking his leg in a home game v Luton Town (2.1.88) and went on to re-establiush himself as a regular as well as a crowd favourite. His best season for the club was probably the 1990/91 promotion-winning term, when he contributed eight goals - more than in all his previous seasons at Upton Park - and finished the campaign as runner-up to Ludo Miklosko in the Hammer of the Year poll. But Hammers' season-long struggle in the top flight the following season was an unhappy time for George personally. Knee ligament damage and then a mystery heart scare restricted his involvement. Even so, he still made 290 League and Cup appearances, scoring 17 goals in his West Ham career. Although he qualified for a testimonial after 10 years at Upton Park, this honest pro accepted a surprise £100,000 move to First Division strugglers Birmingham City in Mar. 1993 in the hope of regaining regular first team football. So while Hammers were clinching promotion back to the top flight, wholehearted "Smokey" was experiencing the blues on his way into Division Two with Barry Fry's beleaguered City side.

Played	League		FAC		LC		Europe		Total	
	App	Gls	App	Gls	App	Gls	App	Gls	App	Gls
1984-85	1	0	0	0	0	0	0	0	1	0
1985-86	26	1	7	0	2	0	0	0	35	1
1986-87	36	2	5	1	6	0	0	0	47	3
1987-88	30	1	0	0	2	0	0	0	32	1
1988-89	27	1	1	0	3	0	0	0	31	0
1989-90	38	2	1	0	10	0	0	0	49	2
1990-91	44	5	7	3	3	0	0	0	54	8
1991-92	21	0	0	0	4	1	0	0	25	1
1992-93	16	0	0	0	0	0	0	0	16	0
TOTAL	239	12	21	4	30	1	0	0	290	17

George Parris

Eric Parson

PARSONS, Eric 1946-50

Born: Worthing, Sussex. 9.11.23
Lge apps: 146 (34 gls)
Cup apps: 6 (1 gl)

■ Signed as a junior for Hammers after being spotted playing for Worthing Boys v West Ham Boys at Upton Park. Given the affectionate nickname of "Rabbit" by the Upton Park patrons, for the way he used to hare down the touchlines, this flying outside-right was sold to London rivals Chelsea in Nov. 1950 for £23,000 - a huge fee for those days. An ever-present member of the Pensioners' 1955 First Division championship-winning side and recipient of two England 'B' caps, he later moved to Brentford where he pushed his total League appearances to over the 400 mark, despite sustaining a broken leg while at Griffin Park. He set up a successful signwriting business when he retired from playing.

PAYNE, Joe 1946

Born: Brinington Common, near Chesterfield. 17.1.14
Lge apps: 10 (6 gls)
Cup apps: 1

■ A name indelibly imprinted in the record books for his 10 goals for Luton Town in his first appearance at centre-forward v Bristol Rovers in the old Third Division South in Apr. 1936. His 55 goals were largely instrumental in Luton winning the Third Division South title and at the end of that season he won

his solitary cap for England, scoring twice in the 8-0 win over Finland. A former Derbyshire coalminer previously with Bolsover Colliery and Biggleswade Town, he joined Chelsea in Mar. 1938 and managed 36 League games for the Stamford Bridge club (21 gls) before war interrupted his career. Signed for Hammers in Dec. 1946, but had his brief spell at the Boleyn beset with injury problems.

He later ended his League days at Millwall but retired through injury without making a first team outing at the Den although he made a comeback with SL Worcester City in 1952. Also a good cricketer (he played for Bedfordshire in 1937) and snooker player. Football League (South) Cup finalist at Wembley with Chelsea (1944, winner 1945).

PAYNE, John 1926

Born: Southall, Middlesex. 3.1.06
Lge apps: 4 (1 gl)

■ Effective on either flank, this speedy winger progressed through junior amateur soccer with Botwell Mission and Lyons Athletic to senior amateur level with Southall. He remained on the Athenian League club's books while he sampled First Division football with Hammers, scoring v Manchester United at Upton Park in Sept. 1928 and making two further appearances that season v. Portsmouth and Derby County respectively. He had earlier made one appearance for West Ham in 1926/27 and had been honoured by representing Middlesex

County. Johnny transferred to Brentford in 1928 and afterwards had the 1930/31 season with Manchester City. He joined Brighton and Hove Albion in Aug. 1934; Millwall July 1935 and Yeovil in May 1936.

PEARSON, Stuart 1979-82

Born: Hull, Yorkshire. 21.6.49
Lge apps: 34 (6 gls)
Cup apps: 16 (4 gls)

■ A goal-scoring striker of proven ability whose time at the club was dogged by injuries. Had already won 15 full international caps for England when he arrived at Upton Park from Manchester United for a big fee in Aug. 1979. First impressed Hammers when he played against them in an FA Cup-tie for Hull City at Boothferry Park in Jan. 1973; but the player spent the intervening years at Old Trafford, appearing in two Wembley Cup Finals for United - a feat he emulated with Hammers. Stuart had a brief spell in South Africa before opening a shop at Whitefield, near Manchester, which sells European tile imports. He was dismissed as assistant manager of Bradford City along with manager Frank Stapleton in Apr. 1994.

PETCHEY, George 1952-53

Born: London. 24.6.31
Lge apps: 2

■ Given only two Second Division outings during his time at Upton Park in the inside-right position, he went on to make over 250 appearances for Queens Park Rangers as a wing-half, who he joined in July 1953. Transferred to Crystal Palace in May 1960, he made a further 153 senior showings for the Glaziers and was an ever-present as Palace won promotion to Division Three in 1961. Also helped them into Second Division in 1964, before injury ended his career in 1965. He then won further fame as manager of Orient and Millwall, after cutting his teeth in management as Bert Head's assistant. In 1986 he was helping to run Brighton's junior teams and is now Youth Development Officer at the Goldstone Ground.

Stuart Pearson

PETERS, Martin
1962-70

Born: Plaistow, London. 8.11.43
Lge apps: 302 (81 gls)
Cup apps: 62 (19 gls)

■ The least famous, but arguably the most complete footballer, of the legendary West Ham/England triumvirate of Moore, Hurst and Peters, which did so much to win the World Cup for their country in 1966 and the European Cup Winners Cup for their club a year earlier. A pupil of Fanshawe School, Dagenham, Peters' career charts a classic course rising from his school side to Dagenham Schools, London, Essex and England Schools and then England Youth after signing apprentice with West Ham in May 1959. Tagged "10 years ahead of his time" by England manager Sir Alf Ramsey in 1966, his career eventually exceeded that milestone and beyond with Hammers, Tottenham Hotspur, Norwich City and Sheffield United. Martin made the first of over 300

League appearances with the club on Good Friday, 1962 against Cardiff City at Upton Park and went on to play in every position - including goalkeeper! In fact, in only his third senior game - in the return at Ninian Park on Easter Monday - Peters found himself deputising for injured 'keeper Brian Rhodes, who had himself come into the side as cover for Lawrie Leslie, hurt v Arsenal two days earlier! He played five times for England Under-23's and 67 times for the full England team after making his senior international debut v Yugoslavia at Wembley (4.5.66) in a 2-0 victory. Martin twice went close to marking his debut with a goal, but he had only to wait for the next game - v Finland in Helsinki (26.6.66) - to open his scoring account for his country in a 3-0 win. The first 33 caps were achieved as a Hammer, the rest with Spurs in addition to representing the Football League on five occasions. Left out of the West Ham side which fought its way to Wembley for the 1964 Cup Final v Preston North End in favour of 'hard man' Eddie

Bovington, he made up for the disappointment the following year by winning a European Cup Winners' Cup medal there after a faultless display against the German side TSV Munich 1860, returning again to the twin towers in 1966 to help his country lift the World Cup. Although he missed the opening game of the tournament v Uruguay, Peters came in for the group victories over Mexico and France but it was the quarter-final success over the ruthless Argentinians that really signalled his arrival on the world stage. It was from a Peters cross that Hurst headed the winner - a goal that had 'made in West Ham' written all over it. The understanding between Hurst and Peters was uncanny and proved so productive for club and country over a long period. Of course, the 1966 final v West Germany belonged to the Hammers' trio. Moore captained the side, Hurst netted a hat-trick and Peters scored the crucial second goal in an epic 4-2 victory. Peters flourished in Ramsey's new 'wingless wonders' system from which the modern-day 'midfielder'

Martin Peters and Chelsea's Ron Harris, March 1968

evolved. Three months before the Wembley highlight Peters had received a League Cup runners-up medal with his club v West Bromwich Albion - his goal in the second leg at The Hawthorns failing to prevent Hammers from losing 5-3 on aggregate. This was the last honour he was to gain as a West Ham player before his record £200,000 transfer to Spurs in March 1970. Spurs paid £150,000 plus Jimmy Greaves, but there was no doubt that Tottenham had the best of the deal. For Spurs, Peters - tall and lean - twice gained League Cup winners' medals v. Aston Villa in 1971 and Norwich City in 1973, both at Wembley. He also won a UEFA Cup winners' medal with Spurs in 1971 v Wolves and a runners up medal in the same competition when Spurs lost to Feyenoord in 1974. Made 287 League and cup appearances at White Hart Lane between 1970 and March 1975 and just over that total with his next club, Norwich City (£50,000), before being appointed player-manager of Sheffield United to end his playing career at Bramall Lane in 1981 (although he did turn out as an amateur for Gorleston for a while). He now works for a Motor Insurance company (originally with Geoff Hurst, who has since left) after a spell with a fruit machine company in East Anglia. He is now also involved in promotional work for Spurs as well as occasional TV appearances as match-analyst. One of the all-time greats at Upton Park, Peters was the complete midfielder - perceptive, an excellent passer with both feet, strong in the air and a sharp eye for goal. He was so difficult for opponents to mark, often arriving in the box late on the blind-side, hence the title of his autobiography 'Goals From Nowhere'. Just look at his scoring record for the Hammers - superb by any midfield player's standards and comparable to many strikers' goals ratio! His only hat-trick came v West Bromwich Albion (31.8.68) - current manager Harry Redknapp got the other in the 4-0 rout.

❏ **England caps:** 1966 v Yugoslavia, Finland, Poland, Mexico, France, Argentina, Portugal, West Germany, Northern Ireland, Czechoslovakia, Wales; 1967 v Scotland, Wales, Northern Ireland, USSR; 1968 v Scotland, Spain (twice), Sweden, Yugoslavia, USSR, Romania, Bulgaria; 1969 v France, Northern Ireland, Scotland, Mexico, Uruguay, Brazil, Holland, Portugal (sub); 1970 v Holland, Belgium. (33).

Played	League		FAC		LC		Europe		Total	
	App	Gls	App	Gls	App	Gls	App	Gls	App	Gls
1961-62	5	0	0	0	0	0	0	0	5	0
1962-63	36	8	1	0	2	1	0	0	39	9
1963-64	32	3	0	0	4	0	0	0	36	3
1964-65	35	5	2	0	1	0	9	1	47	6
1965-66	40	11	4	0	10	3	6	3	60	17
1966-67	41	14	2	0	6	2	0	0	49	16
1967-68	40	14	3	2	3	2	0	0	46	18
1968-69	42	19	3	3	3	2	0	0	48	24
1969-70	31	7	1	0	2	0	0	0	34	7
TOTAL	302	81	16	5	31	10	15	4	364	100

PHILLIPS, Wilf   1931-32

Born: Brierley Hill, West Midlands. 9.8.1895
Lge apps: 21 (3 gls)
Cup apps: 2

■ A famous name from Millwall's Third Division South championship side of 1928, which notched up a record 65 points and 127 goals in winning the title. "Peanuts" Phillips - as he was lovingly tagged by the Dockers' fans - was one of the renowned inside-forward trio which contributed 83 goals towards that total: Wilf hit 26, former Huddersfield, Chelsea and England centre-forward Jack Cock added 25; and another Hammer-to-be, Jackie Landells, weighed in with 32. Switching his allegiance from the Lions to Irons, Wilf scored on his debut in a 4-2 victory v Blackburn Rovers at Ewood Park (28.11.31). Sydney Puddefoot and all! It proved to be one of the few bright spots of a dismal season which saw Hammers relegated to the Second Division at its end, and Wilf departed from the Upton Park scene to join near-neighbours Clapton Orient. Before Millwall, Wilf scored goals regularly for Stoke City, Ebbw Vale, Darlaston, Bilston Unity, Bristol Rovers, cs 1923. Signed for Lions for a £500 fee in Nov. 1925. Joining Thames in June 1930 from where he transferred to Irons for another £500 price tag in May 1931. After Clapton Orient he joined his last club Stourbridge in Aug. 1933. A great practical joker, he was nicknamed 'Winkie' by the fans.

PHIPPS, R.   1919

Lge apps: 1

■ His only League appearance came against Stoke City at the Victoria Ground on 27.9.19 when Hammers went down 2-1.

PIERCY, Frank   1904-1912

SL apps: 214 (7 gls)
Cup apps: 17

■ Signed from Middlesbrough during Hammers' initial season at the Boleyn in 1904, Frank was intimately involved in the affairs of West Ham United up to his untimely retirement through illness in 1931. First took an active interest in the game as a 16-year-old with Southbank, a junior team competing in the Teessiders Minor League. He joined 'Boro in 1898, but retained his amateur status while continuing his trade as a blacksmith until the Teesider left the Northern League to turn pro at the turn of the century and joined Div. 2 of the FL. Frank captained the Reds for the four seasons leading up to his move south, during which time he won several Cleveland Cup medals. Nicknamed the 'Old War Horse' at the Boleyn Ground because of his robust style of defending, he often fell foul of referees and was suspended for one month following an incident in a match v Swindon (1.9.07). The ban had little effect, however, as he got his marching orders again in a bruising encounter with

F. PIERCY,
WEST HAM UNITED.

arch-rivals Millwall (22.2.08). But the enforced absences didn't prevent him from amassing the third highest SL appearance record for the club, behind Herbert Ashton (224) and Fred Blackburn (217). A big crowd favourite, he was made skipper when Dave Gardner left for Croydon Common in 1907. A mainstay of the West Ham defence in the centre-half position during eight Southern League seasons until he packed up playing in 1912, after being awarded his first benefit by the club in Jan. 1910 when he kept the proceeds of the New Brompton match, he was then appointed assistant trainer under Charlie Paynter. The end of WW1 saw him in charge of one of West Ham's most successful reserve XI's in the London Combination during a period when he was often invited to be a "sponge-man" for senior amateur representative sides, including the Isthmian League XI. An all-round sportsman, Frank was prominent in local club cricket, won an Essex County Bowls Badge and held a golf handicap of two at his peak having received expert tuition from golf pro teammate, George Kitchen, to whom he handed over the captain's armband when injuries began to take their toll. One of the club's finest servants, he was awarded a posthumous testimonial match following his death before the start of the 1931/32 season, when an Isthmian League XI provided the opposition to West Ham's First Division side on 1.10.31 at Upton Park.

Played	League		FAC		LC		Europe		Total	
	App	Gls	App	Gls	App	Gls	App	Gls	App	Gls
1904-05	33	2	1	0	0	0	0	0	34	2
1905-06	24	0	2	0	0	0	0	0	26	0
1906-07	37	0	2	0	0	0	0	0	39	0
1907-08	23	0	2	0	0	0	0	0	25	0
1908-09	26	2	0	0	0	0	0	0	26	2
1909-10	29	0	5	0	0	0	0	0	34	0
1910-11	32	2	4	0	0	0	0	0	36	2
1911-12	10	1	1	0	0	0	0	0	11	1
TOTAL	214	7	17	0	0	0	0	0	231	7

PIKE, Geoff   1975-1987

Born: Clapton, London. 28.9.56
Lge apps: 291 (32 gls)
Cup apps: 76 (9 gls)

■ The whole-hearted endeavour and perpetual motion of this key midfield man did much to cushion the blow of losing Patsy Holland through injury. A similar type of player to Pat and his predecessor Ronnie Boyce, Geoff made a major contribution to the club's

Geoff Pike

promotion back into the top flight in 1981. Making his League debut as far back as March 1976 v Birmingham City, he played much of his early soccer in the Thurrock district and later with Gidea Park Rangers, well-known providers of football talent. A member of Hammers' youth side which reached the FA Youth Cup Final in 1975, v. Ipswich Town. Diminutive. Geoff had to wait a further five years for his first senior honour - an FA Cup winners' medal in 1980. He followed it up with a League Cup runners-up medal and Second Division champ- ionship memento the next year, when he was ever-present and runner-up in the Hammer of the Year poll. Transferring to Notts County for £35,000 in July 1987, he scored twice on his debut and went on to appear in 82 League games for the Magpies and score 17 goals in- cluding the only hat-trick of his career v Southend United. In Sept. 1989 Geoff returned to East London to make 44 FL appearances for Orient before taking charge of the Youth team at Brisbane Road.

Played	League		FAC		LC		Europe		Total	
	App	Gls	App	Gls	App	Gls	App	Gls	App	Gls
1975-76	3	0	0	0	0	0	0	0	3	0
1976-77	20	6	1	1	0	0	0	0	21	7
1977-78	28	2	1	0	1	0	0	0	30	2
1978-79	14	1	0	0	1	0	0	0	15	1
1979-80	31	5	8	1	6	1	0	0	45	7
1980-81	42	6	3	0	9	1	6	1	60	8
1981-82	34	2	2	0	5	0	0	0	41	2
1982-83	40	6	1	0	7	0	0	0	48	6
1983-84	28	2	2	1	5	1	0	0	35	4
1984-85	30	2	4	1	4	0	0	0	38	3
1985-86	10	0	5	1	0	0	0	0	15	1
1986-87	11	0	4	0	1	0	0	0	16	0
TOTAL	291	32	31	5	39	3	6	1	367	41

PINDER   1900-02

SL apps: 1
Cup apps: 1

■ This left-back made just one league appearance, in a 2-0 SL win over Queens Park Rangers (23.2.01) at Rangers' Latimer Road enclosure at Notting Hill.

POLLARD, Walter   1929-33

Born: Burnley. 26.9.06
Lge apps: 37 (4 gls)
Cup apps: 6 (2 gls)

■ Signed as a full professional by First Division Burnley at the age of 17 in Sept. 1924, after impressing in the Burnley Sunday School League. Wally formed a memorable right-wing partnership with Clarets' famous England international Bob Kelly while at Turf Moor. Switching his allegiance (but not his colours) when he joined Hammers in the summer of 1929, he made his Upton Park debut later the following season against his former club. A member of the West Ham team which reached the FA Cup semi-finals in 1933, he left the club to take up the appointment of player-coach of Soucaux in France during the 1933/34 season, but did not find the Gallic temperament of some of the players to his liking. Returning to

Walter Pollard

England, he played out the remainder of his career with Fulham, Southampton (where he played 23 FL apps and scored three goals) and Brighton; the latter of whom he was serving when WW2 called an abrupt halt to League football. Finding employment in the Electricity department of Ilford Borough Council, he also coached their works side until he was struck down with a heart attack at the tragically early age of 38, in 1945.

POTTS, Steve   1985-

Born: Hartford, Connecticut, USA. 7.5.67
Lge apps: 235 (1 gl)
Cup apps: 55

■ Steady Steve may have been born in the United States, but he is an East Ender through and through having returned with his family to Dagenham, Essex, at a very young age. Any hope of "Pottsy" earning a place in the host country squad for the 1994 World Cup finals vanished when he appeared for England at Schoolboy and Youth levels. Starred for Barking, Essex and London under-16's before joining Hammers straight from school in 1973. Steve captained the youth team to the South-East Counties Division One title in 1984/85. Made his first team debut in the First Division at Upton Park v Queens Park Rangers on New Year's Day, 1985, as a replacement for Geoff Pike. It was his only senior outing of the season and he got only one sub. outing in 1985/86, coming on for Steve Walford in a 1-0 win at Ipswich Town. But Steve continued to impress in the reserves and skippered the side to the Combination League championship at the end of the most successful season, league-wise, in the club's history. His introduction to the first team was gradual, chances only usually presenting themselves when injury ruled out regular

Steve Potts

right-back Ray Stewart. More often than not, Pottsy found himself filling a midfield slot as the team fought a series of relegation battles in the late 80's. But he adapted well to playing in different positions - just as well, too, because after establishing himself as first choice right-back under Lou Macari in Division Two, Steve's place was under threat again when the next manager, Billy Bonds, made right-back Tim Breacker his first signing in Oct. 1990. They shared the position for a while before Steve again slotted into midfield and then his career took an unexpectedly welcome new turn. Long-term injuries to long-serving centre-backs Alvin Martin and Tony Gale caused Bonzo concern, but he found the answer in the versatile Potts. Gaining in confidence, this shy, unassuming man built a new reputation for himself as an accomplished central defender. He relied on Martin or Gale to win high balls, but made up for his lack of inches by reading dangerous situations in advance of the opposition's players. He brought much-needed pace to the back four and quickly earned the respect of team-mates and fans for his new-found qualities in the centre of defence. Steve's safety-first approach brought more solidarity to West Ham's defence - he prefers to leave the fancy stuff to others - if not goals at the opposite end. In more than 300 senior games for the club, Steve has managed just one goal - a long-range 'bobbler' that crept under the Hull City 'keeper in a 7-1 Upton Park romp (6.10.90) en route to promotion from Division Two. But it would be impossible to count how many times the mild-mannered Potts has stopped goals going in at the other end with his clinically-timed tackles. In the traumatic 1991/92 season, Potts was one of Hammers' few success stories. He ended that term voted runner-up (to Julian Dicks) in the Hammer of the Year poll. A year later he not only became the fans' No.1 choice but also took over the captaincy at Dicks' expense and led the team back into the top flight. Despite reported interest from Birmingham City midway through the 1993/94 Premiership season, Steve has remained faithful and consistent at the heart of Hammers' defence and can look forward to a well-deserved testimonial year.

Played	League App	Gls	FAC App	Gls	LC App	Gls	Europe App	Gls	Total App	Gls
1984-85	1	0	0	0	0	0	0	0	1	0
1985-86	1	0	0	0	0	0	0	0	1	0
1986-87	8	0	0	0	0	0	0	0	8	0
1987-88	8	0	3	0	1	0	0	0	12	0
1988-89	28	0	7	0	6	0	0	0	41	0
1989-90	32	0	1	0	7	0	0	0	40	0
1990-91	37	1	7	0	2	0	0	0	46	1
1991-92	34	0	5	0	3	0	0	0	42	0
1992-93	46	0	2	0	2	0	0	0	50	0
1993-94	40	0	6	0	3	0	0	0	49	0
TOTAL	235	1	31	0	24	0	0	0	290	1

PRESLAND, Eddie 1965

Born: Loughton, Essex. 27.3.43
Lge apps: 6 (1 gl)

■ Tall, adventurous full-back who scored a goal on his League debut v Liverpool at Upton Park in Feb. 1965. He signed professional forms in Oct. 1960 after playing schoolboy soccer for East Ham, London and Essex, and as a junior for Hammers. Eddie was also a fine cricketer, being capped for England Boys and later joined Essex as a professional. Transferring to Crystal Palace in Jan. 1967, he spent three seasons as a first team regular at Selhurst Park, playing 60 League matches before moving on to Colchester United where he played 69 games to conclude his League career. Eddie was encouraged to do work in East End schools by Ron Greenwood in the mid-60's, along with fellow former Hammers John Lyall, Billy Landsdowne, Harry Cripps and Dennis Burnett, so as not to waste their afternoons after their soccer commitments were completed for the day. Now in his capacity of P.E. and games teacher at Stepney Green School, Eddie is reaping the benefits of that policy and is quick to give pupils a viewing of his most cherished possession - a copy of the BBC Match of the Day video for the Liverpool game! On leaving Layer Road Eddie joined up with former Busby Babe and ex-West Ham and Leyton Orient defender Eddie Lewis playing for Guild FC in South Africa. When he returned in the early 70's he was appointed player/manager to Wealdstone, whom he led to the Southern League championship. Similar posts followed at Dulwich Hamlet, Hendon, Gravesend and Northfleet, Dulwich again and then Dagenham. Initially coach at Victoria Road, Eddie was appointed manager in 1980 and led the Daggers to their last major trophy - a 2-1 Wembley win over Mossley in the FA Trophy Final. With West Ham winning the FA Cup the week before, the East End had rarely seen such celebration especially when John Lyall arranged for the two cups to be shown off in a dual display of solidarity. Daggers promptly rewarded him with the sack! After that kick in the teeth, Eddie

Eddie Presland

understandably became disillusioned with the game for a while but is now back in the mainstream scouting and doing opposition assessment for John Lyall, Paul Goddard and Mick McGiven at Ipswich Town.

PROCTER, Norman 1923-24

Born: Alnwick, Northumberland
Lge apps: 7 (1 gl)

■ Equally effective in either of the inside-foward positions, this midfield schemer made a name for himself when he represented Durham County as a schoolboy before being signed up by Rotherham County. Joining Hammers for their initial First Division campaign of 1923/24, he made his debut in a 1-1 draw v Middlesbrough at Upton Park on Sept. 22, and had a further six appearances that season to close his senior account. He joined Leicester City on leaving West Ham.

PROUDLOCK, George 1946-47

Born: Stubswood, Northumberland. 19.9.19
Lge apps: 18 (5 gls)

■ One of a multitude of professionals who had their League careers disrupted by WW2, in which he served in the Essex Regt. and then the R.A. in North Africa. George returned to Upton Park after hostilities had ceased and normal football activities resumed in 1946/47. Signed from Northumberland amateur side Amble in 1937, the clever inside-forward made a small but valuable contribution to West Ham's immediate post-war fortunes before transferring to Workington.

PUDAN ("Dickie"), A.E. 1900-03

Born: Canning Town, London.
SL apps: 7

■ Dickie, as he was affectionately known by patrons at the Memorial Grounds, formed a notable, although short-lived, full-back partnership with Scotsman Charlie Craig during Irons' initial Southern League season in 1900/01. Formerly with amateurs Clapton for the first half of season 1899/1900, he first appeared in Hammers colours at Bristol City (12.1.1901). Made only two appearances that season and five in 1901/2 before transferring to the other Bristol club, Rovers, where he won a SL Championship medal in 1905. Now in demand, he moved on to Newcastle United and appeared in the 1908 FA Cup Final which the Magpies lost to Wolves. Left the Geordies in May 1909 for Leicester Fosse (now City), then playing in the Second Division of the FL. He retired in 1910 to join Huddersfield Town as secretary/manager but returned to Leicester where he eventually became a director and a successful Midlands businessman. In his schooldays Pudan captained the Canning Town XI.

PUDDEFOOT, Sydney 1913-22/1932-33

Born: Bow, London. 17.10.1894
SL apps: 55 (28 gls)
Cup apps: 6 (7 gls)
Lge apps: 125 (67 gls)
Cup apps: 8 (5 gls)

■ A goalscoring legend whose sensational £5,000 transfer to Falkirk in 1922 became the most chronicled event involving an individual in the long history of West Ham United. A pupil of Park School, West Ham, which also produced England international Harold Halse and later Hammers legend 'Big' Jim Barrett, Syd had come to prominence with Condor Athletic and Limehouse Town in local junior football before being discovered playing for London Juniors v. Surrey Juniors by manager Syd King. Young Syd was brought on by Charlie Paynter and George Hilsdon and came up quickly through the ranks to become a force in the Southern League side. How well he settled into the team can be ascertained from an extract of a newspaper report featuring Hammers' 4-1 win over Exeter City at Upton Park on 2.1.15: "In every department the winners showed superiority, and from the beginning to end they dominated the game. For a time the visitors maintained an excellent defence, their backs kicking and tackling finely, while Pym saved several shots in splendid style. Some 14 minutes elapsed before Puddefoot, who completely outshone every other forward on the field, opened the scoring for his side and 10 minutes later he was again successful in finding the net." Syd scored a hat-trick in that match and shortly afterwards established an FA Cup goalscoring record for the club when he scored five times in an 8-1 victory over Chesterfield. Following the disbandment of the Southern League for the duration of WW1 at the end of the 1914/15 season "Puddy," as he was affectionately known by the fans, made 126 appearances in the replacement war-time competition, the London Combination. As he was not recruited into military service until late in the conflict, Syd was able to pursue his football activites to the full and really excelled in war-time soccer as his near-100 goal haul and a sensational seven v. Crystal Palace in Nov. 1918 (a London Combination record), bore ample testimony. When the Great War ended in 1918 he had his first taste of League football the following year when West Ham were elected to the enlarged Second Division. His 21 goals in 1919/20 led to his selection for two Victory Internationals for England v. Scotland and Wales. A further 29 tallies in 1920/21 and 19 more up to Feb. 1922, prompted Falkirk (who Syd had guested for during the war) to make their impertinent transfer bid, which was duly accepted and included Syd's younger brother, Len, going north as part of the deal in Feb. 1925. After three years in Scotland, during which he scored 45 goals in over 100 games for the Bairns, Syd moved to Blackburn Rovers for another big fee, and in addition to winning three more England caps in 1926 (v. Scotland at Old Trafford and Northern Ireland, twice), was a member of the Rovers' side which won the FA Cup with victory

Syd Puddefoot

over Huddersfield Town at Wembley in 1928. Puddy was given his last representative honour when he was selected by the Football League v. the Irish League at Anfield in Oct. 1925. Ten years after leaving Upton Park 37-year-old Syd returned like a prodigal son to help in Hammers' vain fight to stay in Division One at the end of the 1931/32 season. Leaving West Ham for good after making a further 15 Second Division appearances the next season. In 1933 Syd took the ambitious step of becoming coach to Turkish club Fenerbahce of Istanbul and began a volatile association with continental soccer. The following year he joined another Turkish club, Galataseray, but it proved to be a bad move when he was badly manhandled while trying to calm down fighting players and spectators during a big game. 17 players were suspended and Puddy returned to England to take up a safer appointment as manager of Northampton Town in Mar. 1935 in Div. 3 (South). He wasn't frightened off by the experience, however, and returned to Turkey in Mar. 1937 and stayed to the outbreak of WW2. On his return he was employed by the Blackpool Borough Police and later The Civil Service at the Ministry of Pensions but retired in 1963 to live at Southend. He was soon snapped up by Southend United who used his vast experience in a scouting capacity. Syd Puddefoot died in Rochford Hospital on 2.10.72 after putting up a three-week fight against pneumonia, just before his 78th birthday. He had also been an accomplished cricketer, playing for Essex on eight occasions.
❏ ***England caps:*** *1920 v Wales, Scotland.*

PYKE, Malcolm 1957-58

Born: Eltham, London. 6.3.38
Lge apps: 17

■ A steady, constructive defender who provided vital cover for the wing-half berths during the 1957/58 promotion season. Progressed through the junior ranks to make his initial Second Division appearance v Bristol City at Upton Park in Apr. 1957. Won a Second Division championship medal the following year, but didn't have any First Division outings when Hammers returned to the top flight in 1958/59. He subsequently transferred to Crystal Palace in the exchange deal which brought Ron Brett to the Boleyn. Played only two League games at Selhurst Park. Now licensee of the Papermakers Arms at Dartford, Kent.

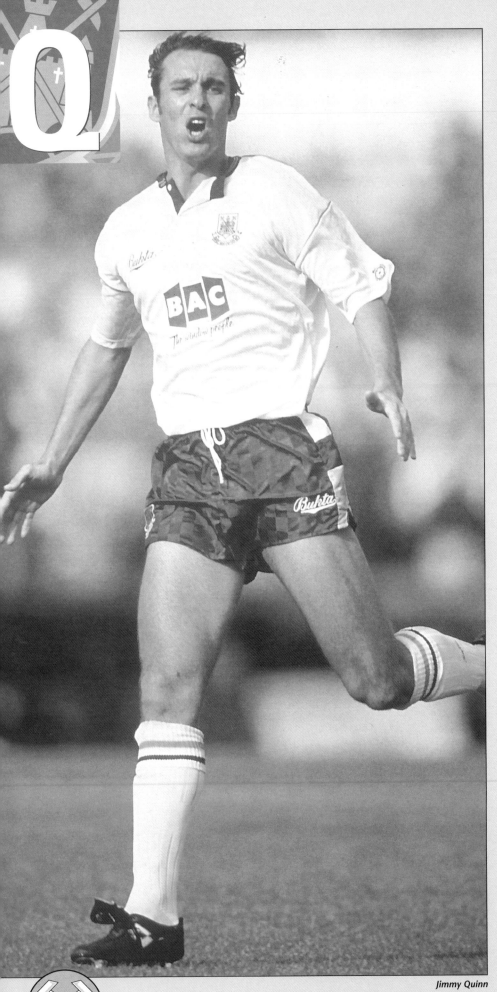

Jimmy Quinn

QUINN, Jimmy — 1989-91

Born: Belfast, Northern Ireland. 18.11.59
Lge apps: 47 (19 gls)
Cup apps: 9 (3 gls)

■ Tall, prolific striker who proved excellent value for the £320,000 fee manager Lou Macari paid Bradford City for him in Dec. 1989. The much-travelled, 'old fashioned'-style centre-forward was a relatively late starter in the game. He was playing for non-league Oswestry Town when Swindon Town spotted him and signed him for £10,000. But he was already 22 years-old by the time he made his debut for Robins in the Third Division v Walsall (9.3.82). The Ulsterman scored 10 goals in 49 league games before a £32,000 move to Blackburn Rovers in Aug. 1984. It was during his spell at Ewood Park that Jimmy made his Northern Ireland debut v Israel in Belfast (Oct. 1984). He netted 17 goals in 71 League games for Rovers before Macari, then manager of Swindon, brought him back to the County Ground at a cost of £50,000 in Dec. 1986. This time, Quinn found the target more regularly, notching 30 in 64 games. But after only 18 months in his second spell with Swindon, Jimmy was on his way again in 1988 - to Leicester City in a £210,000 deal. It was the unhappiest period in Quinn's career, though, as he struggled to score six times in 31 Second Division appearances. He didn't hang around for long at Filbert Street and in Dec. 1988 he joined Bradford, where he contributed 13 goals in 35 league appearances. Next stop Upton Park, where he made his debut in a 4-2 Second Division win v Barnsley on New Year's Day, 1990. Although Jimmy was cup-tied and could therefore take no part in Hammers' League Cup bid (which ended at the semi-final stage), he proved himself in front of goal by hitting 13 in just 20 outings, including two as sub. v. Brighton. But under Billy Bonds the following season, Quinn found himself replaced by the fit-again Frank McAvennie and confined to the subs' bench. And his hopes of a first team run were further hit by the signing of Iain Dowie. Jimmy started only 16 league games, but still weighed in with six goals in the 1990/91 promotion-winning campaign. His last appearance was in the number 12 shirt v Charlton Athletic at Selhurst Park (4.5.91). His next port of call was Bournemouth, where Cherries' manager Harry Redknapp showed his ability to spot a bargain by signing "Quinny" for just £40,000. It was money well spent as the Northern Ireland international scored 19 goals in 43 games in his only season at Dean Court. Yet this footballing nomad was on the move again in July 1992 when ambitious Reading signed him for £55,000. This, too, was a great investment because Quinn - who has now won more than 40 full caps - went on to amass 55 league goals in 88 matches over two seasons. His 35 in 1993/94 (plus five cup goals) saw Royals romp to the Division Two championship.
❏ ***Northern Ireland caps:*** *1990 v Norway; 1991 v Yugoslavia (sub). (2).*

RADFORD, John   1976-78

Born: Pontefract, Yorkshire. 22.2.47
Lge apps: 28 (0 gls)
Cup apps: 2 (0 gls)

■ A famous name from Arsenal's 1970/71 double season, his two years in the claret and blue were dogged by almost unbelievable bad luck. In 30 senior outings he did everything but score. At times it seemed gremlins were at work to prevent him from doing so. As if by magic, his move to Blackburn Rovers in Feb. 1978 saw him regain his scoring touch - including a goal on his debut! His 30 games for Hammers without a goal must remain something of a record for a recognised striker. Became a successful manager with Bishop's Stortford whom he led to some exciting FA Cup exploits. Two England caps with Arsenal. FA Youth Cup finalist 1965. Football League Cup finalist 1968 & 1969. Fairs Cup winners' medal 1970. Double winner 1971. FA Cup finalist 1972.

RAISBECK, Lou   1900

Lge apps: 2 (0 gls)
Cup apps: 0

■ Something of a utility player, performed in any of the half-back positions and also as a forward when the occasion demanded. A product of Scottish junior soccer with Slamanan, he graduated to the professional ranks with Airdrieonians and from the Diamonds moved south to another team with a sharp cutting edge, Sheffield United, in Blades' FA Cup-winning year of 1899. A period spent back in his native Scotland on loan to Third Lanark was followed by a further move to Middlesbrough. It was from Teesside that he moved to the Memorial Grounds in 1900, but his appearance in the number five shirt in the opening two matches of the season v. Gravesend and Millwall were to be his last with Hammers.

RANDALL, Tommy   1906-15

Born: Barking, Essex, 1886
Lge apps: 189 (9 gls)
Cup apps: 16 (1 gl)

■ Tom began his Upton Park career as an amateur inside-forward and, although he scored on his debut in a 4-1 win over the already crowned SL champions Fulham, the fans took an immediate dislike to his thoughtful, slow approach to the game (calling him"Old Mother Randall") and almost drove him out of football with their barracking. Then, at Charlie Paynter's benefit against Woolwich Arsenal (15.11.06), Hammers' trainer persuaded a disillusioned Randall to turn out at half-back as a personal favour. He was such a success in his new role that he was signed as a full pro for the princely sum of 30 shillings a week! Becoming a fixture in the Southern League at left-half, Tom was honoured with the captaincy of the Southern League Representative XI, playing against the English, Scottish and Irish leagues in 1912, and

the English and Irish again the following year. He was also selected for the Football Association XI. The transformation was so complete he was appointed captain and became one of the most popular players at the club. He spent his formative years in local junior soccer with Ethelburgers and Barking St. Andrews, later graduating to Barking in the South Essex League, with whom he was selected for a county match between Essex and Suffolk in which his performance for Essex earned him a trial at Upton Park. Succeeded in the first team by Jack Tresadern, Tommy passed away in 1946.

RATCLIFFE, George   1900-02

Born: Hanley, Staffs. 1877
Lge apps: 41 (14 gls)
Cup apps: 2 (0 gls)

■ Sharing his birthplace with Hanley's most famous footballing son Sir Stanley Matthews,

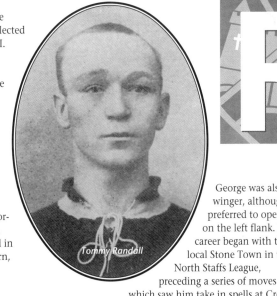

Tommy Randall

George was also a winger, although he preferred to operate on the left flank. His career began with the local Stone Town in the North Staffs League, preceding a series of moves which saw him take in spells at Crewe Alexandra, South Shore and Sheffield United before joining Grimsby Town in May 1898. His time with the Mariners was spent during the club's move from Abbey Park in 1898 to Blundell Park the following year. But he proved to be equally at home on either enclosure as he scored 18 times in 57 Football League appearances following his debut for the Humberside club (3.8.1898). In 1900 George was involved in another exciting new development, transferring to West Ham United in their first year under that title. At the Memorial Grounds George was moved into the middle of Hammers' attack, eventually filling all the inside berths in turn. His goalscoring output remained steady, but not spectacular, and in 1902 he was transferred to Doncaster Rovers where he made 26 appearances in 1902/03.

Tommy Randall, nicknamed 'Old Mother' by the Upton Park fans

Harry Redknapp takes on Sunderland's Martin Harvey

REDKNAPP, Harry   1965-72

Born: Poplar, London, 2.3.47
Lge apps: 149 (7 gls)
Cup apps: 26 (1 gl)

■ West Ham United through and through, this cockney character joined the groundstaff straight from school, went on to become a first team favourite and is now back at Upton Park as manager. As a player flame-haired Harry combined old-fashioned wing play with his own particular brand of artistry to win over the fans. Although not always a first team regular under Ron Greenwood, "Arry-boy" was a popular choice with the Upton Park faithful, particularly fans in the old Chcken Run terrace. A former England Youth international, he was a member of Hammers' sides which lifted the FA and London Youth Cups in 1963. Signing professional forms in Mar. 1964, he made his senior debut in August the following year in a home 1-1 draw v. Sunderland (23.8.65), replacing Peter Brabrook. But it was not until 1967/68 that Harry wore the number seven shirt regularly. The next season was his most successful, appearing in 36 league games and creating plenty of goals for the likes of Geoff Hurst and Martin Peters with his right-wing crosses. The nearest Harry came to winning a major honour was as a member of the Hammers' team that featured in the League Cup semi-final marathon with Stoke City in 1972, failing by a whisker to reach Wembley. It was in fact Harry who was fouled by Gordon Banks for the penalty that England's 'keeper eventually saved from Hurst in the second leg at Upton Park. Transferred to AFC Bournemouth in August the same year, he had a short spell with Brentford before retiring from League football in 1976. Assisted Bobby Moore, another former team mate at Upton Park, at Oxford City after trying his luck in America with Seattle Sounders. Then became manager/coach of Bournemouth, where he made a brief comeback as a player in 1982/83 season for a League Cup tie against Manchester United at Old Trafford. Harry made quite a name for himself at the south coast club. In 1986/87 he led Cherries to the Third Division championship with a record 97 points, taking the club into Division Two for the first time in its history. He earned a reputation as a managerial wheeler-dealer with a keen eye for a bargain. He can boast a number of shrewd signings who have gone on to become stars in the Premier League, including Shaun Teale (Aston Villa) and Ian Bishop (Manchester City & West Ham) and of course his own, son, talented midfielder Jamie, who is a big favourite at Liverpool and leading light for England Under-21's. Harry had been linked with a number of bigger clubs but after nine years with Bournemouth - during which time he opened his own Italian restaurant in the town and owned a couple of racehorses - he was delighted to return to West Ham in July 1992, as assistant to Billy Bonds. Big mates for many years - Harry was Best Man at Bill's wedding in 1967, when they both operated on Hammers' right flank - it seemed the ideal partnership. And it paid immediate dividends for Hammers, who bounced back into the top

Harry Redknapp the manager takes training

flight at the first attempt as runners-up to Newcastle United in Division One 1992/93. The following season they steered the club to a respectable 13th position in the Premiership, before the summer upheaval which saw Bonzo quit the club after 27 years, just 10 days before the start of the 1994/95 campaign. Harry was understandably most unhappy at the time about the circumstances surrounding his appointment as manager, but he agreed to step up into the hot seat and then appointed his brother-in-law, another big former favourite, Frank Lampard, as his new assistant. Harry's 'street-wise' reputation and undoubted coaching ability should stand him in good stead as he battles to re-establish West Ham in the senior division. With relatively little money to spend in comparison to the so-called elite clubs, his ability to strike a hard bargain in the transfer market is just what West Ham need. Having said that, it was Harry who paid a club record £1.5 million to bring Don Hutchison from Liverpool in Aug. 1994, to prove that he will spend big money on the right player. He also brought Tony Cottee and Julian Dicks back to the club in shrewd deals from Merseyside giants, Everton and Liverpool.

REDWOOD, George   1910-12

Born: London, 1887
SL apps: 10
Cup apps: 3

■ This versatile defender was signed from Fulham along with team mate Fred Harrison and made his West Ham debut at right-half in a 4-1 defeat at Swindon Town (25.3.11) - his sole appearance that season. He fared better during 1911/12, however, making 12 more first team appearances, including a return to Swindon's

County Ground in an FA Cup third round replay following a 1-1 draw at Upton Park. But it was another fruitless venture for George - he and his fellow defenders conceded four goals for no reply to go out of the competition after defeating Gainsborough Trinity and Middlesbrough in previous rounds. He also played at right-back and centre-half. George joined Hammers from London rivals Fulham, but we have no record of where he went after leaving the club. However, it is known that he learnt his football at the Page Green Board School, served in the 4th Battalion Royal Fusiliers Regiment and also played for Enfield Town.

REID, James   1900-01

Born: Scotland, 1879.
SL apps:: 13 (5 gls)
Cup apps: 6

■ Jimmy soon discovered his feet could make hs fortune. Petershill (Glasgow) was his first club, followed by Hibernian. He then came south to Burslem Port Vale, now without the Burslem prefix, and from where Hammers also signed Billy Grassam. Very forthright and outgoing, he impressed the secretary of the newly-formed West Ham United assigned to negotiate his transfer by walking up to him on Sheffield Station and shaking hands as though he had known him all his life! Scored in six consecutive games for Watford in 1905/06, and altogether 16 times in 35 games, signing off with a couple v. Millwall. Career took in Hibs, Gainsborough, West Ham, Worskop Town, Notts County, Watford, Spurs (where he played for two seasons and scored 35 goals in 59 League and Cup games), New Brompton and Reading.

REID, Jimmy   1897-99

SL app (TIW): 15 (9 gls)
Cup apps: 3 (1 gl)

■ Another Reid from Reading, inside-forward Jimmy was the most prolific scorer of the trio; scoring ten times in his 18 confirmed League and Cup appearances, but he probably scored more as a member of the TIW side which won the London League by one point from Brentford and competed for the London Senior Cup in 1897/98, losing to Ilford 1-3.

REID, George   1899

SL app (TIW): 6 (1 gl)

■ Following the demise of the Warmley club of Bristol in Feb. 1899, Francis Payne, the Ironworks secretary, signed three of the stricken organisation's leading players: Peter McManus, Henderson and George (Geordie) Reid. Formerly with Reading, George was no relation to Jimmy Reid, who had also played for the Berkshire club at the same time as his namesake and by a strange twist of fate, was also on Ironworks' books and played in the same Irons team on several occasions. George was most at home at inside-left, but he did play one of his six games for Irons at centre-forward. He scored only one goal, v. Southall (25.3.1899). George played for Middlesbrough early 1900's and was in Scotland in 1906/07 with Johnstone (Renfrewshire) but returned south to Bradford Park Avenue in 1907/08.

REYNOLDS   1898/99

SL app (TIW): 12 (5 gls)

■ A tricky winger who was ahead of his time with use of 'screw-shots' and 'benders' to confuse opposing goalkeepers. Amazingly, he was never on the losing side for Irons, being on the winning team in all but one (drawn) of his dozen SL matches in 1898/99. He was formerly with Leicester Fossee and Gravesend United.

RHODES, Brian   1958-63

Born: Marylebone, London. 23.10.37
Lge apps: 61
Cup apps: 5

■ Known as "Bruey" to his team mates, this reliable, unspectacular goalkeeper made over 60 League appearances during his nine years at the Boleyn. A former Essex Schoolboys player and reserve for England Boys, he signed full pro forms in 1954 after joining the staff in Apr. 1952. As an amateur he played for Essex Youth and made an appearance for the Rest v. London, at Stamford Bridge. Brian won an honour in his first season as a pro in 1954/55, gaining a winners' medal in the London Mid-Week League. Making his Football League debut v. Blackburn Rovers in Sept. 1957, Brian made four further appearances in that Second Division championship-winning season, but

Brian Rhodes

RICHARDS, Dick   1922-24

Born: Chirk, Wales. 14.2.1890
Lge apps: 43 (5 gls)
Cup apps: 10 (1 gl)

■ Joined Hammers as an outside-left from Wolverhampton Wanderers during the club's Cup Final season of 1922/23, switching to the opposite flank owing to the brilliant form of Jimmy Ruffell. He had been an automatic choice for his country, Wales, while at Wolves, winning five caps in 1920/22. Dick continued in that vein with West Ham, playing for the Principality when they won the Home International Championship in 1923/24, with victories over England, Scotland and Northern Ireland. His international appearances served to further underline his versatility, as they were all played from the inside-left position. Transferring to Fulham in 1924, Dick found his brief stay at Craven Cottage beset with injury and illness, although his fortunes did improve with his move to Mold in the Welsh League, to the extent of gaining a further cap in 1926, totalling nine full caps. Dick played for a trio of non-league clubs before breaking into League football, Bronygarth, Chirk and Oswestry United. Either side of WW1 he scored 22 goals in 86 League appearances for Wolves. He concluded his career with Colwyn Bay United in 1927/28. Dick took a job with an electricty company in Cheshire and it was while lifting electric light poles that he sustained the serious back injury from which he died at the age of 42. (29.1.34).
❑ *Wales caps:* 1924 v England, Scotland, Northern Ireland (3).

RICHARDSON, Frank   1923-24

Born: Barking, Essex. 29.1.1897
Lge apps: 10 (2 gls)

■ A centre-forward who joined Hammers from Stoke City, Frank made his First Division debut in a 2-0 win over London rivals Chelsea at Upton Park (27.10.23). He totalled 10 League appearances that season before transferring to Swindon. Frank died 19.5.87.

ROBERTS, Bill   1936-37

Born: Connahs Quay, Clywd, Wales. 3.3.14
Lge apps: 1 (0 gls)
Cup apps: 0

■ Hammers signed this rugged Welsh defender from Irish club Newry Town, along with his team mate Paddy Peters, after the pair had impressed in an international friendly v. Olympique de Marseille at Upton Park in Oct. 1936. The pair signed pro forms the following week, and although Peters was not retained at the end of the season, Bill made a solitary Second Division appearance v. Burnley at the Boleyn in Nov. 1937. In the summer of 1939 he transferred to Crystal Palace. But Bill has remained a Hammers' fan all his life, and was still actively supporting the team from the North Bank terrace, at over 80 years-old, in 1993/94. West Ham supporter Terry Connelly,

had to wait two years for his First Division baptism in the 3-2 Upton Park win over Wolves (21.11.59). He returned to first team action for the final 15 matches of the season, when he took over from Noel Dwyer. The following season he missed only six out of 42 League games - his best run in the team. Mainly a reserve, he always performed capably when called up for first team duty, and went to the States when the club competed for the International Soccer League and Challenge Cup in 1963. Rejoined his former manager, Ted Fenton, at Southend United the same year, but played only 11 times in their Third Division side before emigrating to Australia, where he became involved with coaching the Australian Olympic squad. He later settled at Napier, on New Zealand's North Island. Brian tragically lost a three-year fight against leukaemia at the age of 55 in July 1993.

Bryan 'Pop' Robson

Bill Roberts (right) is introduced to Jim Barrett by Paddy Peters (centre)

whose hobby is tracking down former players, brought his presence to the notice of the club who responded by making Bill their guest of honour at a first team match.

ROBERTS, VIVIAN   1920

Lge apps: 1 (0 gls)
Cup apps: 0

■ Not much is known of this goalkeeper, other than that he made his only league appearance in a 0-1 defeat v, Stockport County at Edgeley Park (26.4.20).

ROBERTSON   1907-08

Lge apps: 1 (0 gls)
Cup apps: 0

■ Made his solitary Southern League appearance in a 0-0 stalemate against Southampton at the Dell (21.12.07) in the centre-forward berth.

ROBINSON, Bill   1949-52

Born: Whitburn. 4.4.19
Lge apps: 101 (60 gls)
Cup apps: 4 (1 gls)

■ Held Hammers' post-war scoring record with 26 goals in 40 league games in 1950/51, until John Dick surpassed him in 1957/58. A pre-war pro with Sunderland (with whom he once scored three goals in four minutes against Manchester United), Bill came to Upton Park from Charlton Athletic in Jan. 1949, after playing in a reserve match there the week before his transfer. Seven days later he scored on his debut v. West Bromwich Albion at The Hawthorns. A member of Charlton's FA Cup-winning team of 1947 v. Burnley, Bill was appointed full-time organiser of the youth section when he retired from playing at the end of 1952/53. He was largely responsible for making it one of the finest in the country before being promoted to assistant manager in Nov. 1957. Two years later Bill became manager of Hartlepool. He passed away 7.10.92.

ROBINSON, Leslie   1920-24

Born: Romford, Essex. 2.5.1898
Lge apps: 19 (2 gls)
Cup apps: 0

■ Often a top scorer in the reserves, this clever inside-right served the club well during the early League seasons, after arriving from Dagenham side Stiling Athletic, without being able to lay claim to a regular first team place. He had the honour of scoring their 100th goal in the London Combination in 1923/24. Les later joined Northampton and then Norwich City in June 1927, Thames in Sept. 1928 and finally, Torquay United in July 1929. Chosen to represent the London League vs London Combination, Les also served in the 4th Battalion Essex Regt. during WW1. Died: Barking, Essex, 1965.

ROBSON, Bryan   1971-74/1976-79

Born: Sunderland. 11.11.45
Lge apps: 227 (94 gls)
Cup apps: 27 (10 gls)

■ Better known as "Pop" to the fans, this prolific goalscorer was first signed from Newcastle United, where he had won a Fairs Cup winners medal and a Second Division championship medal, for a then club record fee of £120,000 in Feb. 1971 and scored on his Hammers' debut v. Nottingham Forest (24.2.71). Topped Hammers' scoring charts in 1972/73 with 28 First Division goals before returning to his native North-East with Sunderland in 1974. However, it was not long before the popular Wearsider was back at Upton Park, re-signing for £80,000 in Oct. 1976. Once again he led the scorers' list with 24 Second Division goals in 1978/79, winning an Adidas Golden Boot Award in the process. Although offered a new contract, his amazing career again retraced its steps when he returned to Roker Park for the second time in the summer of 1979 and won another Second Division championship medal. Moved on to Carlisle United in 1980 and was back in London again for 1982/83, still scoring for Chelsea. He then returned to his beloved North-East as player-coach for Sunderland and enjoyed a fairytale return to Upton Park by helping the Wearsiders to a shock 1-0 win. Pop was appointed manager of Carlisle United, but later relinquished the post and played part-time for Gateshead in the Northern Premier league. Afterwards went into business as a newsagent but is now back in mainstream football coaching at Manchester United.

Played	League		FAC		LC		Europe		Total	
	App	Gls	App	Gls	App	Gls	App	Gls	App	Gls
1970-71	14	3	0	0	0	0	0	0	14	3
1971-72	42	9	4	1	10	4	0	0	56	14
1972-73	42	28	2	0	2	0	0	0	46	28
1973-74	22	7	0	0	1	1	0	0	23	8
1976-77	30	14	2	0	0	0	0	0	32	14
1977-78	37	9	3	2	1	0	0	0	41	11
1978-79	40	24	1	1	1	1	0	0	42	26
TOTAL	227	94	12	4	15	6	0	0	254	104

ROBSON, George   1928-31

Born: Newcastle-upon-Tyne. 17.6.1908
Lge apps: 17 (2 gls)
Cup apps: 1 (1 gls)

■ The first of Hammers' trio of same surname signings from Newcastle United, George actually made his West Ham debut v. the Magpies at St. James's Park in the last fixture of the 1927/28 season. His first team opportunities at the Boleyn were limited by the availability of players of the calibre of Vic Watson, Viv Gibbins and Stan Earle, but he proved his worth whenever called upon. In Dec. 1928 he underlined his goalscoring ability in a record 13-2 Football Combination victory over Fulham reserves at Upton Park by scoring five times against the West Londoners, as did fellow-forward Johnny Campbell. But still he failed to secure a regular first XI place, a situation which prompted his move across London to Brentford in Feb. 1931 (where he won a Third Division championship medal). George later became a member of Hammers' scouting staff, retiring from his position in 1971. An ex-lorry driver, George began his career with St. Peters Albion before joining the Magpies.

ROBSON, Keith   1974-76

Born: Hetton-le-Hole, Northumberland. 15.11.53
Lge apps: 68 (13 gls)
Cup apps: 19 (6 gls)

■ Like his namesake George, this aggressive forward was signed by Hammers from Newcastle United. A skilful but temperamental player who had his fair share of flare-ups with opponents and referees, he figured in both of the club's successful cup runs of the mid-70's, but missed the 1975 FA Cup Final v. Fulham. He made up for that disappointment the following year, gaining a European Cup Winners Cup Runners-up medal and scoring Hammers' equaliser in the Brussels final v Anderlecht. His spectacular goal v Eintracht Frankfurt in the 3-1 semi-final, second leg victory at Upton Park clinched a memorable 4-3 aggregate win over the Germans to book West Ham's ticket to the Heysel Stadium. Transferred to Cardiff City in Aug. 1977, he played 21 games for the Bluebirds before moving on to Norwich City in Feb. 1978.

Keith Robson evades a tackle from Liverpool's Phil Neal, December 1976

ROBSON, Mark 1992-93

Born: Stratford, East London. 22.5.69
Lge apps: 47 (8 gls)
Cup apps: 4 (1 gl)

■ Exciting winger who fulfilled a life-time dream when he signed for his local club on a free transfer from Tottenham Hotspur in Aug. 1992. He proved he had fully recovered from a long-term knee injury by playing a starring role in West Ham's 1992/93 promotion-winning campaign. Scored eight league goals himself and set up many others for Clive Allen and Trevor Morley with his pinpoint crosses. Played mainly on the right flank, but blond-haired "Robbo" could also shine on the left, where he would invariably cut inside to shoot. Although slightly built, he was not afraid to run at opponents and torment them with his tricky ball skills. Made his hammers' debut in a pre-season friendly at Leyton Orient (31.7.92) and did enough to earn a one-year contract. His First Division debut came as sub. at Barnsley (16.8.92) and he missed just two other games thereafter. Signed a new contract prior to the 1993/94 season but after just one start and two sub. outings in the Premiership, he was bitterly disappointed to

find himself out of the first team reckoning. He was reportedly in tears when he heard from Billy Bonds that West Ham were prepared to let him go to Charlton Athletic to fulfil his wish for regular first team football. Robbo reluctantly moved to the refurbished Valley in Nov. 1993 for a bargain £125,000. Despite being born only a corner kick away from Upton Park, and training with Hammers as a schoolboy, Mark's pro career started at Exeter City in Dec. 1986. After 26 league games for the Devon club, a £50,000 move to Spurs brought him back to London in July 1987. But he was limited to just three starts and five sub. outings at White Hart Lane, so he gained first team experience in loan spells with Reading, Plymouth Argyle, Watford and Exeter City (again) before Tottenham manager Terry Venables released him. A true East Ender, the chirpy cockney enjoys coaching youngsters in his spare time and managed local boys' side, Senrab, to a number of honours.

ROBSON, Stewart 1987-91

Born: Billericay, Essex. 6.11.64.
Lge apps: 69 (4 gls)
Cup apps: 14 (2 gls)

■ This former England under-21 captain's promising career was blighted by injury, and Hammers rarely saw the best of him following his expensive £700,000 move from Arsenal in Jan. 1987. A wholehearted midfielder who never gave less than 100%, Stewart's talent remained unfulfilled at Highbury where he underwent surgery for a serious pelvic injury even before he arrived at Upton Park. John Lyall hoped "Robbo" would emerge as his driving force in midfield but he missed too many games through injury. Made his debut at Coventry City (24.1.87) - the club he would later join from West Ham -and after 18 league appearances in his first half-season with Hammers, Stewart played 37 games in 1987/88 and won the Hammer of the Year award. But then he featured in only 14 more league games over the remaining three seasons of his time in East London. At one stage, he was sidelined for more than a year with a pelvic injury that required three operations and long

Mark Robson (centre) salutes the travelling fans after a goal at Watford. Also in the picture is Steve Jones.

Stewart Robson shrugs off a challenge from Sheffield Wednesday's Imre Varadi

rehabilitation at a London physiotherapy clinic. Yet Stewart underlined his courage by returning in glorious style for a League Cup fifth round replay at Derby County in Jan. 1989. He continued to be dogged by injury, though, with a virus and knee problems adding to his miserable time with Hammers. His last outing was as sub. at Watford (12.1.91) before Billy Bonds gave the robust Robson the chance to make a fresh start with Coventry City. Robbo initially went to Highfield Road on loan, but did enough to earn a contract with the Sky Blues who snapped him up on a free transfer. Revitalised, Robson was appointed club captain by manager Terry Butcher and finished his first season there as Player of the Year. But the injury jinx struck again in 1992/93, when he was restricted to just 15 league matches and he played only the first match of 1993/94. Yet it was all so different for Stewart as a youngster. A pupil of Brentwood Public School, he captained England youth and made his Arsenal debut, aged 17, ironically at Upton Park (5.12.81). Although very competitive in midfield, Robbo could also adapt to the full-back or central defensive positions when needed, and even played in goal twice for the Gunners (without conceding a goal) when Pat Jennings was injured! Rated one of the best young prospects in the country by former England manager Bobby Robson but, typical of his bad luck, had to withdraw from three full international squads due to injury.

ROBSON, William — 1933

Born: Southwick, County Durham. 1906
Lge apps: 3

■ A former Sunderland Boys star, this fine full-back spent his formative years in Wearside junior soccer - most notably with Castletown St. Margaret's in the United Churches League. A miner by trade, he progressed to his coal works side, Hylton Colliery, competing in the Wearside League. His performances there drew the attention of Derby County who signed him as a pro. It was via the Baseball Ground that he arrived at Upton Park in the summer of 1933 after six seasons with the Rams. Making his Hammers' debut in the opening match of the season v. Bolton Wanderers at Upton Park, he played in the following two matches, away to Brentford and Plymouth Argyle respectively, to complete his hat-trick of first team appearances. Joined Reading cs 1934. Bill died at Oxford (11.8.1960) aged 54.

ROSENIOR, Leroy — 1988-92

Born: Balham, South London. 24.8.64
Lge apps: 53 (15 gls)
Cup apps: 12 (4 gls)

■ Powerful, black striker whose goals did much to keep Hammers in the top flight at the end of 1987/88. Leroy began his career with Fulham in

1982, making his League debut for them at Leicester City (4.12.82). Played 54 League games, scoring 15, before moving to Queens Park Rangers for £50,000 in the summer of 1985. But played only 38 senior appearances before returning to Craven Cottage in 1987 for another 30 matches in Division Three that yielded 20 goals. John Lyall had tried, unsuccessfully, to bring several leading strikers to Upton Park in the difficult winter of 1987/88 before Rosenior answered the call. The £275,000 signing, who was particularly strong in the air, arrived relatively unknown to Hammers' fans but made an immediate impact, alongside the unsettled Tony Cottee, by scoring the winner on his debut v Watford at Upton Park (19.3.88). Added another four First Division goals in eight more remaining games, including a vital double v Chelsea that ensured survival in the final home match. The following season, with Cottee having left for Everton, Rosenior carried the burden up front. He topped the scorechart with seven league goals and eight more in various cup competitions, but it was not enough to keep Hammers in Division One. Then the injury jinx struck Leroy in a big way. Persistent knee and Achilles injuries limited him to just four league starts under Lou Macari in 1989/90 and, worse still, just two sub. outings the following season. With competition for places further intensified by the return of Frank McAvennie, and the signing of Trevor Morley and Jimmy Quinn, Leroy had loan spells with Fulham and Charlton Athletic. There was talk of him going

Leroy Rosenior

experienced David Burrows having replaced Julian Dicks at left-back. Still, Keith underlined his versatility by moving into the left-midfield position on occasions, where his crossing ability led to a number of goals. Unfortunately a broken leg - sustained in a tackle with Everton's John Ebbrell - ended his season prematurely in Apr. 1993. At least Keith could look back on winning his first senior Northern Ireland cap v Latvia in Sept. 1993. The return of Julian Dicks in Oct. 1994 meant that Keith once more had to fight for his first team place.

❑ *Northern Ireland cap: 1993 v Latvia (sub). (1).*

to France to play for Metz, but he received an unexpected recall to First Division action at the start of 1991/92. his last appearance for Hammers came in the role of sub. at Nottingham Forest (28.9.91). Leroy, whose family originate from Sierra Leone, Africa, finally settled at Bristol City, where he played first team football before taking up a coaching role.

ROTHWELL, James   1910-14

Born: Crosby, Liverpool. 1888
SL apps: 88 (4 gls)
Cup apps: 11

■ Jim didn't have the happiest of debuts for Hammers, being in the West Ham team trounced 3-0 at Brentford (13.12.1910), but luckily the scoreline was reversed in the next fixture v. Leyton at the Boleyn which enabled Irons' new defender to settle into the side in the number two shirt. He missed only one match to the end of the season which saw his team finish a respectable fifth in the SL that campaign. He remained more or less a regular until 1913/14 when he played his last match at left-back in a 3-2 win at Southampton (14.2.14).

ROWLAND, Keith   1993-

Born: Portadown, Northern Ireland. 1.9.71
Lge apps: 23 (0 gls)
Cup apps: 5 (0 gls)

■ Signed twice by Harry Redknapp - initially at Bournemouth for whom he made his League debut v Darlington (17.8.91). The slim left-back made 72 appearances for the Cherries, as well as spending one match on loan to non-league Farnborough Town (Aug. 1990) and two on loan to Coventry City (both sub. outings) in Jan. 1993. In the summer of 1993, with Redknapp by then back at West Ham as Billy Bonds' assistant, Rowland earned a permanent move to the Premiership when Hammers signed him for £110,000 and Paul Mitchell for £40,000. Made his debut on the opening day v Wimbledon (14.8.93), but his first season was punctuated by injuries and he found it difficult to hold down a regular first team place with the more

Keith Rowland

Jim Ruffell

RUFFELL, James   1921-37

Born: Doncaster, Yorkshire. 8.8.1900
Lge apps: 505 (159 gls)
Cup apps: 43 (7 gls)

■ Although Jim was born in South Yorkshire, he became an adopted East Ender after his family had moved south and played his early soccer with Essex Road School, Manor Park, Fullers, Chadwell Heath Utd, Manor Park Albion, East Ham and Wall End United before joining Hammers in March 1920. Apart from a brief spell with Aldershot, Jimmy served no other club during his pro career. His League appearances set a West Ham United record which remained unchallenged until Bobby Moore surpassed it in 1973. Making his first appearance in Hammers' colours in a 3-0 victory over Port Vale at the Boleyn in Sept. 1921, Jimmy's League and cup appearances rose steadily in the early 20's - as did his goalscoring record despite having scoreless seasons in 1921/22, 1932/33 and 1936/37. It's doubtful if his career total of 166 in League and Cup will ever be surpassed by an ortho-dox winger. Inevitably capped by his country and a member of the West Ham team which contested the first Wembley Cup Final in 1923, the Hammers' management could hardly have foreseen what lay ahead when they plucked the diminutive outside-left from the works team of the Ilford Electricity Board! Chosen six times to play for England, he made his international debut v. Scotland at Manchester in April 1926, when even the dual threat of Jimmy and former West Ham star Syd Puddefoot in the England side could not prevent the Scots winning 1-0. There can be little doubt that had it not been for the very high standard of competition for the England left-wing spot at that time, with Cliff Bastin (Arsenal), Eric Houghton (Aston Villa) and Eric Brook (Manchester City) all in con-tention, our subject would have won many more caps. In addition to his half-dozen full caps, further representative honours bestowed on him included selection for the Football League v. Scottish League in 1926/27 and against the Irish League in 1928/29 as well as appearances in

English Trial Matches against the North, South and Rest in 1927; The Rest v. England, 1927; and against the Rest and Lancashire in 1929. Matches in which players were literally playing for their international lives. A succinct assessment of Jimmy Ruffell's play was given in a book entitled 'A Century of English International Football 1872-1972' by Morley Farror and Douglas Lamming: "Opponents learned to pay Ruffell the compliment of close marking; it was fatal to let him give full rein to his exceptional speed and flashing shots." His two decades at the Boleyn saw him form many notable left-wing partnerships, numbering among them fellow England internationals Billy Moore, Len Goulden, John Morton and briefly, Syd Puddefoot, when the latter returned to West Ham in 1932. But if Jim had had to make a preference, it would probably have been the first-named Billy Moore. Portraying perfectly the cigarette-card image of the professional footballer, complete with centre-parting in his slicked-back hair, Jimmy set a dashing scene as he tormented his opposing full-backs, often leaving them with muddied backsides as he cut in to score yet another goal. When he left West Ham in 1937 he chose to see out the remainder of his career with little Aldershot, and in a remarkable coincidence he played his last game for the Hampshire club in opposition to the same team that he'd faced 17 years earlier in his first game for Hammers... Port Vale! Jim became involved in the fish trade after he retired from the game he graced with such distinction and was also later a brewery representative and an Essex licensee. The last link with the 1923 FA Cup final team was lost when Jim passed away on Sept. 6, 1989. His death prompted the following tribute from someone who witnessed Jimmy's career at first-hand and who himself holds a unique place in Hammers' history, the late Jack Helliar: "I had the privilege of being a personal friend of Jimmy and his family and can categorically state that Jimmy was the finest winger ever to play for West Ham United - a legend. He will be sadly missed by all his friends and acquaintances throughout football, for as well

as being one of the "Greats" he was also one of the nicest people you could wish to meet. Always smart, a perfect gentleman." A theme reiterated by my father, George Hogg, who also saw Jimmy play before World War II: "He was always well turned out, well-groomed and very gentlemanly. He was the Trevor Brooking of his day, in that respect."

Footnote: Jim's brother Bill was also on Hammers' books, but never made the first team and transferred to Nelson in 1927.

❏ *England caps:* 1926 v Scotland, Northern Ireland; 1928 v Northern Ireland, Wales; 1929 v Scotland, Wales. (6).

Played	League		FAC		LC		Europe		Total	
	App	Gls	App	Gls	App	Gls	App	Gls	App	Gls
1921-22	14	0	1	0	0	0	0	0	15	1
1922-23	33	6	9	1	0	0	0	0	42	7
1923-24	39	2	3	0	0	0	0	0	42	2
1924-25	42	9	6	3	0	0	0	0	48	12
1925-26	40	12	1	0	0	0	0	0	41	12
1926-27	37	13	3	1	0	0	0	0	40	14
1927-28	39	18	2	1	0	0	0	0	41	19
1928-29	37	20	5	0	0	0	0	0	42	20
1929-30	40	13	4	0	0	0	0	0	44	13
1930-31	37	13	1	0	0	0	0	0	38	13
1931-32	39	15	2	0	0	0	0	0	41	15
1932-33	8	0	0	0	0	0	0	0	8	0
1933-34	22	8	2	0	0	0	0	0	24	8
1934-35	36	20	2	0	0	0	0	0	38	20
1935-36	30	10	2	1	0	0	0	0	32	11
1936-37	12	0	0	0	0	0	0	0	12	0
TOTAL	505	159	43	7	0	0	0	0	548	166

Matthew Rush

RUSH, Matthew   1990-

Born: Dalston, East London. 6.8.71
Lge apps: 25 (3 gls)
Cup apps: 1 (0 gls)

■ Strong, pacy right-winger who has taken some time to make the break through at Upton Park after joining the club from school in July 1988. Signed pro. Mar. 1990 and made his first team debut later that year v. Hull City in a 7-1 Second Division slaughter at Upton Park (6.10.90). Started only three games in the top flight in 1991/92 but opened his goal account with two headers in a home win v Norwich City. His form in the reserves didn't escape the notice of Jack Charlton, though, who called Matthew into the Republic of Ireland Under-21 team on two occasions that season. Rush's day at Upton Park appeared to be numbered when he failed to feature in any senior matches in 1992/93. He joined Cambridge United on loan in Mar. 1993, making 10 appearances, and benefited from an 11-game stint with Swansea City a year later. Just when he seemed to be on his way, Rush's Upton Park career received a boost when he was recalled in the spring of 1994 and played 10 Premiership games, scoring a vital goal in a home win v. Ipswich Town. Harry Redknapp gave the enigmatic youngster another extended run in the first team at the start of 1994/95 when he will be finally hoping to establish himself.

RUSSELL, John

1904-05

Lge apps: 16
Cup apps: 1

■ This former Everton defender was on duty for the official opening of the Boleyn Grounds v. Millwall (1.9.1904). Wearing the number six shirt, John helped Hammers win that inaugural fixture against their arch rivals 3-0 and stayed in the side for a 15-match run until losing his place to Dick Jarvis. He was back on duty for the final match of the season when Irons ended the campaign as they had began, with a 3-0 win.

RUTHERFORD, Jack

1933-34

Born: Nanthead, Cumberland.
Lge apps: 33
Cup apps: 2

■ Signed from Watford on the recommendation of former Hammers' goalkeeper Ted Hufton, after the latter had joined the Hertfordshire club in the twilight of his career. Although Ted claimed the credit for sending Jack to Upton Park, it was Gillingham who discovered him originally playing for Crawcrook in the North Eastern League while continuing to work as a coal miner. From the Kent club he transferred to Vicarage Road, and from there to the Boleyn to become regular first choice 'keeper for season 1933/34. Jack made way for a new signing from Burnley, Herman Conway, the following Second Division campaign, and in June 1935 he joined Charlie Paynter's old home town club, Swindon Town.

Jack Rutherford

Alan Sealey (centre) has blood streaming from a stud gash on his right leg after a savage challenge sidelined him during West Ham's Cup-Winners' Cup away leg with Sparta Prague in December 1964. He watches with Ron Greenwood as Hammers are beaten 2-1 on the night but win 3-2 on aggregate.

SADLER, George
1946

Born: Whitwell, Northumberland. 7.5.15
Lge apps: 1

■ Centre-half George just qualifies for this directory, making the necessary one appearance in the 1946/47 season. Signed from Gainsborough Trinity, along with goalkeeper George Taylor, he had to be content with the solitary Second Division outing, there being a glut of defenders at the Boleyn at that time. They included veteran Charlie Bicknell, Arthur Banner, Steven Forde, Johnny McGowan and Ernie Devlin. George subsequently transferred to Southern League Guildford where he came under the managership of another ex-Hammer, Archie Macaulay. Hammers provided the opposition to the Surrey club at his benefit in 1954. George joined the Hammers prior to WW2, and served with his colleagues in the Essex Regt. T.A. and Royal Artillery. He also participated in all-in wrestling during the summer months.

SAGE, G
1895/96 TIW

■ A winger who joined TIW after the break-up of the old Castle Swifts club in 1895. Played in the FA Cup tie v Chatham and the floodlight friendly v Old St Stephens (15.12.1895).

SATTERTHWAITE, Charles
1903-04

Born: 1878
SL apps: 32 (13 gls)
Cup apps: 4 (5 gls)

■ A high class inside-left who joined Hammers from New Brompton (now Gillingham) for the start of the 1903/04 season. He was an immediate success in the claret and blue, scoring on his debut in the opening game of the season v Millwall and finishing the campaign as Hammers' top scorer in Southern League matches with 13 goals to his credit. He met with equal success in cup ties, scoring in all three qualifying rounds of the competition, including a hat-trick against Chatham, before his - and Hammers' - scoring run ended with a 0-1 intermediate round defeat v. Fulham. He also once scored four goals in a SL fixture v. Brighton. His fine form and consistency, in a season during which he missed only two Southern League matches, alerted other clubs and he transferred to Woolwich Arsenal in the following close season. In 1906 Charlie visited Hammers in their new home for a first round cup replay with the Gunners, and helped his new club to a 3-2 win assisted by two other ex-West Ham men, McEachrane and Bigden. Well-known for his thunderbolt shooting, he once broke the goal nets with one of his scoring efforts at Plumstead and in an Arsenal/Sheffield United match he smashed a tremendous 25-yard drive which hit the bar, rebounded against J. Lievesley, the Blades' goalie, knocking him clean off his feet, the ball ending up in the net. With Liverpool in 1900/01 (he was Reds' 12th man for their 1901 FA Cup visit to the

Memorial Grounds), Charlie had an England trial in 1904/05 while with the Gunners, for whom he scored 21 goals in 61 FL appearances between 1904 and 1908. His brother, S. Satterthwaite, also played for Arsenal, 1907/10.

SCANES, Albert
1909-10

SL apps: 3 (3 gls)

■ Bert was one of several number nines drafted in to deputise for England international George Webb, whose business commitments often prevented him from turning out for Hammers. Two goals on his debut at Crystal Palace and a winning counter at Upton Park v. Northampton Town made the former Barking man the most successful by far of that season's understudies, but he wasn't retained for the following campaign and moved to Croydon Common for 1911/12.

SCOTT, Tony
1959-65

Born: Edmonton, London. 1.4.41
Lge apps: 83 (16 gls)
Cup apps: 14 (3 gls)

■ An orthodox right-winger with a penchant for scoring goals. North London-born, he escaped the Tottenham scouting net to join the Upton Park groundstaff in 1957; quickly making his way through the junior ranks and 12 appearances for England Youth. Had his League debut v Chelsea in 1960, going on to make over 80 senior appearances before transferring to Aston Villa for £25,000 and renewing his right-wing partnership with Phil Woosnam at Villa Park.

Tony Scott

SEALEY, Alan   1961-67

Born: Hampton, Middlesex. 22.4.42
Lge apps: 107 (22 gls)
Cup apps: 21 (4 gls)

■ Scorer of the two goals which defeated TSV Munich in the memorable 1965 European Cup Winners' Cup Final at Wembley, his career plummeted after a freak pre-season training accident the same year. The players organised an impromptu cricket match at the Chadwell Heath training ground. Sealey fell awkwardly over a wooden bench and sustained a broken leg. Signed from Leyton Orient in the exchange deal that took Dave Dunmore to Brisbane Road in Mar. 1961, Alan was a frequent member of the Hammers' attack in the 60's. Spotted originally by talent scout Eddie Heath and signed for Orient by caretaker manager Les Gore after scoring five goals in his first trial match, Alan joined Hammers in a somewhat unusual fashion. He arrived at Upton Park just after the departure of Ted Fenton and just before the appointment of Ron Greenwood as new team boss - actually being signed by chairman Mr Reg Pratt! He had been well schooled in the finer points of the game at Orient by master coach Eddie Baily (who went on to become West Ham's chief scout). Transferred to Plymouth Argyle in Nov. 1967, Alan stayed only briefly at Home Park before ending his playing career with his then local club Romford in the Southern League. Alan took over the family business of distributing bookmakers' lists when he retired from playing. He was back at Upton Park for the Bobby Moore memorial match in Mar. 1994, when the 1964 and 1965 cup-winning teams returned for a night of nostalgia and to pay tribute to their former skipper.

SEXTON, Dave   1953-56

Born: Islington, London. 6.4.30
Lge apps: 74 (27 gls)
Cup apps: 3 (2 gls)

■ Transferred to Hammers from Luton Town in Mar. 1953, he had learned his early soccer with Chelmsford City in the Southern League. Son of former professional boxer Archie Sexton, who fought Jock McAvoy for the British Middleweight title in 1933, Dave enjoyed a chequered playing career. A striker of some repute, he scored some valuable goals in his three years at the Boleyn but the only representative honour he won was playing for the FA v the RAF in 1953. Moving to Leyton Orient in May 1956, he later had spells with Brighton & Hove Albion (where he was a member of their Third Division South championship team) and Crystal Palace, where his playing career was ended by injury in Jan. 1962. Dave's managerial career has since overshadowed that of his playing days. As a manager-coach he has seen service with Chelsea (twice), Orient, Fulham, Arsenal, Queens Park Rangers, Manchester United and Coventry City. He was appointed assistant to England manager Bobby Robson in July 1983, and was

Dave Sexton

later put in charge of the revolutionary new "Soccer School" and the Under-21 squad. His greatest triumphs in management were undoubtedly at Chelsea, whom he steered to an FA Cup win in 1970 and a European Cup Winners' Cup success over Real Madrid in 1971. He also led the Blues to runners-up spot in the First Division (1971/72). A feat he repeated at QPR (1975/76) and Man. Utd. (1979/80). He is now coach at Aston Villa.

SHEA, Danny — 1908-13/1920-21

Born: Wapping, London. Nov. 1887
SL apps: 179 (111 gls)
Cup apps: 22 (22 gls)
Lge apps: 16 (1 gl)

■ With his Irish ancestry and inquisitive nature in opposing penalty areas, Dan would have been a certain contender for Jack Charlton's Republic of Ireland team had he been around today. Charlie Paynter discovered this brilliant inside-forward almost on the club's doorstep, playing Sunday morning football for the Builders Arms pub team in Stratford and also for Pearl United and Manor Park Albion in 1908. He progressed almost immediately to Hammers' Southern League side. A superb ball-player, hard to dispossess, he developed into a consistent goalscorer and became the leading light in West Ham's attack. His fine form didn't fail to catch the attention of Football League clubs, and after 166 Southern League appearances for Hammers, Blackburn Rovers duly broke the existing transfer record to take him to Ewood Park for £2,000 in 1913 - in a move which modern day benefactor Jack Walker would have been proud of - and saw Dan pocket £550 as his share of the

fee. It proved to be a shrewd transaction on Hammers' part when, after winning two England caps and a First Division championship medal while at Rovers (scoring 27 goals to help them to the title), he returned south during the war years to make a further 75 appearances in the claret and blue as a guest player in the hastily-formed London Combination. He also had spells with Birmingham, Fulham and Nottingham Forest in WW1 and was in the side which defeated Everton in the final of the Victory Shield. Although Danny went back to Blackburn with the cessation of hostilities to win further England honours in two Victory Internationals v. Scotland, like George Hilsdon, Harry Stapley and Syd Puddefoot before and after him, he returned for a second spell at the Boleyn. It proved to be an abortive reunion, however, for after 16 Second Division outings and a solitary goal to show for his efforts in 1920/21, he transferred to Fulham after a difference of opinion with the West Ham management in Nov. 1920. The move saw him regain some of his old form, and he finished the following season as Cottagers' second top scorer with 11 goals. But he continued to move around, first joining Clapton Orient and later Coventry City. Dan played out the last days of his chequered career with Sheppey United in the Southern League. Worked as a docker during WW1 and after he hung up his boots, he was also a publican in later life. Described as being "An artful schemer and delicate dribbler at inside/right for many seasons. Had the knack of wheeling suddenly when near goal and unleashing a thunderbolt shot." An occasional visitor to Upton Park in later years, Danny Shea died at the age of 73 at Wapping, after being taken ill on Christmas Day, 1960.

SHEARING, Peter — 1960

Born: Uxbridge, Middlesex. 26.8.38
Lge apps: 6

■ An experienced senior amateur goalkeeper with Uxbridge, Hayes and Kingstonian, he played against the last named for Hendon in the 1960 Amateur Cup Final at Wembley. Signed for Hammers after a spell on Spurs' books, making his initial League appearance v. Sheffield Wednesday at Hillsborough. He went on to half a dozen First Division outings before returning to reserve duty. Began a grand tour of the West Country clubs when transferred to Portsmouth, later taking in Exeter City, Plymouth Argyle, Exeter again, Bristol Rovers and finally, Gillingham. He assisted fellow ex-Hammer Andy Nelson at Charlton when the latter was manager at The Valley and also became a fully qualified referee.

SHONE, Danny — 1928

Born: Liverpool. 1900
Lge apps: 12 (5 gls)

■ Stocky inside-left signed from Liverpool. Made a scoring First Division debut on the opening day of the 1928/29 season for Hammers v. Sheffield United at Upton Park.

Although he almost managed a goal every other game in his 12 League appearances in the claret and blue, West Ham transferred the likeable Liverpudlian to Coventry City on 2.1.29 in a double deal which also resulted in James Loughlin joining the Midlanders. He scored one goal in nine matches for City. Began his career with Grayson's in Division One of West Cheshire League before signing for Liverpool as a pro in May 1921.

SHREEVE, Frederick — 1908-11

Born: 1884
SL apps: 65 (4 gls)
Cup apps: 10

F. SHREEVE.
WEST HAM UNITED.

■ Right-back Fred had the unusual distinction of scoring on his Hammers' debut from that position, although as a known penalty-taker, his goal which helped to secure a 2-1 win over Northampton on 24.10.08, probably came from the 12-yard spot. Formerly with Millwall, he went on to form a regular full-back partnership with Bill Taylor that season, ending up with 19 Southern League appearances to his credit. The following term saw him with a new partner in Bob Fairman, and he missed only one match to complete his most successful season at Upton Park. Began his career at Burton United and joined Doncaster Rovers for 1911/12. Fred's son Bert later played for Charlton Athletic and appeared for them in both the 1946 and 1947 FA Cup Finals.

SILOR, William — 1909-10

Born: 1887
SL apps: 6

■ Previously having served Eton Mission, Leyton and Norwich City (with whom he scored seven goals in 26 games in 1908/09). Bill made his first appearance in Hammers' colours in a 1-0 Southern League defeat at Exeter City on 5.3.10 in the centre-forward position. Switched to the outside-left berth for his next outing v. Croydon Common, he remained there for a further four matches to bring his total appearances to a round half-dozen in the claret and blue.

Danny Shea

SIMMONS, Charles   1904-05

SL apps: 34 (8 gls)
Cup apps: 1

■ Inside/forward "Chippy" Simmons was with West Bromwich Albion for six years before signing for Irons. "A wonderful ball player with a deceptive body-swerve. Would have won numerous England caps but for being a contemporary of the great Steve Bloomer." Apart from playing in the first-ever game at the Boleyn Ground, Simmons did likewise with WBA at the Hawthorns (3.10.1900). Only one season with Hammers, Chippy began his career with Worcester Rovers.

SIMMONS, Jim   1920-22

Lge apps: 27 (1 gl)

Jim Simmons

■ Shares a unique and, until now, unrecognised distinction with fellow early-century ex-Hammer, Billy Barnes: BOTH signed for the club from Sheffield United, and BOTH scored FA Cup Final goals for the Blades! Sometimes confused with a predecessor of the same surname, "Chippy" Simmons, who was signed from West Bromwich Albion in 1904, Jim was a nephew of the legendary Sheffield United goalkeeper Bill Foulke. Usually employed in the outside-right position, he realised every footballer's dream when he scored Sheffield United's first goal in their 3-0 1915 FA Cup Final victory v. Chelsea at Old Trafford. Billy Barnes had achieved the feat when he scored Blades' winner in the 1902 final replay v Southampton at Crystal Palace. Jim was forced to retire from the game before Hammers reached their first final in 1923.

SIMPSON, Peter   1935-37

Born: Edinburgh, Scotland. 13.11.1908
Lge apps: 32 (12 gls)
Cup apps: 4

■ Played his first game for West Ham in a 4-3 defeat by Norwich City in the first League match played at Carrow Road, following the Norfolk club's move from their previous ground, The Nest. Although he failed to get on the score-sheet on his debut, Peter gave a good return for the modest fee paid to Crystal Palace by Hammers for his services, being equally at home in any forward positions. Began his career with St. Bernards, where he had two seasons before joining Kettering Town. Palace had signed him with four other players from Kettering in June 1929. He was the most successful of the quintet and scored six goals v. Exeter City in Glaziers' 7-2 win on 4.4.30 and in all scored over 150 League goals for the

South Londoners and was awarded a benefit match by them against the famous amateur club, Corinthians. He later transferred to Reading. A former shipping clerk who began his careeer with Leith Amateurs.

SISSONS, John   1963-70

Born: Hayes, Middlesex. 30.9.45
Lge apps: 213 (37 gls)
Cup apps: 51 (16 gls)

■ Became the youngest player to score in an FA Cup Final at Wembley and the second youngest to appear there (behind his Preston opponent of that May day in 1964, Howard Kendall). His career looked certain to rocket into the international arena the following year when he returned to the twin towers as a vital part of Hammers' victorious European Cup Winners' Cup-winning side. But despite numerous Under-23 appearances, Johnny never won a full cap. Originally an inside-left in his formative years with Middlesex and England schoolboys, he was successfully converted to outside-left by Ron Greenwood after making his senior debut v. Blackburn Rovers at Upton Park (4.5.63). One of the most feared wingers in the League when on song, his form inexplicably waned towards the end of his time at the Boleyn. Transferred to Sheffield Wednesday, he made 115 League appearances for the Hillsborough club before moving on again to join forces with his former team-mate John Bond at Norwich. He managed only 17 games for the Canaries, however, and ended his League days with Chelsea, making a further 10 outings in 1974/75. John later emigrated to South Africa where he built up a successful motor products company of which he is now a partner. He suffered a big blow when his treasured 1964 FA Cup Winners' medal and 1965 European Cup Winners' Cup counterpart were stolen during a robbery at his home on the outskirts of Cape Town, SA. On a nicer note, West Ham paid for John and his former team-mate 'Budgie' Byrne to make a special 11,000 mile round trip from SA for the occasion of the Bobby Moore memorial match, in Mar. 1994, when they were guests of honour along with their colleagues from those two cup-winning teams. John has been in SA for 18 years now, after originally signing a two-year contract to play for Cape Town City. Although he played his last match at the age of 38, he still keeps fit by being a keen cyclist. He entered the 65 mile Argus cycle race, a major event in the African sporting calendar which attracts 22,000 cyclists worldwide. In all, John pedals 150 miles a week to and from work on his Peugeot bike and takes part in 10 races a year.

Played	League		FAC		LC		Europe		Total	
	App	Gls	App	Gls	App	Gls	App	Gls	App	Gls
1962-63	1	0	0	0	0	0	0	0	1	0
1963-64	14	3	7	3	1	0	0	0	22	6
1964-65	38	8	2	1	1	0	9	2	50	11
1965-66	36	5	2	1	9	1	4	1	51	8
1966-67	35	7	2	1	6	3	0	0	43	11
1967-68	37	8	3	2	2	0	0	0	42	10
1968-69	32	4	1	0	2	1	0	0	35	5
1969-70	20	2	1	0	0	0	0	0	21	2
TOTAL	**213**	**37**	**18**	**8**	**21**	**5**	**13**	**3**	**265**	**53**

Bulgarian referee Dinov refuses to allow John Sissons on the field treatment during the 'Battle of Prague' (see page 184). It was Sissons who scored the vital goal in Czechoslovakia to ensure Hammers progress.

SLATER, Stuart
1987-92

Born: Sudbury, Suffolk. 27.3.69
Lge apps: 141 (11 gls)
Cup apps: 33 (5 gls)

■ One of the most exciting products of West Ham's youth system, Stuart (pic left) emerged as a first team star in the early 90's but did not fulfil his full potential in claret and blue. Born and bred in the sleepy Suffolk countryside, the shy, unassuming youngster turned down the chance to join his local club, Ipswich Town, to sign up for Hammers as an apprentice in July 1985. Proved outstanding for the youth and reserve teams, scoring prolifically despite his lightweight build for a striker. Turned pro in Apr. 1987 and John Lyall gave Stuart his first taste of the first team when he introduced him as an 89th minute sub. v Derby County in the First Division at Upton Park (3.10.87). After one other sub. outing that season, "Chopper" featured in 18 games in Lyall's last season with the club, which ended in relegation. But under Lou Macari, Slater continued to blossom into one of the country's most exciting young prospects. In 1989/90 he established himself as a first team regular, playing 40 Second Division matches and scoring seven league and four cup goals. The following season, under Billy Bonds, he had a number of outstanding games. His close control and neat ball skills brought many a match to life. Bonzo thought Slater was at his best playing wide on the left, but the player maintained his preference for an out-and-out striker's role, or a position just behind the front two where he could run at defenders. As word of Slater's pace and skill spread throughout the league, he became more closely marked and found it harder to make an impact, especially in front of goal. One of his three goals in 1990/91 came against Everton in a thrilling FA Cup quarter-final tie under the Upton Park floodlights (11.3.91). Slater murdered the First Division side almost single-handedly with his penetrating runs down the left flank - an outstanding performance capped by his winning goal. Afterwards, Everton boss Howard Kendall told the Press that Slater was worth £3 million. Now everyone had heard of the likeable lad who always let his football do all the talking for him. The former England Under-21 international earned one 'B' cap, as sub. v Switzerland at Walsall in May 1991. West Ham turned down a £2m offer from Glasgow Celtic, but constant transfer speculation clearly had an unsettling effect on Stuart who failed to reproduce his breathtaking Everton display in subsequent matches. Indeed, after scoring v Bristol Rovers (8.5.91) at the end of the promotion-winning season, he went a whole season - 41 league and 12 cup ties - without scoring. When Celtic, by now managed by Stuart's agent, former Hammer Liam Brady, came back in for him with a £1.5m bid in the summer of 1992, West Ham agreed to sell their most prized asset. The move may have been financially very rewarding for Slater, but the Glasgow 'goldfish bowl' didn't suit his laid-back,

quiet lifestyle. As Celtic's big-money buy, and with arch rivals Glasgow Rangers winning everything in sight north of the border, Stuart's performances came under close scrutiny from Parkhead fans and the Scottish media. His difficult 15 months at Celtic brought him only three goals and when his mentor, Brady, resigned amid a well-publicised boardroom battle, it was inevitable that Slater would soon follow. In fact, Stuart was pleased to go 'home' - to Ipswich, where he stood on the terraces and worshipped mid-70's favourites such as Muhren and Thijssen. The £750,000 move, in Sept. 1993, as well as taking him back close to his family home, also reunited him with his first manager, John Lyall, as well as fellow former Hammers McGiven, Goddard, Whitton and Parkes.

SMAILES, Matthew
1929

Born: Durham
Lge apps: 7
Cup apps: 3

■ Made his Hammers' debut in the 8-2 thrashing of Leeds at Upton Park (when Vic Watson struck six goals against the hapless Yorkshiremen), Matt could hardly have hoped for a more memorable first appearance. Beginning his career with Annfield Plain in Northumberland, he then had two years with Blackburn Rovers before joining West Ham in 1928. According to his pen-picture in a 1928 club handbook, he was obtained as an under-study to Collins, Barrett and Cadwell, being equally at home in any of the half-back positions. Together with George Robson, Matt lodged with Jack Hebden and his family in Central Park Road, East Ham. He joined Coventry from Hammers where he played 11 games in the Third Division South. Moved to Ashington FC in Aug. 1931.

SMALL, Mike
1991-94

Born: Birmingham. 2.3.62
Lge apps: 49 (13 gls)
Cup apps: 10 (5 gls)

■ Whatever likeable Mike's critics say about his somewhat ungainly style and difficulty in avoiding offside decisions, no one can take away one remarkable purple period in the club's traumatic 1991/92 relegation season - his first at Upton Park. Signed from Brighton & Hove Albion for £400,000 on the eve of season, Small arrived with an impressive pedigree. In his only season on the south coast, he netted 21 goals (including one against Hammers at Upton Park) in Seagulls' promotion challenge, which ended in the play-offs. And he showed immediate promise once in the top flight with West Ham. After making his debut against one of his former clubs, Luton Town (17.8.91), he went on to score 13 goals in an amazing 20-match sequence, including a notable winner at Arsenal. The flood of goals turned to a trickle after Christmas, although 18 league and cup strikes in his first season at Division One level was very encouraging. Unfortunately for this powerful, black striker, his Upton Park career went downhill from then on. He was sent off in the opening match of 1992/93, at Barnsley, and - with recent arrival Clive Allen forming a new potent strike partnership with Trevor Morley - rarely got another chance. Low on confidence, and plagued by a long-term back injury, Small could not even guarantee himself a regular place in the reserves! He featured in just nine league games in the 1992/93 promotion term - his last at Notts County (13.3.93). West Ham tried to cut their losses and pave the way for the player to try his luck elsewhere after the player had spent a brief loan spell at Wolves (for whom he scored at Sunderland). Billy Bonds even declared that Small could leave on a free transfer, but still there were no takers - except Charlton Athletic, who

Mike Small shrugs off a challenge from Mike Marsh, then of Liverpool but later to move to Upton Park.

briefly took him on loan in 1993/94 - before his Hammers' contract expired. Mike began his league career with Luton, making three sub. appearances in 1981/82, before going on loan to Peterborough United (two starts plus two sub. outings) a year later. He then turned his attention to the continent, playing in Belgium (Standard Liege), Holland (Twente Enschede and Go Ahead Eagles) and Greece (PAOK).

SMALL, Sam   1937-48

Born: Birmingham. 15.5.12
Lge apps: 107 (40 gls)
Cup apps: 9 (1 gl)

■ Signed from Birmingham in the days before they had adopted the "City," Sam was an unselfish, hard-working centre-forward who served the club well, both before and after the war. Indeed, you could add "during" to that sentence, as it was Sam who scored the all-important goal in Hammers' 1-0 Football League War Cup win at Wembley in 1940 v. Blackburn Rovers. Described in the club's 1939/40 handbook as "one of the nicest chaps in the game," he would have undoubtedly made an even bigger impression at the Boleyn but for the outbreak of hostilities. Transferred to Brighton & Hove Albion in Mar. 1948, he made 38 League appearances without scoring for the Seasiders.

SMILLIE, Andy   1958-61

Born: Ilford, Essex. 15.3.41
Lge apps: 20 (3 gls)
Cup apps: 3

■ A skilful, ball-playing inside-forward who had won a host of representative honours with Ilford, London and England Schoolboys before joining the Upton Park groundstaff in 1956. Signed pro in 1958 after adding three England Youth caps to his earlier honours. Made his First Division debut in Dec. the same year v. Spurs at White Hart Lane. Andy refused the terms offered him for 1961/62, and was subsequently transferred to Crystal Palace where he joined up with fellow ex-Hammers John Cartwright, Alf Noakes and George Petchey, and also Hammer-to-be Johnny Byrne. He scored 23 goals in 53 League appearances at Palace and later had spells with Scunthorpe (13 apps, 2 gls) and Southend (163 apps 29 gls) before ending his League career with Gillingham (94 apps 7 gls). Andy now runs a restaurant on the seafront at Southend.

SMITH, D   1919

■ A right-winger who came from Stewarton and played in Hammers' first-ever League match v. Lincoln City at Upton Park on 30.8.19... his only appearance in the first team.

SMITH, Harold   1927

Born: North Shields.
Lge apps: 1

■ Despite having the misfortune of attending a non-football playing school as a lad, Harry quickly made up for lost time in local junior football before graduating to Cullercoats, a senior amateur club. His performances there prompted Newcastle United to sign him as a full professional for the 1925/26 season. He subsequently made several appearances in Magpies' reserve side from the inside-left position prior to his transfer to Hammers the following season. One of a number of North-Easterners on the Upton Park payroll at that time, he made only one First Division outing in the 1-2 home defeat by Manchester United on 29.10.27. Harry returned north to join Blyth Spartans in Aug. 1928.

SMITH, John   1956-59

Born: Shoreditch, London. 4.1.39
Lge apps: 127 (20 gls)
Cup apps: 5 (2 gls)

■ One of the club's finest discoveries, plain John Smith was a major influence during the promotion season of 1957/58. The far from ordinary skills he exhibited that campaign will be long remembered at Upton Park. Joining the ground-staff in 1954 and signing full pro two years later, after he had won hounours with East London, Middlesex and London Schoolboys, he went on to win England Youth and Under-23 caps while with Hammers. On the verge of full England international honours (he was twice named as reserve during 1959/60), his career took a downward spiral after he was involved in an exchange deal

Andy Smillie

played out the remainder of his career in the lower Divisions with Coventry, Leyton Orient, Torquay, Swindon (where he won a League Cup Winners' medal in 1969) and finally Walsall where he was appointed manager, resigning in Mar. 1973. He then managed Dundalk in the League of Ireland. John died at the tragically early age 49 while managing a social club at Harlesden, N-W. London.

SMITH, Mark   1979

Born: West Ham, London. 10.10.61
Lge apps: 1
Cup apps: 1

■ A lad who looked destined to follow in the tradition of a long line of Upton Park full-backs, he instead had a career of latent promise cruelly cut short by injury. A West Hammer by birth, he had won rave notices with Newham, Essex and London Boys, and was an England trialist before signing for his local club in Oct. 1979. After skippering the youth team he made his initial senior appearance v. Southend in a 5-1 League Cup win at Upton Park (8.10.79) and his League bow v. Swansea (17.11.79) before the tragic termination of his career.

SMITH, Roy   1955-56

Born: Rawalpindi, India. 19.3.36
Lge apps: 6

■ An inside-forward of some talent, he retained his amateur status for two years before signing full pro in June 1955. Although of English parentage he was born in India - a somewhat unusual location for a footballer. He played his early soccer with Woodford Youth Club when his parents returned to this country, and from there joined Hereford United before moving to Hammers. Making two League appearances in 1955/56 and a further four the following campaign, he then decided to emigrate with his parents instead of looking for another club after being placed on the transfer list by West Ham. He recommenced his League career in the early 60's with Portsmouth.

SMITH, Sidney   1904-05

SL apps: 2 (1 gl)

■ Inside-right Syd played in the last two matches of the 1904/05 season, making his debut in the 1-1 Boleyn draw with Portsmouth (21.4.1904) and getting on the score sheet with 'Chippy' Simmons and Frank Piercy in the 3-0 win at Watford (25.4.1904).

SMITH, Stephen   1919-22

Born: Hednesford. 27.3.1896
Lge apps: 27
Cup apps: 4 (1 gl)

■ In direct contrast to his fellow winger and contemporary D. Smith, Syd had a good run in the first Team during Hammers' initial League season, making 23 Second Division appearances in 1919/20. Formerly with Portsmouth, he made only one showing the following season, however, and three the next before transferring to Charlton Athletic in 1922. After three seasons at the Valley he joined Southend United in May 1925. Later had spells with Clapton Orient and Queens Park Rangers before signing for Mansfield Town in June 1929. He passed away at Chichester, Sussex in 1980. Footnote: In the 1986 edition of Who's Who of West Ham United, this player was erroneously listed as Sydney Smith and appears as such in other books about the club, but his correct name is actually Stephen Charles Smith.

SMITH, William   1928-29

Born: Corsham, Wiltshire.
Lge apps: 2

■ A West Countryman, full-back Bill has often been confused over the years with a colleague and namesake Harry Smith, an inside-forward who played for Hammers at round the same time. Played as an amateur for Casham in the Wiltshire League before joining Southern League Bath City (still as a member of the non-paid ranks) for a season-and-a-half. He then signed pro forms for Notts County and spent four years on Trentside until his transfer to West Ham in 1927.

SMITHURST, Edgar   1920-21

Lge apps: 3

■ Made his first team debut in a stirring 2-1 victory over Tottenham Hotspur at Upton Park on 13.3.20 - one of Spurs' rare defeats in a season which saw them run away with the Second Division title with a record 70 points. Ed had another League appearance that campaign, in Hammers' concluding fixture at home to South Shields. A right-winger, he played one more League game in 1920/21 before moving to Oldham Athletic.

SOUTHREN, Tommy   1950-54

Born: Southwick, Sunderland. 1.8.27
Cup apps: 2

■ Although a North-Easterner by birth, this speedy outside-right played most of his early football in Hertfordshire junior competitions after his parents had moved to Welwyn. Signed from the quaintly-named Peartree Old Boys, Tommy joined the pro ranks in 1949 and gained a first XI place a year later. A member of Hammers' reserve team which won a unique Combination Cup and League double in 1953/54 season, he also represented the London FA v Berlin FA the same campaign. He joined Aston Villa at Christmas 1954 and had four years at Villa Park, playing 63 League games and scoring six goals before moving to Bournemouth, where he played 64 Third Division games scoring 11 times.

SPEAK, George   1914-15

Born: Blackburn
SL apps: 13

■ Yet another import from Midland League Gainsborough Trinity, George started out with native Lancashire clubs Clitheroe Central and Darwen, and had a trial with Liverpool before joining Grimsby Town in May 1911. After making a mere four Football League appearances for the Mariners, the stocky left-back made the short journey across Lincolnshire to join Trinity in July 1913 and spent 10 months there before transferring to Hammers in May 1914. Beginning the 1914/15 season as West Ham's first-choice left-back, he lost his place after four matches and did not regain it until the end of Mar. to make 13 Southern League appearances in all. He made three war-time outings the next season, but played most of his football during the conflict as a guest of Preston North End and joined the famous Lancashire club permanently for a £25 transfer fee in Mar. 1919. He'd risen in value considerably by the time of his transfer to Leeds United in Jul. 1923, joining the Yorkshiremen for a substantial £250. His career ended on a winning note at Elland Road when he picked up a Second Division Championship medal in 1924 before retiring the following year. Died 10.3.53. George with given the following testimonial in Doug Lamming's excellent *"Who's Who of Grimsby Town"* - "Capital back, quite fearless, kicking an admirable length and placing to advantage. A believer in direct methods, George was a little apt at times to take undue risks. Described as 'a bundle of pluck and energy'."

Tommy Southren

SPEEDIE, David   1993

Born: Glenrothes, Scotland. 20.2.60
Lge apps: 11 (4 gls)

■ One of the most controversial and unpopular players to ever wear a West Ham shirt, this fiery, little former Scottish international striker certainly made his mark in an 11-match loan spell towards the end of the 1992/93 promotion season. A temperamental character who has had more than his fair share of disciplinary problems throughout a long and turbulent career, "Speedo" was never going to win any popularity polls around Upton Park. The fans couldn't forget how he had antagonised them in his previous days with Chelsea in particular. Their anger towards Speedie was never more clearly illustrated than the abuse he received following two bad misses late on in the home game v arch rivals Millwall, which ended in a 2-2 draw. Afterwards, manager Billy Bonds, who stuck by his loanee with typical honesty and integrity, personally apologised to the player for the hostile treatment he received from the terraces. All credit to Speedie, because no one could question his commitment to helping Hammers towards the top flight - despite all the stick he received. He scored twice v Leicester City and also grabbed the winner v Bristol Rovers, but the highlight of his stay came on the last day of the season in what proved to be his final appearance for the club. He netted the opening goal in the 2-0 victory v Cambridge United (8.5.93) that clinched promotion from Division One by the narrowest possible margin - just one goal difference over third placed Portsmouth. Even the fickle fans hailed Speedo a hero that day! In fact, David enhanced his more pleasant reputation as something of a lucky promotion charm. For he had been prominent in getting Blackburn Rovers promotion to the top flight at the end of the previous (1991/92) season - but was then discarded when chairman Jack Walker and new manager Kenny Dalglish joined forces to rebuild the club at the expense of millions of pounds. And after his spell with Hammers, Speedie moved on to Leicester City in 1993/94, when he contributed 12 vital goals to Foxes' promotion charge back to the Premiership - albeit missing the glorious play-off final v Derby County due to injury. Speedie began his long career with Barnsley and also had stints with Darlington, Coventry City and Liverpool.

A goal for David Speedie (right), one of four in his short spell with West Ham

STALLARD, Arthur   1913-15

SL apps: 13 (8 gls)

■ West Ham were tempted to accept an offer from Sunderland for Syd Puddefoot because they had an option on a promising young goalscorer from Chatham, once the Kent club were out of the FA Cup. They duly went out - 9-0 at Sunderland! - and Stallard signed pro for Hammers. Syd stayed, too, and Arthur scored a vital debut goal in a 3-2 Boleyn victory over Millwall deputising for Puddy (14.4.1913). He had to wait until towards the end of the following season before claiming a regular first team spot for the last 11 matches of 1914/15, when Puddefoot switched to inside/right allowing Arthur the number nine jersey. The result was a sensation as Stallard took over the goalscoring mantle of his hero. He hit seven in 11 SL fixtures and it seemed Hammers had unearthed another major find to rank alongside Harry Stapley, George Webb, George Hilsdon, Danny Shea and Puddefoot himself. The horrors of The Great War were to deem otherwise, however, and despite scoring 17 times in just 23 war-time fixtures to underline his rich promise, Arthur Stallard was destined to die for his country during the conflict... falling on the battlefield in France on 30.11.17, just seven months after scoring his last goal for Hammers.

Arthur Stallard

St. PIER, Wally

Born: Becontree Heath, Essex.
Lge apps: 24

■ A reserve team centre-half who spent most of his playing days as understudy to Jim Barrett, but went on to serve West Ham United for 47 years as chief scout to become the greatest star-finder in the club's history. Among his many discoveries, with the help of his vast scouting network, were the legendary trio of Moore, Hurst and Peters . . . but back to the beginning. His first amateur club was Eagle Park, but Wally arrived at the Boleyn from Ilford in Apr. 1929 after selection for Essex County, the Isthmian League and FA XI's. He made his First Division bow at right-half v. Leicester City at Upton Park the following Oct., numbering four senior outings that campaign. The most appearances he managed in any one season was seven. It was when he retired from playing and was

Wally St. Pier

appointed chief scout by his manager and good friend Charlie Paynter that he found his true forte. Beginning as a steady trickle, the flow of talent he brought to the club reached its crescendo in the 60's and 70's, and was evident in all Hammers' cup triumphs over that period. Given a well-deserved testimonial evening in May 1975 (when many of his "finds" turned out to play), Wally retired the following year after a life-time of loyal service. Wally passed away in 1989.

STANDEN, Jim   1962-67

Born: Edmonton, London. 30.5.35
Lge apps: 179
Cup apps: 57

■ An emergency signing from Luton Town after Hammers' regular 'keeper Lawrie Leslie had suffered a broken leg, he performed with such distinction that he made the first XI spot his own. Kept out of the side by brilliant Welsh international Jack Kelsey at his first club Arsenal, Jim was also forced to understudy another international, England's Ron Baynham, at Kenilworth Road. All this reserve duty ended at Upton Park, however, and Jim took part in the club's dazzling cup success of the mid-60's.

An accomplished cricketer, he also won a championship medal with Worcestershire and topped the first class County bowling averages with 64 wickets at an average of 13 runs during the same period. In all Jim took 313 wickets for Worcestershire between 1960 and 1970. Apart from a brief comeback, Jim lost his place with the signing of Bobby Ferguson from Kilmarnock in 1967 and went off to play for Detriot Cougars in the US Professional League. After returning to England for the 1969/70 season at Millwall, he played eight games for the Lions before signing a two-year contract at Portsmouth while continuing with the bat-and-ball game. He made 13 appearances for Pompey before hanging up his boots. Jim settled in Camberley, Surrey, where he had a sports shop, but later returned to the USA. He was coaching would-up goalkeepers at Fresno University, California in 1986 and now lives in California where he works for a Honda car leasing firm. Jim was delighted with the reception he and his mid-60's colleagues received when they returned to Upton Park as guests of honour at the Bobby Moore memorial match in Mar. 1994. Jim's 1965 European Cup Winners' Cup medal was up for auction at Christies in Oct. 1994 valued at between £4,000 and £6,000. Just before the auction, Jim explained: "I'm not desperate, hard-up or on the breadline. I simply want to raise some money for a real estate deal."

Jim Standen keeps a firm grip on the ball at White Hart Lane in April 1966. Martin Peters and Eddie Bovington shield the Hammers 'keeper from Tottenham's Alan Gilzean.

STANLEY, Thomas   1920

■ A left-back signed from Liverpool, "Digger," as he was nicknamed by the Anfield fans, made only one appearance for Hammers - in a 2-1 defeat at Stockport County. An experience shared by fellow debutant Viv Roberts, who also made his solitary Second Division appearance in that encounter with the Cheshire club.

STEPHENS, John William   1947-48

Born: Cramlington, Northumberland. 13.9.19
Lge apps: 22 (6 gls)
Cup apps: 2 (1 gl)

■ One of two footballing twin brothers who played for East Cramlington and Leeds United before the war, Bill suffered what must be the fastest-ever injury to a club player in a competitive match when he broke his left leg five seconds after the kick-off of an Eastern Counties League match at Bury St. Edmunds (22.4.49) - his second leg-break in successive seasons. He was shaping up well at centre-forward before his first mishap in 1947/48 when he made 23 first team appearances (scoring seven times). Bill had only one more senior showing after that and was transferred to Cardiff City in Dec. 1950, but he never made the league side at Ninian Park. Originally signed by Charlie Paynter from the manager's own home-town club, Swindon, where he had scored 25 times in 47 matches. Bill died in 1974.

STEPHENSON, Alan   1968-72

Born: Chesham, Bucks. 26.9.44
Lge apps: 108
Cup apps: 10 (1 gl)

■ A costly acquisition from Crystal Palace who tried in vain to make the number five shirt his own. Despite an impressive pedigree which included seven England Under-23 caps, he largely failed to solve the problems at the heart of Hammers' defence which had prevailed from the time of Ken Brown's departure. Nevertheless, he still managed over a hundred senior appearances - mostly alongside Bobby Moore - and never lacked endeavour. After a period on loan to Fulham, during which he played 10 times for the Cottagers in 1971/72, he was eventually transferred in the close season to Portsmouth for a fee of £32,000, where he logged another 100 senior outings up to 1974. His best years were undoubtedly at Palace as his 185 League and Cup appearances bear testimony. Stephenson went to South Africa in the close season of 1975 before returning to Orient as coach. He left the game to become a licensee.

STAPLEY, Harry   1905-08

Born: Tunbridge Wells, Kent. 29.4.1883
SL apps: 71 (39 gls)
Cup apps: 4 (2 gls)

■ It was considered something of a coup when this famous amateur accepted an invitation to play for West Ham and borne out when he scored the only goal of his debut match v. Portsmouth (23.12.1904). A schoolmaster in private life, he played for Manor Park Albion, Bromley, Norwich CEYMS, Reading and Woodford Town before joining the Hammers. Harry resisted the lure of professionalism throughout his distinguished football career and set a goalscoring record unique in the history of the game. Somewhat slightly-built for a centre-forward, he nevertheless topped Hammers' scoring lists for three successive seasons in the old Southern League and his subsequent transfer to the then Second Division Glossop saw him lead the Derbyshire club's goalscoring charts for a further seven consecutive campaigns - a performance largely overlooked in the record-books. Capped for England as an amateur international before WW1 on 10 occasions: v Ireland, Holland, Wales, Belgium and Germany in 1908; and v. Ireland, Holland, Belgium, Switzerland and France the following year. He added to his total in 1919 when he made a brief return to Hammers and won further caps v Sweden and Holland in the Olympic Games. He once scored five goals in a match for his country. His duties as a school teacher prevented him from playing in midweek matches at distant destinations, i.e. Plymouth Argyle and Bristol Rovers, but his signing was thought to have been a major factor in the club allowing George Hilsdon to join Chelsea. A brother, W. Stapley, also played for West Ham but not in the SL side. He, too, also joined Glossop, having previously been with Dulwich Hamlet. Harry's career also took in King Charles Higher Grade Schools XI, Reading reservers; Reading amateurs. Also a Berks and Bucks Senior Cup winner and represented West Berks League. Scored 67 goals in 135 League games for Glossop. Never selected for a full international although, during the seasons when he was Glossop's leading scorer, England called on eight different centre-forwards. Before moving to Derbyshire, Stapley was a schoolmaster at Woodford. Went to Glossop to become the private tutor and personal cricket and football coach to sons of Sir Samuel Hill-Wood Bt. (the family associated with Arsenal). Particularly successful as a cricket coach - three of his pupils in the Hill-Wood family later going on to win blues at Oxford and Cambridge. As the years passed, he was taken more into Sir Samuel's confidence and served as private secretary when he became an MP for the High Peak constituency. Also served as his employer's nominee on the board of various local companies. Harry died at Glossop on 29.4.39.

STEVENSON R.   1898-98 TIW

Born: Scotland

■ Previously with Woolwich Arsenal whom he captained, Stevenson was the first big-name player to appear for the Ironworks. He had turned out for Old Castle Swifts in 1894/95 but went home to Scotland after the break-up of that club. Returned to play for Irons in 1895/96. Installed as club captain, he filled a number of positions in Ironworks' first season including full-back and centre-forward.

STEWART, W   1899-1900

SL apps (TIW): 16

■ Signed from Luton Town. His debut for TIW was v. Reading (1.3.1900). A wing-half, he played in the last 16 matches of the season as captain but didn't reappear for 1900/01.

STRODDER, Gary   1987-90

Born: Mirfield, Yorkshire. 1.4.65
Lge apps: 65 (2 gls)
Cup apps: 14

■ Tall, slim central defender with closely cropped hair who was originally signed by John Lyall as cover to help solve an injury crisis in the 1986/87 season. "Strodds" arrived from Lincoln City (where he played 132 league games after making his debut v Wigan, 28.8.82) at a cost of £150,000 after fellow central defenders Alvin Martin and Paul Hilton both suffered injuries. Made his First Division debut in the number five shirt at Chelsea (21.3.87), and found himself in the first team reckoning again for much of the following season when Tony Gale became the next long-term casualty. But made only another 23 first team appearances over the next two seasons before Billy Bonds sold him to West Bromwich Albion for £190,000 in Aug. 1990. Gary established himself as a regular in the senior team at The Hawthorns, having now made more than 120 league appearances for the Baggies. Gary's father, Colin, played for Huddersfield and Halifax.

See pages 198 & 199 for RAY STEWART

STROUD, Roy   1952-56

Born: West Ham, East London. 16.3.25
Lge apps: 13 (4 gls)

■ Born within earshot of the West Ham ground, Roy's parents moved to Hounslow when he was a youngster, and it was in the county of Middlesex that he made a name for himself, playing for London and Middlesex Boys before being selected for England Boys in the outside-right position. During the war years he gained invaluable experience with Arsenal and Brentford while still retaining his amateur status. This was rewarded when he won the first of 11 England caps in 1948. He later toured the continent, Iceland and the Far East with Hendon, the Athenian League and Middlesex Wanderers XI's. Making his Second Division debut in Apr. 1952 v. Notts County, Roy eventually took the professional plunge in November the following year, by this time playing at centre-forward. Injuries restricted his early progress and were to prove a bug-bear throughout his time at Upton Park. Roy joined Southern League Chelmsford City in 1957, but his injury jinx followed him to New Writtle Street and, after sustaining a broken leg, he decided to retire from the game - returning to his former trade in the grocery business.

Gary Strodder

SUGDEN, Sidney   1902-03

SL apps: 1

■ "A wonderfully dashing player with a splendid turn of speed and a deadly shot. But not a good team man," centre-forward-cum-inside-forward Sidney Sugden was so described by a contemporary reporter. Played just one game for West Ham, in the 3-1 Memorial Ground victory over Watford (18.10.1902) at number nine. Began his career with Ilford before the turn of the century, he was so keen to remain an amateur he declined an offer from those giants of the Victorian/Edwardians eras, Aston Villa. He changed his tune when he joined Nottingham Forest, however, and signed pro for the Trentside club in 1903/04 when he became their top scorer with 13 goals in 27 First Division matches. His form faltered the next season when he drew a blank in 12 outings and he returned to London to join Queens Park Rangers (14.1.05). After making only a moderate impact with Rangers, he transferred to their near-neighbours Brentford where he stayed for three seasons before transferring to Southend United for 1909/10 (22 games, 5 gls) who were languishing near the bottom of SL Division One. There was an interesting story behind Syd's solitary match for Hammers which came about as a result of William Davidson's dispute with the West Ham management. Davidson left the club in a hurry, John Farrell, his deputy, was unfit and Sugden, then playing for Ilford, volunteered to fill the spot.

SUCKLING, Perry   1989-90

Born: Leyton, East London. 12.10.65
Lge apps: 6

■ Goalkeeper brought in by new manager Lou Macari on loan from Crystal Palace and played six consecutive Second Division games in 1989/90 as cover for the injured Phil Parkes. Unfortunately for Perry - an East Ender - four of those games ended in defeat so Macari turned instead to unknown Czech 'keeper Ludek Miklosko. It left Suckling to move on for another loan spell, this time at Brentford. Perry arrived at Upton Park in Dec. 1989, making his debut in a home defeat by in-form Oldham Athletic (16.12.89), shortly after enduring the nightmare experience of being on the wrong end of Palace's 9-0 First Division crushing at Liverpool. Perry, who also played for Hammers at Ipswich, Leicester and Plymouth as well as at home v Barnsley (the only time he finished on the winning side) and Hull, began his career as an apprentice at Coventry City. He moved on to Manchester City and gained 10 England Under-21 caps before transferring to Selhurst Park in 1987.

Dave Swindlehurst

SUNDERLAND, H.S.   1899-1900

SL apps (TIW): 1

■ Played his single SL (Div. 2) match in the 2-0 defeat at Bristol City (2.12.1899). Previously with Gravesend United and Millwall, the latter with whom he played 12 SL games in 1898/99.

SWINDLEHURST, Dave   1983-85

Born: Edgware, Middlesex. 6.1.1956
Lge apps: 61 (15 gls)
Cup apps: 10 (2 gls)

■ A striker in the Hurst/Cross mould, his signing for a substantial fee from Derby County did much to minimise the effect of the latter's departure from the Boleyn. A Palace youth team mate of Alan Devonshire in the early 70's, their reunion at Hammers proved a fruitful one after a gap of some 10 years. It was after scoring 73 goals in 237 League games for the Glaziers that he moved to Derby in 1980. A similar scoring ratio for the Rams impressed manager John Lyall sufficiently to bring him to Upton Park. A series of injuries kept him out of first team contention, and he was eventually transferred to Sunderland in 1985.

STEWART, Ray   1979-90

Born: Stanley, Perthshire, Scotland 7.9.59
Lge apps: 345 (62 gls)
Cup apps: 86 (22 gls)

■ Became the most expensive teenager in British football when John Lyall signed him from Dundee United for £430,000 in Aug. 1979, but it proved money well spent. Although the young defender was uncapped when he joined Hammers at the age of 19, within two years he had won an FA Cup winners' medal, scored in the League Cup Final and completed the notable achievement of being capped by Scotland at every level. The latter period of his 11 year period at Upton Park was severely hit by injury, but Raymond - West Ham's undisputed Penalty King - certainly earned his place in Hammers' hall of fame. A product of Errol Rovers in the Dundee Sunday Boys' League, he turned down offers from more glamorous clubs, such as Glasgow Rangers, to join his local team, Dundee United, in May 1973. Encouraged by manager Jim McLean, he developed into one of Scotland's most talented defenders, showing maturity far beyond his tender years. He captained Scotland Under-15's to a 1-0 victory over England at Wembley - the first of his five unbeaten appearances at the famous Empire Stadium. Ray's first team debut for the Terrors came just six days before his 17th birthday, in 1976, at Celtic's Parkhead. Playing in midfield - a role he filled on numerous occasions - he was asked to mark a certain Kenny Dalglish! Ray enjoyed his three seasons as a pro at Tannadice, but the club needed to sell its best assets. McLean turned down an original £175,000 bid for Stewart by the East Londoners, plus an improved offer, and it was with extreme reluctance that McLean finally gave permission for Hammers to sign Stewart. Many youngsters would have been daunted by the prospect of leaving their family home in the Perthshire countryside for the challenge of life in the big city of London, but Ray settled immediately. Made his West Ham debut in a League Cup, second round (second leg) tie at Barnsley (4.9.79) alongside Billy Bonds in the centre of defence. But he was used in midfield for his home debut v. Sunderland (15.9.79), when the Upton Park faithful were impressed with the new signing's toughness in the tackle and his ability to fire ferocious shots from long distance. West Ham were in the Second Division then but the good times were just around the corner and Stewart was at the heart of the club's success in the early 80's. He was top scorer in the 1980 FA Cup run, scoring a couple in the fourth round win at Orient and the dramatic penalty winner v Aston Villa in the quarter-final at Upton Park. Ray's coolness under pressure - there was only a minute left - and his deadly shooting - invariably relying on power rather than placement - established him as one of the most successful spot-kick specialists in the country. Ray underlined his versatility again by playing in the centre of defence (in place of the injured Alvin Martin) in the epic semi-final replay win over Everton at Elland Road and of course played his part in the 1-0 FA Cup Final triumph over

Arsenal. Ray's first season in East London went like a dream - and the fairytale continued in 1980/81. Hammers romped to the Division Two title with a record points haul - "Tonka," as Ray was affectionately known to the fans, missed only the home clash with Grimsby Town - and, in Mar. 1981, returned to Wembley to face First Division champions Liverpool in the League Cup Final. Once again the unflappable Stewart showed nerves of steel as he ran up and placed his right-foot shot past Ray Clemence for the last-gasp penalty equaliser in front of 100,000 fans. Liverpool went on to win the replay at Villa Park but no one could deny Ray his moment of glory. His experience had also been enriched by the experience of European football and then, as reward for consistent performances at club level, the first of his 10 full Scottish caps, v Wales at Swansea (16.5.81). Ray believes that his best game for his country came later in that Home International series - a 1-0 win over England at Wembley. He earned seven senior caps under Jock Stein, the old Celtic supremo, but is sure it would have been more but for his fracas with Mark Hateley which resulted in both players being sent off in an Under-21 international at Hampden Park in Apr. 1982. The incident almost certainly cost him a place in Scotland's squad for the 1982 World Cup finals in Spain. It was not until after Stein's death that Ray - who admitted that he was occasionally critical of some of Stein's coaching methods - received a recall, playing a further three matches under Andy Roxburgh. On the domestic front, Ray continued to enjoy life with the Hammers. Promotion to Division One brought out the best in him. He rose to the challenge magnificently, scoring 10 league and three cup goals. Ray thrived on responsibility and whenever Alvin Martin was absent, he assumed the captaincy with ease and a deep sense of pride. A natural leader, he was also prominent throughout the club's best-ever First Division campaign of 1985/86, finishing third top scorer with six - behind Frank McAvennie and Tony Cottee - as Hammers ran Merseyside

giants Liverpool and Everton to a photo-finish at the top. Although high on the all-time appearances list at West Ham, Ray would probably have topped 600 in the league but for the injury that almost threatened his career and severely restricted his appearances in his latter years with the club. Lyall's team were fighting a losing battle against relegation when, in the first half of the game at Derby County (14.1.89), he suffered an agonising injury - rupturing two of the four ligaments around his knee, including the main anteria cruciate ligament. Ray wouldn't listen to the medics who warned he may never play again. Instead, he called on his most determined characteristics to rebuild his shattered knee via a long and lonely rehabilitation programme. Some 14 months had passed when Ray made his first tentative comeback bid, in a reserve fixture at Arsenal (10.3.90). He played seven Combination League games in just a month, but it was too much too soon. A second operation was needed before another comeback attempt followed at the start of 1990/91 - his testimonial season at Upton Park. A hamstring strain added to Ray's frustration but he refused to throw in the towel and did at least manage to play a small part in Hammers' promotion campaign. New manager Billy Bonds recalled Ray for a vital Second Division match at Brighton (10.4.91) and he made four more league appearances as well as coming on as sub. in the ill-fated FA Cup semi-final v Nottingham Forest at Villa Park. Ray Stewart's last-ever game for West Ham United was in a 1-1 draw v Charlton Athletic at Selhurst Park (4.5.91). He didn't feel much like joining in the promotion celebrations, though. At 31, the normally ebullient Scot was saddened by the news that he would be released on a free transfer. When no playing or coaching offers materialised in the south, he returned to Scotland and joined St. Johnstone. Initially signing as a player, Ray also worked in a coaching capacity with the reserves and, making use of his extensive list of contacts and energy in the P.R. field, took up the community officer's role at McDiarmid Park. Hammers' fans of the 80's will no doubt remember Ray best for his unrivalled penalty record. He successfully converted 76 spot-kicks and missed only 10. Quite remarkable.

❏ *Scotland caps:* 1981 v Wales, Northern Ireland, England; 1982 v Northern Ireland, Portugal, Wales; 1984 v France; 1986 v Republic of Ireland, Luxembourg; 1987 v Republic of Ireland.

Played	League		FAC		LC		Europe		Total	
	App	Gls	App	Gls	App	Gls	App	Gls	App	Gls
1979-80	38	10	8	0	8	1	0	0	54	14
198-81	41	5	3	1	9	2	6	1	59	9
1981-82	42	10	2	0	5	3	0	0	49	13
1982-83	39	8	1	0	6	3	0	0	46	11
1983-84	42	7	4	1	5	1	0	0	51	9
1984-85	37	6	4	1	4	0	0	0	45	7
1985-86	39	6	6	1	3	3	0	0	48	10
1986-87	23	4	3	0	3	0	0	0	29	4
1987-88	33	4	2	0	0	0	0	0	35	4
1988-89	6	2	2	0	1	1	0	0	9	3
1990-91	5	0	1	0	0	0	0	0	6	0
TOTAL	345	62	36	7	44	14	6	1	431	84

Ray Stewart scores from the spot v Manchester United at Upton Park (above)...and again in an F.A. Cup fifth round replay at Old Trafford when Hammers won 2-0 in 1986 (left).

Tony Cottee runs to congratulate Ray as he celebrates another successful conversion (right).

Best wishes

Alan Taylor

Lancaster born Alan Taylor created his own little niche in Hammers history by scoring both goals in the 1975 FA Cup Final win over Fulham, having already netted a brace in both the quarter-final and semi-finals.

TATE, Isaac   1927-29

Born: Gateshead, Tyne & Wear
Lge apps: 14

■ Yet another signing from Newcastle United, he had impressed the West Ham management with his safe handling while keeping goal for the Magpies against Hammers. Known as "Ike" to his colleagues, he joined the Geordies at the age of 18 and had three years at St. James's Park before arriving at the Boleyn as understudy to the great Ted Hufton. His quest for regular first team football led to his transfer to Doncaster Rovers.

TAYLOR, Alan   1974-79

Born: Lancaster, Lancashire. 14.11.53
Lge apps: 98 (25 gls)
Cup apps: 25 (11 gls)

■ This speedy whippet-like striker made the transition from Fourth Division Rochdale in true Roy of the Rovers fashion, appearing in the 1975 Cup Final within six months of his transfer. Once rejected by Preston, he had drifted into non-League soccer with Lancaster and Morecambe before Rochdale gave him his chance. But as a West Ham player he hit the headlines. It was Alan's deadly finishing that got Hammers to Wembley. He scored twice in the sixth round victory over Arsenal at Highbury, poached another brace in the semi-final replay v Ipswich Town at Stamford Bridge, and did the same again in the Final against fighting Fulham. Although he played in the 1976 European Cup Winners' Final v Anderlecht in Belgium, his style of play made him very susceptible to injuries, which restricted his first team outings. Transferred to Norwich City in Aug. 1979, he later joined Cambridge United after a spell with Vancouver Whitecaps. Was given a free transfer by Hull City at the end of 1983/84 and then back in the claret and blue for a different cause with Burnley in June 1984. Later had a brief spell with Bury before making an amazing return to Division One with Norwich City in 1988/89. Was recently running his own milk round franchise at Scarning, Norfolk.

TAYLOR, Archie   1906-09

SL apps: 63
Cup apps: 7

■ Archie joined Hammers at the age of 25 from London rivals Brentford, making his Southern League debut v. Bristol Rovers at the Boleyn (15.10.06). Although that match was lost 1-0, the tough-tackling former Bristol Rovers and Bolton Wanderers left-back helped to tighten the

A. TAYLOR,
WEST HAM UNITED.

defence of a Hammers' team which finished a creditable fifth in the Southern League First Division that season. Archie moved to his home-town club Dundee in Mar. 1909, but later returned south to join Barnsley where he filled the number two spot in the 1912 FA Cup Final for the Yorkshire club who defeated West Bromwich Albion 1-0 in a replay at Bramall Lane, after a 0-0 draw at Crystal Palace. Later managed York City. Started with Dundee East Craigie as centre-half in the side which won the Dewar Shield, Forfarshire Cup and the East of Scotland Cup and also produced Sharp of Arsenal.

TAYLOR, Frank   1889-1902

SL apps (TIW): 14 (1 gl)
SL apps (WHU): 12 (4 gls)
Cup apps: 1 (1 gl)

■ The youngest player in Thames Ironworks' last Southern League team, Frank took over the left-wing spot following the tragic death of England international Harry Bradshaw on

Christmas Day, 1899. Tipped by the writer of the club's handbook to become "one of the finest outside-lefts in the kingdom," the former Harwich man served the old Ironworks and the new West Ham well enough, without rising to those somewhat rashly predicted heights.

TAYLOR, George   1938-56

Born: Wigan, Lancashire. 21.3.1920
Lge apps: 115
Cup: 3

■ One of Charlie Paynter's many signings from Midland club Gainsborough Trinity, the career of goalkeeper George at Upton Park was spent mainly as understudy to Ernie Gregory, although he did make 38 appearances in 1954/55 when the latter missed the whole season through injury. It was his reliability as a deputy which made Hammers reluctant to release him. His sound displays aroused the interest of other clubs, but every time he was set for a move Ernie was injured and George had to step in to fill the breach. He was nearing the veteran stage when he eventually left the Boleyn, seeing out his playing days with Southern League Sittingbourne. George died in Oct. 1983 at the age of 63. In addition to his first team matches, George played 231 times for the reserves.

TAYLOR, Tommy   1970-79

Born: Hornchurch, Essex. 26.9.1951
Lge apps: 340 (8 gls)
Cup apps: 56

■ His arrival from near-neighbours Orient in Oct. 1970 for a hefty fee, plus Peter Bennett as part of the deal, solved a long-standing defensive problem for Hammers. Tommy had caught the attention of a number of clubs in his auspicious start with the Brisbane Road outfit, during which time he helped the O's to promotion from Division Three and also captained the England Youth team. He was on the verge of full international recognition after winning no less than 13 Under-23 honours whilst with Hammers, albeit some of which were permissible under the ruling that allowed over-age players in the team. An integral member of the side which brought Cup success to Upton Park in the mid-70's, he returned to his former club in the summer of 1979 after losing his place to Alvin Martin. Later became youth coach

Tommy Taylor

for Charlton Athletic, after a spell in Belgium with Antwerp. He then spent three years in New Zealand football management before returning to fill a coaching post with Football League newcomers Maidstone United in 1989. He was recently in charge of the youth team at Cambridge United.

Played	League		FAC		LC		Europe		Total	
	App	Gls	App	Gls	App	Gls	App	Gls	App	Gls
1970-71	30	1	1	0	0	0	0	0	31	1
1971-72	42	0	4	0	10	0	0	0	56	0
1972-73	37	3	2	0	2	0	0	0	41	3
1973-74	40	0	2	0	2	0	0	0	44	0
1974-75	39	0	7	0	3	0	0	0	49	0
1975-76	42	2	0	0	5	0	9	0	56	2
1976-77	36	0	2	0	3	0	0	0	41	0
1977-78	42	2	3	0	0	0	0	0	45	2
1978-79	32	0	0	0	1	0	0	0	33	0
TOTAL	340	8	21	0	26	0	9	0	396	8

TAYLOR, William   1906-09

Born: Tyneside
SL apps: 63
Cup apps: 7

■ Bill made his SL debut for Irons in the 0-1 home defeat v Bristol Rovers (15.10.1906). He made only four appearances that season, but made the left-back position his own over the next two years before being superceded by Bob Fairman.

THIRLAWAY, William   1921-23

Born: Burham
Lge apps: 36 (2 gls)
Cup apps: 3

■ An outside-right signed from Unsworth Colliery, Billy made 33 Second Division appearances in 1921/22. But a subsequent loss of form saw his first team outings reduced to two in 1922/23, down to a solitary one game the next season - his last as a Hammer. He then joined Southend United where he made seven appearances at the beginning of 1924/25 in Division Three South. He then became a soccer nomad as he went on his travels with Luton Town, South Shields, Birmingham, Cardiff City (Mar. 1927), Tunbridge Wells Rangers (July 1930) and Unsworth Colliery (Aug. 1931).

W. THIRLAWAY
WEST HAM

THOMAS, Mitchell   1991-94

Born: Luton, Bedfordshire. 2.10.64
Lge apps: 38 (3 gls)
Cup apps: 9 (0 gls)

■ Arriving from rivals Tottenham, and as an expensive £500,000 replacement for injured crowd favourite Julian Dicks, Mitchell always had a lot to prove to Hammers' fans. He started reasonably well in the left-back spot and within weeks of making his debut v. Luton Town (17.8.91) - his first club - the tall, slim black defender delighted the Upton Park faithful by scoring the winner . . . against Spurs! Also on target v. Crystal Palace and Oldham Athletic and even after Dicks returned in Jan. 1992, Thomas kept his place by switching to midfield. After losing his way at White Hart Lane (where he was third choice left-back when Billy Bonds came in with his half-million pound offer), the gangling Thomas made 35 First Division appearances in his first season for Hammers. But they were difficult days at West Ham. Against a background of unrest on the terraces, where the fans were revolting against the club's ill-fated bond scheme, the team's miserable performances on the field culminated in relegation. As an out-of-form ex-Spurs player, the critics saw Thomas as an ideal scapegoat. He played just three more league games in 1992/92 (when Dicks was suspended) and never made the first team again after appearing v. Crewe Alexandra in the League Cup tie at Upton Park (23.9.92). Despite the club's efforts to try and recoup some of the money they paid for Thomas, there was little interest in him outside Luton, whose manager David Pleat initially took Thomas on loan before finally agreeing to buy him outright at a cut-price £50,000 in Mar. 1994. Pleat was in his first spell as Hatters' manager when Thomas joined the club from school and made his league debut - ironically, at Upton Park (4.1.83). And Pleat's first signing when he became manager of Tottenham, in 1986, was . . . Mitchell Thomas. He made 157 league appearances for Spurs and played left-back in the team defeated by Coventry City in the 1987 FA Cup Final.

THOMPSON, A   1903-04

SL apps: 10 (1 gl)

■ Arrived in mid-season from Middlesbrough, centre-forward Thommo had to wait until his third match in the claret and blue before scoring what proved to be his only goal for the club in the 4-1 Boleyn win over Wellingborough Town (30.1.1904). Was a colleague of Chris Carrick and Frank Piercy at 'Boro. Scored two goals in three outings for the Teessiders in 1902/03.

THORPE, Peter   1933-34

Born: Nottingham.
Lge apps: 3

■ An experienced right-back who had represented Nottingham Boys before graduating to League standard with Blackpool, Reading and Sheffield Wednesday, captaining the former and latter. He made his trio of Second Division appearances in quick succession v. Bolton Wanderers, Brentford and Plymouth Argyle at the start of the 1933/34 season.

TINDALL, Ron   1961-62

Born: Streatham, South London. 23.9.1935
Lge apps: 13 (3 gls)
Cup apps: 1

■ A stockily-built centre-forward who had a great goalscoring record with his first club, Chelsea. After a humble beginning as an office boy at Stamford Bridge, he went on to score 68 times in 160 first XI appearances for the Blues and won representative honours for the Football League v League of Ireland. Ron arrived at Upton Park in Nov. 1961 as part of the exchange deal which took Andy Malcolm in the opposite direction, scoring three goals in 13 outings that season. A first-class cricketer, his commitments to Surrey in their fight for the County Championship clashed with the start of the 1962/63 campaign. When they were finally resolved he decided to transfer to Third Division Reading to ensure regular first team soccer. After serving the Elm Park outfit well, he moved on again to Portsmouth in 1965, where he successfully converted to a defensive role. He made 162 League appearances for Pompey before taking up coaching appointments at Fratton Park, which culminated in him becoming general manager for the start of 1970/71. One of his first signings for the south coast club was former Hammer and cricketer, goalkeeper Jim Standen. The scorer of 5,000 runs and taker of 150 wickets for Surrey in the late 50's and early 60's, Ron left football for a time to manage a golf club at Watelooville, Hants. Ron later emigrated to Australia and was made director of coaching for Western Australia after settling in Perth at a place called Wembley! Ron now organises coaching programmes for the 107 sports officially recognised by Western Australia, a state which is 10 times bigger than the UK.

TIPPETT, Thomas   1933-35

Born: Gateshead, Tyne & Wear
Lge apps: 27 (10 gls)
Cup apps: 1

■ A goal-scoring outside-right who progressed through a number of Tyneside junior teams before turning pro for Craghead United in the North-Eastern League. It was only apt that this former blacksmith should sign for Hammers after spells with Doncaster

Thomas Tippett

Rovers, Rochdale, Port Vale and their Potteries neighbours, Stoke City. An all-round sportsman, his direct style of wing-play made him an able deputy for England international Johnny Morton.

TIRRELL, Alfred — 1913-15

SL apps: 7

■ A full-back transferred to Upton Park from Peterborough City (South Eastern League) during the cs of 1913. Made his debut Feb. 28, 1914 at Crystal Palace (2-1), his only appearance that season. Played six SL games in 1914/15. Turned out a few times during the war, mostly in 1918/19 when he was the most regular player with 30 appearances. Was still with the club when peace-time soccer resumed in 1919 but didn't play in any first team matches that year. Transferred to Luton Town in the cs 1920 and played in over 120 SL and FL games (six goals) up to the end of 1924/25.

Alfred Tirrell

TIRRELL, Patrick — 1908-09

Born: 1885
SL apps: 13 (1 gl)

■ Signed from Southern League rivals Northampton Town, Pat had the pleasure of scoring one of the goals which enabled Hammers to defeat his former Cobblers' team-mates 2-1 at Upton Park on 24.10.1908. Operating with equal efficiency at either right, or left-half, he got stuck on 13 appearances that season, his last as an Iron. Arrived at Upton Park during cs 1908. Already fully experienced having made 95 Southern League appearances for Northampton Town. Before Northampton he had a short spell at Kettering. At Northampton he was a team-mate of Herbert Chapman, who later managed Arsenal, and of James Frost, who preceded him to Upton Park by a couple of months. Tirrell played six times against the Hammers between 1905 and 1908, four times as a half-back. Turned out 14 times in Southern League games for West Ham in 1908/09 but was part of a huge clear-out at the end of that season.

TONNER, Arthur — 1933

Born: Glasgow, Scotland.
Lge apps: 1

■ Originally a goalkeeper in schools soccer, he was converted to full-back by his first junior club Stafford in the Tradeston and District League. His move to St. Anthony's - who had earlier provided forward Hughie Mills - led to his discovery by West Ham and his eventual move south. An apprentice sawyer before signing pro forms for Irons, he helped to cut down Forest in his only first team outing in the 5-2 Upton Park win over the Nottingham men in Sept. 1935.

Arthur Tonner

TRANTER, Walter — 1897-99

Born: Teesside
SL apps (TIW): 20

■ Said to have "rushed in where others feared to tread," Wally was left-back in the Thames Ironworks team which won the London League Championship in 1897/98, losing only one match in the process. A good story was told of his carrying off, in "error," the Dewar Shield amid high spirits at the League's presentation concert to honour the triumph. Appointed club captain, the Middlesbrough-born defender led Hammers to the Second Division championship of the Southern League, but surprisingly threw in his lot with the top section with Chatham the following season. He returned to the Memorial Grounds for 1900/01, although there is no record of his appearing at senior level for the new club, West Ham United. Later went to play in Northern Ireland for a Belfast club.

Don Travis

TRAVIS, Don — 1946-48

Born: Manchester. 21.1.1924
Lge apps: 5

■ Another centre-forward, Don holds the unique record of being the only Hammer to score four goals on both his reserve and first team debuts. To chart his amazingly chequered career we must go back to 1940, when he played for the first of his 12 clubs whilst still an amateur at the age of 15... Blackpool. His apprenticeship with the Seasiders was disrupted when he was called up for National Service with the Army in 1944, serving as a gunner in the Royal Artillery. It was around this time that he played for Plymouth Argyle, and was saddled with the nickname of "Sailor" after being wrongly reported as being in the Navy by the local press! He made his initial appearance for West Ham in a Combination match v. Chelsea Reserves in Sept. 1945, and scored his first quartet. No sooner had Charlie Paynter signed him for Hammers than he was whisked away and posted to Scotland with his unit, where he made guest appearances for St. Mirren and Cowdenbeath. It was whilst on leave in Feb. 1946 that Don made his first team bow against.... Plymouth Argyle. Apart from Don's feat of again scoring four, the match threw up another Hammers' record, winger Terry Woodgate scoring a hat-trick in seven minutes.

TRESADERN, Jack   1913-26

Born: Leytonstone, East London.
SL apps: 6 (0 gls)
Lge apps: 144 (5 gls)
Cup apps: 16 (0 gls)

■ Despite the intervention of two world wars, the first of which badly interrupted his playing career and the second his managerial progress, Jack Tresadern eventually made his mark in both spheres without gaining the honours his talents fully deserved. "Tres," as he was popularly known, joined Hammers from Barking in 1913 after helping that club win the London Senior Cup and South Essex League in 1911/12. Represented Essex and London and in 1912 scored one of the goals by which Barking defeated Brentford 3-2 in the London Challenge Cup. A former cashier with a firm of London ship repairers, he later ran a poultry farm in Essex. He began life at Upton Park as understudy to the great Tommy Randall in the left-half position. Although small in stature, his lack of physical attributes did not prevent him being commissioned to the Royal Garrison Artillery during WW1, along with future team-mate George Kay. Indeed, after the war and when he had won a regular first XI place, his robust play prompted his trainer and mentor Charlie Paynter to remark that it must have been Jack who inspired the maxim: "The bigger they are the harder they fall!" In his youth Jack captained his school team and also appeared in West Ham's English & Corinthian Shield XI's under Harry Earle, the father of famous Hammer, Stan Earle.

He had a trial with Southend United but elected to stay an amateur to join Barking. Jack's finest hours as a Hammer came in season 1922/23, when his sterling displays in Irons' promotion to the First Division and winning through to the first Wembley Cup Final, gained him well-deserved international recognition against Scotland. Jack had one of his rare off-days v. the Scots, however, and although England managed to draw the match at Hampden Park 2-2, Jack often recalled ruefully afterwards: "I was the best player Scotland had on the field." Even so, his off-colour performance against the Scots did not stop his inclusion in the England side which defeated Sweden in Stockholm the following month in a match when team-mate Billy Moore scored one of the goals in a 4-2 victory. In Oct. 1924, Jack swapped clubs when he transferred to Burnley before joining Northampton Town as player/manager, where he played with former Hammer colleague Percy Allen at the County Ground. Incidentally, it was around this time that Jack's career was running parallel with the aforementioned George Kay who had managed Southampton and later bossed Liverpool. In fact, it could be claimed the pair were the forerunners of the now famous West Ham managerial Academy. Jack later held the reins at Crystal Palace, Spurs (who gained promotion to the First Division under his guidance) and Plymouth Argyle. It was at the latter port of call that Jack Tresadern stood his greatest test of character... and came through with flying colours. When he took over at Home Park war clouds were already gathering on the horizon, but it would have been hard for anyone to imagine the extent of the devastation the forthcoming blitz was to have on the fortunes of Plymouth Argyle. It is now a recognised fact among football folk that had it not been for the efforts of "Tres," in somehow seeing the club through that nightmare transitionary season of 1945/46 and convincing the Football League legislators that the game was still a viable proposition at Plymouth, the Argyle would not be in existence today. It is said Jack had to literally scour the dockyards and local leagues on many occasions that campaign to raise a side. After saving the Pilgrims he later managed three Southern League clubs, Chelmsford City, Hastings United and Tonbridge - the latter of whom he was serving when he suffered a heart attack at his home in the town on Christmas Day, 1959, and died the following day at the age of 67.
❏ *England caps:* 1923 v. Scotland, Sweden.

Don Travis (*continued from overleaf*)

He also scored again the following match v. Portsmouth, seemingly saving it up for the Navy towns! A long post to the Middle East followed, and on his return he found competition for the number nine shirt from Sam Small, Frank Neary and Bill Stephens. Despite making another four Second Division appearances and scoring heavily for the reserves, he was somewhat surprisingly transferred to Southend United at the end of 1947/48. He played only once for the Essex club, however, before beginning a transfer trail across Northern England, taking in spells with Accrington Stanley, Crewe, Oldham, Chester and Oldham again. He returned South for one last taste of glory with Southern League Yeovil in 1959, being in their side which performed a giant-killing on his old employers, Southend. But his travels were still not over as he played for SL Trowbridge Town and Western League Dorchester Town after leaving Huish. Don Travis played five times for West Ham during the transitionary, regionalised Football League South tournament, scoring seven goals in 1945/46. These are not recognised in official Football League records, however.

TUCKER, Ken   1947-57

Born: London. 2.10.1925
Lge apps: 83 (31 gls)
Cup apps: 10

■ Ken's career had a sensational if somewhat unusual beginning in that he scored a hat-trick on his debut v. Chesterfield at Upton Park in Oct. 1947, and then did not score again for another four years (in 14 appearances during that period). A fast, powerful winger signed from Finchley, his scoring exploits in the reserves (73 goals in 191 matches) finally won him regular first team recognition in 1955/56. His success when scoring 15 in 37 appearances was due largely to his decision to change from part-time to full-time training. Ken transferred to Notts County in Mar. 1957, and later joined the enclave of ex-Hammers at Margate just after WW2. He went into the newsagents' and then the Licensed Victuallers' trade when he retired.

TURNER, Charlie   1938-39

Born: Athlone, Republic of Ireland.
Lge apps: 11

■ West Ham signed this experienced Republic of Ireland international centre-half from Southend United for extra defensive cover following the retirement of Jim Barrett. Although he was mainly the understudy to Dick Walker during his two seasons at Upton Park, he was capped five times by the Republic of Ireland over the same period to add to the nap hand he had already gained while with the Shrimpers. In the summer of 1939 Charlie transferred to Hartlepool United and after WW2 he returned to Ireland to manage League of Ireland club Shelbourne. He left Irish football to join Stalybridge Celtic and then moved to Leeds United before teaming up with Southend in cs 1935 and played 110 League and Cup matches for the Shrimpers.

❏ *Republic of Ireland caps: 1937 v Norway (2); 1938 v Czechoslovakia, Poland; 1939 v Hungary (5).*

TURNER, Cyril

1919-21

Lge apps: 7 (1 gl)

■ This right-back made his Hammers' debut v. Stoke City at the Victoria Ground on 27.9.1919. He was on duty again v. the Potters in the return fixture at the Boleyn Ground the following week, when a 1-1 draw went some way to avenging the earlier 2-1 defeat on the Staffordshire club's enclosure. The legendary Syd Puddefoot was Hammers' marksman on both occasions. It was Cyril who was the unlikely goalscoring hero in the next match, however, when deputising at centre-forward for "Puddey" (who was either injured or, more likely, on international duty) he scored the only goal of the game against Grimsby Town at Blundell Park.

TYLER, Dudley

1972-73

Born: Salisbury, Wiltshire. 21.9.44
Lge apps: 28 (1 gl)
Cup app: 1

■ Signed for £25,000 - a record at the time for a non-League player - largely on the strength of his performance against Hammers for Southern League Hereford during their historic FA Cup run of 1971/72. His rise to stardom was even more remarkable, taking into account a "hole in the heart" operation while he was still a junior player. Dud's brief sojourn at the Boleyn was made memorable despite the shortness of his stay. His return to Edgar Street and his former club was sweetened when they celebrated their newly-won League status with a thrilling FA Cup victory over West Ham in 1973/74 (after a draw at Upton Park). He retired from the game after sustaining an ankle injury in 1977.

Above: Dudley Tyler

Left: Ken Tucker

VAN DER ELST, Francois 1981-83

Born: Belgium
Lge apps: 62 (16 gls)
Cup apps: 8 (3 gls)

■ Most remembered for his stunning performance against Hammers in the European Cup Winners' Cup Final for Anderlecht at the ill-fated Heysel Stadium in 1976. West Ham signed their tormentor-in-chief and architect of their defeat for £400,000 from New York Cosmos six years later (Jan. 1982). His appearance for the Belgians that night versus his club-mates-to-be (although he could hardly have realised it at the time) was the first of a unique hat-trick of appearances in successive seasons in the final of that competition. "Frankie" was on the losing side v.Hamburg in 1977 and a winner again the following year v. WAC Austria. Also in the Anderlecht team which won the UEFA Super Cup v. Liverpool in 1978, Francois was an automatic choice for his country until his move to the States. His form at Upton Park saw him resurrect his international career, however, culminating in his appearance in the 1982 World Cup in Spain (where he had two outings as sub.). Made his Hammers' debut at Brighton (16.1.82) and after five goals in the second half of that campaign, he contributed a useful nine league and five cup goals as West Ham climbed to eighth position in the 1982/83 First Division. Considered by many to have been one move ahead of many of his colleagues at the Boleyn, it's doubtful if the brilliant Belgian would have returned to his own country with Lokeren so soon if his family had been able to settle here.

WADE, Don
1947-50

Born: Tottenham, London. 5.6.1926
Lge apps: 36 (5 gls)
Cup apps: 4 (2 gls)

■ A maker, rather than taker, of goals, this inside-forward was born near the Tottenham ground. It was West Ham who signed him as a pro, however, after he had played for Spurs' juniors and Edgware Town. Prominent in Army football, he made his Second Division baptism in 1947/48 v. Fulham after his demobilisation. An all-round sportsman, he also played on the wing on occasions. Moved to Bedford Town after his service with Hammers.

WADE, Reg
1929-32

Born: Ilford, Essex
Lge apps: 32
Cup apps: 1

■ Signed pro for Hammers in 1929, after gaining an FA Amateur Cup winners' medal with Ilford in that year's final v. Leyton at Highbury. Taking the step up to professionalism in his stride, he made his First Division debut in the left-back position in a 4-1 victory over Liverpool at Upton Park (18.1.29). His best run in the first team was in 1930/31 when he made 28 appearances. He transferred to Aldershot in 1932. Also had a spell with Millwall whom he joined from Barking in 1925, but failed to make the first team.

WADE, William
1929-32

Born: Jarrow. 22.3.1901
Lge apps: 16

■ Sometimes confused with his namesake and contemporary, fellow full-back Reg Wade. Bill was a big, beefy defender who came to Hammers from Preston North End. He had previously played as an amateur for Smith's High Docks, Bertram (in the South Shields Combination) and Jarrow (in the North-Eastern League). Mainly a reserve at the Boleyn, he returned North to join the newly-formed Wigan Athletic in 1932. Bill passed away at South Shields 23.8.1958.

WAGGOTT, David
1908-10

Born: 1885
SL apps: 10 (3 gls)
Cup apps: 1

■ Signed from West Stanley (North Eastern League) after having previously had experience with Wednesday (then without the Sheffield prefix). Made his SL bow for Irons in a 1-0 Boleyn Castle defeat v. Crystal Palace in his normal inside-left position, but the following season made his last two appearances at outside-left.

WAGSTAFFE, George
1909-10

Born: Bethnal Green, East London. 1887
SL apps: 3

■ Formerly with South Weald, Hammers signed this well built centre-half from Norwich City. Making his debut in a 4-2 reverse at Luton, he went on to make a trio of outings that season. Moved to Doncaster Rovers, then a Midland League club, in cs 1910.

WALDEN, George
1911-12

SL apps: 2

■ George was an amateur throughout his career who made occasional appearances in West Ham's South Eastern League XI and made two showings in the SL v. Watford (11.3.14) and Brentford (27.3.14). A right-winger with Clapton, he played in the Spotted Dog club's victorious FA Amateur Cup Final-winning team v. Bishop Auckland in 1915.

WALFORD, Steve
1983-87

Born: Highgate, North London. 5.1.1958
Lge apps: 115 (2 gls)
Cup apps: 14

■ A £165,000 buy from Norwich City, where he had proved his predigree in over 100 league appearances, at the beginning of 1983/84. Steve settled in well at left-back. Once on the Upton Park staff as a junior, he broke into league football with Spurs in 1975/76, but played only two league games at The Lane. Followed manager Terry Neill to Arsenal in 1977 and gained experience in all defensive and midfield roles while clocking up almost 100 league and cup outings with the Gunners. A very economical player, he used the ball with telling effect and stunned his team-mates by scoring a spectacular only goal of the match v. Everton at Goodison Park (29.8.1983) in only his second game for Hammers. He went on to perform

Steve Walford

consistently well in 129 league and cup games in the old First Division until losing his place to George Parris midway through the club's most successful season to date - 1985/86. Had loan spells at Huddersfield Town (where he played in Terriers' record 1-10 Second Division defeat v. Man. City, (7.11.1987), Gillingham and West Bromwich Albion before being given a free by West Ham. In 1989 Steve joined the Lia Sun club of Hong Kong, but after playing in Turkey he returned to the UK with Wycombe Wanderers. In Mar. 1992 he joined Wealdstone on loan.

WALKER, Albert
1932-37

Born: Little Lever, Lancashire
Lge apps: 162
Cup apps: 12

■ This stout-hearted defender began his playing career amid humble beginnings in his native Lancashire during the late 1920's. Signing

Albert Walker

memorable partnership with Alf Chalkley. After six season's sterling service with Irons (he was an ever-present in the side which finished third in the Second Division in 1934/35), the former engineer returned north again in 1938 to sign for Doncaster Rovers. But after spending the war years in the National Fire Service, he moved back south to join Colchester United, then the talk of the football world for their daring FA Cup exploits as a Southern League outfit. Albert linked up again with former West Ham and England wing-half, Ted Fenton (then in charge at Layer Road and later to succeed Charlie Paynter as Hammers' manager in 1950). In 1952 Ted duly asked Albert to join him at Upton Park as coach to the Metropolitan League side. Coming up through the ranks as he had done as a player, he took charge in turn of the Eastern Counties League XI, the reserves in the Football Combination and was finally attached to the first team. Albert retired in 1980 after 34 years combined service as player and coach. He passed away in Apr. 1993, aged 83.

amateur forms for Southport after progressing from his school side to Little Lever United in the Bolton & District League, Albert spent just over a year at Haig Avenue before making an exciting move to First Division Bolton Wanderers. Alas, his initial taste of the big-time with Wanderers, already well-served at full-back by Haworth and Finney, was a brief one. Twelve months later he had exchanged the wide open spaces of Burnden Park for the more cramped confines of Barrow's Holker Street in the old Third Division North. But again it was only a short stay, for with Barrow unable to pay his wages, Albert could hardly refuse when Hammers' scout Ned Liddell arranged for him to travel south to join West Ham for a bargain fee in the summer of 1932. Newly-relegated to the Second Division, Hammers struggled at the start of 1932/33, as the previous season's disastrous form began to spill into the next. Changes were called for, and the likeable Lancastrian made his debut in a 5-2 victory over Oldham Athletic at Upton Park to begin a

WALKER, Charlie 1936-39

Born: Nottingham
Lge apps: 110
Cup apps: 8

■ Reckoned in the club handbook for 1938/39 to be one of the best left-backs ever to don the claret and blue, Charlie was signed from Arsenal in 1936 after finding his first team opportunities limited at Highbury by the outstanding presence of England captain Eddie Hapgood. He had no selection worries at Upton Park, and soon settled down to form a memorable full-back partnership with Charlie Bicknell. Indeed, the pair missed only two matches between them in the last pre-war season of 1938/39, and were on duty at Wembley in June 1940 when West Ham

annexed the Football League War Cup. Charlie played in all but one of the ties leading up to that triumph and went on to compete in 38 further war-time fixtures before signing up for the RAF. He returned after an extended tour of duty in the Far East in time to participate in the first peace-time season of 1945/46 in the 22-club Football League South, which comprised pre-war First and Second Division clubs. He played in 21 of that season's fixtures, but after appearing in an exciting 3-3 draw v Wolves at Molineux, departed to join the club he had left to sign for Arsenal before the conflict, Kent League Margate Town, as secretary/manager - under the proviso that he could play for the Kent club as long as his league rights were retained by West Ham.

WALKER, Dick 1934-53

Born: Hackney, London. 22.7.1913
Lge apps: 292 (2 gls)
Cup apps: 19

■ A name indelibly written into the history of West Ham United in an association which spanned three decades and almost 600 matches in all competitions. Despite being born near the famous Hackney Marshes, Dick Walker was a comparatively late starter for a footballer - especially as he was destined to become one of the most famous of all club servants. It wasn't until he moved with his family to Dagenham that Dick took up the game seriously, playing for the local Becontree Athletic as an inside-forward on Sunday mornings. It was in that role he was spotted by one of the club's scouts and brought to Upton Park for an extended trial. He played half-a-dozen or so games in the London Mid-Week League during the 1932/33 season, but signed at the end of that campaign for West London club Park Royal, the birthplace, incidentally, of former Hammers' star Alan Devonshire. However, after actually playing for the Royals against West Ham at the Boleyn, the club brought him back to the fold to begin an association which was to span more than two decades. Dick made his first XI debut as right-half v. Burnley at Upton Park in Aug. 1934, and filled a number of defensive positions before finally taking over from the redoubtable Jim Barrett at centre-half in 1936. Had it not been for the war it is highly probable that he would have been capped for England and also challenged Jimmy Ruffell's appearance record for Hammers. A ready wit and practical joker, his leave from the Paras during war-time to play the occasional match for Hammers was always accompanied by speculation as to what rank he would hold, fluctuating as it did in those days between Private and Sergeant with alarming regularity! There's no doubt, however, that he was as professional as a soldier as he was a footballer, often being mentioned in military dispatches. After WW2, and when things had returned to near normality, it was Dick who was elected to take up the team captaincy following the retirement of Charlie Bicknell. When his own career neared its end and he was no longer an automatic choice, he switched his attention to helping the younger players with the same enthusiasm as before. It must have been a sad departure from first team football for Dick when he made his last Second Division appearance, before one of the lowest crowds ever to assemble for a League match at Upton Park, v. Plymouth Argyle in Feb. 1953. Hammers lost 0-1, but Dick turned in his usual immaculate performance, earning the respect of every one of the 8,000 attendance. It was to be another four years before he hung up his boots completely, continuing to chalk up another 200-plus appearances for the reserves and "A" team until the end of 1956/57. He was given a well-deserved testimonial match in Oct. 1957. Became coach to Dagenham and later a full-time

Dick Walker

WALLBANKS, Fred 1935

Born: Wigan, Lancashire. 1909
Lge apps: 0
Cup apps: 1

■ One of the six famous footballing brothers who played league soccer in the 30's and 40's, Fred had a brief but unusual sojourn at Upton Park, making his solitary first team appearance in an FA Cup tie. An aspiring left-half with his local Chopwell Boys while at school, the versatile Lancastrian converted to the centre-forward position when he went to live in the North-East, and enjoyed successs in that role with Spen Black & Whites and later Consett in the North-Eastern League. His next port of call was with legendary amateurs Crook Town, with whom he gained further experience as an inside-forward in the Northern League before signing pro forms with Bury. After a spell with Chesterfield, Fred went back to non-league fare with Scarborough, where his 34 goals in one season again attracted league clubs. Bradford City duly signed the young sharp-shooter, but converted him to the full-back berth. By now a recognised utility player, he travelled south to join West Ham in Dec. 1934, and made his first appearance in the claret and blue against Brighton reserves at Upton Park two days before Christmas in a 4-0 win. The following month Ted Fenton was injured in a home third round FA Cup tie with Stockport County, and Fred was drafted into the side at right-half for the replay after the Cheshire club's shock 1-1 draw at the Boleyn. Worse was to follow at Edgeley Park, with Hammers being dumped out of the competition in true giant-killing fashion. It was Fred's first and last senior outing and at the end of the season he transferred to Nottingham Forest. One of six footballing brothers: James Wallbanks played for Norwich City, Northampton Town, Wigan Athletic, Millwall and Reading; Horace Wallbanks for Aberdeen and Luton; Harold Wallbanks for Fulham, Southend United and Workington Town; and John Wallbanks for Barnsley, Chester and Bradford City; while an adopted brother, surname Harvey, also played for Barnsley.

WARD, Mark 1985-89

Born: Prescot, Lancashire. 10.10.62
Lge apps: 165 (12 gls)
Cup apps: 38 (2 gls)

■ Bargain signing from Oldham Athletic in the summer of 1985, Mark cost only £225,000 initially plus £25,000 more after his 25th appearance. Diminutive, though very competitive, right-winger, the tenacious "Wardie" made his debut at Birmingham City (17.8.85) and went on to play a prominent part in Hammers' most successful-ever First Division season. Although never a regular goalscorer himself, his ferocious shooting made him especially dangerous from set pieces, while his crosses created plenty of chances and goals for strikers Frank McAvennie and Tony Cottee. Mark made many of his runs from deep positions and showed a willingness to work back in

member of Spurs' scouting staff for many years. Dick's later life was an unhappy one, beset as he was with ill-health which required him to spend long spells in hospital. His death, in Feb. 1988 at the age of 75, represented a sad demise for a man whose greatest legacy was the help he gave to young players making their way in the game.

Played	League		FAC		LC		Europe		Total	
	App	Gls	App	Gls	App	Gls	App	Gls	App	Gls
1934-35	3	0	0	0	0	0	0	0	3	0
1935-36	2	0	0	0	0	0	0	0	2	0
1936-37	27	0	2	0	0	0	0	0	29	0
1937-38	32	0	1	0	0	0	0	0	33	0
1938-39	38	0	5	0	0	0	0	0	43	0
1945-46	0	0	4	0	0	0	0	0	4	0
1946-47	34	0	1	0	0	0	0	0	35	0
1947-48	39	1	1	0	0	0	0	0	40	1
1948-49	40	1	1	0	0	0	0	0	41	1
1949-50	39	0	2	0	0	0	0	0	41	0
1950-51	33	0	2	0	0	0	0	0	35	0
1951-52	4	0	0	0	0	0	0	0	4	0
1952-53	1	0	0	0	0	0	0	0	1	0
TOTAL	292	2	19	0	0	0	0	0	311	2

WALKER, Len 1900-01

SL apps: 1

■ Len made only one SL appearance for West Ham, playing at inside-left in the 2-0 defeat at Bristol Rovers' Eastville enclosure (24.11.1901). He joined Brentford in 1903.

WALLACE, J 1901-03

SL apps: 17 (3 gls)

■ This inside-forward made his initial Irons appearance in the 3-0 defeat at Reading (23.11.1901) in the number eight shirt. It was the only SL game he played that season. The following term he switched to the inside-left berth and had a 16-match run in the first team in which he scored three goals, the most notable of which was the only goal of the match v Spurs at the Memorial Grounds. He joined Luton Town with Billy Barnes during the cs 1904.

Mark Ward in action against Nottingham Forest

support of his full-back - usually Ray Stewart. But after McAvennie left for Celtic in 1987 and Cottee joined Everton a year later, Ward, too, became unsettled, particularly when West Ham were relegated at the end of 1988/89 and manager John Lyall got the sack. It was not long before Mark - sometimes fiery on the field - clashed with new manager Lou Macari. Their dispute came to a head in Oct. 1989 when Wardie missed the team coach travelling to Aston Villa for a midweek League Cup tie and the PFA were called into mediate. Although Mark resumed his place in the side for a handful of games, he was determined to get away from Upton Park. His last appearance for the club came at Ipswich Town on Boxing Day, 1990. Four days later he was back north making his debut for Manchester City after new Maine Road boss Howard Kendall had agreed a £1 million-rated swap deal that took Ian Bishop and Trevor Morley to Upton Park. Ward was only with City for 18 months and 55 league matches, though, before he was on the move again - this time back to his native Merseyside to join Everton for £1.1m. Ironically, Wardie had been overlooked by the Everton management while on Goodison books as a schoolboy. He drifted into non-league football with Northwich Victoria, who sold him to Oldham for £10,000 in July 1983. Now Everton were paying 100 times that figure to bring him back to Goodison! Two-and-a-half seaons on and Mark had lost his way at a club in turmoil. Ambitious Birmingham City signed him on loan in Mar. 1994 to help boost their Second Division promotion bid. He played nine league games for Barry Fry, who saw enough in the little scouser to splash out £500,000 on him the following August.

WARD T.G. 1901-02

Cup apps: 1

■ Usually a centre-forward, this player made his solitary appearance for Hammers in the infamous 2-1 FA Cup defeat v. Grays at the Memorial Grounds (16.11.1901), playing on the right-wing. Joined West Ham from Ilford (14.9.1901).

WATSON, George 1932-35

Born: Forest Gate, East London. 1907
Lge apps: 33
Cup apps: 5

■ George began his football career as a bustling centre-forward with his local junior side, Whycliffe Albion, scoring 69 goals for that club when they won the Forest Gate and District League championship. Despite this success, it was when

George joined his next club, Abbey Langthorne Works team, that he realised his true ambition - to be a goalkeeper! Proving to be as efficient at stopping goals as he had been at scoring them, he came to Hammers as an amateur during the 1929/30 season, and after being sent back to Ilford to gain experience, was signed as a pro. Given the unenviable task of replacing Ted Hufton after the latter had transferred to Watford following Hammers' relegation to Division Two in 1932, George did well in his initial season as a first team regular and was in the side which reached that year's FA Cup semi-finals. A good swimmer, he won the "White" Cup for the Hammers' club championship three years running.

WATSON, Lionel 1905-08

Born: Southport, Lancashire. 1881
SL apps: 76 (26 gls)
Cup apps: 4 (1 gl)

■ Joined Hammers with Harry Hindle and Fred Blackburn from Blackburn Rovers (cs 1905) in an Edwardian version of Billy Bonds' triple transfer swoop of more recent times. Watson had a good scoring record with the Lancastrians prior to moving south, scoring four goals in 14 First Division games in 1904/05 and was Rovers' leading scorer with 16 tallies from 31 starts in 1903/04. He maintained a similar scoring rate at Upton Park after making his debut there v. Swindon Town (2.9.1905). An infant prodigy who had won three soccer medals before the age of 10, he began his career in earnest with Southport Central. Later moved to Manchester City, but retained his amateur status while with the Mancunians. A great practical joker, he signed pro with Blackburn.

George Watson

WATSON, Victor   1921-35

Born: Girton, Cambridgeshire. 10.11.1897
Lge apps: 462 (298 gls)
Cup apps: 43 (28 gls)

■ Of all the great centre-forwards who have worn the number nine shirt for West Ham Utd over the years, Vic Watson stands out as the finest. Spotted playing for Wellingborough Town having earlier turned out for Girton, Cambridge Town, Peterborough and Fletton United and Brotherhood Engineering Works, he was duly signed for a £50 transfer fee in Mar. 1920, to give cover for the then leader Sydney Puddefoot. Vic later became as big a star as the man he was to replace so dramatically when the latter signed sensationally for Falkirk. Scoring on his first team debut from the inside-left position v. Port Vale at Upton Park in Sept. 1921, he was a former Army Sgt. Instructor during WW1. Vic even played three games at outside-left over the Christmas holiday fixtures before claiming the centre-forward spot when Syd moved north of the border. From then on the goals and honours followed thick and fast, with his 22 League goals being largely responsible for Hammers' promotion to the First Division, and five counters in the FA Cup contributing likewise to the club's appearance in the first Wembley Cup Final during that doubly-memorable 1922/23 season. Capped for England v. Wales and Scotland, he had no trouble keeping up his scoring rate in the First Divison, notching over 200 goals during nine seasons in the top flight. The highlight of those gala years came on a rain-lashed afternoon in an unforgettable 8-2 thrashing of Leeds United at Upton Park (9.2.1929), when Vic scored six times against the hapless Yorkshiremen. Inexplicably overlooked by England, still the selectors remained unmoved, but a club record

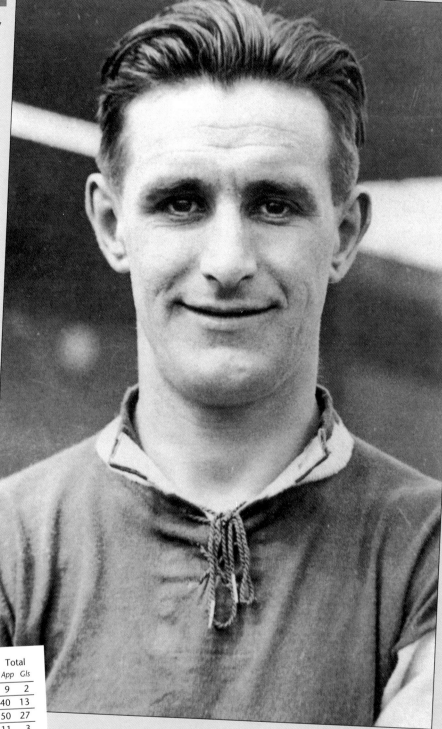

Played	League		FAC		LC		Europe		Total	
	App	Gls	App	Gls	App	Gls	App	Gls	App	Gls
1920-21	9	2	0	0	0	0	0	0	9	2
1921-22	37	12	3	1	0	0	0	0	40	13
1922-23	41	22	9	5	0	0	0	0	50	27
1923-24	11	3	0	0	0	0	0	0	11	3
1924-25	41	22	6	1	0	0	0	0	47	23
1925-26	38	20	1	0	0	0	0	0	39	20
1926-27	42	34	3	3	0	0	0	0	45	37
1927-28	33	16	2	0	0	0	0	0	35	16
1928-29	34	29	5	1	0	0	0	0	39	30
1929-30	40	42	4	8	0	0	0	0	44	50
1930-31	18	14	0	0	0	0	0	0	18	14
1931-32	38	23	2	2	0	0	0	0	40	25
1932-33	35	23	6	4	0	0	0	0	41	27
1933-34	30	26	2	3	0	0	0	0	32	29
1934-35	15	10	0	0	0	0	0	0	15	10
TOTAL	462	298	43	28	0	0	0	0	505	326

42 First Division goals the following season saw him back in an England shirt in 1930. The six-goal blast against Leeds apart, Vic scored four goals in a match on three separate occasions, and tallied an astonishing 13 hat-tricks during his Hammers' career. Transferred to Southampton in 1935, where he scored on his debut v. Swansea Town (31.8.36) and 14 times in 37 League and Cup games. He had one season with Saints before retiring to grow tomatoes and cucumbers in his native Cambridgeshire - after a brief spell as trainer/ coach with Cambridge City after the war... no doubt to the accompanied relief of defences throughout football. Described by a contemporary scribe: "Dashing centre-forward whose tactic was to persistently harass the opposing defence." Vic died on 3.8.1988 at the age of 91.

❑ *England caps: 1923 v Wales, Scotland; 1930 v Scotland, West Germany, Austria. (5).*

WATTS, Ernest   1903-04

SL apps: 25 (1 gl)
Cup apps: 4 (1 gl)

■ Joined Hammers from Reading, but prior to his time with the Berkshire club served Notts County in the Football League. Made skipper of Irons in 1903/04 season, the last at the Memorial Grounds and also his with the club, as he joined New Brompton for 1904/05. A sterling centre-half and an ex-soldier, Watts played for the Royal Berks Regiment Cricket XI and held an RHS certificate for life-saving. Took part in the North v. South match of 1903.

WAUGH, R.   1922

■ Previously with amateur side Bedlington United, this right-back made his Second Division baptism for Hammers in a 2-1 defeat v. Leicester City at Filbert Street (14.1.1922), and went on to complete half-a-dozen league appearances in the claret and blue.

WEALE, Robert   1925-26

Born: Troedyrhiw, Wales. 9.11.1903
Lge apps: 3

■ A former Welsh Schoolboy international, this tricky outside-right filled the place vacated by Bill Edwards in the London Combination side when the latter stepped up to the first team. Signed from his home town team, Troedyrhiw, Bob was later given a taste of First Division football, but after marking up his debut v. Notts County (10.10.25), made only two further league appearances before joining Swindon in June 1927. His form must have improved dramatically at the County Ground, for in Dec. 1928 Southampton paid a club record fee of £1,000 to take him to The Dell. Despite scoring a hat-trick soon after his arrival, he failed to live up to expectations, however, and after a dispute over terms and making 48 league and cup appearances, scoring 10 goals, he decided to move back to his native Wales with Cardiff City in Aug. 1930. But he didn't stay long at Ninian Park, playing for Boston Town and Guildford City in 1931, before moving on to Newport County in 1932, making 26 League appearancess, and the next year he was in North Wales with Wrexham, where he had 23 League outings. He continued life as a soccer journeyman, playing for Glentoran in 1935 and Bath City the following year. His younger brother Tom also played league soccer before the war with Cardiff City and Crewe. Bobby died at Merthyr Tydfil in 1970.

WEBB, George   1908-12

Born: Poplar, East London. 1888.
SL apps: 52 (23 gls)
Cup apps: 10 (9 gls)

■ Rightly revered as the first West Ham United player to win a full international cap for England, centre-forward George was selected for his country v. Scotland and Wales in 1911 - a busy year for the famous amateur in terms of representative honours. "Amateur centre-forward and a power in the land in the pre-1914 era. Fast, had a great shot while hefty physique made him even more redoubtable." So described by a football historian from a later era. Honoured at English Amateur international level in 1910 v. Switzerland, four times the following year v. Wales, Belgium, Germany, Holland and Denmark, and Holland in 1912. He joined team-mate Danny Shea and George Kitchen in representing the Southern League v. Irish League in 1911. Born and bred in the East End of London, he first showed his talent with his Shaftsbury Road School side before graduating to the local Ilford Alliance and then on to the renowned Wanstead club. Attending a pre-season trial match at Upton Park in Aug. 1905 at the age of 18, he impressed sufficiently to be given a run out in the reserves v. Reading, but had to wait another three years for his full Southern League debut, when he scored the only goal of the match against the then powerful Leyton side at Upton Park. The stepson of George Hone, an early administrator of TIW and a director of West Ham, he was well connected in business circles as a toy manufacturer and freemason. He hung on to his jealously-guarded amateur status throughout his career, even after an ill-fated taste of Football League soccer with Manchester City, whom he joined in July 1912, and played for City in their two opening games of the season - both 1-0 wins away to Notts County and deadly rivals Manchester United. While out of the side injured, Webb was horrified to learn that a transfer fee had been paid for his services and promptly "resigned" from City. Not only was there a cash payment, but the deal also led to the first ever meeting between the two sides, a friendly being staged at Upton Park in Nov. 1912. City won 4-2. Despite his reluctance to relinquish his amateur status and a tendency to put his business interests before football, George impressed many of the 'old school' by refusing to allow the lure of professionalism to weaken his corinthian spirit and it came as a great shock to all at the Boleyn Grounds when he died of consumption at the age of 28.3.1915.
❏ *England caps:* 1911 v Wales, Scotland (2).

WEARE, Arthur J. ("Jack")   1936-38

Born: Newport, Wales. 21.9.1912
Lge apps: 58
Cup apps: 2

■ A fine custodian whose youngest brother, Len, made 524 League appearances between 1955 and 1969 for Newport County. Jack began his career with Lovells Athletic before signing pro forms for Wolves in 1933/34 season, from where he joined Hammers. A healthy 35 Second Division outings in 1936/37 was followed by a further 23 in 1937/38. But the following season the agile Welshman lost the first team spot to Herman Conway and Harry Medhurst, who each made 21 appearances in the last pre-war League programme. After the war Jack played a further 141 games for Bristol Rovers before retiring to let young Len carry on the family trade of football. Jack joined the RAF for his war-time service and reached the rank of Sergeant as well as becoming a qualified physical training instructor. During service in the UK he played as a guest for Bournemouth, Bristol Rovers, Hibernian and St. Mirren. Whilst with Saints he played in the side which defeated Glasgow Rangers in the Scottish Summer Cup at Hampden Park 1-0, having beaten Greenock Morton in the semi-final who included Sir Stanley Matthews and Tommy Lawton in their line-up. Later during the conflict he was posted to India where he met up with his former-Hammers team mate, full-back Charlie Walker. The pair were selected to play for England v. Scotland (the selectors didn't realise Jack was a Welshman!) at Irwin Stadium, New Delhi and after the game were presented with trophies by Lord Louis Mountbatten then Vice-Roy of India. In 1952 he emigrated to South Africa and worked for a food processing company in Estcourt Natal. Then in 1957 he applied for a job in Rhodesia (then Salisbury) and was a production manager there until he retired in 1987. Jack is now living in Harare, Zimbabwe.

WEBSTER, Joe   1914-20

Born: Nottingham, 1883.

■ A goalkeeper who had served the club from Southern League days, he made two Second Division appearances as deputy for Ted Hufton, v. Huddersfield Town and Port Vale respectively at Upton Park in season 1919/20. He joined Hammers from Watford in 1914 and played in the first 17 fixtures of 1914/15. In 1912/13 Watford were fined by the SL authorities for failing to forward Webster's name at the start of the season. Was a colleague of the famous Spurs and England international, Arthur Grimsdell, in his Watford days. Began his career with his local club Ilkeston and had three years active service in France in WW1 and played with the 'Footballers Battallion.' Re-joined Hammers after the Armistice but went back to Watford as trainer after one season. He died at Northampton (15.10.27).

WEBSTER, Simon   1993-

Born: Earl Shilton, Leicestershire. 20.1.64

■ This commanding central defender is still anxiously awaiting his first team debut for Hammers - 16 months after joining the club from Charlton Athletic for £525,000. His absence from the senior side has nothing to do with form - only a cruel injury blow. "Webbo" had been with Hammers for just 14 days in July 1993 when he suffered a broken leg in a pre-season training accident involving Julian Dicks. It was the second time in his career that Simon has had to battle back from a broken leg, having suffered a similar injury while with Sheffield United. He had arrived at Bramall Lane in Mar. 1988 from Huddersfield Town, who collected a £35,000 fee, having previously signed him for a mere £15,000 from Tottenham in Feb. 1985. The former White Hart Lane apprentice appeared in three first team matches, making his Spurs' debut v. . . . . West Ham at Upton Park (1.1.83)! How unlucky Simon would love to be playing Premiership football there again. He did manage a comeback in Apr. 1994, playing 12 Combination matches until the end of the season. But he was still troubled by the leg in pre-season friendlies and his frustration was compounded early in the 1994/95 season when his ankle had to be plastered. While on the long road to recovery, Simon has been spending his spare time taking A-level human biology with a view to becoming a physiotherapist.

WELDON, Anthony   1931-32

Lge apps: 20 (3 gls)
Cup apps: 2 (1 gl)

■ Tony Weldon began his career with Scottish junior side Kilsyth Rangers before moving on to Airdrieonians for the princely sum of £5 in Dec. 1924. At Broomfield Park he succeeded in turn two full Scottish internationals in Willie Russell and Hughie Gallacher, until a thumping £2,000 transfer to Everton in Mar. 1927. His partnership with fellow compatriot Alex Troup made a major contribution to the Toffeemen's league championship success the following

Simon Webster

Joe Webster

year. In June 1930 he was on his travels again when a £1,000 fee took him to Hull City, where he made 31 League appearances and scored six goals, before joining West Ham in June 1931. He battled bravely on Hammers' behalf in 20 league appearances during the disappointing 1931/32 campaign. In the following close season he moved on again, this time to Welsh side Lovell's Atheltic, serving his by now customary year's stint, then transferring to Rochdale in the summer of 1933. The following summer he joined Dundalk as player/coach, and late in 1934 was appointed player/manager of Bangor (Northern Ireland), thus becoming one of the few players to play for clubs in England, Northern Ireland, Scotland, Republic of Ireland and Wales. Incidentally, Tony is the father-in-law of former Leeds United centre-forward Jim Storrie.

WHITBREAD, Adrian   1994-

Born: Epping, Essex. 22.10.71

■ Arrived from newly-relegated Swindon Town in Aug. 1994, just after the start of the season, in part-exchange for the beleaguered Joey Beauchamp, who was relieved to be heading for the Wiltshire club without even making a competitive appearance for Hammers. For this powerful central defender it was a case of returning to his East London roots. Adrian began his promising career with near-neighbours Leyton Orient, whom he had captained at the age of 21 and made 125 league appearances prior to his £500,000 transfer to Swindon in July 1993. With the veteran Alvin Martin and Steve Potts already occupying the central defensive positions at West Ham, Adrian started the 1994/95 term on the subs' bench. He got on for the last 21 minutes of the opening home game v Leeds United (20.8.94) and made his first full appearance in the 2-0 League Cup, second round (second leg), win over Walsall at Upton Park (5.10.94), collecting the sponsor's man-of-the-match award in the process.

WHITCHURCH, Charlie 1944-46

Born: Grays, Essex. 29.10.1920

■ Charles joined Hammers from Portsmouth as an amateur left-winger in the 1944/45 season, after beginning his career with Ford Sports before WW11 and making guest appearances for Charlton and Southend United during the conflict, signing pro the following summer. Although he had left Upton Park for Spurs before full League football was resumed in 1946/47, he was a regular member of the side which competed in the Football League South tournament during the first post-war season of 1945/46. After scoring twice in eight appearances for Tottenham, the former English Schoolboy international moved on to Southend United, where he scored a further five times in 17 outings for the Shrimpers before bowing out of league football in 1948. Employed at the Ford Motor Company in Dagenham, he continued to play for their works team until he emigrated to Canada in 1951. Charlie passed away in July 1977 in Michigan, USA, where he was involved in rocket research with General Motors.

WHITEMAN, Robert 1909-15

SL apps: 136 (3 gls)
Cup apps: 10

■ In common with George Wagstaff, Bob also served South Weald and Norwich City, and was by far the most successful of several signings made by Hammers from the Norfolk club. Counting his 10 FA Cup outings and four appearances in the first war-time season, he made exactly 150 appearances for the club. A fine total for the times, and nearly all from the right-half berth. Described as "a consistent performer, a good interceptor with no frills." Played locally for Manor Park Albion before joining South Weald.

Adrian Whitbread

WHITTON, Steve   1983-86

Born: Plaistow, London. 4.12.1960
Lge apps: 39 (6 gls)
Cup apps: 7 (2 gls)

■ Although he was born in the East End of London and played for Newham Boys, Steve decided he would have a better chance of advancement with Coventry City than a London club, signing apprentice for the Midlanders in Apr. 1977. Signed as full pro the following year, he duly made his First Division debut v. Spurs in 1979. A flankman of great power and pace, he really came into his own in 1982/83, and was the Highfield Road club's top scorer with 12 goals in 38 league matches. He signed for Hammers for £175,000 in the summer of 1983, making his first team bow in the initial fixture v. Birmingham City. Had a period on loan to Birmingham during the 1985/86 season and joined the Blues for £60,000 in Aug. 1986, playing 95 League games and scoring 28 goals before moving on to Sheffield Wednesday in Mar. 1989 for £275,000, where he played 32 times scoring four goals. In Jan. 1991 he teamed up with former manager and coach, John Lyall, and Mick McGiven at Ipswich Town in a £150,000 deal. Steve made 130 League appearances for Town and scored 23 goals before joining Colchester United in Mar. 1994 for £10,000.

Steve Whitton

WILDMAN, William   1906-08

Born: Liverpool. 1883
SL apps: 39
Cup apps: 2

■ Bill played two seasons with his local Queens Road team before joining Everton. He had four seasons at Goodison Park before signing for Hammers in 1906. Missed just one match in his first season at Boleyn Castle playing at right-back, but an unfortunate injury sustained in the second match of the 1907/08 season v. Spurs effectively ended his career in the claret and blue.

W. WILDMAN,
WEST HAM UNITED.

WILLIAMS, Harry   1951-52

Born: Salford, Lancashire. 24.2.1929
Lge apps: 5 (1 gl)

■ Discovered by Manchester United during an England Youth trial game, he spent a little under a year at Old Trafford without playing in the league side. Left them to join Cheshire League Witton Albion, where his exploits aroused the interest of West Ham. After scoring heavily for the "A"team and Combination side, the young inside-forward was drafted into the first XI for his debut v. Rotherham at Millmoor in Oct. 1951. He made another four appearances that season and scored a goal v. Southampton, that being the sum total of his Second Division outings for Hammers. Transferred to Bury in 1953, and from there to Swindon Town the following year.

WILLIAMS, Ron   1937-38

Born: Wandsworth, London.
Lge apps: 9 (5 gls)
Cup apps: 1

■ This robust centre-forward cracked five goals in nine Second Division appearances for West Ham in the 1937/38 season underlining the availability of goalscorers in those days. Previously with Reading, he made his initial appearance in Hammers' colours in a 0-0 draw with Coventry (13.11.37) at the Boleyn after signing for £4,000, and proved an able stand-in for Sam Small. In the summer of 1938 he transferred to near-neighbours Clapton Orient, and was O's top scorer with 17 goals in 1938/39. Before

joining Reading, Roderick, as he was christened, played for Sutton United, Epson Town, Uxbridge Town (with whom he represented the Athenian League), Crystal Palace (as an amateur), Norwich City (106 goals for reserves) and Exeter City, where he scored 36 goals in 1936/37.

WILLIAMS, William   1922-26

Born: Leytonstone, East London
Lge apps: 34 (7 gls)
Cup apps: 9 (1 gl)

■ Billy became the youngest-ever full professional when he signed for Hammers in 1921, at the age of 15, from Fairbairn House Boys' Club. A former England Boys star, he made his Hammers' debut v. Blackpool at Bloomfield Road and scored in a 3-1 defeat (6.5.22) - his only Second Division appearance in the claret and blue. In Mar. 1925 he made another entry into the record books as a member of a party which embarked on the trip to Australia. Returning home in Sept. after several Test matches down under, the experiment brought the following comment from the club's 1925/26 handbook: "Has had a unique experience for so young a player, having had a glorious time in Australia since April last, where he has been finding the net frequently. We hope that continuous football has not affected his efficiency." The writer's fears may not have been altogether groundless, as Bill only made a further 14 first team outings before his transfer to Chelsea in 1927. After one year at Stamford Bridge he became a free agent in amateur football, and among others served Dartford, Guildford and Dagenham. Eventually retiring at the age of 40, he went into the haulage business and later ran a tobacconist and confestioner's shop in Ilford. Billy eventually retired to live at Frinton-on-sea and passed away there 8.3.94. The club were informed of his death by his grand-daughter, Miss Lisa Gordon, of Harold Hill, who showed club historian John Helliar a fascinating collection of pictures depicting her grand-father's career. The oldest photo was taken in 1919 and recorded the impressive catalogue of success by Billy's school football team, Central Park School of East Ham, which held the Dewar Shield - the trophy presented to the winners of the London Schools' Championship. In 1917/18 and 1918/19 they also won the Robert Cook Cup which was competed for by Essex Schools. During this period they had also won the Bethell Shield on four occasions, in addition to three times winning the White Cup. So Billy came to West Ham as something of a schoolboy prodigy.

Danny Williamson

WILLIAMSON, Danny   1994-

Born: West Ham, London. 5.12.73
Lge apps: 3 (1 gl)

■ The first youth product at Upton Park to score on his home debut since Tony Cottee (1983) when he netted the first v Southampton (7.5.94) in the final game of the 1993/94 season. This promising midfielder had made his first team bow a week earlier, as sub. in a 2-0 victory at Arsenal, and also impressed in a midweek goalless draw at Queens Park Rangers. A schoolboy star for Newham and Essex, Danny gained experience earlier in the 1993/94 season during 13-match loan spell with Third Division Doncaster Rovers, making his league debut v. Lincoln City (9.10.93).

WILKINSON, F   1905-06

SL apps: 14 (2 gls)
Cup apps: 1

■ A slightly built outside-left, "Snowball," as he was affectionately known by early-century Hammers' fans, was a steal from Second Division Manchester United who had put a £150 fee on his head but had to let him go to West Ham, FOC as they (as a SL club) were not bound by Football League rules. Began his football life in the puritanical surrounds of St. John's Sunday School team which won the Walter Spencer Challenge Cup and thus

Wilkinson became the owner of his first football medal. In 1902 he signed for Manchester League club, Newton Heath, as an amateur and won a runner-up medal with them. He signed pro for Manchester United but was allowed to join Hull City who were at that time playing friendly matches, so again no fee was due. But when Hull joined the Second Division of the FL they could not afford the £150 United wanted. So the former pattern maker at an iron foundry befittingly joined the Irons. "Snowball" soon saw familiar faces at the Boleyn Ground, including the famous Fred Blackburn who was his wing partner and an old adversary in a Lancashire Cup Final. A former sprint champion, his speed served him well during his 15 SL appearances during 1905/06.

WILSON, Arthur   1932-34

Born: Newcastle-on-Tyne
Lge apps: 29 (14 gls)
Cup apps: 6 (2 gls)

■ Yet another member of the considerable North-East England enclave which assembled in increasing numbers between the wars at Upton Park. A Geordie by birth, Arthur was a talented inside-forward who liked a crack at goal. His early honours included selection for both Newcastle and Northumberland Boys, and he was with Newcastle United Swifts before being snapped up by his local club - Scotswood - when he left school. He then made the long trip south to sign pro forms for Southampton,

where his fine form and 12 goals from the wing-half and inside-forward berths in 65 league and cup appearances attracted the attention of West Ham's management and an invitation to Upton Park for a fee of £500. Making his initial Irons' appearance v. Swansea Town at the Vetch Field on the opening day of the 1932/33 league campaign, he went on to score a creditable 15 goals in 33 League and Cup games that season. Arthur later joined Chester and in Nov. 1937 he joined Wolverhampton Wanderers where he stayed until January 1939 when he transferred to Torquay United.

WILSON, Ron   1946-47

Born: Sale, Cheshire. 10.9.24
Lge apps: 3

■ A useful player who could fill any of the defensive duties, but was most at home at wing-half. Made his debut in the troubled 1946-47 season, which saw the resumption of normal League matches for the first time since 1938/39 and Hammers fighting off the threat of relegation to the Third Division (South). Although he was retained for the following season, Ron did not appear for the First XI again. Afterwards coached Hornchurch and Upminster, Aveley and Barking. A keen photographer, Ron was recognised as the club's unofficial 'snapper' the short time he was at Upton Park.

WINTERHALDER, Arthur 1906-07

Born: Oxford, 1885
SL apps: 10 (5 gls)
Cup apps: 2 (1 gl)

■ Strange as it may seem, Arthur was no relation to his namesake, Herbert Winterhalder, and the fact that these two players with such unusual names played on the same stage within a year of each other, seems to be just another of the amazing coincidences thrown up in the history of the game. A pupil of Oddessa Road School who represented West Ham Schools XI in February, 1899, Arthur made a sensational SL debut on the left wing when he scored a hat-trick v. Spurs at the Boleyn (29.12.1907) and almost emulated the feat of Billy Grassam six years earlier who went one better and scored four on his debut v. Gravesend (1.9.1900). Even so, with Ken Tucker (v. Chesterfield, 4.10.47) and Tudor Martin (v. Newcaster, 9.9.36), Arthur goes down in Hammers history as one of the only three players to score that dream of all forwards - a debut hat-trick. Arthur also signed off his West Ham career with a goal, in a 4-1 Upton Park victory over SL champions Fulham on the last day of the season 1906/07. So ended his short, but sensational sojourn as an Iron. Footnote: Don Travis scored four goals in his debut for Hammers in a 7-0 League South victory v. Plymouth Argyle at bomb-damaged Upton Park (16.2.46). Terry Woodgate also hit a seven-minute hat-trick in the same match, but these feats are not recognised in official football League records due to the regionalised temporary nature of the competition.

WOOD, Edward John ("Jackie") 1937-49

Born: West Ham, East London. 23.10.19
Lge apps: 58 (13 gls)
Cup apps: 3 (2 gls)

■ An outstanding outside-left with an eye for scoring goals, this colourful character was also a great practical joker who, along with Dick Walker and "Big Jim" Barrett, symbolised the happy spirit that existed at the Boleyn in the late 40's. Born and bred in West Ham, Jack was connected with the club as a youngster, but as there was no youth policy in those days, he went into amatuer soccer with Leytonstone - winning an England cap in the process. Having signed pro in 1937, Jack's career, like so many other players of his generation, was badly disrupted by WW2 when called up with the Essex Regt. Territorials in 1939. He returned for 1945/46 season, and made a fair total of first team appearances in the immediate post-war years to add to the 10 already gained before hostilites, although by this time he had converted to inside-forward. In Oct. 1949 he transferred to Leyton Orient, where he made a further 10 League appearances.

WINTERHALDER, Herbert 1905-06

Born: Kettering, Northamptonshire. 1880.
SL apps: 12

■ Grammar school educated Herbert preceded his unrelated namesake to the Boleyn Grounds by some 15 months, but the two wingers' West Ham careers overlapped into the same season in 1906/07, although they never appeared in the same team. A fact that saved contemporary football reporters from a deal of potential confusion! After making a name with his school side, young Herbert signed for Kettering Athletic in 1895, a junior team competing in the Kettering Combination and later amateur forms for Kettering Town, with whom he won a Midland League Championship medal during his three-season stay with the Poppies - his home town club. His form there attracted the attention of Sheffield United for whom he signed and stepped out in 13 First Division matches. At Brammall Lane Herbert was a team mate of Fred Milnes, the famous amateur full-back who also served Hammers briefly. Herbert made the long journey to Plymouth to assist the Argyle in their first season of 1903/04. In 1904 he joined the ill-fated Wellingborough Town who folded in 1904/05 after suffering from lack of funds. Our subject succinctly summed up his season there to "Rambler" of the East Ham Echo in Aug. 1905: "The least said about Wellingborough, the better. It was a disastrous year right through, financially and otherwise." Making his SL bow in a 2-1 home defeat to Luton Town (16.9.1905), Herbert went on to make 10 appearances that season playing at centre-forward and on both wings, but had to wait until the next season and his last match in the claret and blue to score his only goal for the club - in a 1-1 draw at the Crystal Palace (29.9.1905) during Glaziers' second season at the famous old venue. Herbert's father was a jeweller from the Black Forest area of Germany and when he retired from playing Herbert ran a photographic and art shop in Kettering for some 40 years until his death in Sept. 1946.

WOOD, Jimmy 1930-35

Born: Royton, Lancashire
Lge apps: 63 (13 gls)
Cup apps: 1

■ This speedy outside-right gave six seasons of loyal service to West Ham without ever being able to lay claim to a regular First XI place. After learning the basics of the game with Crompton Albion in the Oldham Amateur League, he signed pro forms for Hyde. He left Hyde for a season and went to Bournemouth, but returned to his first pro club before transferring to Hammers in July 1929. The highlight of his career with West Ham must have been his inclusion in the team which did battle with Everton in the FA Cup semi-final at Molineux in 1932/33. Drafted into the team as a replacement for the injured Tommy Yews, he turned in a fine display as Irons went down 1-2 and unluckily missed out on Wembley. In June 1935 Jim transferred to Crystal Palace, and scored four goals in 10 matches.

Ron Wilson

STEPHEN MARSH

WOODARDS, Dan 1907-21

Born: East Ham, East London
SL apps: 109 (3 gls)
Cup apps: 14

■ A product of local junior football, Dan was an outstanding wing-half at the height of his career, winning the nicknames of 'Dapper Dan' and 'Beau Brummell', because of his well-groomed appearance. He assisted Plashet Lane School when they won the East Ham Shield and in 1904 was playing for East Ham Excelsior before moving on to St. Ethelburgas. He first joined West Ham in 1905 but made no first team appearance, waiting until 23.3.1907 before making his SL debut v Brighton. Played for Hastings in 1908/09 but returned to Upton Park in 1910. Still on the staff when Hammers joined the League in 1919, having played in 180 games including war-time, and was still playing

Dan Woodard

for and coaching the reserves. In later years the Boleyn Ground bore testimony to his fastidious nature when he was appointed club groundsman. The luftwaffe rearranged his handiwork in August 1944, however, when a VI landed on the south/west corner of his beloved Boleyn pitch. Dan was the only person at the ground when the missile exploded and caused a huge crater on the field. He was said to have been badly shaken by the blast and indignant at the damage done to his finely manicured playing surface. Hammers had to play all their matches away from home while emergency repairs were done, but amazingly, won nine consecutive matches, then lost 1-0 to Spurs on their return to Upton Park in December - despite Dan's efforts to restore the coveted greensward to its former glory.

WOODBURN, J 1919-20

Lge apps: 4

■ A right or centre-half signed from Hurlford, he made his Second Division bow in a 1-0 victory over Birmingham at St. Andrews on (25.10.19). Completed a quartet of league appearances that season before being transferred to Peterborough and Fletton United.

WOODLEY, Derek 1959-62

Born: Isleworth, Middlesex. 2.3.42
Lge apps: 12 (3 gls)
Cup apps: 1

■ An extremely fast flankman who had won England Schools honours before joining Hammers. While still on the groundstaff he added six England Youth caps and an FA Youth Cup runners-up medal to his earlier triumphs and looked set for a big future. Two goals on his League debut in Oct.1959 v. Luton Town did little to dispel that view, and it was something of a surprise when he eventually left Upton Park. Former Hammers' manager Ted Fenton swooped on the eve of the 1962/63 season to

WOODGATE, John Terence ("Terry") 1939-53

Born: East Ham, East London. 11.12.19
Lge apps: 259 (48 gls)
Cup apps: 16 (4 gls)

■ Another local product, this flying forward was equally at home on either wing. Actually making his Second Division debut before the war v. Bradford Park Avenue on Good Friday 1939, Terry won a regular place in the first team after the conflict, having served for more than six years in WW2 with the Essex Regt and Royal Artillery. The experience he had gained guesting for many clubs during the war-time period kept him in good stead for the Second Division campaigns that followed. But first he caused a sensation by scoring a seven-minute hat-trick v. Plymouth Argyle in a Football League South fixture at Upton Park (16.2.1946) and thus emulated Syd Puddefoot's feat of WW1. He became a regular in Hammers' post-war Second Division side and was ever-present in 1950/51. Able to perform on either wing with equal efficiency, he was an asset not least for his welcome input of goals. However, the emergence of Harry Hooper and Malcolm Musgrove as regular first-team contenders prompted his transfer to Peterborough United in Mar. 1954. After hanging up his boots he took over a public house in March, Cambridgeshire. Sadly, Terry passed away at the age of 62, in April 1982.

Played	League		FAC		LC		Europe		Total	
	App	Gls	App	Gls	App	Gls	App	Gls	App	Gls
1938-39	4	0	0	0	0	0	0	0	4	0
1945-46	0	0	4	0	0	0	0	0	4	0
1946-47	41	5	1	1	0	0	0	0	42	6
1947-48	38	7	2	0	0	0	0	0	40	7
1948-49	38	9	1	0	0	0	0	0	39	9
1949-50	29	4	2	2	0	0	0	0	31	6
1950-51	42	12	2	0	0	0	0	0	44	12
1951-52	38	8	3	1	0	0	0	0	41	9
1952-53	29	3	1	0	0	0	0	0	30	3
TOTAL	259	48	16	4	0	0	0	0	275	52

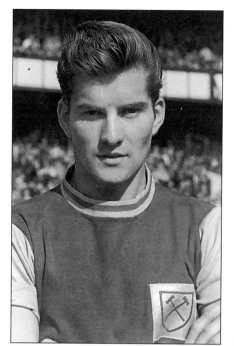

Derek Woodley

take Derek and his colleague Mick Beesley to Southend in a dual transfer. Derek left the Shrimpers (after scoring 24 times in 181 league and cup games) for Charlton in 1967, only to return to Roots Hall four months later. He finally finished his League career at Gillingham in 1970.

WOOLER, Alan 1973-75

Born: Poole, Dorset. 17.8.53
Lge apps: 4
Cup apps: 1

■ Signed by Hammers from Reading in Aug. 1973 after beginning his career with Southern League Weymouth, Alan was given the unenviable task of taking over Bobby Moore's number six shirt at Upton Park. After a spell with Boston Minutemen in the North American Soccer League in 1974, he moved to Aldershot and made over 200 League appearances for the Hampshire club.

WRAGG, Doug 1956-59

Born: Nottingham, 12.9.34
Lge apps: 16 (0 gls)
Cup apps: 0

■ This popular winger was spotted by Hammers' playing in the "Star" Youth Final at Wembley in 1953, and was duly signed pro in June the same year. Doug was prominent in schools football and played for Nottingham and England Boys. He was also a fair boxer, being a former Hyson Green and England representative in his native Nottinghamshire. His career benefited enormously when he was demobbed from the Army in 1955 and able to return to full-time training. After proving himself a capable first XI deputy and nearly seven years with Hammers, Doug was

WOOSNAM, Phil 1958-62

Born: Caersws, Montgomeryshire, Wales. 22.12.32
Lge apps: 138 (26 gls)
Cup apps: 15 (3 gls)

■ The original "Welsh Wizard," Phil was a footballing genius who almost single-handedly controlled Hammers' destiny from the inside-right position in the immediate post-promotion years, and was the first Hammer to play for the Principality since Wilf James in 1932. A relatively late starter, he did have one game for Manchester City as far back as 1952, after moving to Maine Road for trials while still retaining his amateur status. Woosie's talents were evident at an early age and he graduated from Montgomeryshire Schoolboys through to Wales Schoolboys to Youth international honours at the time he won a scholarship to Bangor University reading physics. While at college, he won the first of eight amateur caps v. England at Bangor in 1951. He also captained the varsity side to the Welsh Universities' Championship. Outside of campus he played his early soccer with Wrexham, Peritus, Manchester City, amateur Sutton United and Middlesex Wanderers. Graduating with a BSc degree, Woosnam joined the Royal Artillery as a 2nd Lieutenant to complete his national service, during which time he played for the Army XI with Maurice Setters (WBA) and Eddie Colman and Duncan Edwards (Man. Utd.). Phil's career really took off at Leyton Orient although he continued to teach at Leyton County High School. It cost Hammers a then club record fee of £30,000 to persuade O's to part with their star performer in Nov. 1958, and he made his debut v. Arsenal at Upton Park the same month. Phil relinquished his teaching career just before his move to Hammers, and although he had signed pro forms with O's, it wasn't until he had joined West Ham at the age of 26 that he was free to concentrate on the game on a full-time basis. Few players can have crammed so much into their lives at such an early age, although it was relatively old to be embarking on a first class soccer career. He was chosen for Wales on 15 occasions during his four years at the Boleyn, having already won one cap while at Brisbane Road and also represented the Football League. The arrival of Johnny

Byrne in Mar. 1962 seemed to hasten Phil's departure, which to many appeared premature, the pair's link-up in Hammers' attack having become the highlight of the London scene by the time of his move to Aston Villa. He gained another two caps and scored 23 goals in 111 League matches while with Villa. In 1966 Phil emigrated to the States to take up the post of player/coach to Atlanta Chiefs, who won the North American Soccer League two years later under his guidance. He was then appointed Commissioner of the League and since then probably did more to further the game in the States than any other single person. The staging of the 1994 World Cup finals in the USA has seen much of Phil's groundwork come to fruition and in his role as a soccer marketing consultant based in Atlanta, one of the proudest spectators at the tournament. The ironic thing is Woosie nearly didn't go to the USA at all, as he explained at the World Cup: "I wanted to continue my playing career in Division One and one week after agreeing to join Atlanta Chiefs, Tommy Docherty asked me to join him at Chelsea. I hadn't signed anything with Atlanta, but I had given them my word and I stuck to it. But more than once I moaned: 'Why didn't you come in for me earlier' at Chelsea." American soccer chiefs will be thanking their lucky stars and stripes that the Blues delayed.
❏ *Wales caps:* 1958 v. England; 1959 v. England, Scotland; 1960 v. Northern Ireland, Republic of Ireland, Scotland, England; 1961 v. Northern Ireland, Spain, Hungary, England, Scotland; 1962 v. Northern Ireland, Brazil. (14).

transferred back to his home county via Mansfield Town in Mar. 1960. He later moved on to Rochdale and then Chesterfield, before going out of the League with Grantham. Nicknamed "Oily" by the fans, Doug was in Fourth Division Rochdale's team which battled through to the Final of the 1962 League Cup Final and played in the first match of the two leg final v. Norwich City at Spotland, which the East Anglians won 3-0 and the final 4-0 on aggregate. Doug is now employed by a subsidiary of Raleigh, making car seat covers at Bilborough, Notts.

WRIGHT, George   1951-58

Born: Ramsgate, Kent, 19.3.36
Lge apps: 161 (0 gls)
Cup apps: 9 (0 gls)

■ An excellent full-back signed from Southern League Margate after beginning his career with Ramsgate Athletic and then Thanet United, who gave good return for a small transfer fee. His debut v. Hull City at Boothferry Park in Sept. 1951, was the first of a remarkable appearance total for Hammers. A great servant, the nearest George got to international honours was when he was selected for an England 'B' Trial XI v Olympic Trial XI at Highbury in 1952, although he also turned out on two occasions for the Football Association v. Cambridge University and then represented London in the final of the 1958 Inter Cities Fairs Cup v. Barcelona. After playing eight times in the 1957/58 promotion season, George transferred to near neighbours Leyton Orient, where he made 87 league appearances, making an unfortunate debut when he put through his own goal v. Bristol Rovers in Aug. 1958. Leaving in 1961 for Gillingham, he ended his league career at the Kent club with four more appearances. George then went back to finish his career with Ramsgate Athletic in the summer of 1963. He now has his own cabinet-making business in Kent.

George Wright

Ken Wright

WRIGHT, Ken   1946-49

Born: Newmarket, Suffolk. 16.5.22
Lge apps: 51 (20 gls)
Cup apps: 1 (0 gls)

■ Awarded the Distinguished Flying Cross for his heroic deeds during the war while in the RAF, he joined West Ham from Cambridge City as an amateur, but signed pro forms in 1946. A forward with an eye for goal, he maintained a good scoring ratio during his four seasons at the Boleyn.

WRIGHT, P   1914-15

Lge apps: 10 (1 gl)
Cup apps: 0

■ Making his first appearance in the 2-1 home win over Gillingham on the opening day of the 1914/15 season at outside-left, he scored his only goal in a 4-1 win over Bristol Rovers at Upton Park (24.10.1914) when Leafe, Bailey and Burton also got their names on the scoresheet.

WYLLIE, Robinson ("Bob")   1956-57

Born: Dundee, Scotland, 4.4.29
Lge apps: 13 (0 gls)
Cup apps: 2 (0 gls)

■ Scottish custodian who began with junior side Monifieth Tayside FC before transferring to Dundee United. His displays at Tannadice were impressive enough to send Blackpool over the border seeking his signature as a deputy for Scottish international George Farm. He played 13 First Division matches for the Seasiders up to his transfer to Hammers in May 1956. Required to do a similar job at Upton Park - this time as deputy to Ernie Gregory - it was unlucky 13 in league matches again for Bob, as he moved on to Plymouth at the end of 1956/57, before finally settling down for a lengthy stay at Mansfield Town.

YENSON, William 1902-1904/1908-09

Born: Kingston Bagpuize, Oxfordshire. 1880.
SL apps: 50
Cup apps: 7

■ Another early-century Iron who made an FA Cup Final appearance, albeit a losing one, after leaving the confines of the Memorial Grounds. Bill swapped his defensive duties for an attacking role on his departure to Bolton Wanderers, lining up in the centre-forward position for the Lancastrians in their 1904 Cup Final meeting with Manchester City at the Crystal Palace after scoring two of Trotters' goals on the way to the Final. City's 1-0 victory (inspired by the legendary Billy Meredith) prevented what would have been a remarkable hat-trick of winners' medals gained by players with West Ham connections: Bill's appearance having been preceded by those of Billy Barnes for Sheffield United in the 1902 Final at Crystal Palace (Billy joined Hammers the following season) and goalkeeper Hughie Montieth's appearance in Bury's record breaking win of 1903, also at the famous London venue. Bill later came back to the capital to play for Queens Park Rangers and returned to Upton Park when he re-joined Hammers for the 1908/09 season.

The 'Sportsman' pen pictures of the 1904 FA Cup Final teams included: "Yenson came from West Ham at the beginning of the present season. Originally a full-back he was tried for Bolton at 'half' then falling in the centre-forward position. He is scarcely an orthodox centre, but a robust and useful player, fond of throwing his weight about and worrying the full-backs." Bill had captained Rangers when they won the SL championship in 1907/08 and made 26 appearances in 1908/09 before returning to Irons. But he didn't stay long, moving to Croydon Common where he made 36 appearances and scored two goals in 1909/10. "A tall, well-built player although a trifle slow at times. He played some excellent games for the Hammers."

YEOMANSON, Jack 1947-50

Born: Margate, Kent. 3.3.20
Lge apps: 106 (1 gl)
Cup apps: 5

■ An immediate predecessor of George Wright, both at Margate and West Ham, it was Jack who set the high standards for his successor to follow. It would be a toss-up between these two fine full-backs to find who gave Hammers the best service; certainly Jack's 106 League appearances, spread over four seasons, were invaluable in helping Hammers through the tricky post-war period. And he did achieve something his replacement never managed... he scored a goal!

YEWS, Thomas Peace 1922-33

Lge apps: 332 (46 gls)
Cup apps: 29 (5 gls)

■ With Jimmy Ruffell on the opposite wing it was small wonder that centre-forward Vic Watson claimed all Hammers' goalscoring records during an era of wing-service unsurpassed to this day. Vic headed countless goals from Tommy's runs along the touchline and crosses from near the corner-flag - a ploy nicely summed up by manager Charlie Paynter when he once commented: "Tom could pick a fly off Vic's eyebrows!" Scorer of a near half-century of goals himself during his 330-odd appearances in the claret and blue, he made many more goals than he scored. Signed by Hammers at a fee of £150 from Hartlepool United in the club's Cup Final year of 1923, he also had other talents, being a "rag-time" pianist of some note. His renditions were very much in demand during frequent continental tours of those happy days. After ending his playing days with nearby Clapton Orient in the mid-30's (he joined the O's in 1933), Tom became an engineer at Briggs Motor Bodies. At the time of his death, in Aug. 1966, Tom was a charge-hand at the Ford Motor Company.

Played	League		FAC		LC		Europe		Total	
	App	Gls	App	Gls	App	Gls	App	Gls	App	Gls
1923-24	12	1	0	0	0	0	0	0	12	1
1924-25	33	1	6	1	0	0	0	0	39	2
1925-26	32	1	1	0	0	0	0	0	33	1
1926-27	39	8	3	0	0	0	0	0	42	8
1927-28	42	11	2	0	0	0	0	0	44	11
1928-29	41	10	5	3	0	0	0	0	46	13
1929-30	41	3	4	1	0	0	0	0	45	4
1930-31	37	7	1	0	0	0	0	0	38	7
1931-32	23	2	2	0	0	0	0	0	25	2
1932-33	32	2	5	0	0	0	0	0	37	2
TOTAL	**332**	**46**	**29**	**5**	**0**	**0**	**0**	**0**	**361**	**51**

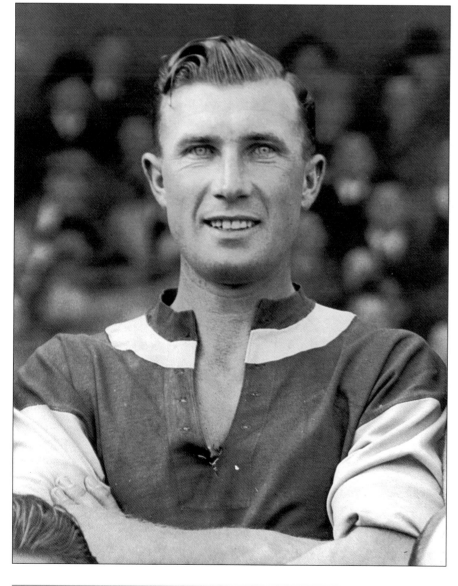

Jack Yeomanson

YOUNG, Jack
1920-25

Born: Tyne and Wear. 1895.
Lge apps: 124 (3 gls)
Cup apps: 14

■ Dashing, left-winger who converted to full-back with considerable success. Signed for a sizeable - for those days - fee of £600, his switch of positions brought the following comment in Jack's pen-picture in the programme for the 1923 FA Cup Final: "He played for Southend United at outside-left, and went to Upton Park as a forward; but he displayed his aptitude as a defender, and well-earned the position he now occupies." By the mid-20's ill-health had eroded his First Division appearances, and he played his last game for West Ham at Elland Road v. Leeds (19.9.25) before transferring to QPR. In 1929 he joined Accrington Stanley. After retiring from playing due to ill-health, Jack continued his links with the game by scouting for Liverpool, whose manager George Kay was his former captain at West Ham. Jack's

Jack Young

daughter, Miss Dorothy Young, still lives in the same house that her parents occupied when her father returned to his native town of Whitburn, Tyne and Wear, and was the guest of honour of West Ham United when entertaining Newcastle United in Feb. 1993. She later donated the original shirt that Jack wore in the 1923 FA Cup Final to the club. Jack had passed away in 1952 at the age of 57.

YOUNG, Len
1934-35

■ A former Essex Schools player, Len was a well-built centre-half who had two seasons at Upton Park as understudy to Jim Barrett. Locally-born, he was one of the club's many captures from Ilford. Transferred to Reading, he was still playing for the Berkshire club in the old Third Division South after the war, and later joined Brighton & Hove Albion - where he retired from playing in 1949.

YOUNG, Robert
1907-09

Born: Swinhill, Lanarkshire, Scotland. 1886.
SL apps: 42 (1 gl)
Cup apps: 2

■ Bob made his Hammers' debut v. Spurs at left-half, but being something of a utility man, filled all the defensive berths with the exception of goalkeeper during his two years at the Boleyn Ground. Joining Hammers from St. Mirren at the beginning of the season in which his former Saints team mates were destined to reach the Final of the Scottish Cup at Hampden Park v. Celtic, the 21 year-old set about establishing himself in Irons' Southern League side to finish the term with 33 appearances to his credit. First team outings were scarcer the following season, however, and a 6-3 defeat at Norwich (12.12.08) signalled the end of his career in the claret and blue, in which his only goal was scored v Norwich (4.4.08). Transferred to Middlesbrough, he stayed on Teesside until 1910 when he joined Everton for a massive (for those days) fee of £1,200. Quite a transformation for someone who didn't play any football until he was 17. He had been a keen athlete and won several half mile races. Turned out for Swinhill Hearts and Larkhall Thistle before joining Saints.

PROGRAMME & PLAN OF THE FIELD OF PLAY

BOLTON WANDERERS

Goalkeeper
R. H. Pym

Right Back
R. Howarth

Left Back
A. Finney

Right Half-Back
W. Rowley

Centre Half-Back
J. Seddon

Left Half-Back
W. Jennings

Outside Right
W. Butler

Inside Right
D. B. N. Jack

Centre Forward
J. R. Smith

Inside Left
J. Smith (Captain)

Outside Left
J. Ruffell

Inside Left
W. Moore

Centre Forward
V. Watson

Inside Right
W. Brown

Left Half-Back
J. Tresadern

Centre Half-Back
G. Kay (Captain)

Right Half Back
S. Bishop

Left Back
J. Young

Right Back
W. Henderson

Goalkeeper
A. E. Hufton

WEST HAM UNITED

Miss Dorothy Young, the daughter of John (Jack) Young who played left-back in our FA Cup Final side of 1923. Mrs Young is pictured here with West Ham United Chairman Terence Brown and the shirt that her father wore in that epic Wembley match against Bolton.

WAR-TIME GUESTS

The following players appeared as guests for West Ham United during World War Two:

Player	Club (if known)	Apps.	Gls.
A. AIKEN		1	0
L. ARMESON	Blackpool	4	0
Sam BARTRAM	Charlton Athletic	1	0
Samuel BRIDDEN	Swansea City		
Alan BROWN	Burnley		
Oliver BROWN			
R. BROWN		1	0
W. BROWN		1	0
Peter BUCHANAN	Chelsea & Scotland	1	0
Charlie BURKE	Ardeer Athletic	1	0
John BURKE	Millwall		
J. BURNETT	Tooting & Mitcham		
Alistair CAMPBELL	Southampton		
Bert CANN	Charlton Athletic	4	0
Louis CARDWELL	Blackpool	1	0
Tom CHEETHAM	Brentford	1	1
Willie CORBETT	Celtic	12	0
George CURTIS	Arsenal	19	2
C. DAVIES		1	0
Tommy DEANS	Celtic	8	1
Jock DODDS	Sheffield United	9	10
Peter DOHERTY	Manchester City		
Ted DRAKE	Arsenal	2	0
Maurice DUNKLEY	Manchester City	11	1
A. FERRIS		1	0
Bern FENTON	Millwall	2	0
Bob FERRIER	Huddersfield Town	1	0
Alf FITZGERALD	Queens Park Rangers		
Doug FLACK	Fulham	2	0
Ian GILLESPIE	Ipswich Town	1	0
Howard GIRLING	Crystal Palace	1	0
G. GLADWIN		7	0
George GRAY		1	1
G. GREEN	Charlton Athletic	3	0
R. GRIFFITHS			
Almeric HALL	Tottenham Hotspur	6	0
J.L. HALL		1	0
Eddie HAPGOOD	Arsenal	2	0
Les HENLEY	Arsenal	1	0
Syd HOBBINS	Charlton Athletic	6	0
Harold HOBBIS	Charlton Athletic	23	3
Percy HOOPER	Tottenham Hotspur		
Idris HOPKINS	Brentford	2	0
L. HOWELL		1	0
William HUGHES	Huddersfield Town		
Doug HUNT	Tottenham Hotspur	2	0
Jimmy JINKS	Millwall	1	0
Dai JONES	Leicester City	42	0
E. JONES		1	0
L. JONES	Arsenal	1	0
Joe JOBLING	Charlton Athletic	1	0
Bernard JOY	Arsenal	2	
F. KIPPAX	Burnley	8	2
Arnold LOWES	Sheffield Wednesday	1	1
George LUDFORD	Tottenham Hotspur	3	3
J. MAHON	Huddersfield Town	18	6
Joe MALLETT	Queens Park Rangers		
D. McGIBBON		4	0
J. McLEOD		1	0
Leslie MEDLEY	Tottenham Hotspur	1	0
R. MORRIS		1	0
Ernie MUTTITT	Brentford	3	3
Berry NIEWENHUYS	Liverpool	16	3
J. OAKES		1	0
J. OSBORNE		1	1
Albert PAGE	Tottenham Hotspur	3	0
Harold PEARSON	Millwall	1	0
R. PENNY		1	0
Ernest PHYPERS	Tottenham Hotspur	1	0
Paul POWELL-BOSSONS		1	0
H. PRITCHARD	Wolverhampton Wanderers	1	0
Bob PRYDE	Blackburn Rovers	1	0
Lawrence RAYMOND		1	0
S. RICHARDSON		1	0
Horace RICKETTS	Reading	2	0
Alf RIDYARD	Queens Park Rangers	1	0
J. RIORDAN		1	0
Albert ROLES	Southampton		
J. SAUNDERS		1	0
R. SAVAGE		1	0
Laurie SCOTT	Arsenal	1	0
Bill SIDLEY	Arsenal	1	0
A. SLIMAN		1	0
C. SMITH		1	0
E.J. SMITH		2	0
J.C.R. SMITH		1	0
J.T. SMITH			
James SMITH	Millwall & England		
Bert TANN	Charlton Athletic	1	0
D.W.J. THOMAS			
Robert THOMAS	Fulham	1	0
Laurie TOWNSEND	Brentford	1	0
Cyril TRIGG	Birmingham	1	2
Tommy WALKER	Chelsea	16	0
H. WALLER		9	0
S. WATSON		1	0
William WHATLEY	Tottenham Hotspur		
Sam WEAVER	Wolverhampton Wanderers	1	1
Ernie WILKINS	Brentford	2	1
Bill WHITTAKER		1	0
H. WRIGHT		2	0
Ken WRIGHT	(As amateur)	5	5
Benny YORSTON	Middlesbrough	2	0

CUP FINAL TEAMS

The players who have represented West Ham United in a final.
(European Cup Winners' Cup, FA Cup, Football League Cup and FA Youth Cup)

EUROPEAN CUP WINNERS' CUP

■ **1965**
v **TSV Munich** (W.Germany)   Won 2-0
at Wembley
Scorer: Sealey (2)
Team: Standen, Kirkup, Burkett, Peters, Brown, Moore (capt), Sealey, Boyce, Hurst, Dear, Sissons.

■ **1976**
v **Anderlecht** (Belgium)   Lost 2-4
at Heysel Stadium, Brussels
Scorers: Holland, Robson
Team: Day, Coleman, Lampard (A. Taylor), Bonds, T. Taylor, McDowell, Holland, Paddon, Jennings, Brooking, Robson.

FA CUP

■ **1923**
v **Bolton Wanderers**   Lost 0-2
at Wembley
Team: Hufton, Henderson, Young, Bishop, Kay, Tresadern, Richards, Brown, Watson, Moore, Ruffell.

■ **1964**
v **Preston North End**   Won 3-2
at Wembley
Scorers: Sissons, Hurst, Boyce
Team: Standen, Bond, Burkett, Bovington, Brown, Moore, Brabrook, Byrne, Hurst, Boyce, Sissons.

■ **1975**
v **Fulham**   Won 2-0
at Wembley
Scorer: A. Taylor (2)
Team: Day, McDowell, Lampard, Bonds, T. Taylor, Lock, A. Taylor, Paddon, Jennings, Brooking, Holland.

■ **1980**
v **Arsenal**   Won 1-0
at Wembley
Scorer: Brooking
Team: Parkes, Stewart, Lampard, Bonds, Martin, Devonshire, Allen, Pearson, Cross, Brooking, Pike.

FOOTBALL LEAGUE WAR CUP

■ **1940**
v **Blackburn Rovers**   Won 1-0
at Wembley
Scorer: Small
   Team: Conway, Bicknell, C. Walker, Fenton, R. Walker, Cockcroft, Small, Macaulay, Foreman, Goulden, Foxall.

FOOTBALL LEAGUE CUP

■ **1966**
(1st Leg) v **West Bromwich A.**   Won 2-1
at Upton Park
Scorers: Moore, Byrne
Team: Standen, Burnett, Burkett, Peters, Brown, Moore, Brabrook, Boyce, Byrne, Hurst, Dear.

(2nd Leg) v **West Bromwich A.**   Lost 1-4
at The Hawthorns
Scorer: Peters
Team: Standen, Burnett, Peters, Bovington, Brown, Moore, Brabrook, Boyce, Byrne, Hurst, Dear.

■ **1981**
v **Liverpool**   Drew 1-1
at Wembley
Scorer: Stewart (pen)
Team: Parkes, Stewart, Lampard, Bonds, Martin, Devonshire, Neighbour, Goddard (Pearson), Cross, Brooking, Pike.

(Replay) v **Liverpool**   Lost 1-2
at Villa Park
Scorer: Goddard
Team: Parkes, Stewart, Lampard, Bonds, Martin, Devonshire, Neighbour, Goddard, Cross, Brooking, Pike (Pearson).

FA YOUTH CUP

■ **1957**
(1st Leg) v **Manchester United** Lost 2-3
at Upton Park
Scorers: Cartwright, Fenn
Team: Goymer, Kirkup, Howe, Lewis, Walker, Lyall, Rowlands, Smith, Fenn, Cartwright, McDonald.

(2nd Leg) v **Manchester United** Lost 0-5
at Old Trafford
Team: Goymer, Kirkup, Howe, Lewis, Walker, Lyall, Rowlands, Smith, Fenn, Cartwright, McDonald.

■ **1959**
(1st Leg) v **Blackburn Rovers**   Drew 1-1
at Upton Park
Scorer: Smillie
Team: Caskey, Cripps, Burkett, Bovington, Moore, Brooks, Woodley, Cartwright, Beesley, Smillie, Scott.

(2nd Leg) v **Blackburn Rovers**   Lost 0-1
at Ewood Park
Team: Caskey, Cripps, Burkett, Bovington, Moore, Brooks, Woodley, Cartwright, Beesley, Smillie, Scott.

■ **1963**
(1st Leg) v **Liverpool**   Lost 1-3
at Anfield
Scorer: Britt
Team: Mackleworth, Burnett, Kitchener, Dawkins, Charles, Howe, Redknapp, Bennett, Britt, Sissons, Dryden.

(2nd Leg) v **Liverpool**   Won 5-2
at Upton Park
Scorers: Britt 3, Dawkins, Dryden
Team: Mackleworth, Burnett, Kitchener, Dawkins, Charles, Howe, Redknapp, Bennet, Britt, Sissons, Dryden.

■ **1975**
(1st Leg) v **Ipswich Town**   Lost 1-3
at Upton Park
Scorer: Sharpe
Team: Danson, Smith, Tuddenham, Fraser, Martin, Domfe, Hill, Curbishley, Sharpe (Hurlock), Pike, Brush.

(2nd Leg) v **Ipswich Town**   Lost 0-2
at Portman Road
Team: Danson, Smith, Tuddenham, Fraser, Martin, Domfe, Hill, Curbishley, Sharpe (Hurlock), Pike, Brush.

■ **1981**
(1st Leg) v **Tottenham H.**   Won 2-0
at Upton Park
Team: Vaughan, Keith, La Ronde, Reader, Ampofo, McPherson, Barnes, Allen, Milton, Burvill, Schiavi.

(2nd Leg) v **Tottenham H.**   Lost 0-1
at White Hart Lane
Team: Vaughan, Keith, La Ronde, Dickens, Ampofo, McPherson, Barnes, Allen, Milton, Burvill, Schiavi.

Billy Bonds

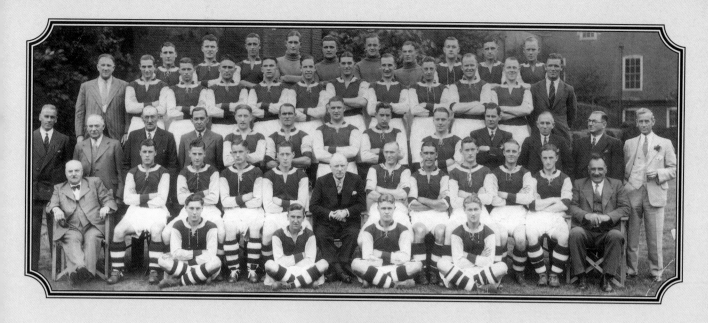

TEAM GROUP GALLERY

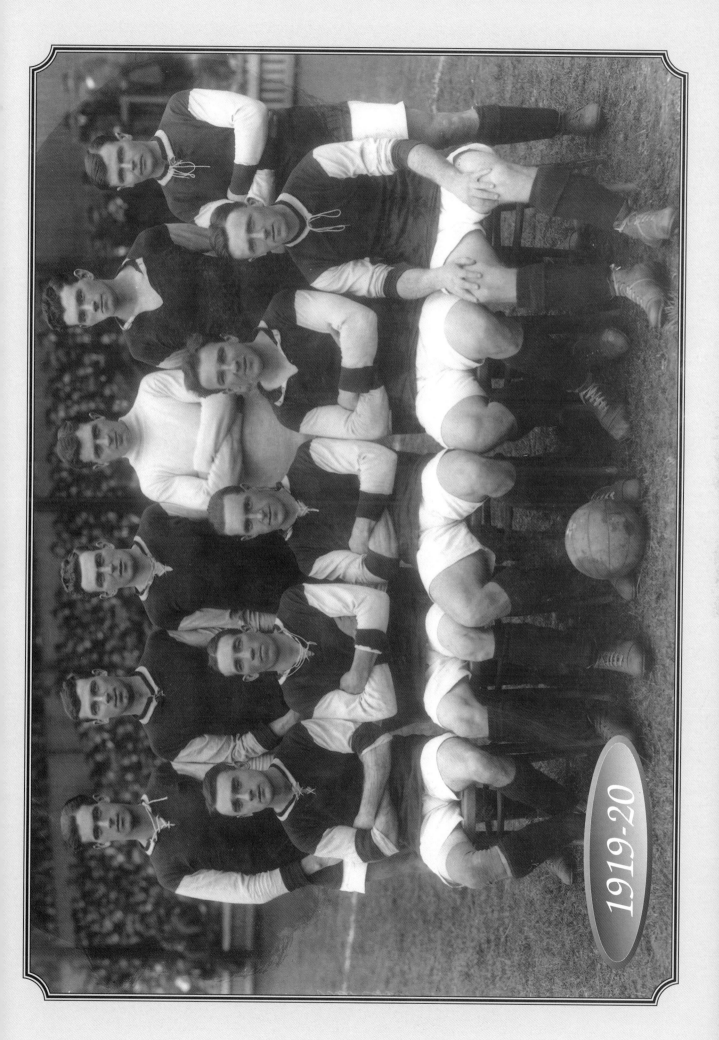

1919-20

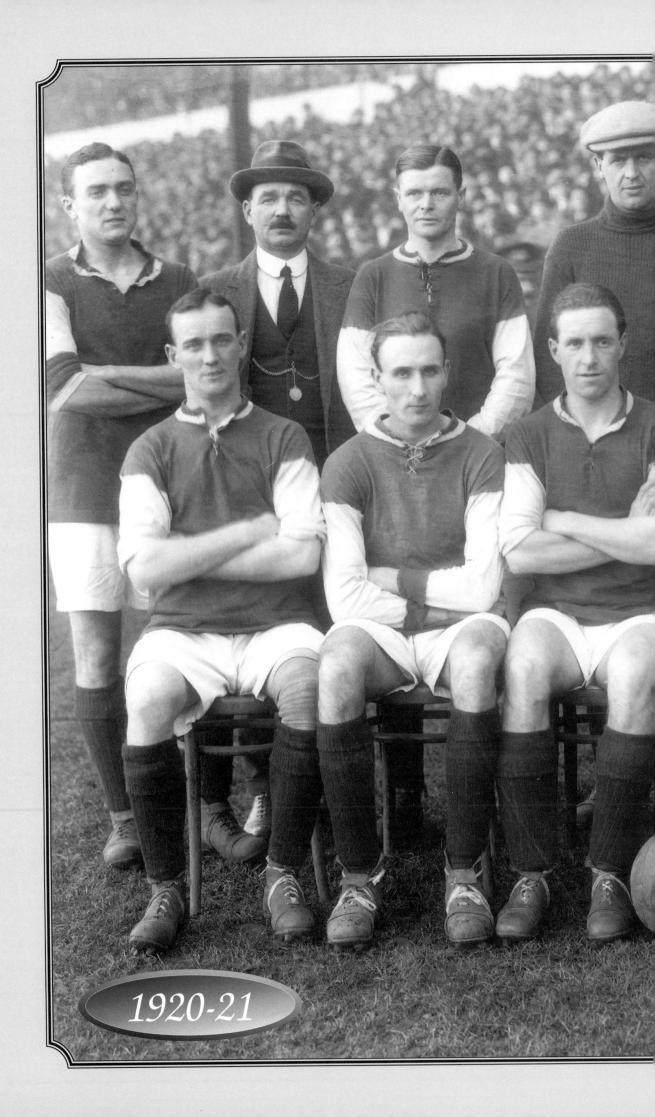

1920-21

228

1922-23

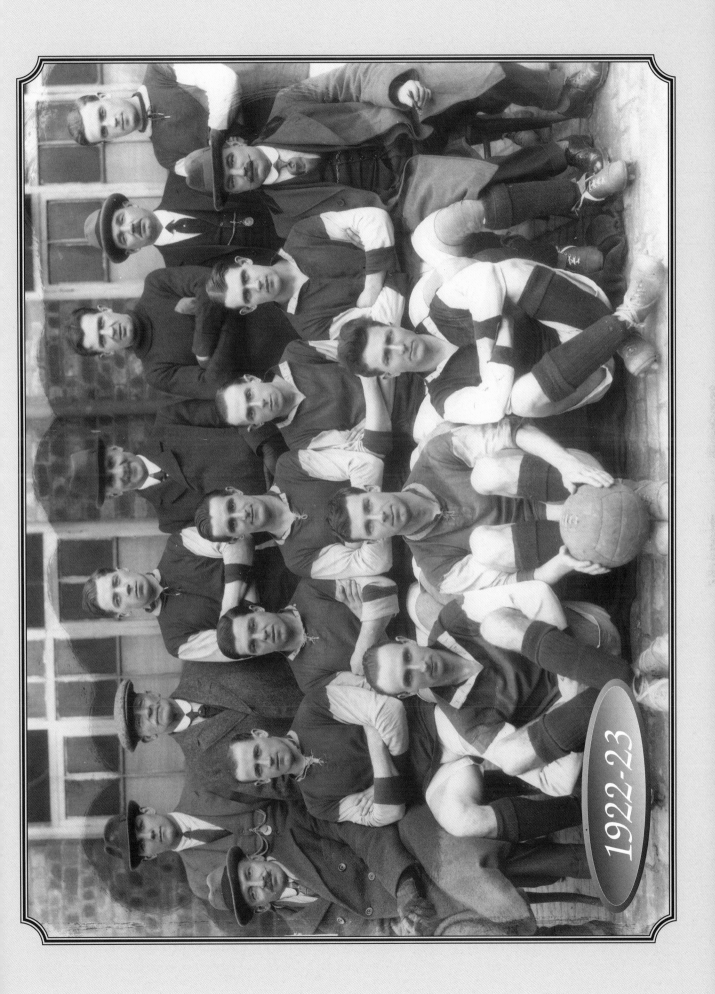

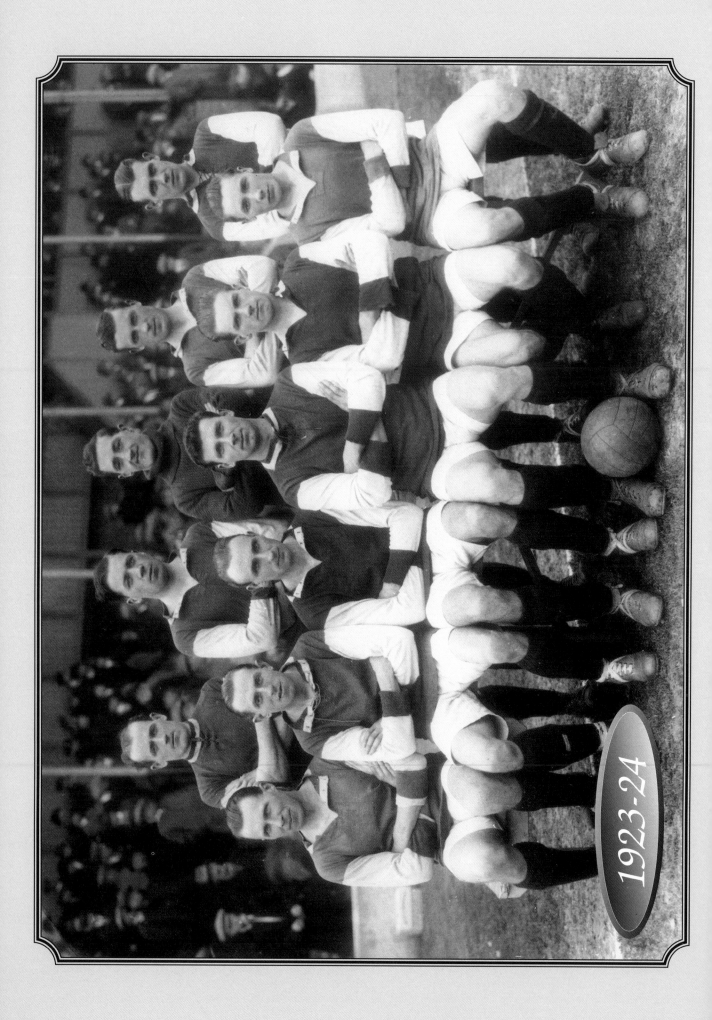

1923-24

1924-25

233

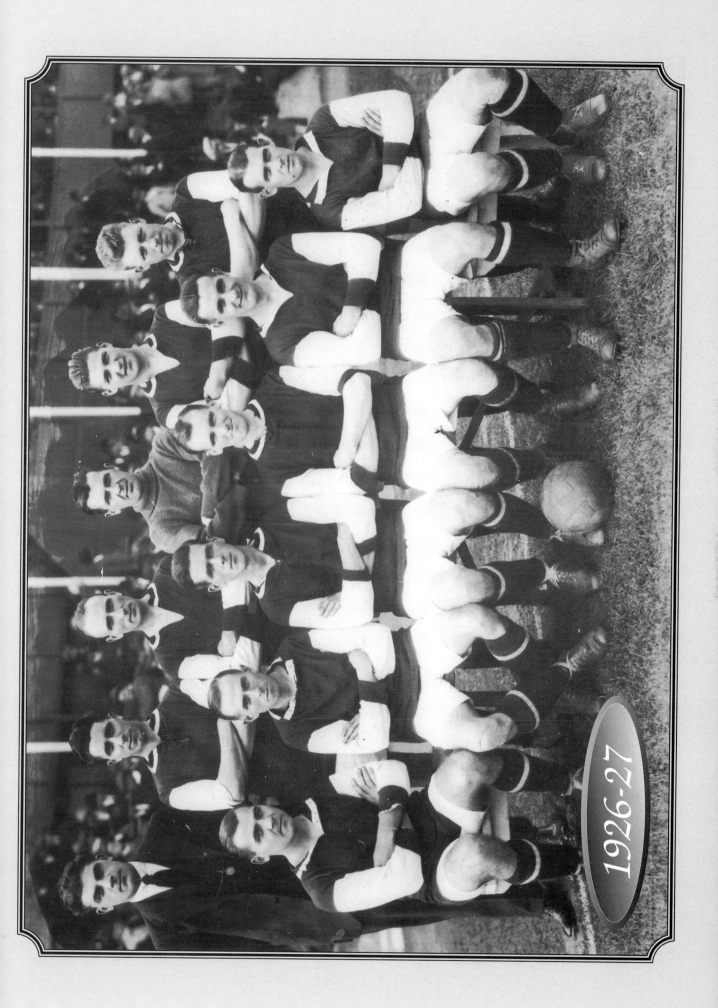

235

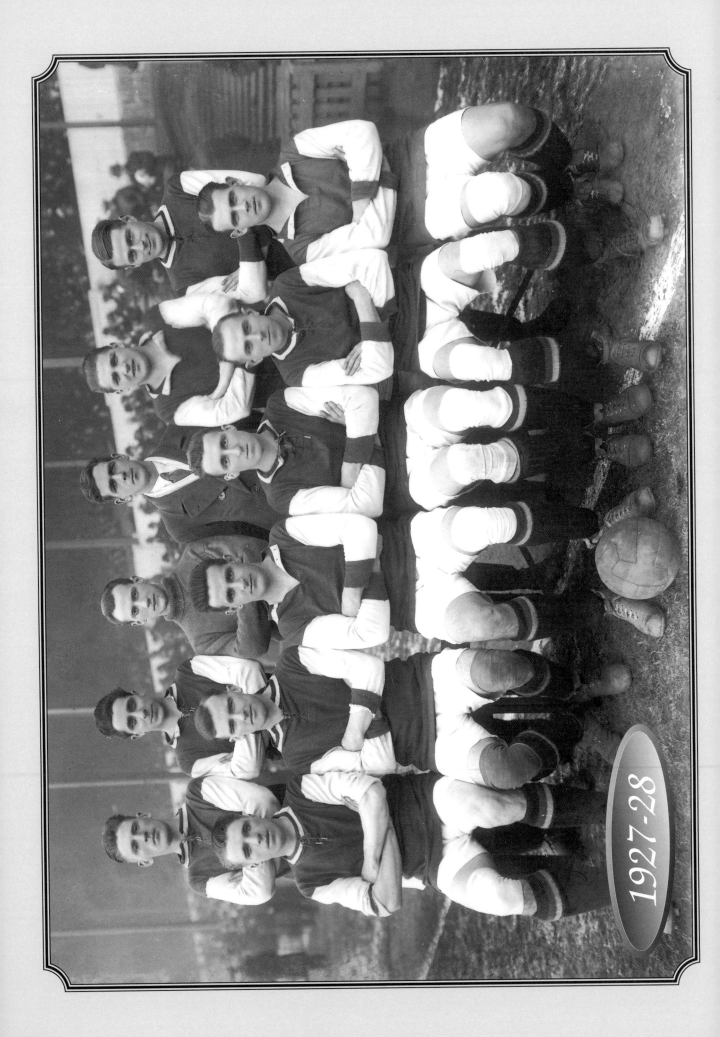

1927-28

1928-29

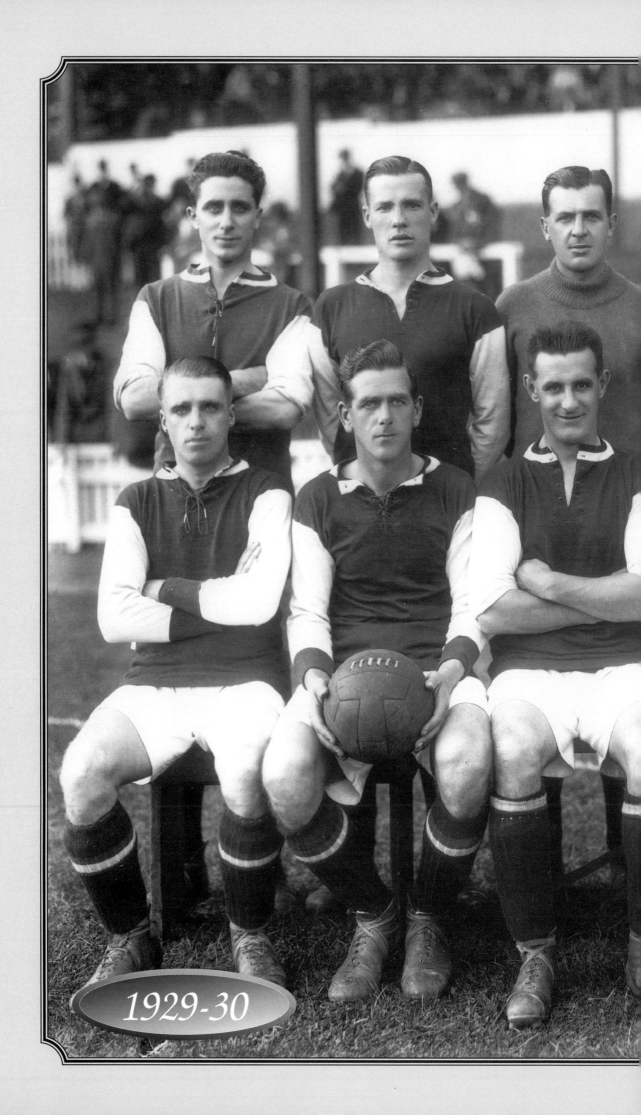

1929-30

1930-31

1931-32

1935-36

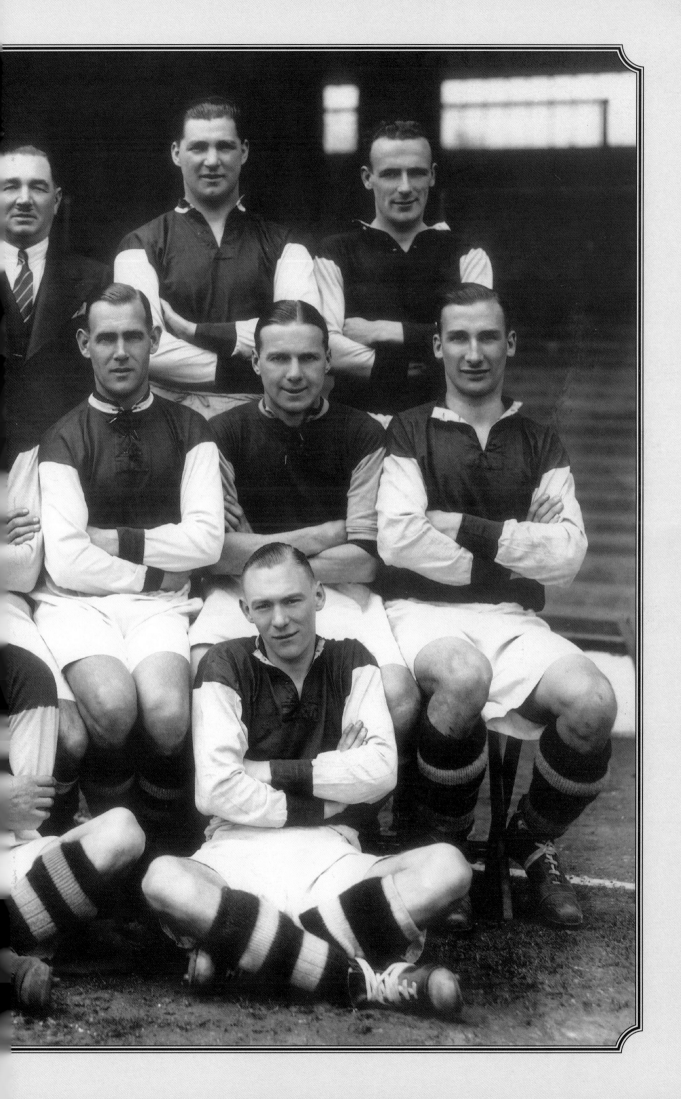

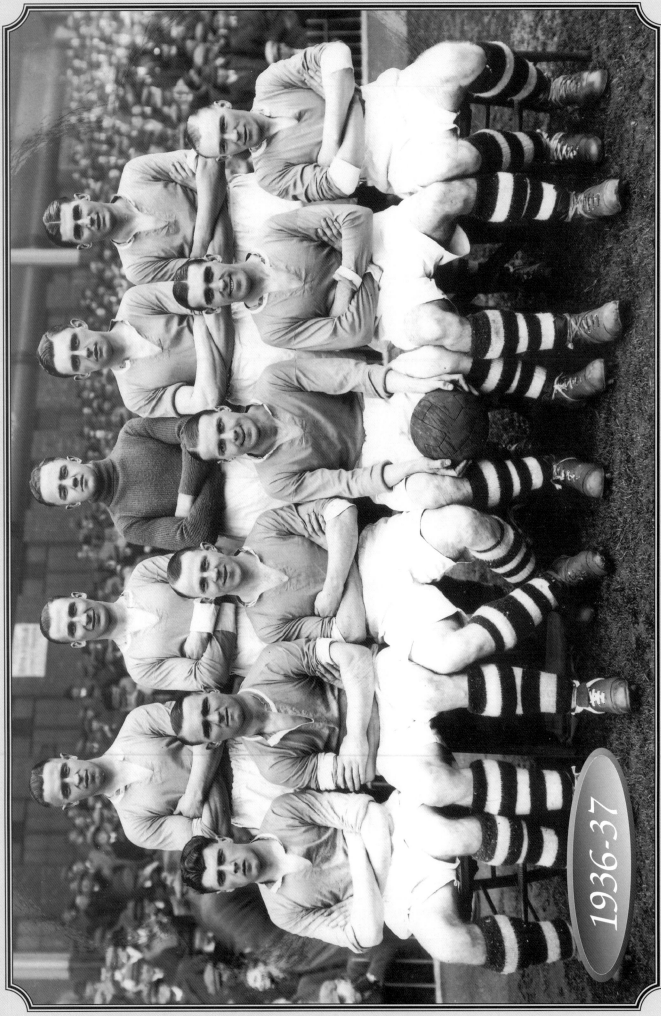

1936-37

245

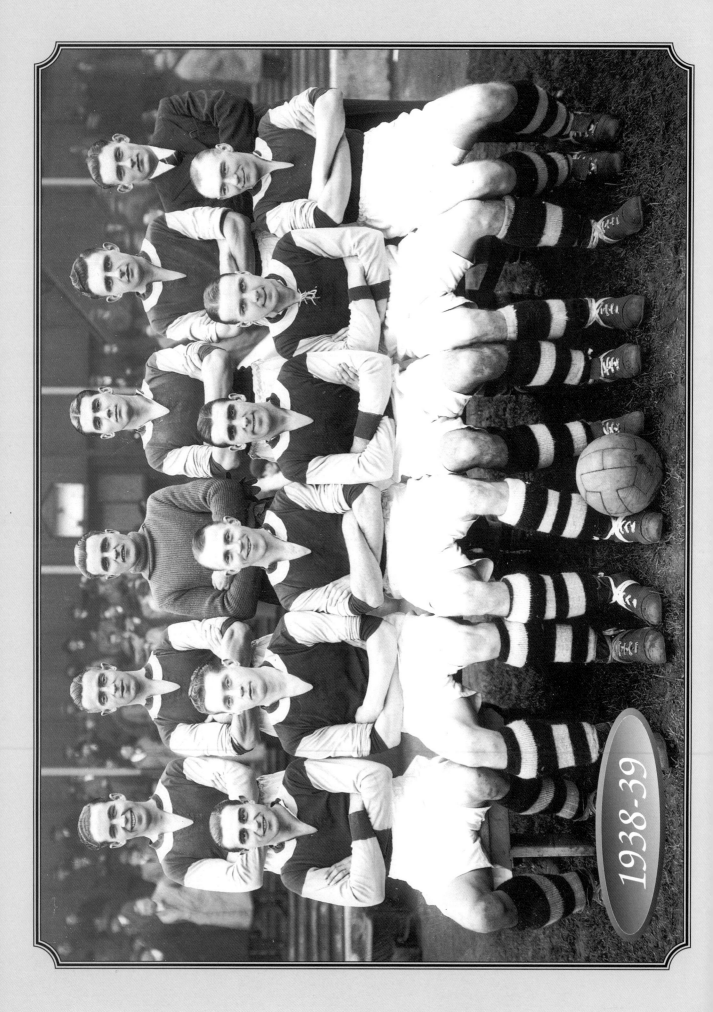

1957-58

1963-64

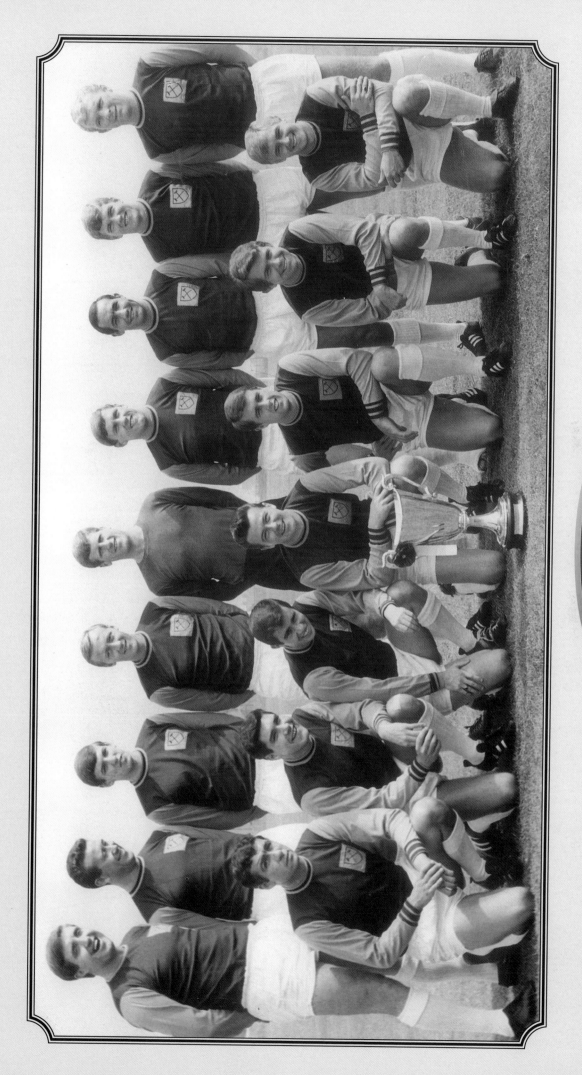

1965-66

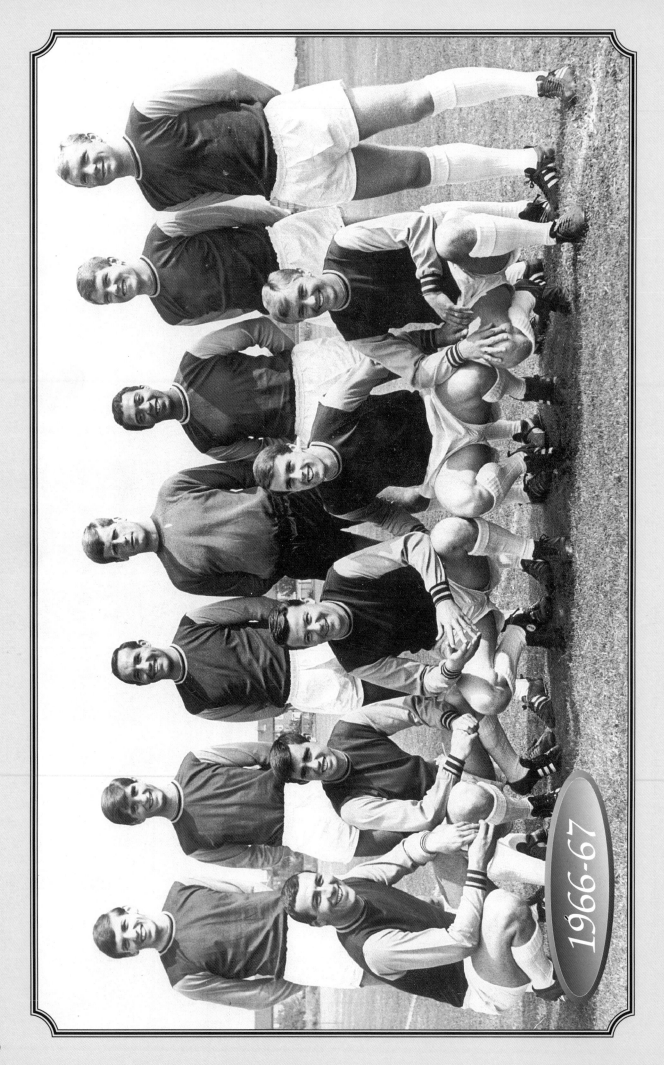

1971-72

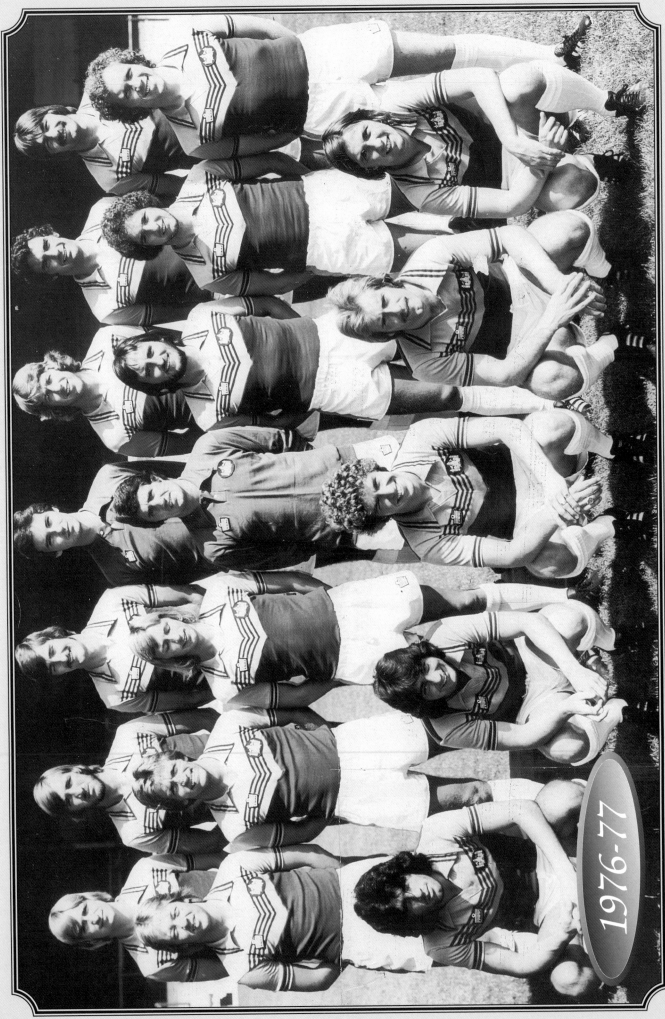

1976-77

1979-80

1981-82

254

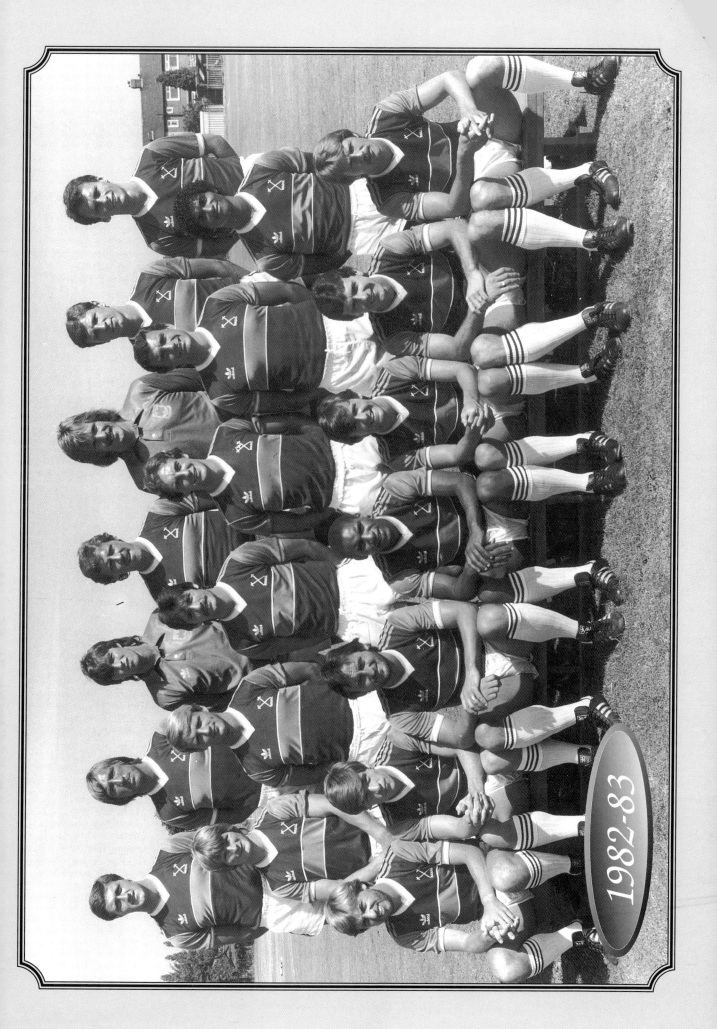

1982-83

WHO'S WHO SUBSCRIBERS

PRESENTATION COPIES

Terry Brown
Peter Storrie
Martin Cearns
Charles Warner
Tom Finn
Harry Redknapp
Frank Lampard
Billy Bonds
John Lyall
Terry Connelly
Roy Shoesmith
Stephen Marsh *(West Ham United Autograph Society)*
John Northcutt
John Helliar
Alan Jacobs
Alvin Martin
Ray Stewart
Tony Gale
Phil Parkes
Alan Devonshire
Geoff Hurst
Martin Peters
Trevor Brooking
Lawrie Leslie
Dr. A J F O'Reilly
Liam Healy
Brendan M A Hopkins
Terry Grote
Paul Gwinn
Steve Gunter
Gerald Toon
Julian Baskcomb
Trevor Hartley
David Philip

SUBSCRIBERS

V Lindsell
Miss K Avon
A R Chapman
R F Lewis
Eric Townsend
Terence Mark Jonas
Andrea Nelson-Harris
G B Miller
Chris Frearson
Kevin Uren
Peter Trevillion
Trev Paul
Stephen Crowe
Keith Meredith
P A F Clarke
C Goodwin
J Burrows
Gary Bush
Laura Brooks

Reg E Marsh
Per Netzell
Theresa Carey
Lee Gibson
Thomas Murphy
Paul Argent
Michael Oliver
Michelle Thomas
Mark Brown
Dennis J Curtin
Stephen Benham
Liam Tyrell
A Hickson
Antony Beaman
Jonathan P Bill
David Bean
D Harrison
F W Martin
M Beerkens
Paul Warman
Susan Hart
Hans Peter Rohner
G M Hansman
Laurence Munroe
David Hedge
Jeremy S Fisher
Sigve Kloven
J M Borley
Gary Paine
Stephen George Burton
Simon J Bremner
Bernard Mayo
Nigel Lawrence
Guy Western
Tony Western
Charlie Morris
Jeremy Alexander Seaburg
W J Copping
Barry Norwin
Mark S Humphreys
R Dale
E J Smith
D J King
Mark Vandenpump
J P Noble
Keith Martin
Simon Goodley
John Goodwin
Terry Coster
N Stock
Alfie Ray Brooks
Michael Pritchard
W F Morgan
Allen Scott
D Rix
S C King
R Brown
Don Roberts
Gareth Farrant
Gary Pearce
Jurgen Hohmann
P Jackson
J H Eldred

P B Bickford
Gavin Alexander
Philip W Blewett
Steve Stirman
Peter Goswell
Mark Sandell
Ian King
A Fleckney
Tony Jagger
(Yorkshire Iron)
T N Lilley
J Haynes
Michael R Wilson
Charlie Barrett
Steven Bern
John P Reynolds
C Ashby
Martin Gallagher
Paul Whiteman
Terry Hatcliff
Alan Henry
William George Buttle
Christer Holmlund
Lyn Turner
J Staunton
Julia Postlethwaite
Paul Blundell
Duncan Smith
Mark Randall
Eric Casbolt
David Maddocks
Tony Rickwood
Paul Bounden
Steven Nelson
Michael J Toms
David T Monk
S G Tipple
Lesley Baliga
Mark Beeby
Darren Webb
Yap Mun Wai
Ian Buckle
Justine Costerd
David Lawson
Kevin Eade Lark
K G Nelson
A Palmer
Mark Foreman
W C Duhme
Colin Cassell Jnr
Peter Jones
Jayne Lloyd
Trevor Pope
Martin Gerrard
Peter Sawford
James Weight
Richard White
Colm Power
Moshe Shamai
Miri Shamai
J R Maskell
M R Bartram
R L J Coffey

Trevor Gregory
Tom Emery
Greta Bryan
Paul Gibbs
Martin Goode
Tony Barritt
Terry Denham
I A Hunt
Marcus Hamilton
Bob Warnick
Martin Paul Mason
P Hart
Neil Gurling
Toni Monteiro
John Bayley
Dave Brown
Len O'Halloran
Neil Regelous
K Bennett
Dave Barlow
Mark Crocker
Jackie Cearns
D M Byford
Alan Gardner
S King
G E McGregor
D J Lee
Jamie William Meechan
Robert Smith
Geoff Thompson
Valerie Seltzer
Christopher Seltzer
Jean Hogg
Christopher Hogg
Dulcima Hogg
Mandy Rutledge
Sandy Rutledge
Peggy Worman
Terry McDonald
Jean McDonald
Mia McDonald
George McDonald
Jack McDonald
Mrs E. McDonald
Eddie Hollingsworth
Connor Lewis
Dennis Farrow
Tony Lee
Paddy Craven
Tony Cable
Brendan Cable
Pete Kirkman
Martin Rowe
Lee Caddy
Jane Clark
F R Lee
Alvin David Easterbrook
I D Friend
Steve Blowers
Brian Martin
Brian Taylor
D G McGreevy
Alan Davidson